D0020384

SOCCER
MEN

Profiles of the Rogues, Geniuses, and Neurotics Who Dominate the World's Most Popular Sport

SIMON KUPER

NATION
BOOKS
New York

New York
www.nationbooks.org

Published by Nation Books,
A Member of the Perseus Books Group
116 East 16th Street, 8th Floor
New York, NY 10003

Nation Books is a co-publishing venture of
the Nation Institute and the Perseus Books Group

Books published by Nation Books are available at special discounts for
bulk purchases in the United States by corporations, institutions, and
other organizations. For more information, please contact the Special
Markets Department at the Perseus Books Group, 2300 Chestnut Street,
Suite 200, Philadelphia, PA 19103, or call (800) 810-4145, ext. 5000, or
e-mail special.markets@perseusbooks.com.

Designed by Pauline Brown
Typeset in 9.5 point Meridien LT Std by the Perseus Books Group

Library of Congress Cataloging-in-Publication Data

Kuper, Simon.
    Soccer men : profiles of the rogues, geniuses, and neurotics who dom-
inate the world's most popular sport / Simon Kuper.
        p.   cm.
    Includes index.
    ISBN 978-1-56858-458-4 (pbk.)—ISBN 978-1-56858-459-1 (e-book)
    1. Soccer players—Biography. 2. Soccer coaches—Biography. I. Title.
    GV942.7.A1K87   2011
    796.3340922—dc23
    [B]
                                                                2011018789

10 9 8 7 6 5 4 3 2 1

SOCCER MEN

ALSO BY
SIMON KUPER

Soccer Against the Enemy

Ajax, The Dutch, The War

Soccernomics
(with Stefan Szymanski)

To my father, who suggested the
idea for this book, as he did for so many other
projects; to Pamela, for tolerating me while
I wrote it; and to Leila, Leo, and Joey,
who I hope will read it one day.

CONTENTS

PART II: Managers and General Managers

PART III: Some Other Soccer Men

SOCCER MEN

INTRODUCTION:
ORDINARY MEN AND CRAFTSMEN

In his book *The Football Man*, published in 1968, Arthur Hopcraft marvels at the fame of soccer players—at least in countries other than the United States. Say the word *Georgie* in Manchester, Hopcraft writes, "or in close proximity to some kind of [soccer] activity in any other British town," and everyone will know at once that you are talking about Best. If you say *Matt*, they think Busby. *Denis* evokes Law, *Nobby* means Stiles, and so on. Hopcraft explains this "not by the fanaticism . . . but by the deep and lasting impact made by men of extraordinary personality in the context of sport."

Hopcraft began covering soccer at the age of sixteen. English talk show host Michael Parkinson, an early colleague at a local paper in the tough miner's town of Barnsley, remembers him as "the first reporter I had encountered who wore a bow tie, which took courage in Barnsley in the 1950s."

Later Hopcraft became a well-known writer for television; in 1979 he wrote a famous adaptation of John Le Carré's *Tinker, Tailor, Soldier, Spy*. But before abandoning soccer he packaged much of his best work in *The Football Man*, and it's that book that made me decide to write this one.

In his book, Hopcraft anatomizes English soccer of the time in a series of profiles: "The Player," "The Manager," "The Director," "The Referee," "The Fan" (mostly about hooligans), and so on. Hopcraft meets and describes George Best, Alf Ramsey, a young Ken Bates (then chairman of Oldham), and many others. He takes them seriously, not as demigods but as ordinary men and craftsmen. His overly polished prose is now a bit dated, and we no longer need his assurances that soccer is important enough to write about (quite the opposite: We now often need to be told that it isn't). Still, *The Football Man* is a wonderful book, and prescient in places. Hopcraft tells us that contrary to what many people in 1968 thought, a European Super League would never happen, but he adds, "A more likely suggestion is that a domestic Premier League may hive off from the English Football League to confine top-quality soccer to perhaps a dozen of the country's major areas of population. This is a perfectly rational idea, and one which is known to find favour among a number of men in influential positions in soccer."

I would never dare compare myself to Hopcraft, and I don't wear bow ties, but men of extraordinary personality still make an extraordinary impact in the context of sport, and in *Soccer Men* I give my take on the soccer men of our day. I have done my best to understand what they are like, not as demigods but as ordinary men and craftsmen.

Like Hopcraft, I began writing about soccer at the age of sixteen: a profile of Dutch player Ruud Gullit, published in *World Soccer* magazine in October 1986, for which I think I was paid about $40, which was a lot of money to me then. (I'll come clean straight away and say that a lot of the profiles in this book are of Dutchmen. Just be thankful I didn't grow up in Panama.) I've been profiling players, and managers, and directors, and sometimes even fans ever since. I joined the *Financial Times* newspaper in 1994, and am there again today, but in between I've had stints at the *Observer* (one of Hopcraft's old papers) and the *Times* (London). I have also written for innumerable magazines and papers from Japan (good pay) to Argentina (not so good).

I have never thought that most soccer players have anything special to say. I know a colleague who believes that only by speaking to a real live player can you access truths about the game. This man is forever texting players, and saying things like, "If you speak to Franz Beckenbauer, he'll tell you that . . ."

I reject that idea. I do believe that you can access truths about the game by speaking to Arsène Wenger, if he feels like telling you, which he probably doesn't. I don't believe you can access them by speaking to Wayne Rooney.

In fact, now that I have reached middle age, I've increasingly given up chasing interviews with players. It isn't worth the humiliation. Sometimes a magazine will call and ask, "Can you get an interview with X?" I always say that you can: if you want to spend weeks sending faxes that somehow never arrive, phoning impatient agents on their cell phones, hanging around training grounds, and trading favors with boot sponsors. In the end you'll get an interview with X. He'll probably turn up hours late, say, "I hope we'll win on Saturday," and then drive off again.

Another colleague of mine describes acting as an interpreter for a star who had just joined Real Madrid. As the two of them sat in the car heading for the press conference where the star was to be presented, my colleague asked him what message he wanted to convey to the waiting media. The star looked surprised at the thought. "The aim," he explained, "is to say nothing."

Soccer players almost never say, "No comment." As the English play-maker Paul Gascoigne once pointed out, if you do that, the newspaper will report that the player said, "No comment," which makes him look suspicious. Instead, the player says sweet nothings.

I live in Paris, and the other month I caught Franck Ribéry being inter-viewed on French television. It was impressive to see how fluently the phrases rolled out: "We played well. . . . Another big game coming. . . . Let's hope we can win. . . . Only the team performance matters." In its way, it was a perfect performance. This kind of drivel often satisfies interviewers, too. Many news-papers and television stations barely worry about the content. What they are trying to show is access to players—or the appearance of access. That by itself is enough to sell. I think I sold my interview with Kaká to publications in eight countries.

Of course, sometimes you catch a player on a good day, often after he has retired, and then the interview is a pleasure. I felt that in some of the profiles in this book: going around Cape Town with Bruce Grobbelaar, around Rotterdam with Johnny Rep and Bernd Hölzenbein, or sitting in the Polo Bar in Ascot, England, with Glenn Hoddle. Soccer players tend not to respond well to abstract questions about emotions ("How did you feel when? . . ."), but if you ask about specific moments or places or people, they sometimes get going. Even interviewing active players can be worthwhile. These people are roaring with energy, almost never have low blood sugar or a hangover, and are fascinated by what they do. Nicolas Anelka and Rivaldo were not pleased to see me, but they did say interesting things.

Then there is the intangible sense of a person that you can get only from actually meeting him: his aura, if you like. Once in the Nou Camp stadium someone introduced me to a bandanna-wearing Ronaldinho. While we ex-changed pleasantries, I had nearly a minute to take him in from point-blank range. As he stood there, his legs were constantly in motion. He was bounc-ing, almost dancing on the spot. He also couldn't stop looking around. This may just have been desperation to escape a British geek, but I risked an instant psychiatric diagnosis: attention deficit disorder.

After interviewing great players, we journalists often compare notes. We rarely ask each other what the guy said, because we know it was probably boring. Players today are such corporate men—more of which later—that they usually say exactly what you know they are going to say. Instead, the first question from journalist to journalist is usually, "What was he like?"

After I interviewed Kaká (who said little of interest), I duly reported back to colleagues that he'd been an extremely pleasant, polite bloke. A while later, a German friend of mine interviewed Lionel Messi in Barcelona. "What was he like?" I asked. Well, my friend admitted, Messi had said nothing of interest. But otherwise he had done everything he could to make his guest happy. "What a sweet little man!" my friend marveled.

We ask, "What was he like?" in part because we are looking for the secret of the man's success. We want to believe that great players become great in part because of the men they are. They cannot just be good at kicking a ball. We assume their characters must also be conducive to great achievement. Surely, there are personality traits that unite the firecracker Maradona with the brooding Zidane and the homeboy Messi. In other words: Are superstars exceptional people?

I hope this book adds up to something like a group portrait of the profession. Let's start with the players' life paths. Malcolm Gladwell, in his book *Outliers: The Story of Success*, popularized the "10,000-hour rule." This is a notion from psychology, which says that to achieve expertise in any field, you need at least 10,000 hours of practice. Gladwell quotes neurologist Daniel Levitin: "In study after study, of composers, basketball players, fiction writers, ice-skaters, concert pianists, chess players, master criminals, this number comes up again and again. . . . No one has yet found a case in which true world-class expertise was accomplished in less time." The 10,000-hour rule has since been questioned in various fields. It may indeed not apply in highly physical sports like running or jumping, where somebody with perfect genes can become world-class without much training. However, in a highly skill-based sport such as soccer, Gladwell's essential point is correct: practice makes perfect.

One constant of players' autobiographies is therefore a childhood spent kicking a ball around and, in a cliché of the genre, sometimes sleeping with one. There's one thing all the great players, from Maradona to Messi, have in common: They hit the 10,000-hour mark, at least.

Hitting that mark has consequences for character. Few of the game's superstars have broad life experience outside soccer. From their early teens, when they typically start the move into top-class soccer, they are actively discouraged from developing interests outside the game. One friend of mine, who had a modestly successful playing career, says it's not that players are stupid. Rather, they're blinkered.

That characteristic has probably worsened over time, as the sport has become ever more professional. In various ways, the superstar has changed over recent decades. In particular, two superstar types have all but died out: the leader and the rock star.

From the 1960s, when media attention for players began to grow (see *The Football Man*), until the 1990s, when television money began to flood the game, the profession that soccer resembled most closely was rock music. Like rock stars, players were pursued by fans and groupies. Like rock stars, they tended to peak in their twenties. Like rock stars, they could say and do and drink and take drugs almost as they liked. Strange to tell, few clubs before the 1990s demanded that players looked after themselves. And so you got rock-star players like George Best and Maradona, and even rock-star managers like Malcolm Allison.

These men lived hard. Not only did the clubs allow it, but players had little to lose by ruining their bodies. After all, few made much money from soccer. Best was "young, popular and rich by lower-middle-class standards," notes Hopcraft in his profile. "It is only because the pay and conditions of leading [players] were so recently those of moderately skilled factory helots that Best and his contemporaries look so excessively and immodestly affluent." Soccer had given these players a brief window in which they could live like rock stars, and so they did.

The other type of superstar common from the late 1960s until the 1980s was the leader. Maradona was one (being a rock star didn't get in the way), but the ultimate leader-superstars were Johan Cruijff and Franz Beckenbauer. Both men were born just after the Second World War, as part of western Europe's baby boom. By the late 1960s, in a world growing in prosperity and shedding deference, the boomers were seizing power for themselves. They demonstrated against Vietnam and led the street revolutions of 1968. On the soccer field, too, they made a power grab.

Cruijff and Beckenbauer didn't only take responsibility for their own performances, but did so for everybody else's as well. They were coaches on the pitch, forever pointing and telling teammates where to move. They helped the nominal coaches make the lineups. They didn't do deference. They demanded a greater share of the game's profits. Cruijff shocked his club, Ajax Amsterdam, by bringing his father-in-law in with him to conduct his pay talks.

Yet when soccer changed in the 1990s, both leaders and rock stars were doomed. With all the new money coming in, clubs became better organized. They regained control over their players. Often the manager—typified by Alex Ferguson at Manchester United—became a sort of dictator over his team. Clubs also began to focus more on the physical and demanded that their players abandon rock-star lifestyles. Even Ronaldinho had to leave Barcelona when the club grew fed up with his partying every night, particularly after he began to take along the teenage Messi. In soccer, the rock star was ousted by the corporate man. Liverpool's long-serving defender Jamie Carragher, in his autobiography *Carra*, describes the "robotic, characterless ideal [that] modern coaches want."

Soccer players today are almost all followers rather than leaders. Joan Oliver, when he was Barça's chief executive, insisted to me that Messi was a leader. But it turned out that by *leader*, Oliver meant something very different from a Cruijff or a Beckenbauer. Messi, Oliver explained, was a "twenty-first-century leader": someone who didn't speak much but led by example. That's not what Cruijff would have called a leader.

So today's superstar—Lampard, Kaká, Messi—is a slightly monomaniacal corporate man and yes-man. (In my profile of Florent Malouda, I describe his battle to turn himself into just that person.) Sure, they want to win. Like all good corporate executives, they take their jobs seriously. And they're paid a lot to win. They practice hard. A few are driven fanatics—Edgar Davids, profiled here, for example. But anecdotal evidence doesn't suggest that all superstars are like that. Boudewijn Zenden, who played alongside Davids on the great Dutch team of 1998, told me that it simply wasn't true that everyone on the team was a driven fanatic. The one thing they all had in common, Zenden said, was that they were very good at soccer. Davids was known inside the game as a driven fanatic. Other superstars, by contrast, give every appearance of being relaxed. Wayne Rooney emphasizes in his autobiography how "laid back" he is. Steven Gerrard (himself a "twenty-first-century" leader by example only) confirms, "What I love about Rooney is, however big the occasion, he's relaxed. . . . No warm-up, no tension, let's get cracking, lads. No worries." If you have the gifts of a Rooney, you probably don't need the personality of a Davids.

The myth of the superstar as driven fanatic is one that sports fans like. It suggests an explanation for how these legends got where they are: a route we could all follow to succeed in life, no matter how much or little talent we have. This was the myth behind those ubiquitous advertising posters featuring Tiger Woods: "We know what it takes to be a Tiger." The idea was that Tiger lived every second of his life in devotion to golf and had gotten where he was thanks to fanatical drive. Then it turned out that Tiger spent much of his time picking up girls in bars. In other words, he is a slightly monomaniacal corporate man who got where he is through a natural gift, good coaching, and hitting the 10,000-hour mark (or in his case, given that he started when barely out of the crib, more like the 20,000-hour mark). He works very hard and relaxes the rest of the time, like millions of successful people in all fields. Other than being a brilliant athlete, Tiger has no special characteristics.

I suspect that's true of most of soccer's superstars. "The very rich are different from the rest of us," Scott Fitzgerald mused to Ernest Hemingway. "Yes," said Hemingway. "They have more money." Great soccer players are different from the rest of us, too: They have more talent. Otherwise, the scary truth seems to be that they really are rather like you and me.

It's still worth reading about them. First, these are the heroes of our time—in countries other than the United States and, increasingly, inside the United States, too. We all want to be them; we want to understand them better. Second, each one is shaped by his background. Xavi is a different kind of central midfielder than Gerrard largely because they come from different places. Just as any biographer of anybody would do, I have tried to locate these players in their origins. With David Beckham and Eric Cantona, I was most interested in how others respond to them.

Once I've met the guy, or have watched him play, and I've read and spoken to a lot of other people about him, I am free to go off and write what I like. That is because soccer players almost never read me. Hopcraft points out the problem of reporters who follow one club all year. They are the journalists who are most likely to get access but are least able to write honestly. "The mere preservation of a tolerable social connection between such a man and the club's players and officials means that he is unlikely to be uncompromisingly critical of them," says Hopcraft. I don't have that problem. I show up at the club, do the interview, leave forever, and then publish it in the *Financial Times* or a little Dutch magazine. I can be uncompromisingly critical.

"In the main in this book I am more concerned with people than technique," writes Hopcraft, and so am I in mine. I am also concerned with technique, with the craft of soccer: what distinguishes Rooney or Rio Ferdinand from other English players, or why Lampard and Gerrard are so good for their clubs and so disappointing for England. But most of the time, I try to describe these players as if they were human beings. What would you think of Xavi or Robin van Persie or José Mourinho if he lived next door to you, or worked in your office? There are no demigods in this book, just ordinary men, successful professionals pursuing their careers, often rather bemused by the world's response to them. Hopcraft died in 2004 at age seventy-one, but I hope he would have approved.

A NOTE
ON THE TEXT

Most of these profiles were previously published in the *Financial Times*, the *Observer*, the *Times* of London, *Hard Gras* in the Netherlands, and an array of other publications. I thank them all for permission to reprint the articles here. I have tidied up the odd phrase and corrected some errors, but I haven't tried to make myself seem more prescient than I was at the time.

A few pieces—including many of the ones about English players—were written especially for this book.

Throughout I have used the word *soccer* to describe the sport. Many fans—including many Americans—assume this is some cringeworthy American invention. It isn't. *Soccer* is originally a British word, a contraction of *association football*, and until about 1970 it was the most common word for the game in Britain. There's nothing wrong with it. However, I have kept the word *football* whenever it appears as part of a proper noun, a set phrase, or a title: for instance, the magazine *France Football*, the style "total football," or the book *The Football Man*.

PART I:
The Players

Bert Trautmann and Helmut Klopfleisch
September 1997

It's a couple of days after Germany knocked out England at Euro 96. The German team is staying three hundred yards from my London front door, in the Landmark Hotel. I walk past the Allsop Arms and the local tramps, who are wearing discarded England caps and scarves, and turn into the Marylebone Road. At the Landmark I have arranged to meet Helmut Klopfleisch.

I know Klopfleisch from a year I once spent in Berlin. He is a moonfaced electrician who was born in East Berlin in 1948 and became a Hertha Berlin fan soon afterward. On August 13, 1961, the Berlin Wall went up, separating him from his club. For a while Klopfleisch spent Saturday afternoons huddled beside the Wall with other Eastern Hertha fans, listening to the sounds coming from the stadium a few hundred yards away in the West. The border guards soon put a stop to that.

For the next twenty-eight years Klopfleisch followed Western teams around Eastern Europe. The Stasi, the East German secret police, followed him. Klopfleisch was often arrested—in 1986, for instance, for sending a good-luck telegram to the West German team at the World Cup in Mexico. In 1989, months before the Wall came down, he was expelled from the German Democratic Republic (GDR). Since then he has followed the German national team around the world. He has become the unofficial team mascot, licensed to hang around the hotel and chat with players.

This evening he is sitting at a table in the lobby of the Landmark with the president of Werder Bremen and an old man in checkered trousers. Fritz Scherer, the former president of Bayern Munich, is with them, but excuses himself as soon as I arrive. The old man in checkered trousers is tall and tanned, with elegant gray hair and a perfectly buttoned shirt. It is immediately obvious from his aura that he is a legend.

When we are introduced I fail to catch his name, and so I guess that he is Fritz Walter, captain of the German team that won the World Cup in 1954. But after a couple of minutes I realize that this man is Bernd Trautmann,

"Bert" to the English. He is indeed a legend: a German soldier in World War II who was taken prisoner by the British, he stayed on in Britain after the war ended, turned out to be a promising goalkeeper, and ended up joining Manchester City. Most famously, he broke his neck during the FA Cup final of 1956 but played on as City held on for victory.

Trautmann talks like a legend, slowly and ponderously, knowing that whenever he talks, people will listen. It's a style common among very beautiful women.

The conversation turns to Nelson Mandela. Trautmann coughs, and the rest of us fall silent. "I have ordered Mandela's book," Trautmann says. "In my house in Spain I have two thousand books, and I have read most of them. When I come home," and he looks around our little circle, "I will read that book." With great formality he takes a handful of nuts from the bowl on the table.

This goes on for a couple of hours, yet I find it interesting. First of all, Trautmann really is a legend, so nothing he says is dull. But also, the atmosphere at our table is calm and soothing. I assume that this is typical of team camps when everything is going well. The Werder president and Trautmann occasionally order rounds of beer, nobody looks around to see if he can see anyone more interesting (Jürgen Klinsmann, say), and every speaker is permitted time to hold forth.

Klopfleisch alone says little. The general opinion—which I think he shares—is that as a simple electrician, he should be grateful to be here at all.

When Trautmann doesn't have anything more to say, the Werder president explains to me why the German camp is so calm: The Bayern players are behaving themselves. It was different in the past, he assures me. He can say that because his good friend Fritz Scherer has left. "Uli Hoeness—that's the arrogance of Bayern in one man," says the Werder president.

"Paul Breitner," says Trautmann. The Werder president shivers as if he has food poisoning.

The Werder players are very serious characters, he says. Sometimes there'll be a talk on religion in town, and a group of them will go along. Not the Jehovah's Witnesses or anything like that. No, serious theological evenings. Not really Bayern's thing, he thinks. The Werder president says that Werder and Bayern represent two sides of the German character.

"North and South?" I guess.

"I'm afraid I must correct you," he says. "Werder is the Germany of the collective. No stars. Everyone works hard to build something together. The Germany of the 1950s, as it were."

"And Bayern?"

"Bayern is the Germany of today. Too rich, spoiled, always quarreling, and disliked everywhere. And yet they usually win."

That leads us to the great question: Why do Germans always win? Surely, these men must know.

Trautmann takes some more nuts. Klopfleisch and the Werder president look polite but uncomprehending. They don't see my point. After all, Germany doesn't always win. They didn't win the last World Cup, for instance. No, things are not going well for Germany at the moment. The new generation doesn't want to work, and . . .

I give up.

Have they had a nice time in England?

Oh, yes. They are all Anglophiles. There is a tranquillity about this country that Germany lacks.

"You know," says the Werder president, "I grew up in East Berlin. Later I fled to the West. So the division of Germany determined my life. It was the same, of course, for Herr Klopfleisch. And Herr Trautmann became a legend as a result of being taken prisoner in the war. But in England nothing has changed for a hundred years. It's the Old World. I like that so much. The war put an end to all that in Germany."

I learned one thing during my time in Berlin: When it gets late and there is beer on the table and a foreigner present, German conversations turn to war.

"I am a simple man," says Trautmann. He pauses. "This is what I have always remained, but I read my books, and what I read is this: The French, the Americans, the English, they all knew exactly what Hitler was going to do. And so as a simple man I ask myself: Why didn't they do anything? If France had chased him out of the Rhineland in 1936 . . ."

At eleven o'clock he goes to bed. The Werder president follows, but first he puts our beers on his room bill. It's easy when the German soccer federation is paying, but even so . . .

Klopfleisch and I have a last cup of coffee. He grumbles, "It's always the same with these old Germans. If this, if that, then Hitler would never have happened, and they could sleep easily at night."

Klopfleisch is bitter. The lives of these three men may have been determined by Hitler, but only Klopfleisch's life was ruined. He was not allowed to go to university, and when he was kicked out of the GDR, he lost everything he had. He's pleased that he can go to a tournament in the West with the national team, he says, but it means less to him than it would have in the days of the Wall.

Klopfleisch's complaints are starting to bore me. He is not a legend. The legend has gone to bed, and so I leave too. "Good luck on Sunday," I say, as if Germany needs it.

Late-night German conversations no longer invariably turn to war, and Germany's victory in the final of Euro 96 (the whole of Wembley booed when Oliver Bierhoff scored their golden goal) was the last time they won a trophy.

I last saw Klopfleisch in Berlin in 2009. He was in a hospital bed. He still enjoyed talking about soccer, but kept returning to his pain at seeing former communists live happily ever after. He had been a hero of the cold war, and after the Wall fell he thought that justice would at last be done. He was wrong. As part of the deal on German reunification, most East German communists and spies were left unpunished.

A Stasi agent, who had spied on Klopfleisch from the church beside his flat, had taken over his summer house outside Berlin, his "Little California." Klopfleisch has been trying for twenty years to get the house back.

Someone in the hospital room asked if he saw his battle with the late GDR as a sort of soccer match. "A match lasts ninety minutes," Klopfleisch sighed. "This one just went on forever."

Bert Trautmann died in Spain at the age of eighty-nine on July 19, 2013, widely mourned in both Germany and Britain as a symbol of reconciliation between the two countries.

Johan Cruijff
January 1999

When Johan Cruijff was a young player and still rather naive, Dutch journalists used to tease him by asking him what was the last book he had read.

Invariably, he would cite the now-forgotten American novel *Knock on Any Door*. Sometimes the journalist would say: "But you said that last time!" and Cruijff would reply, "I've read it again. It's a very good book."

So it is ironic that Cruijff—voted European player of the century last week by the International Federation of Football History and Statistics—is responsible for the Dutch publishing sensation of this winter.

The book, *You Have to Shoot, or You Can't Score, and Other Quotes from Johan Cruijff*, first appeared in October. It sold out instantly. It was reprinted twice in November, sold out again, and now sits once more in piles beside the tills in half the bookstores in Holland.

The quotes were assembled by Henk Davidse, who collected Cruijff interviews for decades and found rich material. Cruijff talked a lot. Even on the pitch, on the ball, with three men on him, he was always gesticulating and shouting advice to teammates. His whole life has been a conversation.

He talked about everything. The chapter headings include "On Guilders, Pesetas, and Dollars," "On Tar and Nicotine," "The Dutch Team: A Difficult Relationship," and "On His Youth, Father Manus, Brother Henny, Wife Danny, the Children, and Health."

And Cruijff said things that no one else did. "Even when he talked nonsense," wrote Nico Scheepmaker in his biography *Cruijff, Hendrik Johannes, 1947–1984, Fenomeen*, "it was always interesting nonsense."

Cruijff understood soccer better than anyone, but he also thought he understood everything better than anyone. He told a Chicago taxi driver the quickest way into town, advised Ian Woosnam to change his swing, and before having heart bypass surgery debated the method of operation with his surgeon.

He not only said new things but also said them in his own words. Being a genius who left school at the age of twelve, he often found that his thoughts ran ahead of his vocabulary. In Holland in recent months, various learned essays have appeared on the topic of Cruijff's Dutch. Its main characteristics are his frequent use of the word *you* to mean *I* ("That was the worst thing, that you always saw everything better"), his outdated Amsterdam working-class formulations (*ken* instead of *kan* for *can*), and his penchant for apparently random words ("Them on the right is goat's cheese"). Cruijff himself is oblivious to these defects. "Talking," he muses in the book, "if I could do everything as well as talking . . ."

His Spanish is more flawed than his Dutch, but in a different way. He relies too much on the word *claro* (meaning "of course"), pronounced in an Amsterdam accent with a shrug of the shoulders, and on the self-invented phrase *en el este momento* (meaning "now"), used as a delaying tactic.

In fact, his best language may be English, which he learned as a child hanging around Ajax's English coaches Keith Spurgeon and Vic Buckingham. He still makes the odd mistake, though. "Why should I gone back when everything they are doing with soccer in Holland is wrong now?" he once asked the *Washington Post*. But shining through the errors, always, are remarkable formulations.

Like many great philosophers, Cruijff has mastered the apparent paradox. Thus: "Chance is logical."

"Italians can't beat you, but you can lose to them."

"Before I make a mistake, I don't make that mistake."

And, on turning fifty in 1997: "Really I haven't lived fifty years, but one hundred."

Cruijff now feels himself to be an old man, and this is the sadness that underlies the book, the reason it was published now. Davidse is celebrating a mind that no longer exists. "The tooth of time has done its work," Cruijff said in 1996, shortly before being sacked from his last job as coach of Barcelona.

Instead of having original thoughts, he now spends his time taking his grandchildren to the zoo and commentating on Dutch television, often continuing to speak after the microphone has been turned off, because he has never understood how TV works.

Davidse's book is part of Holland's attempt to thank him at last. As a player, Cruijff was often maligned as greedy, and at Ajax he was stripped of the captaincy by his teammates. Fans used to shout "Nose!" at him.

There was delight in 1979 when it turned out he had lost all his money to a French-Russian con man called Basilevitch. This winter, the tens of thousands of Dutchmen dropping into bookstores are, in a quiet way, saying good-bye and sorry. As Cruijff might tell them: "You only start to see it when you get it."

Bruce Grobbelaar
March 1999

B loody mist, eh?" says Bruce Grobbelaar, jumping out of his car just in time for training. "You can't see a golf ball on the fairways." Behind him Table Mountain is indeed shrouded in the stuff, and across the bay from the training ground Robben Island is barely visible, either. The former Liverpool keeper has landed in Cape Town, where he now coaches the Seven Stars.

A Grobbelaar training session goes something like this: Grobbelaar spins a ball on his finger, frowning in concentration while the players stretch and run laps. Grobbelaar places a ball on an orange post and kicks it into the distance while the players pass to one another. Grobbelaar performs the kickoff for two five-a-side games simultaneously, by punting two balls out of his hands at the same time. Grobbelaar watches the five-a-sides, saying "Goal" when appropriate. When a shot goes high over the bar he says, "Boom!" At the end, Grobbelaar selects five players to run short sprints and do push-ups as punishments for unspecified sins.

"Whole team must run!" some players protest, but Grobbelaar ignores them. Twenty-five years ago, one recalls, he was a corporal in the Rhodesian army.

"He's still got a way to go as a coach," one Seven Stars player concedes. Afterward, Grobbelaar chucks me and two of his players in his car, drops them at the supermarket—they have no cars—and drives me into Cape Town for a night out. The city, he says, is one of the six best in the world, along with Vancouver, Perth, London, and Paris. "The sixth one I have not been to yet," he adds, lifting that trademark Zorro mustache for the trademark toothy grin beneath the trademark bald head. At forty-one, with only the merest hint of a beer belly, he is still unmistakably Bruce Grobbelaar, and he is stopped in Cape Town all the time by local Liverpool fans.

The drive into the city is an experience. While reversing at high speed, Grobbelaar can swing the car five inches to his left and then immediately back again to save a side mirror. He can read street signs from nearly a hundred yards. As we drive down the waterfront in the dark, he entertains himself counting the prostitutes: thirty-three, he says. "If my eyesight fails, I don't think I'd be half the man that I am." He was a child prodigy at baseball and cricket, too, better, he says, as a teenage wicketkeeper than David Houghton, who went on to an international career with Zimbabwe.

We sit down to fish and a lot of wine in the Dias Tavern, a Portuguese bar that is showing Spurs beat Leeds, and as Spurs' manager George Graham mistakenly celebrates David Ginola's drive against the post, Grobbelaar roars with laughter. "That'll be one for *Bloopers*!" Grobbelaar would love to be managing an English side himself, living with his wife and daughters in Lymington, Hampshire. The problem, he says, is the damage he suffered from being tried on charges of throwing soccer matches. Although he walked free in 1997 and is now suing the *Sun*, the newspaper that accused him, he cannot find an English club that will have him. "Your name has been tainted with the stigma," he grumbles, emphasizing every word like a true white South African.

And without any prompting, he recalls how the saga began, one day in November 1994, when he arrived at Heathrow to catch a plane to Zimbabwe and was confronted by two *Sun* journalists who told him they had videotapes of him purportedly telling his former business partner, Chris Vincent, about match fixing. This merely compounded Grobbelaar's problems, because he knew that the *News of the World* was about to run a sex story about him. "I had given Vincent a false account of sexual allegations with other people," he explains. He flew his wife and daughters to meet him in Zimbabwe, hoping to shield them from the sex story, but a lawyer told his wife about it on the airplane, and at the Harare airport she walked straight past him. Later that day he had to play a World Cup qualifier against Zaire. It was, he says, hard to motivate himself.

He is still not over the trial. Recently, he dreamed that he was sitting in a cell and waiting again for the jury's verdict, but this time, in the dream, he was found guilty. In real life, Grobbelaar, who had previously lost his money setting up a safari park with Vincent, lost more in the case, together, he believes, with a portion of his reputation. He does not spend a lot of time worrying about it, chiefly because he never expected to live to be forty-one. In the Rhodesian war, he explains, "you went out and survived that day. And the rest is bonus." He fought the war against the black guerrillas who would later lead Zimbabwe. Is it not surprising, then, that he is now the most popular white man in the country?

"Listen," he says, "even my houseboy's son joined the other side. We met in my house during the war. I said, 'If I see you in the bush, I will kill you.' He said, 'Yes, but I will kill you too.' I said, 'Okay, we will see who comes first.' I didn't see him, but he was killed in the war. His younger brother, Gordon, told me.'"

In the war, because of his eyesight, Grobbelaar worked as a tracker, gauging when and where guerrillas had passed from the state of their footprints and food remains. It was a job normally done by black hunters. Although Grobbelaar speaks no language fluently, in the war he picked up some of the Zimbabwean languages—Shona, Ndebele, and Nyanja—to go with his English and Afrikaans.

When English clubs rejected him, he decided to start his coaching career in Zimbabwe. Last year he briefly acted as caretaker-manager of the national team, sending himself on for the last twenty minutes of a game against Tunisia in November, and he spent months trying to negotiate a job as assistant coach. But the Zimbabwean dollar kept plunging, and in the end the country could not pay him enough. As one official at the Zimbabwean FA asked me, "Born in Durban, grew up here, then went to Canada, spent fourteen years at Liverpool—is he a local man?" In fact, Grobbelaar is a local man in many places.

He throws me into his car again, and as we shoot down the highway, overtaking on both sides, he points to the Cape Castle and says, "That's where my grandfather was born. His father was a fusilier in the British army, and the castle was a British stronghold in the Boer War." The birth in the castle, Grobbelaar says, entitled him to a work permit when he joined Liverpool.

In June, Seven Stars will disappear, merging with local rivals Spurs to form Ajax Cape Town, a feeder club of which Ajax Amsterdam will own 51 percent. In the short term, therefore, Grobbelaar plans to win some matches with Seven Stars, playing with a back four. Then, when the club is safe from relegation, he will start them playing the Ajax system with three defenders. Next, his plan is to become head coach of Ajax Cape Town. Then, back to Europe. And the ultimate goal? Grobbelaar is not a man for coyness. "My ambition," he says, "is to take the reins at Liverpool."

He tells me that the training methods I saw in action earlier that evening were learned at Anfield from Bob Paisley, who in turn had learned them from Bill Shankly. Not that Grobbelaar is sentimental about Liverpool. He played in the games at Heysel and Hillsborough, and still has nightmares about them, as well as about the war. "Even today. You are lying down by yourself and thinking about your career, and the three things you think of are Heysel, Hillsborough, and the war."

We end the evening in Grobbelaar's apartment, which he has borrowed from a friend, and sit by the pool listening to the crickets and drinking whiskey. It is the time of night to philosophize. Twenty years ago, says Grobbelaar, his then girlfriend, a Rhodesian woman, became pregnant, and just before he could propose to her, he discovered that the father was his best friend. What, he muses, if he had married her? "I would never have gone to Liverpool. I'd have been somewhere in Africa now. Probably Bulawayo. Running my own business. With five children." Would that have been a good thing? "Yes," he says, "because I would never have met that crazy arsehole Vincent, who nailed me." But he doesn't mean it.

Sadly, Grobbelaar's coaching career has tailed off in recent years, and he no longer seems to work for anybody. Last heard, he was living in Newfoundland, Canada.

Edgar Davids
March 1999

The last time Edgar Davids and I talked, the subject was fashion. "You!" he said. "You're badly dressed!" Surely, I replied, he could not be referring to me. And in his best black American English he shouted: "Damn, yes!"

The Juventus midfielder, who faces Manchester United in the Champions League semifinal next month, is as important to his side as Roy Keane is to United. He is also paranoid, aggressive, and occasionally violent.

When Davids played youth soccer at Ajax, he was sent off so often that a club official took him to Milan and Juventus to show him how good life was for players who made it big. He also devoted a lot of energy to beating opponents by putting the ball through their legs. "Masturbation," his coach Louis van Gaal called it.

Around the same time, Davids strode up to tennis player Richard Krajicek in an Amsterdam bar and said, "I bet you don't know who I am." Krajicek confirmed that he did not.

"My name is Edgar Davids," said Davids. "In a few years' time I'll be playing for Holland and driving a big car. You'll be hearing more from me." Then he stalked off again.

This anger within has made him the player he is today. Left out of Holland's squad for the World Cup of 1994, he spent the tournament on Amsterdam playgrounds practicing what he saw on television. Davids scorns players like Danny Blind who collect soccer trivia; he himself collects tricks, and in big games he can suddenly produce a ten-yard backflip on the turn or swivel a full circle through two opponents.

He was part of the Ajax team that won the Champions League in 1995, and when they lost the '96 final to Juventus, Davids missed the decisive penalty. All the while he remained a difficult character, living in a mental world populated almost exclusively by true mates (the other black players at Ajax), jerks (almost everyone else he knew), and heroes (people he read about in books).

An autodidact, Davids was obsessed with basketball players and rappers. His biggest hero was Dennis Rodman of the Chicago Bulls, whose autobiography, *Bad as I Wanna Be*, he knew by heart. Davids yearned to appear in an advertisement wearing nothing but a pair of sports socks, in imitation of a Rodman pose.

This era culminated at Euro 96 when he walked out of the Dutch training camp in St. Albans, advising the coach, Guus Hiddink, to remove his head from other players' backsides. It was, though he did not acknowledge it, a quote from Rodman.

Then he began a vendetta against Dutch journalists. At press conferences he would seek out foreign reporters and talk in fluent Italian or English until a Dutchman tried to listen in, whereupon he would instantly shut up.

His personality adulterated his soccer. He no longer tried nutmegs, but he did like to stand around with his foot on the ball, pretending to be the Boss. Johan Cruijff said he dribbled too much.

In 1996, Davids left Ajax for Milan. Things began well, with George Weah nicknaming him Big E Small in honor of the rap artist, but later he broke a leg and ended up on the bench. In December 1997, Milan let him go to Juventus for a transfer fee of just $5 million and their good riddance. During transfer talks he turned up at the Milanello training ground with a Juve shirt under his arm.

In Turin, his lurch to sanity began. As a little black boy growing up in Amsterdam-North he had thought of Juventus as the ultimate, or, as he would put it, "cool," club. Suddenly, he found himself among the heroes from his books. He was not about to run with the ball when it was clear even to him that Zinedine Zidane and Alessandro del Piero could do it better. So he played in their service, tackling, intercepting, passing cleanly, and showing once in a while that he could do more than that.

And by the time he reached his third Champions League final, against Real Madrid last May, he too had become a hero. Juventus lost, but he was excellent. The team won Serie A. The jerks who had "dissed" him in the past were sorry now.

Adriano Galliani, vice chairman of Milan, joked, "I shall give orders for Davids to be brought back to Milan." Hiddink recalled him to the Dutch team. Davids started the World Cup on the bench and ended it as his country's best player, a tackler for whom there is no such thing as a fifty-fifty ball. Now he is also the Dutch vice captain.

Last week Davids turned twenty-six. If Juventus overcomes Manchester United in May, he will play his fourth Champions League final in five years. He will not relax—he can never relax—but by now he must know that he has made it.

He really doesn't seem able to relax. In January 2014, aged forty, he resigned as player-coach of the English non-league team Barnet. In the last nine matches he played, he was sent off three times and complained he was "a target."

Rivaldo
December 1999

Monday, December 20, 1999, was a busy day for Rivaldo. He awoke in the Princesa Sofia Hotel around the corner from the Barcelona stadium, because his family had already left for a vacation in Brazil and he didn't want to be alone in the big house.

He had to be at the club at nine o'clock. Louis van Gaal, Barcelona's manager, wanted to analyze the match of the previous evening, a 2–1 victory over Atletico Madrid. The Brazilian player had been substituted after seventy-two minutes.

After the match analysis was finished, the shy Rivaldo asked for permission to speak. Listen, he said in his Portuguese-tinted Spanish, I have respect for the coach and for everybody here, but I won't play outside-left anymore.

A light training session followed, after which Rivaldo appeared before the press. Twenty journalists, still ignorant of his speech, interrogated him about the vote for European Player of the Year. The prize has been awarded by the magazine *France Football* since 1956, and past winners include Stanley Matthews, Raymond Kopa, and Franz Beckenbauer. Whoever wins it becomes a legend.

No comment, said Rivaldo. The result of the vote isn't known yet. "Everybody knows it's you," pleaded the journalists. Rivaldo said nothing.

Magazines like *World Soccer* and *Onze* had already made him their Player of the Year, but the only prize that really counts is *France Football's* Golden Ball.

Then he drove to the airport to collect handball player Iñaki, the son-in-law of the king of Spain. That afternoon they were going to do something for charity. Rivaldo and his agent, Manuel Auset ("I'm not his agent. I'm his friend"), don't want me to say anything about that. Rivaldo doesn't do these things for public relations.

And then, three hours late, dressed in black, the tall Brazilian finally appears on the nineteenth floor of the Princesa Sofia. Iñaki was delayed, and the charity event ran over schedule, says Manuel, a brisk little Spanish lawyer. Rivaldo sits down, groans when he sees my long list of questions, but in the end, on this day of days, agrees to tell his story.

You're tired. Are you often tired?
"No. Today I am. Today I have to do so many things. I am almost always well rested."

The pressure at Barcelona is greater than anywhere else in the world.
"I don't think so. The greatest pressure I experienced in Brazil, at Corinthians and Palmeiras. The pressure in Brazil is a little complicated. They threaten your family, they damage your car, and it's a little complicated. If you were to have the results at Palmeiras that we've been having at Barcelona recently, you wouldn't be able to walk down the street."

So you don't want to finish your career at a Brazilian club?
"Yes, I do. If I could choose a club in Brazil, I'd choose Palmeiras."

You're from Recife. Do you plan to return there later? I think: a house in Recife and a house in São Paulo. São Paulo for work and Recife to relax, with the beach.

And a house in Barcelona?
"No, I don't think so, eh?"

You are a player who plays by instinct, and Barcelona has a thinking coach. That's the way it is, isn't it? (When I ask the question I don't know anything about Rivaldo's speech of that morning.)
"No, he's a coach I respect very much and a coach who looks at tactics. He likes it when players have to do something in his system, in his *tactica*.

It's different in Brazil. There people don't talk about tactics, and that means freedom. But you have to have it in you to take that responsibility. If you have the quality to do more than other players, the coach will give you freedom. So that you can beat three, four, five stars to score. A spectacular goal, an amazing goal, a beautiful goal.

"Here it's a bit complicated, it's more tactical. It's a bit like the *mister* [the Spanish slang for "coach"] says one thing, and the player does the other. I'd like to be more comfortable, to have more pleasure. Because you can't enjoy so much, I try to enjoy when I can."

You want to play in the center.

"I have played on the wing for a while, and now I want to play in the center again. Not with the shirt number 10, but as a number 10. Here, well, here I've never played in the center. For years I have been doing things for the team, and I do nothing for myself. I want to enjoy more, to play in my own position. For me, for the team, for everybody."

Are you happy in Barcelona?

"Yes. I, the family, the children—we are all happy with the club and the city."

Soccer has become very demanding with so many games.

"Yes. I think that is bad for a soccer player. If you are thirty-four or thirty-five, it is a bit complicated. We are not machines."

Several magazines have already voted you their Player of the Year. (I don't mention *France Football*, but in retrospect it is clear Rivaldo's answer refers to that.)

"It's very important for me, because of everything that has happened in my life, all the difficulties I have overcome. And now, I have to be very proud of this prize, very happy. I have to go on with what I do, to keep the will to work. I think."

Do you see qualities in other great players like Ronaldo or Zico that you would like to have yourself?

"Yes, I think so. I used to try a bit to be a copy of Zico, tried to acquire his calm. Zidane is a very calm player. Luis Figo I like too: a player with very good feints, who has great speed. And Ronaldo, who is always near goal, who scores a lot and has great speed. So what I lack, I think, is speed. In a race over long distance, I have speed. In the sprint, not so much."

Now he has to be photographed in the gear of his sponsor, Mizuno. His Nokia phone keeps ringing, so he gives the thing to Manuel. Everyone is calling to congratulate him, because various media are reporting that he has won the Golden Ball. Manuel reads Rivaldo the telephone numbers that appear on the screen. I'm not here, says Rivaldo, who is posing with a ball that unfortunately is flat. "Is he now officially Player of the Year?" I ask Manuel. "Well, I don't know," says Manuel. "We haven't heard anything."

"Call *France Football*," Rivaldo suggests. Good idea. Manuel enters the number, and the telephone rings for a long time. Finally, somebody in Paris answers.

"Vincent!" says Manuel. Rivaldo goes and stands next to him and listens in. Vincent confirms that Rivaldo is the European Player of the Year. We congratulate Rivaldo.

"Thank you," says Rivaldo. He takes the phone from Manuel and walks onto the roof terrace. Alone he looks across the city toward the dark mountains. Directly in front of him is a branch of El Corte Ingles, a Spanish department store. The clock on the outside wall of the store states that the time is 7:23 p.m. and the temperature 10.5 degrees Celsius. From now on Rivaldo is officially a legend, a player who forty years from now will still be discussed in taxis in Montevideo and Damascus.

"Did you already know he'd won?" asks Mark Kaiway of Mizuno.

"Yes," Manuel grins. "He had to pose for a photograph with the Golden Ball."

"Has he celebrated yet?" I ask.

"Celebrated? He hasn't even had his lunch today! He's just been busy."

Rivaldo gives the phone back to Manuel and resumes posing. Manuel shows me the thing. The screen constantly reports that three callers are waiting. When one of them hangs up, a new one appears immediately.

Then Rivaldo has to sit for an hour in a small, dark, hot room under a barrage of television lights. It's like a scene from the Marx Brothers: a roomful of people having themselves photographed with Rivaldo, getting his autograph, kissing him. At about nine o'clock Rivaldo finally reaches the hotel lobby, where he skillfully feints his way past a group of journalists. He has almost made it to his Mercedes SUV when the hotel concierge tackles him.

Rivaldo is imprisoned in his hug. The journalists catch up. Rivaldo struggles into his Mercedes, but they go and stand in front of it. The standoff lasts minutes, but then he is finally allowed to drive to his empty house. In the bath he'll have a chance to think about the day.

The next day Van Gaal kicks him out of the Barcelona squad. It's a bit complicated.

Ruud Gullit
February 2000

A confused old man remarks to another spectator, "Do you know, that could be Ruud Gullit's brother."

"It is Ruud Gullit," the spectator replies.

"Are you kidding me?" demands the old man.

"It's true. He plays for the AFC fifth team now."

The old man takes another look at the large, dreadlocked sweeper in the red shirt and exclaims: "He was on the Dutch team!"

We are in a sports park just outside Amsterdam, two miles down the highway from the Ajax stadium, on a glorious, still winter's Saturday. In the canteen beside the ground old men play cards and ignore the soccer. OSDO third-string versus AFC fifth-string has drawn twenty spectators, most of them the toddler offspring of the players. The toddlers join in the warming up.

They have caught Gullit on a bad day. Even as the Felliniesque figure performs his unmistakable broad-shouldered jog onto the muddy pitch, his team is falling apart: Before the game can start, the woman referee dispatches several AFCers to find shin pads.

The AFC coach, a bad-tempered man with a cell phone, confides that, because of vacations, he has had to call up reinforcements from lower teams. Granted, his sweeper is the European Player of the Year from 1987, still only thirty-seven years old and not given to Maradonaesque dietary excesses. But having Gullit on your park's side is apparently a mixed blessing.

"AFC 5 is not AFC 5 anymore," one player told me. "Now the boys are nervous in the changing room. No one dares to sit next to him."

The former manager of Chelsea and Newcastle, and probable future manager of Fulham, made his AFC debut in September, soon after getting kicked out of St. James's Park. A couple of his friends, fifth-team regulars, got him to play in a friendly against ABN-Amro sixth XI, which had been threatening to field a ringer named Marco van Basten.

That game kicked off with Gullit but without his former teammate at Holland and Milan, who had fallen asleep on the sofa at home. However, woken by a phone call, Van Basten tore to the ground, where he was immediately brought on as a substitute. Eleven seconds later he had scored. He got another later, but Gullit's team won 6–2.

Gullit also scored twice, enjoyed the game, and decided to join AFC. He paid the membership fee of nearly two hundred dollars a year, high by Dutch standards, because this is a chic club. Chelsea, the last team he played for, consented to the transfer.

And so he became the sweeper of AFC fifths, much to the delight of a friend of mine who plays for the AFC fourth team and had always known that he was a better player than Gullit.

He could be right. Against OSDO, the AFC defense marshaled by Gullit concedes two goals in the first five minutes. Gullit, who for several games had maintained an uncharacteristic silence, has recently begun expressing his views.

"Inside! Inside! Inside!" he tells one of his defenders. Then, sighing: "I said inside." One of his enduring themes is that his teammates must learn to mark opponents on the inside.

It is to no avail. The AFC defense is what Johan Cruijff would call "goat's cheese," and when an OSDO forward next sweeps into the penalty area, an exasperated Gullit stands aside and lets him score.

"The cream has gone," comments the confused old man.

It would be wrong to say that Gullit is playing, as he would phrase it, "like a turd." Several times he sweeps a fifty-yard pass onto his outside-left's left toe, an eerie sight in this setting. "Good ball!" the AFC coach shouts reflexively.

However, the winger can never control the ball. Several times Gullit overhits. If you had to guess which of today's players had played sixty-five times for Holland, you would probably pick one of the OSDO forwards.

A spectator tells his son that Ruud Gullit is playing. "Does he play for OSDO?" the boy asks.

The father is shocked. "Ruud Gullit, who played in Italy and for the Dutch team! You know him, don't you?"

"Yeah, yeah, you're kidding me," says the boy.

Finally, AFC get a cross into the box, and Gullit, hurtling in, almost heads it into the top corner. Except that he misses the ball. The coach turns to me, beaming hugely, "It almost makes you think of old times!"

OSDO makes it 4–0. By now AFC has begun the running commentary of mutual criticism traditional in a losing Dutch soccer team.

"Goddammit! What was that?" shouts a forward.

"Well, do something up front!" suggests a defender.

"Referee, that man always has his flag up!" says another forward.

Gullit tries to be positive. He does not want to destroy anyone's confidence for life. After an AFC shot sails twenty yards over the bar, and some OSDO players joke about going home early, he laughs and shouts, "They're getting tired!"

Halftime comes with the score 5–0, and an OSDO striker walks up to shake Gullit's hand. "I was thanking him for all the pleasure he's given me," forty-year-old Thieu Heuijerjans reveals later. "That man meant so much for Dutch soccer."

Heuijerjans and Gullit walk off arm in arm, chatting. Like Cruijff, Van Basten, and Rinus Michels, Gullit has become a very nice guy by the simple expedient of retiring from top-class soccer.

Walking back out for the second half, he throws a glance at the men playing cards in the canteen. They don't look back. They should have, though, because in the second half AFC is transformed. Is it creatine? In any case, the outside-right Alfons soon creates a goal with a brilliant solo run.

"Alfie!" bellows Gullit. "He is fit! He is sharp!"

AFC wins a penalty. Not Gullit, but Guido, the center-forward, takes it. He scores.

Then Guido makes it 5–3. Gradually, however, the AFC revival stalls. As the end approaches, the OSDO players' wives start singing the club song: "OSDO is our club / We have won!"

Then, with only a minute to go, a cross from Guido reaches Ruud Gullit alone in front of an empty goal. This is his moment. But he is caught flat-footed. He tries to jump, cannot get off the ground, and as he contorts his body the ball sails over his head. Ruud Gullit has become a parks soccer player.

The referee ends the game. AFC has lost 5–3, and Ruud goes around shaking hands. He congratulates the referee at length, and to no one in particular he exclaims, "The second half was better!"

He pops into the canteen afterward wearing a gray woolen Italianate coat: the Best Dressed Man in Britain 1996. He has a drink with his teammates (not alcohol, never alcohol) and after five minutes says good-bye and is off in his "people carrier" (the new thing among continental players, who are emerging from the Sports Car Age), which has what looks like a small boat strapped to the roof. From the canteen there is nary a backward glance.

It is not that the Amsterdammers have forgotten Gullit. They just don't go in for idols. This is a town where if you spotted Jesus Christ having a drink with Nelson Mandela at the next café table, it would be uncool to notice. Rembrandt was declared bankrupt here, Spinoza expelled from the synagogue, Cruijff nicknamed the Money Wolf, and when John Lennon and Yoko Ono left town after their bed-in for peace at the Hilton, they had to return their honorary white bicycles to the local hippies. So nobody mobs Gullit. An Amsterdammer himself, he says he likes that about the place.

He could easily slip into former celebritydom. He is no longer even the most famous Ruud in Holland, having been outstripped by the brilliant young goalscorer Ruud van Nistelrooy (who should command the biggest transfer fee in Europe this summer) and Ruud, the character in the real-life soap opera *Big Brother*, who vomited on national television.

He probably shouldn't go to Fulham.

*The year 2000, incidentally, was the year Dutch television invented "Big Brother."

I last spoke to Gullit in the summer of 2013 in Miami, where he was working as a television pundit for beIN Sport and generally hanging out for a month. He'd come up with quite an interesting take on American football, which he enjoyed watching on TV. Being a soccer player, he explained to a bunch of us in the newsroom over coffee, was all about spotting patterns: the opposing right-back was probably going to pass into the middle, so he'd step in and close off that angle. But in American football, he said, most players seemed to have their every move prescribed by coaches. In other words, they were making no or almost no attempt to spot patterns and were therefore not using much of their brains. To him, that was a big shortcoming of the sport. It seemed a peculiarly Dutch take on gridiron.

Lothar Matthäus, the Tabloid Reader
June 2000

Y ou know what?" suggests Lothar Matthäus. "Let's go 'round the room one more time, and everyone can ask a question about his own country." We all shake our heads. We already know everything we need to know about Matthäus.

It's a Monday evening in February 2000, and seven journalists from around Europe are sitting in the Atlantic meeting room of a neo-Stalinist hotel outside Amsterdam. Matthäus, who is preparing for a Holland-Germany friendly, has summoned us here. In seventeen days the best German player of his era will end his European career at the age of thirty-nine, to go off and have some fun in New York.

Our interview was supposed to start at eight o'clock, but at eight a line of German players trudges into the Atlantic for a tactical talk. At the back of the group is a small middle-aged man with a big head, who waves at us and makes funny faces. This is Lothar Matthäus.

One crucial attribute that every aspiring soccer journalist needs is what Germans call *Sitzfleisch*: sitting flesh. We spend an hour and a half getting bored in the hotel bar. At half past nine the German group trudges out of the Atlantic. We trudge in, but are immediately ordered out again by Oliver Bierhoff. Germany's captain is having a sort of after-party with Matthäus and the German coach, Erich Ribbeck, an elegant man who would have been better suited as ambassador to Washington than in his current job. We go back to the bar.

At about ten—though by this time, nobody's keeping track anymore—Bierhoff emerges from the Atlantic. When he sees us he raises his eyebrows in the manner of Roger Moore and says, "An interview with Lothar. Always interesting." Then Bierhoff reaches for his cell—his *Handy*, Germans call it—and starts speaking Italian. He's a cultivated man, Bierhoff. His father was a big fish in an energy company. The child Bierhoff took guitar and tennis lessons, studied corporate economics, and in his first few seasons as a professional player earned less than his dad. Not like Matthäus at all.

Gingerly, we reenter the Atlantic. Now Matthäus is listening with fake humility to the German press officer, but we are allowed to hang around until the press officer disappears. It's ten o'clock, players' bedtime, but Matthäus motions us to sit down and relax.

"Interesting team talk?" asks the journalist from Germany's legendary soccer magazine *Kicker.*

"As you see," says Matthäus, gesturing to the hotel notebooks that are still lying on the tables. They are full of talentless doodles. Don't give up the day job, guys.

Matthäus wants us all to go and get something to drink for ourselves. I take charge of the task. I grab bottles of water from the fridge in the room and try to open them. Inevitably, the bottles turn out to be Kuper-resistant. Finally, someone manages to open a couple of cans of Coke. Matthäus makes sure everyone has a bottle, open or not.

We take our seats around him in a big U. Matthäus checks our tape recorders. Only when he is sure that they all work are we allowed to begin.

But first let's go back to March 21, 1961, the day Matthäus was born in Herzogenaurach. Not much had ever happened in the thousand-year existence of the tiny town near Nuremberg. It hadn't even been bombed in the war.

On March 21, 1961, Herzogenaurach had barely twenty thousand inhabitants and was known for just two things: Adidas and Puma. Both companies were headquartered there. In the 1920s, just when many of the locals had lost their jobs, Herzogenaurach was saved by the rise of sport.

In March 1961 most locals still worked in the sector. Heinz Matthäus was a janitor at Puma. Katharina, his wife, sewed the leather panels of balls at home. It was the era when Germans were working hard and starting to get rich. In the Matthäus home, people worked. Early in life, Matthäus got his own paper route—the start of a lifelong fascination with media.

Heinz, who sometimes had a glass too many, was a strict father. His son would later recall, "If something went wrong, I'd get a thick ear." The smallest boy in his school class joined FC Herzogenaurach, the Puma factory club. When his team lost, he cried.

Our first question this evening is why on earth Matthäus is going to play in New York. After all, against Holland on Wednesday he'll win his 144th cap (the world record if you don't count certain Africans, which FIFA doesn't), while the New York–New Jersey MetroStars are like Hartlepool United. The American media proudly call them "the world's worst soccer team."

Matthäus speaks quickly, fluently, in clichés. Perhaps he hasn't won more caps than any other player, but of all the players who have ever lived, he's surely spoken the most words to journalists. Matthäus rattles off dozens of reasons to move to New York. Man, he thought, New York, it's a big city, an interesting city; you can learn something there. Really, we should all go there. America is the land of opportunity, and in New York he can go out for dinner without the whole restaurant checking out how good he is with a knife and fork.

There are other motives he doesn't mention. In the course of the past twenty years, Matthäus has gradually worked out why everyone in Germany always laughs at him. There are many reasons for that too, and one is his Franz Beckenbauer complex.

A century ago, the mental hospitals of Europe were full of men who thought they were the German Kaiser. They cultivated their mustaches, let one arm hang limply as if paralyzed, and ordered their regiments into battle.

Matthäus, too, has always wanted to be the Kaiser. Nobody laughs at Beckenbauer. Beckenbauer speaks English. Beckenbauer is a man of the world. And Beckenbauer spent five years of his playing career in New York. Matthäus wants to be Beckenbauer.

One of us asks whether Matthäus, in moving to New York, has Beckenbauer in mind.

No, says Matthäus.

And it's partly true: It's also about Maren. Maren is the gorgeous twenty-two-year-old daughter of sports doctor Hans-Wilhelm Müller-Wohlfahrt. Matthäus has known Maren since she was seven. Now she's his girlfriend, and Maren wants to live in New York. Maren is a cultivated woman who wants to study theater in New York. She also wants to see Woody Allen play the clarinet in the Carlyle Hotel on Monday nights. That's not the sort of thing that would occur to Matthäus. He might go and see Pamela Anderson play the clarinet in the Carlyle Hotel. But now he's in love. In the past, this is news that he would have instantly shared with us seven journalists. He once let the German television channel RTL make a documentary about his failed marriage to Lolita. He'd already let a TV crew film him on his wedding day—"out of sheer loneliness," as someone pointed out. The entire German nation laughed, so he won't do that again.

He tells us that David Beckham must avoid the mistakes that he, Matthäus, made. "Beckham must keep his private life out of the media. There'll always be something in the papers, but he has to keep his curtains closed. Why are Beckham's five Ferraris always in the paper? He can have ten Ferraris—I'm happy for him—but they shouldn't be in the paper. How do they say it in English? *My house is my castle?*"

Nowadays Matthäus's house is his castle. That is, he only tells his secrets to *Bild*, the biggest tabloid newspaper in continental Europe. That's how we know that he's going to live in the Trump Tower at 721 Fifth Avenue, which is a good seventy minutes drive to training in New Jersey because New Yorkers clog up their streets with yellow taxis.

In Munich the streets are empty. One spring evening in 2000, my friend Philipp and I stroll along the boulevards of the Bavarian capital. Occasionally, a BMW sails by at eighty miles an hour. Otherwise, you don't feel you're in Germany at all. Munich is full of elegant women, eighteenth-century palaces where you can still imagine the carriages waiting outside the front gate, and delicious Italian restaurants stuffed with local soccer players. Only the many parks hint at the holes made by bombs.

Earlier that evening in Munich, I got into a taxi driven by an obese blonde woman, who told me that she'd driven Matthäus around for a day shortly before he left for New York. His main task was to try on shoes: His many injuries had swollen his right foot one size bigger than his left. The driver didn't think New York would suit Lothar. He's a Bavarian nature person, she explains.

Oh, yes, laughs Philipp, who is from Cologne, when I tell him the story. A Bavarian nature person! Philipp knows Matthäus. Matthäus isn't the sort of man to rise at five in the morning, pull on his hiking boots, and go off and climb a mountain. But Matthäus is the sort of nature person that Bavarians imagine nature people to be: a Bavarian with sunglasses on his head and a sweater slung over his shoulders who gets into his sports car and drives his beautiful girlfriend to a beer garden, where they drink wheat beer in sight of a mountain. Then the Bavarian nature person thinks, like the clerk in a Heinrich Heine story, "How beautiful nature in general is!"

Munich has become Matthäus's hometown. He left Herzogenaurach for good when he was eighteen, after getting a diploma as a painter and decorator. He was given a modest contract at Borussia Mönchengladbach. Without soccer, he'd have laid carpets.

The young Matthäus rose fast: In May 1980, sitting in the German national team's bus, he heard that he'd been picked for that summer's European championship. He burst into tears. "Why?" asked veteran defender Bernard Dietz. Matthäus explained that he and his girlfriend had already booked their summer vacation.

In 1984 he signed for Bayern Munich. He spent a total of twelve years there and became the best player in the world. Had he left it at that, there would now be a statue of him in every town in Germany.

"And yet the last two or three years I no longer hear those jeers and whistles," he reflects in the Atlantic room. "I think that now I've become a sort of role model for people in other professions, too." He tells us about the letter he got recently from a man in his fifties, who like many Germans of his age couldn't find work. At a job interview, the question of the man's age had been raised yet again. "Look at Lothar Matthäus," the man had replied. "He's proving that age has nothing to do with performance." The man had gotten the job.

Matthäus says, "Bixente Lizarazu has said that when he's thirty-eight, he hopes to be able to play like I do now. It's nice to read something like that." But it wasn't always like that: At a Bayern practice a couple of years ago, Lizarazu gave Matthäus a thick ear.

Matthäus's troubles began early. At a very young age, he developed a gift for articulating dumb and irritating thoughts. At the European championships of 1980, Ribbeck, then a sort of jumped-up equipment manager, had said, "Even when we're talking about the meal plan, he quacks something." At the time Matthäus still had no status on the team. He won his first cap during the tournament, against Holland, and almost immediately gave away a penalty. Afterward, the German captain, Karl-Heinz Rummenigge, told the press, "You can't be that stupid."

Rummenigge was then the *Chef* (boss) of the German team. The German team almost always has a *Chef*: a man who tells the coach what the lineup will be, punishes dissidents, and makes the financial decisions. In the 1950s Germany's manager Sepp Herberger used to say, "Fritz Walter *ist mein Chef.*" But the German obsession with *Chefs* derives from somebody else: It comes from Franz Beckenbauer.

It's hard for non-Germans to fathom the extent to which Beckenbauer towers over German soccer. He's the Kaiser, but with more power than the nickname implies. The son of a Munich postal worker, conceived in the final months of war, he is the sort of person who would have become a *Chef* even if he had been an accountant or a machine operator at BMW.

When West Germany lost to East Germany at the World Cup of 1974, Beckenbauer decided the lineup needed to be changed. He had a chat with his pal Gerd Müller, who had a soccer brain but no visible personality. Then Beckenbauer gave the new lineup to the coach, Helmut Schön, because it was Schön's job to fill in the team sheet. Bernd Hölzenbein and Rainer Bonhof replaced Heinz Flohe and Bernd Cullmann. In the final Hölzenbein won the German penalty, and Bonhof gave the cross for Müller's winning goal.

Later, when Beckenbauer coached Germany, his official title was *Der Teamchef.* Ever since Beckenbauer, every German national team has had to have a *Chef* or *Chefs.*

Matthäus, in the grip of his personal Kaiser complex, always wanted to be *Chef.* When he tells us about his international career, the main thing he talks about is his changing status. "Whereas under [manager] Jupp Derwall I was the fifth wheel on the wage, under Franz Beckenbauer I became a regular," he says in fluent tabloidese. Matthäus usually calls him "Franz Beckenbauer," in full, perhaps from uncertainty over whether they are on a first-name basis.

"My breakthrough was the World Cup '86. But I think it was a mistake of Franz Beckenbauer to have me mark Maradona in the final. I concentrated on Maradona, but we neglected our own game. After the 2–0 we changed that: I think that Karl-Heinz Förster took over Maradona, so that I could attack. We made it 2–2, then made a stupid mistake, and lost."

The point is that Matthäus had become Germany's *Chef.* The transfer of power officially took place on June 17, 1986, in the final minutes of the game against Morocco, when the Germans were given a free kick. Rummenigge was getting ready to take it when Matthäus shoved him aside and scored. After that Beckenbauer, the coach, sometimes had a word with Matthäus about the lineup.

But the problem with being *Chef* is that other people want to be *Chef*, too. Rudi Völler did. He and Matthäus would sometimes fire balls at each other in practice. Later, when Jürgen Klinsmann's game improved, he wanted to be *Chef*, too. Eventually, Germany had enough *Chefs* to open a restaurant.

Even at Bayern, Matthäus was always having to fight to stay *Chef*. Sometimes he leaked nasty things about his rivals to the press. *Bild* once reported that the other Bayern players called Klinsmann "Flipper," after a performing dolphin then on television, because his ball control was so poor. The newspaper also announced that Matthäus had placed a bet on the limited number of goals that Flipper would score that season. (Matthäus won the bet.)

The power struggles were bitter. Here are a few of the things the other *Chefs* said about Matthäus:

"Tell it to the toilet seat." (Rudi Völler)
"He who talks a lot, talks a lot of nonsense." (Franz Beckenbauer)
"Our new press officer." (Uli Hoeness)
"My philosophy of life is that you have to help sick people."
(Thomas Helmer)

When I ask Matthäus about all his rows, he tries to act the Kaiser. *Ach*, he says, there are tensions in every group. There are tensions in every family. Everywhere there is a certain hierarchy. It's probably the same at your work, too, he says. You surely have a *Chef* and a secretary, who both do their jobs. And you need them both, don't you?

We all nod obediently, whether we have secretaries or not. Matthäus has sidestepped the question, given the standard answer, has spoken as if he should be playing for the Washington Diplomats. And then he says, "But it's logical that the *Chef* has more to say to you than to the secretary!" And his buckteeth shape into a huge cheeky grin.

It's not just the other *Chefs* who are always attacking Matthäus. The rest of the German population does, too. Foreigners tend to think that all Germans are just Germans, but in reality there are several different kinds of Germans. There are old Germans and young Germans, *Ossis* and *Wessis*, respectable citizens and alternative types, the Cultivated and the Uncultivated, and they tend not to get on. "You Germans really don't get on!" I once commented to a table full of fellow students at the Technical University of West Berlin. They laughed uneasily, because they didn't get on.

You can categorize a German by his attitude to Lothar Matthäus. Cultivated Germans despise Matthäus because he is Uncultivated: He turns his *k*'s into *g*'s, his *t*'s into *d*'s, and he has almost no grasp of the conjunctive tense!

Alternative types despise Matthäus because they despise most Germans. Haters of Bayern Munich (possibly the most significant single group in German society) despise him because he is Bayern. And Bayern fans aren't too keen on him, either, because he spent twelve years pissing in his own tent.

The Dutch don't like him, either. "Matthäus = Hitler," said a banner at a Holland-Germany game in 1989. Tonight, two nights before what will surely be his last Holland-Germany (although with Matthäus you can never be sure), a Dutch journalist asks why he has such a bad image in Holland. "I'd rather ask the Dutch themselves," replies Matthäus, obliging as ever, "because it's a mystery to me. The Dutch people I know personally, whether they are fans or people from the hotel or journalists, are always very positive."

I have to tell him, "It's because for Dutch people, you *are* Germany. You are the country. You are the team."

I mean a lot by it: white shirt with Prussian eagle, dives, hard work, winning, a certain ugliness (although Matthäus is popular with German women). The Dutch see Matthäus as the embodiment of everything they dislike about Germany, everything they don't want to be themselves.

"Matthäus = Hitler" is too strong. Really, the banner meant to say, "Matthäus = A German."

I don't tell him all this, because I remember Paul Simon's story about running into the legendary baseball player Joe DiMaggio in a New York restaurant. In "Mrs. Robinson," Simon had sung:

Where have you gone, Joe DiMaggio?
A nation turns its lonely eyes to you.
Whoo whoo whoo

When he saw DiMaggio in the restaurant, he worried that the old man would be angry with him. It turned out DiMaggio wasn't. He liked the song. But he didn't understand it. The lyrics made no sense, he told Simon. Everyone knew where he was. People saw him on television commercials every day, he pointed out.

DiMaggio had taken the song literally, whereas Simon had meant it metaphorically. Simon had meant to say that the DiMaggio-type hero had disappeared from American life. In the restaurant, Simon realized that sportsmen can't think about themselves as metaphors. They think they really exist.

That's why I just tell Matthäus, "You are the country. You are the team." He looks at me with wide eyes: "So every whistle is a nice compliment to me? Really I should feel honored."

It was a Dutchman who gave Matthäus the most awkward moment of his public life. Not Ruud Gullit, but the man who filmed Matthäus with a video camera at the Oktoberfest in Munich in 1993.

"They forgot you with Adolf!" Matthäus yelled at the Dutchman, forgetting the video camera for a moment. It wasn't the first incident in the course of a public speaking career that has veered from racism to sexism and back again. Once, at a German airport, he called out to a passing women's basketball team that "our black guy" (Adolfo Valencia, his teammate at Bayern) "has one this long."

Inside the German team, only Klinsmann would object to this sort of thing. But most Germans outside soccer have a low tolerance for public racism. The German musician who registered in an Israeli hotel under the name Adolf Hitler was instantly expelled from the Berlin Philharmonic. However, Matthäus was one of the world's best players, *Chef* of the German team, and so he couldn't be expelled.

Yet most Germans—even *Bild* readers—hate Nazi-type jokes. They cringe when English or Dutch people make them. To most Germans, Hitler is still real. It bothers them that their best player, running from microphone to microphone, might blurt out something dumb about Nazis at any moment.

Matthäus isn't a Nazi. Nobody who knows him thinks he has anything against black people. But he is a naughty boy who is attracted to taboos, just as he feels the urge to say mean things about Klinsmann in *Bild* ("He thinks too much").

I had assumed that Matthäus would have his fair share of national pride—perhaps because he was captain of Germany, perhaps because he reads *Bild*. In the Atlantic room I ask him if his heart beats faster when he hears the German national anthem, the way Italians feel about their anthem.

He jokes, "It's only because of the rhythm of the Italian anthem that it makes your heart beat faster."

But isn't he proud to represent Germany?

"It's an honor to represent a whole country, such a big country where so many people play soccer. I don't feel more than that."

I guess Germans born in 1961 aren't big on nationalism.

Now Matthäus is waving about one of our tape recorders. "Look, this one's full. Do you have another tape?" He changes it himself.

The Italian journalist asks Matthäus for his Greatest This, Best That. Best international: against Yugoslavia at the World Cup 1990. Best opponent: Maradona. Favorite club in childhood: Borussia Mönchengladbach. Biggest mistake: his public squabble with Berti Vogts and Jürgen Klinsmann. "We were old enough. We should have talked to each other."

The squabble lasted years. Vogts and Klinsmann got irritated during the 1994 World Cup when they realized that every conversation in the locker room was appearing in *Bild*. They may have been relieved when Matthäus was seriously injured after that World Cup. He was then already thirty-three and surely nearing the end. Just to be sure, the internationals from Bayern and Dortmund, led by Klinsmann and Matthias Sammer, reportedly agreed that he would never play for Germany again.

Matthäus missed Euro 96. On July 21, 1996, he wrote in his (published) diary, "Today the European champions have arrived. Helmer, Ziege, Babbel, Kahn, Strunz and Scholl. There was a big hello at Munich airport. And sincere congratulations from me. European champion, for all of them it's the highlight of their careers."

Translation: None of them has been world champion.

His diary covers the season after Euro 96 and is the main source for anyone wanting to write the definitive story of Lothar Matthäus. "I believe," he writes in the foreword, "that this diary gives an insight into my thoughts." It does. I learned at school that every literary work has a theme. *Mein Tagebuch* (My Diary) has two: cell phones and the German tabloid press.

The diary is itself written in the style of a tabloid newspaper. Day 1: "Friday, July 12: Franz-Josef-Strauss airport in Munich. It's ten a.m. The loudspeakers announce 'Last call for LH 410 through Düsseldorf to New York.'"

This may be because the book was ghosted by *Bild* journalist Ulrich Kühne-Hellmessen. But I suspect that is more or less how Matthäus dictated it.

The greatest influence on his thinking seems to be the German press. On Wednesday, August 14, he writes: "*Bild, TZ, AZ* [the three Munich tabloids], the *Süddeutsche*, the *Merkur, Kicker* and *Sport-Bild*—for me these are more or less required reading."

Seven publications! Later he reveals that he buys the Italian sports daily *La Gazzetta dello Sport* as often as possible. Matthäus is like an academic keeping up with the literature of his field.

In his defense, whereas normal people say things to each other—"talking," as it's known—all communication at Bayern Munich is done through the media. Matthäus learns from the newspapers that Mehmet Scholl's wife has left him, that Karl-Heinz Rummenigge is considering selling Scholl, and that Klinsmann wants a transfer.

It's noticeable how nasty everyone at Bayern is. The funniest character in the diary, besides Matthäus himself, is Beckenbauer. The Bayern president is constantly popping up to say something mean, in words dutifully recorded by Matthäus.

Wednesday, August 21: "After the final whistle Franz Beckenbauer enters the changing-room as usual, and says: You can be very pleased you didn't lose."

Tuesday, September 10 (after a defeat to Valencia on Beckenbauer's birthday): "Franz stands up, and says just one sentence: I didn't get the present I had in mind. He sits down again and the dinner is opened."

Friday, March 14: "At a certain point Franz bursts out: You are a shit team."

But cell phones get almost as much attention. In fact, whereas the most common word in many books is *the* or *is*, in *Mein Tagebuch* it is *Handy* (cell phone).

Here's the entry for Sunday July 28: "We have the new Bayern-*Handys*. All my friends already have my number. But now that I'm in Zurich I notice: the *Handy* has not yet been authorised, I cannot yet be reached. Kreuzer and Helmer were smarter, brought their old *Handys* with them. Now I have to let myself be teased."

Later that day, at Zurich's airport, his eye falls on the Swiss tabloid *Blick*, which has put his wife, Lolita, on the front page. There are photos of her vacation on the Maldives beneath the headline, "Because of Lothar I Had to Let My TV Career Go."

All year, the themes of the diary remain constant:

Thursday, October 3: "I have settled in the Limmer Hof, our training camp. I always think positive. So I must make the best of this situation too. The best thing: my *Handy* works here, so each one of my friends can reach me."

Monday, October 21: "In the Swiss Air plane there's a copy of *Blick*. There are three pictures in it of Lolita, in the cockpit of a private plane. And there's an interview: *Lothar knows that I fly. But it's none of his business. We're now each going our own way.*"

Saturday, January 4, 1997 (when he runs into Matthias Sammer in a restaurant in Kitzbühel): "I go up to him, congratulate him with his European Player of the Year. Tell him his *Handy* number off by heart, that's how often I called him. Now I know why I couldn't reach him: *Handys* can't get reception in Going."

Friday, March 14 (after a crisis meeting at Bayern in which his teammates have accused him of leaking everything to the press): "Of course I know that my contact with journalists offers points of attack. Still, I've been around long enough to know what I can pass on and what not. Often enough at breakfast, the egg stuck in my throat as I read which secrets had got out. I lie in bed and cannot sleep. The accusations have really hurt me. It's one of the greatest disappointments of my life. I stare at the ceiling and think. Then it becomes clear to me: tomorrow against Schalke I won't be captain anymore."

Reading *Mein Tagebuch,* you look into the soul of Lothar Matthäus. And what you find is this: he is a *Bild* reader.

Nonetheless, Vogts, the German coach, called him up for the World Cup of 1998, on the condition that he'd occasionally keep his mouth shut.

I spent a week of that World Cup staying with six German journalists in a villa in the Riviera village of Saint Paul de Vence. The villa had a barbecue, a big garden, and a pool, in which we played water polo at midnight. It was a good villa.

The German team's hotel was three minutes away. One evening Jürgen Klinsmann came to sit in our garden. He drank our beer and said that in the future he'd come around every evening, because our villa was so much nicer than the team hotel. We never saw him again.

A couple of nights later, defender Christian Wörns came to sit in our garden. He drank our beer and told us that the atmosphere on the team really wasn't so bad. That was because Matthäus had stopped making trouble. Why had he stopped? we asked.

"I think," mused Wörns, reclining in his deck chair in shorts and bath slippers, beer bottle in his hand, "that if everyone keeps beating up on you, you learn to shut up."

It's true that by 1998, Matthäus wasn't Germany's *Chef* anymore. Klinsmann and Bierhoff were the *Chefs*, while the team had enough old blokes like Jürgen Kohler and Thomas Helmer to beat up on him when necessary.

But after that World Cup, only Bierhoff was still there. Matthäus was allowed to keep playing, and in February 1999, on the night that Germany lost 3–0 to the United States, the phone rang in his Florida hotel room. It was Erich Ribbeck, asking him to come to his room and explain how Germany should play. Matthäus had become the *Chef* again.

In the Atlantic room it's half past eleven. Matthäus is still bursting with energy, but we're dropping from exhaustion. Because he was an important player, we manage one last question: "What kind of player were you?"

Matthäus likes the question. He thinks about it. Tonight is his night. "Today I'm saying everything. I'm putting it all out there," he's told us.

"I certainly wasn't a Maradona," says the man who in 1990 became World, European, and German Player of the Year, as well as World and European Sportsman of the Year. "I was a very fast player. If I saw space, I used it. If I beat someone, he didn't catch me again. I was a player who came with a run-up. What Maradona saw in a small space, I saw over long distances.

"I'm small, but for instance I'm good with my head. Yes, what made me strong is that I could do all sorts of things. I always had a weak left foot, but when I was twenty-eight Trapattoni taught me to play with my left."

Matthäus rewinds a tape and makes sure everything is on it. Then it's time to say farewell. When it's my turn, he puts both his hands on my shoulders, practically hugs me. I tell him I'm going to be in New York in a couple of months. "Come 'round!" says Lothar. I promise I will.

In New York I'm too busy to meet Matthäus, but I do want to see him play. The MetroStars are playing the Kansas City Wizards in Giants Stadium. I get into a taxi at Times Square. Then I get into another. It turns out that Lothar isn't the only New Yorker who barely speaks English. "Giants Stadium," the Indian taxi drivers repeat the unfamiliar words. They've never heard of the place. Finally, I find an Indian who is willing to let me guide him.

In Giants Stadium there are eight thousand spectators. On the field I spot a small midfielder with a big head who is charging around the field— as they say in New York—like a crazy. Every time a teammate touches the ball, he throws up his arms and screams with rage.

The MetroStars score. Matthäus's teammates are pleased and cheer. On the big screen two 1930s comedians dance around a table. But the goal only makes Matthäus angrier.

Then Kansas City scores twice. Matthäus (as they would say in the States) freaks. He chucks his captain's armband at the linesman, Chip Reed. Reed, who looks like a U.S. marine, chucks it right back at him. The rest of the match, Matthäus wanders around the field mumbling to himself like a bum with a shopping cart on the subway.

Our final farewell took place in the hotel bar outside Amsterdam. My friend Bart has been sitting there all evening, hoping for a glimpse of Lothar Matthäus.

It's midnight, and Lothar is now drinking beer at the bar with two *Kicker* journalists. I carefully put my hand on his shoulder. "Lothar," I ask, "would you mind, for Bart here . . ."

Lothar throws himself on Bart. He wants nothing more from life than to give Bart an autograph. "How you write name?" he asks in English.

I write Bart's name on a magazine: *B-A-R-T.*

"I haf to be right," Lothar explains.

"For Bart," he signs my notebook.

Lothar bangs Bart on his shoulders. He hugs me one more time. Then we're finally allowed to leave.

Poor old Matthäus is still not taken seriously in his own country, and his career as a manager has suffered accordingly. As I write, he isn't managing anywhere. When the German authorities failed to locate him over a court case involving alimony payments to his ex-wife, they even stamped his papers as "deceased." An angry Matthäus retorted, "This is outrageous. Everyone can see that I'm alive." But in soccer terms, sadly, he doesn't seem to be.

Jari Litmanen
October 2000

Edgar Davids, who thinks there is something funny about players who know a lot of soccer trivia, would have smirked had he seen Jari Litmanen entering a canal-side house in Amsterdam one spring evening last year.

Litmanen had come to compete in a soccer quiz, but first he toured the house, exclaiming at its beauty. Perhaps, he said, he would buy one just like it. In seven years at Ajax, it had never previously occurred to him to move into Amsterdam. Instead, he had lived in the unlovely commuter town of Diemen, because all he thought about was soccer.

The home that evening was stuffed with Holland's most august soccer trivia experts. Some of them, at an Amsterdam dinner years before, had shamed Nick Hornby with their grasp of Arsenal history. But in this toughest of contests, the greatest Finnish player ever held his own. He would have done even better had he been a less generous man. When the question designed for him came up—"Who is Finland's most-capped international?"—it turned out that the other player present, the then Ajax captain Danny Blind, knew the answer, too. (It's Ari Hjelm, with one hundred caps, as everyone knows.) Litmanen turned to Blind in amazement. "But," he stammered, "it's months since I told you that."

That level of obsession is probably required if you want to become a great Finnish player. There are no one-man teams in international soccer, but as England may discover on Wednesday, Finland is probably the closest thing to it. Christoph Daum, the German coach-elect who watched them beat Albania 2–1 in their first World Cup qualifier last month, wrote afterward, "Jari Litmanen is the heart and soul of the team."

To some degree this was predestined twenty-nine years ago, when Litmanen was born the son of two soccer players. His mother, Liisa, was a gifted defender, while his father, Olavi, played for Reipas Lahti, the club founded by Finns expelled from Karelia by the Russians in World War II. Litmanen's Karelian heritage has made him a Finnish patriot, who always sings the national anthem. "With gooseflesh," he adds.

As a child, he kicked a ball around in the family's vast back garden, where he imagined, in the place of the usual snow, the grass of his beloved Anfield. In a school essay he wrote that he would be a team player, not an individualist. That he nonetheless acquired the nickname "Diego" seems to have been a tribute to his dark hair.

He planned his career with the care normally associated with young politicians. In his late teens, he set off on a veritable European tour to find the club where he would learn the most. Leeds United, managed by Howard Wilkinson, rejected him, as did Bobby Robson's PSV Eindhoven, while Litmanen had never expected to win a contract at Barcelona. However, the club's manager, Johan Cruijff, recommended him to Ajax, and in 1992 Litmanen landed in Amsterdam.

Ajax then already possessed a decent number 10, Dennis Bergkamp. It was as a substitute for him that the Finn made his club debut on August 23, 1992, in the eighty-seventh minute of a 3–1 victory over Go Ahead Eagles. For most of that season, however, he sat on the bench, studying Bergkamp like a stalker.

A year later he replaced him, and by 1995 Litmanen was probably the world's best attacking midfielder. There is an anonymity to his brilliance: Litmanen seldom dribbles or flies in with a tackle or fires home from thirty yards. Typically, he sends a precise ball out to the wing, and then surges stiffly into the box to finish off. Passing and scoring, passing and scoring. He says, "Zidane is fantastic on the ball, he also defends well, but he scores too little. Verón passes with feeling, is an outstanding playmaker, scores too little."

Litmanen scored twenty-four goals in forty-four European matches with Ajax, a club record. Of all the players they lost in the nineties—Davids, Bergkamp, Kluivert, Kanu, the De Boers—the crowd misses the Finn most. Occasionally, the Amsterdam Arena still resounds to his special song, "Oh oh Litmanen, oh oh oh oh."

Last year, virtually every self-respecting club in Europe courted him. He chose Barcelona, partly because they have a large squad. When it comes to injuries, Litmanen is the Finnish Bryan Robson, and he did not want to join a club like Liverpool, where he would have been under pressure to play weekly. But his choice of club worked rather too well. He barely plays at all.

Barça now want to sell him, but Litmanen feels mistreated and insists on staying while pocketing his weekly net salary of $60,000.

This may make the above paean to his brilliance sound hyperbolic. However, Litmanen's main problem at Barça is probably that he is a Finn. Being a great Finnish player is like being a great Czech car: You never get the respect you deserve. Had Litmanen not been Finnish, he would surely have been voted European Player of the Year in 1995, when Ajax won the Champions League and World Club Cup. Instead, George Weah won, and the Finn came third.

Notionally, Wednesday's game is a World Cup qualifier. In fact, the closest Litmanen will ever get to a World Cup is his hard-drinking tour of France 98 with a bunch of old ice-hockey friends. Bound for undeserved oblivion, poor old Litmanen will soon be just a quiz question himself.

*In 2011, aged forty, Litmanen won what will probably prove the final league championship of his career with HJK Helsinki in Finland. He had still been appearing for the Finnish national team in 2010, which meant that he had played international soccer in four decades and (in case you ever get asked this quiz question) had long since broken Ari Hjelm's Finnish record of caps. He now appears to be retired, but don't bet on it. The man just really likes playing soccer.

Juan Sebastián Verón
July 2001

In the first minute of the Arsenal-Lazio match last year, Juan Sebastián Verón lofted a fifty-yard free kick with the outside of his right boot that landed at the feet of the sprinting Pavel Nedved. It was the sort of pass Michel Platini used to make. Verón, the twenty-six-year-old Argentine midfielder who joined Manchester United last week for $39 million, is potentially the world's best player. He is a two-in-one, combining much of Zinedine Zidane with something of Roy Keane. Painfully thin and six foot two, with a tattoo of Che Guevara, a shaven head, and a goatee, he looks as if he should be a pirate, but in fact his physique is designed for soccer. However, there is a reason he is joining United for a little more than half the price that Real Madrid just paid for Zidane—three years his senior—and it is not just that Real is more profligate than United (although it is).

Verón's career began before he was born. His father, Juan Ramon Verón, an Estudiantes left-winger known as La Bruja (The Witch), scored the goal at Old Trafford on September 25, 1968, that deprived United of the World Club Cup (a trophy taken seriously in South America). Sodden Argentine fans at the ground sang, "If you see a witch mounted on a broomstick—it's Verón, Verón, Verón."

Juan Sebastián Verón was born in La Plata in 1975 and before long had scored thirteen goals in a game. He would steal his father's car ("I've always been a nut"), skip school ("My marks were about zero"), and at the age of fifteen embark on a remarkable sex life ("Like everybody, with a prostitute"). However, the boy could read the game, pass, and tackle, too. Brujita (Little Witch) had barely turned pro with Estudiantes when Diego Maradona pronounced, "I've seen a brave and young player. He's called Verón. He'll be successful."

Six years, six clubs, and several Ferraris later, that is only arguably true. Viewed one way, Verón's career has been a steady forward march: from Estudiantes through Boca Juniors, Sampdoria, Parma, and Lazio to Manchester United. He is no longer a walking tabloid story. Everyone ranks him among the world's best players. Impressively, he's managed this while playing below his potential. There was another telling moment at Highbury in that Champions League game when he fired the ball forty yards at the head of a teammate on the touchline. A beautiful strike, impossible to control, it was hit to show off. Lazio, a flaky team, lost 2–0.

This is at odds with Sir Alex Ferguson's assessment of the player when he signed. "You need one player who can make a difference. The people watching United only want to see the best, and we've got that today." But have they? Viewed another way, players measure each other in medals. Verón's trophy cabinet—if he has anything so passé—is filled mainly with the panties he used to collect. He has won two Italian Cups (no big deal in Italy), a UEFA Cup with Parma, and Lazio's league title. His haul makes him one of United's least-decorated players. But then medals never seemed the point. Renewing his Lazio contract in 1999, he said, "Since I really like Rome, which reminds me of Buenos Aires, I decided to stay."

Earning millions in a beautiful city where the fans didn't demand trophies, he could shine while playing at 75 percent. He was allowed off-days. That's why he is currently valued at half the price of Zidane. Sergio Cragnotti, the Lazio owner, called him "the new Platini." But the comparison quickly breaks down. Platini scored goals; Verón does not. Despite a mean shot, he has only twenty-four league goals in the past six years. Platini, furthermore, could take free kicks. Verón, who was once bored by training, began staying on after Lazio's Saturday practice to hold free-kick contests with Sinisa Mihajlovic, but the loathsome Yugoslav generally won.

Verón might have enjoyed life at Lazio forever had it not been for some forged genealogy. During the late nineteenth century, an Italian, Giuseppe Antonio Porcella, set off for South America. Verón's people, claiming that Porcella was his great-grandfather, secured him an Italian passport. Unfortunately, Porcella never seems to have arrived in South America, and Verón's great-granddad was actually an inhabitant of Rio de la Plata named Ireneo Portela. Verón had to appear in court, and a ban from soccer seemed likely.

The affair was traumatic and damaged his relations with Lazio. He was eventually cleared of any wrongdoing, despite possessing false documents, but had already decided to leave. In January his agent visited England, trying to hawk the player to Liverpool or Manchester United. Later Verón said he wanted to join Barcelona, and Real Madrid had a sniff. But Real went for the top of the market instead, and Verón remembered that United had maintained their interest even when a ban seemed imminent.

So it was that Verón was unveiled last week. In signing, Verón has made a leap of faith, moving to a country he barely knows to join a club he had never visited before his medical exam, but Ferguson, in signing a player who has consistently played below his best, is making the bigger leap. The person who seems to have convinced them both is Sven-Göran Eriksson. The Swede managed Verón at Lazio. Now he visits United more often than probably any other club. "He practically has a seat with his name on it in the director's box," says a United insider. Eriksson and Ferguson respect each other and talk often. Eriksson will have assured Ferguson that he can make an honest pro of Verón, and will have helped persuade Verón of the benefits of playing for United. Great players regularly snub Manchester. As Dutch midfielder Phillip Cocu said last week, "Being allowed to live in the sun of Barcelona is different from having to live in the drizzle of northern England." Nor does the club pay as well as its peers—Roy Keane's $70,000 a week would be an insult to Verón.

What United has to offer is prizes and a life. No club in Europe has won more trophies in the past decade. And as Fabien Barthez has found, in Manchester a great player can live almost as he likes. Whereas players in Italy are forever in training camp, United's players gather at Old Trafford only a few hours before kickoff, even for big Champions League matches. "Everyone is very friendly and just sort of chilled," says the United insider. "There isn't much tension." On the other hand, and this is crucial in Verón's case, Ferguson and his players exercise strong social control. Mark Bosnich was doomed when he arrived out of shape for training. When Dwight Yorke became a little too chill last season, the other players let him know. Anyone who relaxes during practice will have Keane on his case. At United, Verón won't be allowed to hit pretty fifty-yard passes to no particular end: He will be made to perform to his potential or leave, his talent wasted. Perhaps he needs United more it needs him.

Watching the thirty-five-year-old Verón play for Argentina at the World Cup in South Africa, I was strangely reminded of England's long-ago cricket captain Mike Brearley. Brearley read cricket brilliantly but didn't play it brilliantly. He was almost a nonplaying captain, and so was Verón. In old age, the shaven-headed one played at a walking pace. Still, it was enough for his old friend Maradona to pick him.

Ruud van Nistelrooy
August 2001

Ruud van Nistelrooy still can't understand a word Nicky Butt says. So dense is Butt's Mancunian mumble that the Dutch striker has to ask Jaap Stam to interpret. However, Van Nistelrooy is learning fast. Every day he practices his Mancunian accent, teaching himself to say "Butty" while distorting the *u* and omitting the *t*'s: "Boo'ey." After just one month at Old Trafford, his English is already deteriorating.

Ian Rush said of his time in Italy that it was like a foreign country. Van Nistelrooy must know what he means. Although his whole life has been a preparation for this moment, he has never experienced anything like Old Trafford before. No player in the United squad has traveled farther to arrive here.

On July 1, 1976, the day Patrick Kluivert was born in Amsterdam, Van Nistelrooy came to earth in the southern Dutch town of Oss. (That's the story anyway; it's more likely that they were separated at birth.) Kluivert's parents were Surinamese immigrants, his father a former player whose name is still legendary in the Dutch West Indies. While in elementary school, the boy joined Ajax. Kluivert was born to greatness. Van Nistelrooy had to achieve it through his deeds. His father was a radiator mechanic, his grandfather a cattle farmer, his first soccer club named Nooit Gedacht (Never Thought of It), and he grew up in entirely the wrong place.

Van Nistelrooy was raised in the village of Geffen near Eindhoven, south of the great rivers that dissect the Netherlands. This is the province of Brabant, where the people are Catholics, more friendly and much less arrogant than in the North. They are more like Belgians than Dutchmen. The Dutch South doesn't produce soccer players, just cyclists. Almost all the country's great players—Cruijff, Van Hanegem, Krol, Rensenbrink, Van Basten, Gullit, Rijkaard, the De Boers, Bergkamp, Kluivert, and Davids, to name a few— are from north of the great rivers, mostly from Amsterdam or neighboring towns like Utrecht. Of current Dutch internationals, only Van Nistelrooy and Boudewijn Zenden (a Maastricht boy) come from south of the rivers.

The South doesn't produce players because it doesn't educate them properly. At Nooit Gedacht, Van Nistelrooy was raised by cheerful volunteers who, the Dutch would say, knew no more about soccer than the average Englishman (sorry). Van Nistelrooy, though not an exceptional talent, was dedicated to becoming a professional. He was diligent at school, but spent the rest of his time kicking balls against garage doors and writing to players for autographs. "On my birthday a picture with autograph arrived from John Bosman," he recalled recently in the Dutch magazine *Voetbal International*. But he remains critical of the former Ajax keeper Stanley Menzo: "Menzo had been trying to see if his pen worked, so there were scrawls on the photograph. I thought that was very careless."

This is how Dutch kids follow soccer: They follow players rather than teams. When Van Nistelrooy joined Manchester United, the British press ritually asked him whether he had supported the club as a child. To Van Nistelrooy, the question made no sense. He had supported Marco van Basten.

At fourteen, he left Nooit Gedacht for mighty Margriet in Oss. Soon FC Den Bosch, a local professional club, invited him for a trial match. The Den Bosch youth coach still remembers that after Van Nistelrooy scored in the game, instead of remaining blasé like a normal Dutch kid, he raced off cheering.

At seventeen, Van Nistelrooy made his debut for Den Bosch. He spent two more years at the club, mainly playing in central midfield, while Kluivert was scoring the winner in a Champions League final and playing for Holland. Then, to Van Nistelrooy's tremendous excitement, he was signed by Heerenveen. It was there that a metamorphosis began. Until then Van Nistelrooy had been a clumsy player, quick and eager but with mediocre ball control and a modest reading of the game. In 1997, one Kluivert was worth about thirty Van Nistelrooys. But Foppe de Haan, the Heerenveen manager, decided that the player had something—in particular, his peculiar broad feet, which, the manager thought, had as much feeling as other people have in their hands. He sent Van Nistelrooy to a Holland match to study Dennis Bergkamp.

Desperate to learn, developing from slender youth into brawny man, and blessed with those broad feet, in nine months Van Nistelrooy outgrew Heerenveen. In 1998 PSV Eindhoven bid $7.8 million for him. It was the highest fee ever paid by a Dutch club, and everyone said it was ridiculous, but he went to Eindhoven and was told he would start on the bench. He was then still mainly an attacking midfielder.

Bobby Robson was lucky enough to be PSV's manager that year. Muddling along without discernible tactics, the club was saved by Van Nistelrooy, who scored thirty-one league goals. He got to this point without much coaching, and it shows. Van Nistelrooy is a player from the Netherlands but not a "Dutch" player, just as Stam (another Dutch provincial) isn't a "Dutch" player, while David Beckham (blond, beautiful pass, can't tackle, in love with himself) is a Dutch player.

Again, the comparison with Kluivert is useful. Kluivert was raised the archetypal Dutch player. He is always looking for the clever pass and never blasts at the goal from a stupid angle or tries to beat two defenders for speed. That would be vulgar. Kluivert misses simple chances because anyone can score from a simple chance. Only proper players can give a clever pass. Van Nistelrooy plays like a South American: sprinting, pushing, throwing himself every which way, shooting all the time. His physique is similar to Kluivert's (are they by any chance related?), but he uses it more. Van Basten is his hero, yet the striker Van Nistelrooy resembles most is Gabriel Batistuta. Both are all-around players built like bulls (both, curiously, with a family background in cattle farming), and neither wastes many shots. They almost always put the ball between the posts. It is a directness that other Dutch players disdain. Van Nistelrooy knows this. By the end of the 1990s, he was a more effective striker than Bergkamp, but he would have been horrified at the thought of taking Bergkamp's place on the Dutch team. Bergkamp is Dutch soccer made flesh (or at least bone). Van Nistelrooy was just a country bumpkin who scored goals.

In October 1999 I saw him play for Holland against Brazil. He had obviously decided that in this exalted company his method of bursting through defenses and scoring had to be ditched. Instead, he played like a third-rate Kluivert, passing to no discernible end.

Yet by this time the Eindhoven airport was virtually scheduling extra flights to accommodate the influx of foreign soccer managers. Arsène Wenger came to watch PSV, Gianluca Vialli saw him for Chelsea, Real Madrid wanted him for their collection, and he was fashionable in Italy. No wonder: Twenty-three matches into the 1999–2000 season, he had twenty-nine league goals and was chasing the forty-three-year-old Dutch record of forty-three. Spookily, it was the third time in a decade that the Eindhoven club had found itself with the best young striker in the world: The previous two had been Romario and Ronaldo. This augurs well for the twenty-two-year-old Yugoslav striker Mateja Kezman, who in his first season with PSV last year scored twenty-four league goals.

Van Nistelrooy could have gone anywhere. He thought the Italian league was the best in the world, but feared that it was too difficult for strikers.

English soccer seemed more suited to his direct and simple style. He was probably won for Manchester United by his meetings with Alex Ferguson. To Van Nistelrooy, it must have been like meeting Van Basten, or even Stanley Menzo. Ferguson was a famous soccer manager! Of course Van Nistelrooy agreed to sign. Maybe he got an autograph in return.

In his autobiography, Ferguson writes, "I was quite excited, for I could tell just by looking into his eyes that this was a young man of substance." One sees what he means. Van Nistelrooy lives for soccer. An intelligent and sensible man, he never gets into the scandals that have embroiled Kluivert. The one blemish on his reputation is the claim by opponents two years ago that he occasionally dived. This briefly earned him the nickname Ruudje Matthäus, after the former German player who is regarded in Holland as the consummate diver.

In March 2000 things began to go wrong for Ruudje Matthäus. First, he injured a knee and failed his medical exam at United. Then, on the morning of Friday, April 28, while he was practicing headers at PSV, his cruciate ligament gave way. By chance a local television station was filming him, and many Dutch fans can still hear him scream. The next day at eight o'clock, Van Nistelrooy was awakened by a phone call from Ferguson, who promised that whatever happened, he would be coming to United. Soon afterward, Ferguson visited the player at home. Van Nistelrooy had surgery in Vail, Colorado. While there he watched Euro 2000 on satellite television, touching the Dutch by waving his crutches frantically in the air whenever Holland scored.

It took nearly a year for his knee to recover. In March 2001 he returned to soccer. In April, in camp with the Dutch national team preparing for a match against Cyprus, he told his teammates at lunch that he had signed for United. They gave him an ovation. Maybe it's a front and perhaps Van Nistelrooy is a bad guy underneath, but everyone who has met him seems to like him. "He's just a good spontaneous guy," says Stam.

Van Nistelrooy came on as a sub for Holland against Cyprus and scored. In June, he came on as a sub against Estonia and scored twice. This is worth mentioning because these are his sole appearances in competitive internationals. He has also played a handful of matches in the first round of the Champions League. In all his career he has played perhaps six competitive matches against top-class teams. In short, at twenty-five he has less big-match experience than Luke Chadwick, baby of the United squad. Van Nistelrooy may look a great striker, but he has never been tested. He also has a damaged knee. On paper, he isn't worth $27 million (but then they don't play on paper).

If anyone knows what it's like to return from serious injury, it is Ronaldo. After watching Van Nistelrooy play for Holland this spring, the Brazilian remarked, "I was impressed by his eagerness. It showed that he doesn't have any more fear. That's the most important thing. That you can do what occurs to you, that you feel your body won't let you down." (Ronaldo added that he wanted one of Van Nistelrooy's shirts. He may need it: Collecting clothes is the Brazilian's hobby, and he changes outfits about six times a day.)

Van Nistelrooy is indeed playing like a man who has never been injured. The Dutchman has scored freely in the preseason, and already United's fans have invented a chant for him ("Ruuuuud!"). He is also bonding with the players. In Singapore, they went out one night as a group, starting in the bar of the Raffles Hotel and proceeding through town. Both Van Nistelrooy and Verón—who speaks no Mancunian—said they were impressed. This did not happen in Italian teams, Verón conveyed.

Van Nistelrooy has begun making friends with Butt and Gary Neville— more influential off the field at United than on it—and he hasn't stopped there. He has gone around Old Trafford and the training ground at Carrington shaking hands with secretaries, security men, and groundsmen: "Hello, I'm Ruud." He and Fabien Barthez (a friendly man with a gift for physical comedy beloved by children) are improving United's image. Van Nistelrooy isn't soft, though. At a recent training session, he chastised Roy Keane about a pass. Untried and damaged he may be, but he will be fine at United.

Michael Ballack
April 2002

Michel Platini, innocently attending the Germany-Argentina game on Wednesday night, was cornered by German journalists and asked a tricky question: What did he think of Michael Ballack?

"I really don't know much about him," the Frenchman stammered. Suddenly, Platini had a characteristic flash of inspiration: Ballack was that big German who had scored those goals against Houllier's team, what was it called, Liverpool, the header and the drive.

Ballack, said Platini, had scored "two different goals" against Liverpool. "Different goals—that's important."

Before leading little Leverkusen to the Champions League semifinals, Michael Ballack had managed to reach the age of twenty-five largely unnoticed abroad.

Few Germans consider this particularly strange. In German soccer, twenty-five years old is unfeasibly young, almost like being fourteen. Ballack is still considered a prodigy. Great hope is attached to him, though this does not mean that German fans like him.

Like many of his country's best players, Ballack is an East German. He was raised in a Saxon village as the son of a construction engineer, played his early soccer for a communist corporation club called Motor Karl-Marx-Stadt, and also attended the local sport school.

This proved the perfect soccer education. Talented East German players were made to train and play nonstop, and those who did not burn out emerged with a wider range of skills than their Western counterparts, whose coaches were always trying to keep things fun. German soccer today depends heavily on *Ossis* such as Jens Jeremies, Carsten Jancker, Alexander Zickler, and Ballack's Leverkusen teammate Ulf Kirsten, who at thirty-six is old enough to have once been an informer for the Stasi secret police.

Ballack was thirteen when the Berlin Wall fell. But when he arrived in the West at FC Kaiserslautern, he was still the stereotypical shy East German. When the club won the Bundesliga in 1998, he had yet to become a regular. Ballack was gifted but inconsistent, a little soft, and Kaiserslautern eventually sold him to Leverkusen for $4 million.

There he chose the number 13 shirt, once the property of local hero Rudi Völler, "to provoke a little." Then he got injured. He went on to score an own goal that cost Leverkusen the Bundesliga title—he cried on the pitch afterward—and at Euro 2000 was granted only sixty-three minutes of play.

Then something happened. Ballack suddenly became a great player, courted by Real Madrid and Barcelona and signed by Bayern Munich for about $40 million, a move he will make after seeing out this season with Leverkusen. (The deal was before the company holding the rights to live Bundesliga matches collapsed, so Bayern may now regret the price.)

His transformation seems to have coincided with his move to attacking midfield. A player of enormous range, who can fly into the box and score with headers, he had previously been wasted at libero or in defensive midfield. Now he is the two-in-one, a central midfielder as good attacking as he is defending: the new Lothar Matthäus.

The other change occurred in Ballack's mind. "I now see myself as a player who has self-confidence," he says. So much so that *Spiegel* magazine, the guardian of German democracy, has published a long feature arguing that Ballack is arrogant. His father called the notion "rubbish with sauce," but many still believe it. A sports magazine ranked Ballack third in a list of players most disliked by Bundesliga players.

This is partly a matter of appearances. To the untutored eye, Ballack resembles a caveman, but Germans think he is handsome, and he dresses well, which in Germany is considered suspect. He is also an elegant player, whose straight-backed run and curly dark hair have prompted comparisons with the young Franz Beckenbauer. Rainer Calmund, Leverkusen's general manager, has called him "the little Kaiser."

But he has a genuine egotistical streak, too. Though a team player, Ballack has never quite assimilated soccer's collectivist ethic. Bayer Leverkusen, the works team of a chemicals company, is not a club anyone dreams of playing for as a child, and to say you would die for the jersey would sound hilarious, but Ballack takes his individualism a bit far.

After Euro 2000 he grumbled that the tournament had "brought him nothing," which was true but tactless given the atmosphere of national mourning. At Bayer, he once Ballacked his coach, Berti Vogts, after being substituted. And when Real Madrid offered Leverkusen an astronomical transfer fee, he turned it down personally, saying that what mattered more was "what you earn yourself."

"You can't tell him anything anymore. He's already a world champion," says Christian Ziege of Spurs, a teammate with Germany. Asked about this, Ballack said Ziege was just angry because of a tackle at training. "I mowed him down. He said, 'Are you crazy?' I said, 'Shut up. What do you want?'"

None of the criticism has unsettled Ballack. His father told *Spiegel* that his son was fortunately "not someone who thinks too much" and, furthermore, was "übercool."

This has been his season. Having underperformed for Germany for years, culminating in that 5–1 defeat in Munich, he scored three goals in the playoff matches against Ukraine to take his country to the World Cup. Playing in midfield, he is the second-highest scorer in the Bundesliga with fifteen. Thanks largely to him, Leverkusen is close to the league title and still in the Champions League.

To the 99.9 percent of German soccer fans who are not Leverkusen supporters, the semifinal against Manchester United is a mere prelude to the greater event of the summer. Germany is short on sporting heroes just now, not even very good at tennis anymore, and a nation's sporting self-esteem has been resting on the Schumacher brothers.

Ballack has emerged just in time for the World Cup. The German team is starting to look respectable again. But they aren't about to win the World Cup, are they?

Rio Ferdinand
June 2002

Even Brazil must be wondering how to penetrate this England defense, which has not conceded a goal in three games. You might beat Danny Mills or possibly Ashley Cole to the byline, but then Rio Ferdinand and Sol Campbell will eat up the cross. The route through the middle, guarded by Nicky Butt and Paul Scholes, looks daunting even for Rivaldo and Ronaldo.

Yesterday Sol Campbell took the left side of the central defense, Rio Ferdinand the right, and they provided a study in contrasting styles.

Campbell was usually marking Denmark's striker Ebbe Sand, but there was more to it than that. While Campbell stands by his man, Ferdinand watches the whole game.

He moves the other defenders around, and when an extra Dane popped up in attack, Ferdinand seldom showed much interest, nor did anything more than glance at him. He generally watches as Campbell and Mills dive in.

Ferdinand is a supervisor, not a cleaner. Like David Beckham, he has blossomed as a leader thanks to Sven-Göran Eriksson's rejuvenation of the team—and he is a more verbal leader than the captain.

Jimmy Floyd Hasselbaink says the two best center-halfs in England are Ferdinand and Martin Keown. Against Keown, says the Chelsea striker, you end the match covered in bruises. But Ferdinand "you almost don't notice."

The Leeds player is the thinking man's center-back, who might barely touch you all game yet not give you a sniff of a goal.

Ferdinand is more interested in the direction of the attack than whoever happens to be in his neighborhood. While Campbell tends to go to where the ball comes, Ferdinand covers space behind and around him.

In his ease of movement he resembles Italy's Alessandro Nesta: tall, fast, and comfortable on the ball, he is nearly the complete defender. Like Nesta, he does not merely defend but organizes his defense.

In the air Ferdinand and Campbell may be the defensive combination of the World Cup. Together they nullified Argentina's policy of hitting crosses for Gabriel Batistuta, and yesterday the Danes won no headers. Ferdinand and Campbell have also scored two of England's five goals so far from corners. ("Rio's goal was an own goal!" insisted Kieron Dyer. "So don't give it to him.")

In Niigata Ferdinand was even granted a couple of brief chants of "Rio!"—a rare honor for a defender. And Dyer gave an unprompted encomium. Without anyone even having asked him about Ferdinand, Dyer said, "I honestly believe that on present form we have the best player in the world, in Rio Ferdinand. Not just the best defender, but the best player."

Dyer said the England squad, which received British television channels in their hotel, had seen Viv Anderson state before the tournament that Ferdinand was "not world-class."

"After forty-five minutes against Nigeria, Anderson came on air and said, 'He is world-class,'" the Newcastle player concluded triumphantly. Foreign journalists concur that Ferdinand is one of the two or three best defenders of the competition. They are struck by his aura. One told me that Ferdinand appears even taller than he is, while a German journalist said that Ferdinand, like Oliver Kahn, is acquiring the sort of mythical status that discourages strikers even before he dispossesses them.

But before we get too carried away with the twenty-three-year-old "New Bobby Moore" (and I gather the nation is getting a bit carried away), it is worth pointing out some shortcomings.

Ferdinand is not a great tackler. He almost always remains upright. This contributes to his elegance, but sometimes a center-half needs to get his shorts dirty. Just before halftime he let a Dane nip dangerously past him to the byline, and when Sand or Jesper Gronkjaer brought the ball into the box, Ferdinand tended not to confront them but to stand off, trying to guide them away from the goal. At moments like that you wish he were more of an old-fashioned English center-half.

He seldom hits a lazy pass, but nor is he a Baresi or Beckenbauer. In the first half he regularly collected the ball from David Seaman, curbing the keeper's love of punting long. But he tends to slot the ball short distances, ideally into midfield or (more perilously) to Mills or Campbell. Still, it is nice to see England defenders pass the ball around with an air of knowing more or less where it is going.

Brazil (unless Belgium stuns the world tomorrow) will be the biggest test of Ferdinand's career. Not just because it is Brazil in a World Cup quarterfinal, but because Brazil is rare at this World Cup in fielding two center-forwards, one of them a genius. Behind them is Rivaldo, who likes nothing better than dribbling through the center of a defense (unless it is shooting from fifty yards). Against Brazil on Friday, Ferdinand will have to do some tackling.

Roberto Carlos
December 2002

It's not about me," Roberto Carlos says, warming himself over a coffee in the Real Madrid canteen (these Spanish winters are tough). "The award is not about Roberto Carlos himself. I think the time has come to honor the job of the defender. Also, I won't have a better chance of winning it. I can't do more than I have done this year. It's impossible to win more titles in just 365 days! I have been a starter in every game, with my club and with my national side. I worked my socks off in every match. What else do I have to do to get the award?"

The Golden Ball for European Player of the Year ought indeed to end up in the trunk of his red Ferrari, but it won't. Today, Ronaldo will be declared the winner. Carlos will finish second and Oliver Kahn, the Germany goalkeeper, third. However, Real Madrid's supermidget—winner of the European Cup, the World Cup, the European Supercup, and the World Club Cup in recent months—unquestionably deserves the prize.

Born in a small town near São Paulo twenty-nine years ago, Carlos was named after a one-legged Brazilian crooner. Perhaps in compensation, he developed thighs the size of Muhammad Ali's at his peak, which is impressive for a man just five feet six. He himself attributes his build to a childhood spent cycling and hauling heavy pieces of farm machinery, but if that were true, every third world village would be thronging with cartoon superheroes.

The thighs took him to Palmeiras, and by the time he toured Europe with the Brazilian national team in the summer of 1995, he was telling everyone, "I'm going to be the best left back in the world. I'm better than Paolo Maldini."

If this was youthful hubris, he never lost it. Like Ali himself, Carlos is forever trash-talking opponents and predicting easy victories. Before the World Cup semifinal, he said Brazil would need only 60 to 70 percent of its potential to beat Turkey, and even that was kinder than the 40 percent he had estimated previously.

Opponents generally remain silent, because they know he is right. Carlos has the simplicity of an untortured soul who has become a multimillionaire thanks to natural gifts. Consequently, he is always smiling. The staff at Real's canteen prefer him to the prissy introvert Raul. So do most journalists, though one Brazilian says that while watching Carlos chuckling in training camp all day with his chum Denilson, he was reminded of "two idiots."

In 1995, Carlos joined Inter Milan, whose manager, Roy Hodgson, practically forbade him to cross the halfway line. A year later, Inter sold him to Real Madrid for $5.4 million, less than they paid for him.

Of all the walking reproaches to Inter's transfer policy, Carlos remains number 1. Perhaps no other human being packs more potency per inch. Carlos runs the hundred meters in 10.6 seconds, his throw-ins regularly travel thirty yards, and his tiny feet—small even by the standards of great players or ancient Chinese ladies—can send a ball flying ninety miles an hour. And he never gets injured. No one else has played more top-level matches in the past five years.

Unfortunately, nobody cares about left backs. It is the position for hiding the feeble. Hence, Carlos passed largely unnoticed until the age of twenty-four, when he hit a free kick for Brazil against France that was speeding well past the goal before changing its mind and bending several yards to finish in the net. France's keeper, Fabien Barthez, never moved.

Carlos imparts the swerve by hitting the ball with his outside three toes. This is a pretty inefficient way of taking a free kick, and he nets fewer than Sinisa Mihajlovic or Gianfranco Zola, but no one else shoots more thrillingly. To quote a great malapropism of British soccer commentating: "He is one of those players who is so unique."

In fact, it comes as a surprise when he names a role model: "Branco, who played in my position just before me for Brazil," he says. "He used to join the attack as often as I do and was also considered a free-kick specialist."

Oh, and Carlos can tackle, too. Because of his unmatched reflexes, he can wait until the last split second when the striker has committed himself. Wherever you are on the field, you are never safe from him. Perhaps the definitive moment of the European Cup final of 2000 occurred somewhere in midfield. Gaizka Mendieta, of Valencia, popped up in yards of space down Real's left, and just as he was about to do something clever, there was a flash of white and Carlos went steaming off in possession. (Only Ronaldo runs as quickly with the ball; without it, practically only Tim Montgomery does, and he is the 100 meters world record holder.) By the time Mendieta turned to see what had happened, Supermidget had almost vanished from sight. Psychologically, the final was over.

Carlos has three Champions League medals, but until this summer he had never won the World Cup. In Brazil, this marks you out as a mediocrity who gets snickered at in the street. "Brazilians aren't so fond of him. He is one of those players that has been away so long that he's almost considered a European and not a Brazilian," says Alex Bellos, author of *Futebol: The Brazilian Way of Life*.

Carlos may look like the average stunted Brazilian pauper—a posh Rio woman, encountering him at the apartment of his Real teammate Flavio Conceicao, took him for a servant—but his lifestyle of Rolexes and jewelry irks people back home.

To get a little respect, he had to win the World Cup. Quite early in this year's competition, he seemed to know he would. Pundits said after the first few matches that Brazil was weak at the back, but in fact Carlos and Cafu just could not be bothered to defend against teams like Belgium or Costa Rica. They would rather have fun, and who cared what Brazil's manager, Felipe Scolari, thought? (Who is bigger, metaphorically speaking anyway, Carlos or Big Phil? Carlos or Vicente del Bosque, the Real boss?) When Brazil met England, things got marginally more serious, and Carlos revealed his gift for irritation. Behaving as if he owned the pitch, he would pick up the ball whenever the referee awarded a free kick to either team. Everyone else who wasted time at the World Cup got a yellow card, but no referee had the nerve to penalize Carlos. (Who is bigger, metaphorically speaking? . . .) Even after Michael Owen's goal, Carlos continued to delay every England free kick. At first, the English players would instinctively wrestle for the ball, but after a while, realizing they were ahead anyway, they began wandering off and leaving him to it.

Whereupon Carlos began pressing them to take their free kicks instantly. His aim, it emerged, was not to waste time but to control the pace of the game, as well as to patronize opponents and referees in the spirit of Stephen Potter's *Theory and Practice of Gamesmanship*. If there were an award for the world's most irritating player, Carlos would win it annually, and Jose Luis Chilavert, the Paraguay goalkeeper, must reflect with satisfaction at having spat in his face during an international, even if this meant that he started the World Cup suspended. "I'd do it again because Carlos showed me his testicles and insulted my country," Chilavert explained.

Speed, power, and gracelessness: It is a recipe for success. In fact, the only qualities Carlos lacks are vision and concentration.

Playing AC Milan in the Champions League last month, he kept hitting beautiful fifty-yard square balls. All were pointless, and a couple were intercepted in dangerous positions, but no one else could have hit them more sweetly. The most surprising aspect of the Milan match was that he was there at all. He had just flown back from a friendly in South Korea with Brazil and was about to return to the Far East for the World Club Cup final in Yokohama. However, Carlos does not miss matches. You would have thought that winning a World Cup might be tiring, but which Real Madrid player has played the most matches so far this season? Yes, it's Carlos, with twenty-three. A trickier question: Who is Real Madrid's reserve left back? Perhaps there is no such thing.

Carlos is more useful to a manager than the cameo genius Ronaldo, and he also saves money on employing a left half, who would only get trampled underfoot anyway. Real's left flank consists of a midget and a pretty winger.

That Carlos was denied the Golden Ball because he is a defender is doubly frustrating, since he is not primarily a defender. Since hardly any team is crazy enough to field wingers against Brazil or Real Madrid, he is usually free to make the play. Yet Johan Cruijff blithely judges, "He is a defender, and I think he has less qualities than the other candidates."

In the canteen, Carlos says, "It seems that soccer has just an attacking face, and that's not right. I also think there are weird things going on in this voting. I have a feeling that this award could be dominated by marketing interests."

Still, it could be worse. "Ronaldo is a very good friend of mine and a teammate. What more can I ask for from a Golden Ball winner?" he said. "He also became the World Cup top scorer and scored in the Intercontinental Cup final, though people shouldn't forget that I gave him the pass for that goal. At that moment, I realized I had clinched the award for him."

In short, he has only himself to blame.

Zinedine Zidane
April 2003

The night after France won the World Cup final, I sat in a chic café near the Paris Opera watching a beautiful blonde Frenchwoman dance for hours in a "Zidane 10" French shirt. France had changed in an evening. Millions of people had suddenly materialized in Paris's streets, for the first time ever demonstrating for soccer, and for one player in particular: "*Zidane Président!*" Zidane has since become the property of the world. Today he is usually imagined in the Real Madrid shirt. Yet his role on the French team—and in French life—is greater. The French just hope it won't end this summer.

Zinedine "Yazid" Zidane is the product of Marseille's Place Tartane, a square now famous as the backdrop to some of his Adidas advertisements. What mattered on the square was not winning, but how you controlled the ball. Yazid was not the best player on the square, just bigger and more diligent than the others. His signature trick, the *roulette*—rolling the ball back beneath his right sole, pirouetting, then dribbling off—he has practiced every day for more than fifteen years. "What counted for him was soccer, and perhaps also judo," recalls his mother, Malika. But it was a particular type of soccer. On the Place Tartane, Zidane rarely bothered using his left foot, and he never headed. When at the age of fifteen he moved two hours up the coast to play for Cannes and a coach first threw a ball at his head, he ducked.

The teenage Yazid was polite, shy, and apparently without ego. Cannes made him complete a 240-question personality test, which found that he was very motivated, had low self-esteem, and never placed his own interests above other people's. The last quality was rare in such a gifted player. Zidane was a queen bee with the attitude of a worker. To this day, he usually passes when he could shoot. This helps explain why his scoring record for France lags behind that of Michel Platini, his predecessor: "Zizou" has twenty-two goals in eighty-seven internationals, while "Platoche" got forty-one in seventy-two.

Zidane progressed from Cannes to Bordeaux and in 1994, at age twenty-two, made his debut for France. Coming on for the last half hour of so against the Czech Republic, with the French losing 0–2, he scored twice to tie the match. Afterward, he phoned the coach who had scouted him for Cannes: "Did you see? One goal with my head, and one with my left foot!" Zidane has such balance, and diligence, that a few years after belatedly starting work on his wrong foot, he could prompt Franz Beckenbauer to remark, "He has equal precision and power in both feet. I have never seen anyone else like it except Andreas Brehme."

He gradually emerged as France's playmaker. In the crowded midfield of modern soccer, which Real Madrid's technical director, Jorge Valdano, calls "a good place to meet people," Zidane alone regularly finds the time on the ball to make telling passes. It's a matter of both vision and unearthly technique.

It was supposed to come together at the 1998 World Cup, in his own country. However, after a match and a half Zidane got himself sent off for retaliation against Saudi Arabia. Suspended for two matches, he was then quiet in the quarterfinal against Italy and the semi against Croatia. France's best player—or so the French had been assuring an unconvinced world—had a forgettable tournament before those two goals in the final. His manager, Aimé Jacquet, noting that the Brazilians marked laxly on corners, had advised him to "take a stroll towards the front post." If fifteen years earlier you had seen a skinny dark Arab boy doing step-overs on the Place Tartane, you might have imagined him scoring twice in a World Cup final. But never with headers.

That night Zidane's picture was projected onto the Arc de Triomphe. In the years since it has been plastered all over France. He is replacing Marianne as the national symbol. You see him on the front door of elementary schools, promoting some worthy goal or other; on television, criticizing the Far Right leader Jean-Marie Le Pen; and as a rather apelike puppet on the French version of *Spitting Image, Les guignols de l'info.* Nicolas Cantaloup, who mimics his voice on the program, explains, "He speaks very little, in a very low tone of voice. So to imitate him, you have to accentuate that. Make him almost apologize for speaking. It's difficult for an imitator to parody Zinedine Zidane because he doesn't have much asperity. It's also hard because everybody loves him. So I've chosen to provoke humor by playing on his relentless stardom. There's a scene at an airport where he unthinkingly signs an autograph for a dog."

This is not far from the truth. Euro 2000, Zidane's best tournament, made him a French immortal. Not injured, not sent off, not even particularly tired, he led France to a second prize in two years. The day after the final he delayed his holiday to go and say farewell to a dying old man he had known in Marseilles. Each six months the French now vote for Zidane as their favorite Frenchman in the regular poll held by the *Journal du Dimanche* newspaper. He is seen as humble and kind, and however deeply you probe, it seems genuine. Nobody has ever come forward to say, "Actually, Zizou is an arrogant wife beater."

His personality is more than a detail. It has helped make *les Bleus* into a unit. You see the team's collective personality at work when an unfortunate opponent wins the ball and is immediately submerged under a swarm of blue shirts.

As Lilian Thuram, the most thoughtful of *les Bleus* (he had once hoped to become a priest), explained in his autobiography, "We have that spirit because our emblematic player is humble. I think Zidane has obliged each of us to carry ourselves irreproachably on the pitch. In the past the French side had some very skilful generations, but their star players lacked modesty. Zidane never throws a dirty look at a player who makes a bad pass. He never neglects to try to win the ball simply because his name is Zidane. On the contrary."

All his colleagues seem to regard Zidane with that sort of reverence. Soccer is about the ball. Everyone who has ever touched the thing has struggled to master it. Zidane comes closest to achieving it. His fellow players can therefore best appreciate his gift. Didier Deschamps, captain of France in 1998 and 2000, remarks, "Zidane achieves on the field what everyone dreams of doing just once. Even if I had trained day and night, I would never have got there."

Deschamps was the first of Zidane's footmen, later succeeded by Patrick Vieira and Claude Makelele. The job does not just entail bringing the master the ball. In a friendly against England in 2000, a couple of minutes after Dennis Wise had overturned Zidane, Deschamps practically murdered Wise. "You don't touch Zizou" was the message.

Yet it didn't help the French at the last World Cup. Zidane landed in Asia exhausted, injured, and distracted by the birth of his third child; missed France's first two games; and after the third flew home with his eliminated team. The French had shown again how strangely dull they can be without him. Henry, Vieira, Robert Pires, et al. just aren't quite enough. And the team's spirit had dissolved in Seoul's Sheraton Walker Hill Hotel under the self-absorbed captain, Marcel Desailly.

The big question after the tournament was who would replace Desailly as captain. The answer turned out to be Desailly himself. The thirty-four-year-old, distinctly past it, was just too powerful to jettison in public. But France's new coach, Jacques Santini, did get in the habit of not picking him. The captain's armband—an important piece of cloth on this team—descended not on Vieira, as everyone had expected, but on Zidane, a man who hates speeches and fuss and who, as Valdano told me, "speaks only with the ball."

Yet as captain, Zidane reunited the French side. He chats with new players, making them feel welcome, and sometimes even addresses the team. People listen when he speaks.

This summer, now mostly from the left flank, he again leads an unfairly strong French side. But this may be the last time. Zidane used to talk about retiring from the national team this year, and from club soccer the next. Then, this winter, he suddenly extended his contract with Real Madrid until 2007, when he will be thirty-four. Now the French hope he might play the World Cup in Germany after all.

It is hard to believe. You often feel that Zidane's physique has limits, that he is too delicate to keep carrying two such demanding teams, that one day that bent back will cave in. His talk of early retirement shows he feels age encroaching. Asked whether he will retire from *les Bleus* this summer, he replies: "I haven't taken any decision. For the moment I am only thinking about the European championships."

Just in case this turns out to be the last time, watch carefully.

Dennis Bergkamp
May 2003

It was Dennis Bergkamp's first match at Highbury, a friendly against Inter Milan in August 1995. He had just fled Inter, where he had been teased as the dressing-room geek, and that evening in London, Nicola Berti, Inter's midfield player, continued the treatment. When Berti began trash-talking him again, Bergkamp jogged off. Berti followed. Bergkamp led him to Tony Adams, who ordered the Italian to leave the lad alone. Berti ran off, so humiliated that minutes later he cuffed a ball boy.

It was an early sign that Bergkamp was going to feel at home at Highbury. Eight years later, two days after his thirty-fourth birthday, perhaps about to collect his second FA Cup winner's medal, he can reflect on a period that has defined his career. There has been no other player like the one Bergkamp became at Highbury.

After that Inter match, two Dutch journalists and I sneaked into Highbury's marble halls. Bergkamp's family was already there, waiting for their boy to finish changing. The father, an electrician, was standing with his hands folded behind his back, studying framed pictures of Arsenal greats.

He would have known most of them. Like many Dutchmen of his generation, Bergkamp Sr. is an Anglophile who named one son after Denis Law (the name became Dennis Nicolaas Maria Bergkamp) and each summer crammed his boys into the car for a pilgrimage to England.

While we waited for Bergkamp to arrive, Glenn Helder, the Dutch winger, and Ian Wright appeared. Wright shook our hands and addressed us slowly and loudly, as you do with foreigners or morons. Then Helder said, "Ian, show these guys what I taught you." Wright concentrated intensely and began bouncing on the marble and shouting in Dutch, "Bog off! Dirty monkey!" Helder looked on like a proud father. The Dutch newcomers felt welcome at Highbury.

Later that night, in the Highbury car park, Bergkamp recalled an article that had once appeared in Amsterdam's local newspaper. Beneath the headline, "Does Dennis Bergkamp Like Girls?" it had identified him as the only Ajax player without a girlfriend. The article still bugged him. Bergkamp had never been at ease at Ajax. The club's "pearls-and-poodles set" alienated the shy child from the Catholic family. Bergkamp was often on Ajax's reserve and youth teams, was sometimes played at right-back, and was always on the verge of being kicked out.

Summoned to the first team at seventeen, his response was, "I don't want to." He wasn't worried about the level of play. What scared him was that he did not know anybody on the first team. That debut season, 1986–1987, he played mostly at outside right, away from scary central defenders. On May 13, 1987, he came on as substitute as Ajax beat Lokomotiv Leipzig 1–0 in the Cup Winners' Cup final in Athens. Bergkamp was then still at school, taking his homework along on away trips.

He played for Ajax until 1993, winning a lot of domestic prizes and a UEFA Cup, and scoring goals—often lobs—that some Dutch fans still remember. Then came Inter, where he was nicknamed Beavis after the cartoon character, and failed, though he did win another UEFA Cup in 1994. A year later Bruce Rioch, in his brief stint as Arsenal's manager, liberated him. "It was good that my first manager here was an Englishman," Bergkamp told the Dutch magazine *Johan*. "Rioch guided me through English soccer culture." (Rioch is a Scot, but same difference.)

English soccer culture turned out to consist of fourteen-pint sessions, tabloids that wrote off the "Flying Dutchman" after he failed to score instantly, and a Highbury crowd forever urging John Jensen, the nonscoring Danish midfield player, "Shoot!" The rest is history: Jensen's banishment, Arsenal's metamorphosis, and the renditions of "Walking in a Bergkamp Wonderland." Bergkamp called Arsenal his "natural home."

Off the pitch, he has been just as happy. He turned out to be a southern Englishman with a Dutch passport. Bergkamp is a private person who tends his own garden. He is Suburban Man. Hertfordshire is his spiritual home. He has a dry, understated "English" wit. (Players think his jokes are nearly as funny as setting somebody's underpants on fire. Dutch internationals still fondly recall a lunchtime double act between Bergkamp and Clarence Seedorf, discussing their plans to install chapels at home.)

Bergkamp also liked the way the English experience soccer: with passion, but never really as a matter of life and death. Told about the replica shirts bearing his number and the name "God," the pious Christian remarked, "Luckily in England there's a bit of irony behind it. In Italy they really believe it."

The British press suited him, too. The tabloids proceed on the good-boy, bad-boy theory of human nature. After discovering how boring Bergkamp's private life was—he is married with three children—they ignored him. In addition, having little interest in soccer itself, they did not judge players match by match, as the Italians had done. Once Bergkamp had revealed his quality, nobody demanded consistency. The odd flash was enough. And whereas the Italians had judged him primarily on goals, the British realized he was a more exotic animal.

In fact, the Premiership allowed Bergkamp to effect a transformation: from a nippy, goalscoring "shadow striker" into a man of moments. Decades after this Saturday's FA Cup final is forgotten, people will still remember a few of those moments: the instant flick and full-circle spin around Nikos Dabizas of Newcastle United, the instant flick and half-volley with the outside of the foot that took Holland past Argentina in the last minute of a World Cup quarterfinal, or the loblet that put Fredrik Ljungberg alone in front of the Juventus goal. "His moments are as great as anybody's who has ever lived," says David Winner, Arsenal fan and author of *Brilliant Orange: The Neurotic Genius of Dutch Soccer*.

Winner thinks Bergkamp has an "aura." Ludicrous as this is, he may be right. Bergkamp's pale face, sparse hair, and splinterlike build contribute to an impression of ethereal fragility. "It's almost mathematical," Winner says. "It's not about taking your shirt off or falling to your knees or making the sign of the cross or belting it in from thirty yards like Roberto Carlos, or all the normal signs of greatness. It's something interior. He has this vision. And when he scores one of his goals or does one of his passes, you realize he's seen something that nobody else in the stadium could have seen."

To his compatriots, Bergkamp epitomizes Dutch soccer. Whereas Seedorf and Ruud Gullit were jeered when they came to play in the Amsterdam Arena, Bergkamp was applauded there in February, even after committing two bad tackles on Ajax players in the preceding match at Highbury.

Like Bergkamp himself, the Dutch cannot understand why Arsène Wenger ever drops him. When Bergkamp is sent on with twenty minutes left, it seems an indignity, like keeping a Vermeer in the cellar.

Not that Bergkamp is a great player—just a beautiful one. Henk Spaan, who compiled an all-time "top 100" Dutch players, ranked him only twelfth. Bergkamp never won the biggest international prizes, Spaan explains. He was seldom Arsenal's most important player. At times, even Ray Parlour was more important to the team.

You would never want Bergkamp playing for your life. To achieve his great moments, he appears to enter a trance, shutting out the match. "People really have no idea what goes into the making of those goals like that," he told *Johan*.

"My gift is not subject to decay," Bergkamp once said. In fact, he probably has one last season to add some moments to our memories of fifty years from now.

Clarence Seedorf
May 2003

On Wednesday, Clarence Seedorf could win his third European Cup with his third club. He is still only 27. He is a complete player. Yet in his native Netherlands, he is despised. "That Clarence Seedorf might win three Champions Leagues means nothing to me," says Henk Spaan, compiler of the authoritative top 100 of his country's best players and a guardian of Dutch soccer culture. Even Simon Zwartkruis, author of a hagiography published this month, *Clarence Seedorf: De Biografie*, said that the player has "pissing-post status" at home.

Seedorf was always going to win a lot of European Cups. On October 28, 1992, at the age of 16 years and 211 days, he became Ajax's youngest player, ahead of Johan Cruijff, Marco van Basten, Dennis Bergkamp, and so on. "For me, Clarence Seedorf is the player of the year 2000," Louis van Gaal, the Ajax manager, said.

Playing at center-back, left-half, winger, wherever Ajax needed him, Seedorf seemed to have nothing left to learn. Already he had a much bigger build than most players, not to say the most prominent backside in the game. In interviews—there was never any question of Rooneyesque protection—Seedorf sounded like a retired cabinet minister, pontificating about discipline, responsibility, and respect. It emerged, inevitably, that he had been de facto manager of his kindergarten, asked to skip a year in elementary school, and voted to his high school student council, as well as captaining all the national youth teams.

He belonged to a brilliant generation. Since childhood he had played in Ajax's youth teams with Patrick Kluivert, enjoying the best soccer education possible. In the first team they joined the De Boer twins, Edgar Davids, Frank Rijkaard, Edwin van der Sar, Kanu, Jari Litmanen, and the others who, in 1995, would win the European Cup, Seedorf's first.

However, an early warning of future troubles, documented by Zwartkruis, came when Seedorf was substituted during the final against AC Milan. While the match raged on, he rose from his seat on the bench to go and debate his substitution with Van Gaal. An alert reserve goalkeeper caught him and held him down until Seedorf, always an obliging character, decided to drop the matter. He was leaving Ajax anyway. After all, he was already nineteen. Sven-Göran Eriksson took him to Sampdoria, where Seedorf took four seconds to adjust. "I was able to develop my personality further, largely thanks to Eriksson," Seedorf told Zwartkruis. "He is not a man who imposes things on you, not a man for whom there is no vision besides his own."

Innocuous as all this sounds, a problem was emerging. Soccer is a hierarchy topped by the manager, but Seedorf understood it as a sort of discussion group in which people could grow their personalities. Even more than soccer, he loves communication. His favorite mode is abstract speech about "positive energy" and how certain events are predestined and assist personality growth.

This was calculated to irritate Dutch fans (who dislike psychobabble), other players (ditto), and managers (who hate players saying anything at all). Yet when Seedorf joined Real Madrid after a year at Sampdoria, five years after they had first tried to sign him, he took his psychobabble with him. A polite and painfully well-meaning man, he did not imagine that it would upset anyone. When he tried to explain tactics during one halftime to Fabio Capello, the Real manager, Capello tore off his jacket and chucked it at him, shouting, "If you know it all so well, you be the coach!"

Although Seedorf won the European Cup with Real in 1998, beating Juventus in the final, he was not really accepted. His teammate Steve McManaman told me that at training sessions, after the manager had spoken, Seedorf would step forward and say, "You don't want to do it like that. You want to do it like this. And then you want to pass to me." He was sold to Inter Milan in January 2000.

Meanwhile, despite having been a regular international player since the age of eighteen, he had alienated virtually his entire home country. One problem was his "Zidane complex." A wonderful athlete, a sort of extremely fast concrete wall who could play one-touch, Seedorf wanted to be an old-fashioned playmaker. Some players have a personality that matches their style of play. Davids and Roy Keane, for instance, are extremely aggressive men and extremely aggressive players. Cruijff was a bossy man and a bossy player. But Seedorf's personality—an extreme version of the responsible eldest son—impels him to play like a chief when he could be a great Indian.

Holland's managers would usually put him at right-half, but Seedorf, in the spirit of personality growth, would constantly pop up at number 10 instead. Because he can outrun opponents without any apparent effort and never seems to tire, he often seems not to be trying. His penchant for humorlessly declaiming boring abstractions in a monotone also annoyed the Dutch, as did his habit of taking and missing other people's penalties and his activities as spokesman for black players.

Seedorf was seen as the leader of a Surinamese separatist movement within the team. This was unfair. He was speaking for Kluivert only because he thought Kluivert was too dumb to speak for himself and for Davids because Davids was too tactless. The widely held opinion that he and Davids are best friends—"twins"—is a misconception derived from the fallacy that all black people are the same. "Edgar and I are two different personalities," Seedorf said politely.

Holland's white players are mostly fond of Seedorf. When I asked Van der Sar about splits within the team, he said, "Those players you're talking about— we've been through a lot with each other." When Van der Sar and Davids were at Juventus, it was Van der Sar whom Seedorf used to phone. Yet Seedorf is often jeered during international matches (by Holland's mostly white crowds), and in a poll during Euro 2000, 81 percent of the public voted him out of the national team. No Dutch player of recent decades has been more despised.

Seedorf went through hard years. His mother would cry in the stands during international matches, and his father begged him to stop playing for Holland. Even Seedorf himself was affected. One Christmas he considered writing a poem to the Dutch people. (Speech not being enough for him, Seedorf is always doing extra communication through poems and songs.) At Inter he was getting on people's nerves, too. He was often left on the bench. He has won nothing since the World Club Cup of 1998.

Yet since he joined Milan last summer, everything seems to have come together for him. He was put in left midfield, with orders to attack and defend, but allowed to drift to the center when his personality impelled him. Milan loved his body—the club's computer program found that he had the maximum desirable amount of muscle, and he was banned from doing weight training. The club can also live with his growing personality.

When Seedorf joined the club, Bruno de Michelis, Milan's sports psychologist, told Zwartkruis: "He talked 10 per cent like a player, 70 per cent like a coach and 20 per cent like a general manager. But I also saw that he was doing it with a positive intention. In the years I've been working with Milan, I've never seen such a strong personality."

De Michelis said that the way soccer works is that if the manager tells the players to defecate in a corner of the practice field, everyone would oblige without question, and only the bravest player would ask: "Certainly, mister, but what colour should our shit be?" Only Seedorf would dispute the very principle of defecation. Soccer is not yet ready for him, but after a few more European Cups, recognition awaits as a psychotherapist or prime minister.

Seedorf won four Champions Leagues before leaving Europe in 2012 to join Botafogo in Brazil. He played there for eighteen happy months (inevitably, he speaks fluent Portuguese), and as I write in January 2014, he has just begun his first job as coach, aged thirty-seven, back home with AC Milan. He is no longer hated in his home country, and indeed risks becoming something of a Dutch national treasure.

Freddy Adu
November 2003

I asked James Will, a Scottish policeman, what he thought of Freddy Adu. "Who's he, then?" Will responded.

Adu is a fourteen-year-old American soccer player hailed as the new Pele. This week he signed his first contract with DC United in the United States. He should achieve the rare double of playing professional soccer and graduating from high school before he turns fifteen. But first it is worth introducing James Will, because his story gives a sense of Adu's chances of becoming Pele.

Will was Scotland's goalkeeper in the Under-17 World Cup final in 1989. They lost to Saudi Arabia in front of a crowd of fifty thousand, in Glasgow, but Will received the Golden Ball as the competition's best player. "I didn't know there was such a thing until I'd actually won it," he recalls by telephone from the Highlands. "It looks nice on the mantelpiece. That's the one thing."

At thirty-one, Will should now be at his keeping peak. But he plays for Turriff United, his village team. What went wrong? "I dunno, mate. The wrong career moves was one thing."

Will joined Arsenal at sixteen, "a guy from Northeast Scotland who was hundreds of miles away from anybody. However well a club looks after you, they can't replace your family." He stayed five years, spent a season at Dunfermline, and then quit. "I got a bit disillusioned with soccer. If one or two persons didn't like you, it could affect your livelihood."

Did he make the most of his talent? "I probably didn't. It was a pity that at seventeen I didn't have the head I have now. You take an awful lot for granted at that age. You don't actually realize what is happening."

Does he regret anything? "Certainly not. If I didn't take the course I'd taken, I wouldn't have married the person I have, and I wouldn't have these two lovely kids."

What does he advise Adu? "He's really got to treat every game as if it was his last and put everything into it."

Will is fairly typical of Golden Ball winners of the Under-17 World Cup. Other laureates include Philip Osundo of Nigeria, William de Oliveira of Brazil, and Oman's Mohammed Al Kathiri, none of whom I had ever heard of. Another, the Ghanaian Nii Lamptey, hailed at fifteen as the new Pele, is now twenty-eight and playing out an unhappy career in the United Arab Emirates. The adult Lamptey turned out to be the wrong shape for soccer.

The only Under-17 Golden Ball winner to enjoy much subsequent success is the American Landon Donovan, who impressed at the last World Cup, but, at age twenty-one, he remains with the San Jose Earthquakes. Cesc Fabregas, the Spaniard who won the award this summer, is now a sixteen-year-old at Arsenal, hundreds of miles from home.

On Wednesday Adu, who despite being so young played brilliantly at the Under-17 World Cup, was presented to the press at New York's Madison Square Garden. A video loop showed him scoring cartoonlike goals at the tournament: a stocky figure endlessly dribbling through entire defenses, a sort of black Maradona.

More surprising though, was Adu the man. Probably the world's best soccer player of his age, he is undoubtedly the world's most mature person of his age. Before the television cameras he gave a long, fluent speech without notes in which he thanked everyone, but particularly his mother. She brought Adu and his brother to the United States from Ghana after winning a green card in a lottery six years ago. She did it to give the boys a better education. In Potomac, Maryland, she worked seventy hours a week at two jobs. This was the American dream, pure.

Beaming at the tearful woman in the front row, Adu said, "We've been through some tough times, Mom, and here's your son, standing right here, smiling back at you. Thanks a lot, Mom. I love you." There wasn't a dry eye in the press conference.

Adu spoke with more articulacy than I have heard from any adult England player. He revealed that he still makes his bed and takes out the garbage. He scorned the idea of hiring a cleaning lady, even now that he has signed a contract with Nike worth $1 million over four years, and will earn similar amounts playing for DC United, his local professional team—until he is eighteen.

"Be humble" is his mantra. "'Normal' is like me," he elaborated. "Always smiling, playing video games, talking trash back and forth with my friends. There are more important things in life than soccer."

Clearly, he may not make it, but Adu is exactly what U.S. soccer needs to compete with the country's bigger sports. Americans are getting a little tired of their athletes going on strike, shooting limousine drivers, and blowing their fortunes on defense lawyers. Finding heroes in American sports can be hard.

The day after the press conference, the United States picked Adu for the Under-20 World Cup, which kicks off in the United Arab Emirates on Thursday. Perhaps Lamptey will be watching.

As of January 2014, Adu was looking for a club. His last employer, the Brazilian club, Bahia, had released him from his contract citing "technical deficiencies." Aged twenty-four, he has played for nine clubs on four continents and succeeded at none of them. He's still young, and yet the end of the road might already be in sight.

Johnny Rep and Bernd Hölzenbein
June 2004

Long time no see!" calls out Johnny Rep, as Bernd and his wife walk into the Hong Kong restaurant in Rotterdam. It will turn out later that the two former players have in fact seen each other once or twice since they met thirty years earlier in the World Cup final of 1974, including one encounter in Ivory Coast. But tonight Rep's opening gambit falls flat, because Hölzenbein doesn't understand Dutch, and Rep speaks barely a word of German.

The two men don't have a natural click. The German looks like a member of the board of Deutsche Bank: red tie, dark suit, and bald head, even if there's something angelic about his rosy cheeks and round face. You see at once that this is a man who takes himself seriously. The cheery Rep isn't like that. This could be a long evening.

The day before, the Hölzenbeins drove to Rotterdam from Frankfurt in just three hours (or so Hölzenbein claims). Then Hölzenbein went missing for a while. This afternoon I finally tracked him down in the lobby of our hotel. It turned that like almost every other German or Dutchman who was already alive in 1974, he had been locked into a room by Dutch state television and interrogated about the World Cup final. The Dutch are hitting the game's thirtieth anniversary hard. The interviewer knew the answers to every question already, and had even told Hölzenbein what the Germans had had for breakfast on the morning of July 7, 1974. "If that's what you say, I'm sure that's right," the flabbergasted Hölzenbein had replied.

He'd also been asked about Jan van Beveren, the great Dutch goalkeeper who in true Dutch 1970s tradition had boycotted the national team and so had missed the World Cup of 1974. Later, Van Beveren and Hölzenbein played together for the Fort Lauderdale Strikers.

"Van Beveren's become a stamp dealer in Dallas," I tell him.

Now Hölzenbein is even more flabbergasted. "You must have heard that from the guy who interviewed me, because he told me the same thing!"

"I knew it already," I say nonchalantly.

You can see Hölzenbein thinking: "What on earth is going on here?"

In the Hong Kong restaurant we order several dishes to share—which creates a little bit of a bond—and for an hour hardly talk about the final at all. Hölzenbein does reveal, thirty years too late, that the German team revolved around Gerd Müller. The aim was to get the tubby striker the ball as fast as possible. Hölzenbein says, "Müller would turn and go 'Boom.' That wasn't a secret." Yet it was Müller who scored the winning goal in the final.

Otherwise, though, there is just polite chatter about modern soccer, chatter that doesn't really interest anyone at the table, except perhaps the soccer-mad Mrs. Hölzenbein. "Sometimes she'll go to a match while I'll stay home," says Hölzenbein.

Rep seldom watches games, either. Contemporary soccer barely interests him. He lives on the chilly Dutch vacation island of Texel, where he coaches a team in the fourth division of the amateur league, about as low as you can go down the Dutch soccer pyramid. Hölzenbein doesn't work for a club at all, though he is Frankfurt's "city ambassador" for the coming German World Cup of 2006.

He grows animated only when he seizes an opportunity to pull a photograph out of his wallet. "Look!" On the picture, taken at the Helsinki airport, Hölzenbein is standing next to German chancellor Gerhard Schröder. The chancellor, a former amateur center-forward, is grinning, and Hölzenbein is staring solemnly into the lens. Behind them on the tarmac is Schröder's private jet. Perhaps the chancellor carries the same snap around in his wallet and sometimes shows it to Tony Blair: "Look! This is me with Hölzenbein. And my private jet."

The picture was taken in Helsinki, where Schröder and Hölzenbein were stopping over on the way back from the World Cup final in Japan in 2002. Hölzenbein had been invited to the match as a representative of the German world champions of 1974. On the plane he and the chancellor had spoken "very intensively" about soccer. Schröder had asked if Hölzenbein's tumble in the box in '74—which produced Germany's equalizing goal from the penalty spot—had really been a foul.

After dinner it's just a short totter from the Hong Kong to Rotterdam's Goethe-Institut. This evening, the German cultural center is hosting a panel about the final of '74. My German colleague Christoph and I are the moderators. As we leave the restaurant, we warn Hölzenbein that the Dutch audience will want to talk only about his famous "dive." In Dutch soccer terminology, a dive is a *Schwalbe*—the German word for "swallow," as in the diving bird. Because the Dutch regard diving as an authentically German pursuit, they feel it's appropriate to describe it with a German word. We hope Hölzenbein doesn't find the topic of the famous penalty too boring.

"No," he sighs. "Not anymore."

The chief dignitaries tonight are sitting in the audience: the German ambassador, the mayor of Rotterdam, the global number two of the Goethe-Institut. These are men who went to college and are now doing better than their contemporaries who wasted their youth playing World Cup finals. First the dignitaries are allowed to give speeches. Then Rep, Hölzenbein, Christoph, and I take our places at an overlit table at the front of the hall.

After Hölzenbein has elaborately denied that it was a *Schwalbe*, Rep says he always turns off the television anyway when scenes from the final come on. Pointing at Hölzenbein: "Then you see him tripping over his own feet again." There's laughter, but not from Hölzenbein, who doesn't understand what Rep is saying. Rep continues, "No, I'm sick to death of it. In the final I could have scored a hat trick, because I missed several chances. Also in '78, [in the final] against Argentina, I had a header that just shaved the post. I still sometimes dream of it."

It's a nice quote, but I'm not sure it's true: Rep is such an obliging man (that's why he has driven all the way from Texel to be here today) that he will say whatever we want to hear.

I ask Rep if he ever did a *Schwalbe* himself.

"What do you think?" he asks.

"Yes?" I guess.

"Against Scotland in 1978 I let myself fall in the penalty area."

"So you got Holland to a World Cup final with a *Schwalbe*?"

"No, I got Holland to a World Cup final with that stunning second goal against Scotland."

Then, gesturing with his thumb at the *Schwalbe* king: "He'd done it in the previous match as well! He was brilliant at that." Even Hölzenbein laughs a little now.

Then Hölzenbein tells the old story of how the German coach Helmut Schön told his players to look the Dutch in the eye in the tunnel before kickoff.

Rep says, "And still we were 1–0 up after the first minute."

The audience takes the final very seriously, but the players just seem to want to tell jokes. Winning the World Cup must have been the highlight of Hölzenbein's career, I suggest. Perhaps even the highlight of his life?

Hölzenbein doesn't think so: "In the World Cup team the big figures in the hierarchy were Beckenbauer, Müller, Overath. I myself was younger, less important." (There is barely a player on earth who can say of himself, even decades later, "I myself wasn't as good.") "But at Eintracht Frankfurt I was captain, and I must say that winning the UEFA Cup as captain was almost as important to me as winning the World Cup."

Look, he says, for Germans the world championship of 1954 towers over the victory of 1974. And he feels the same way. "Just like everyone else I saw the final of '54, as a small boy, on the only TV set in a radius of perhaps ten kilometers. Those players were my idols. I devoured the books of Fritz Walter [Germany's star of 1954]. 1954 was a symbol of resurgence. 1974 was less important. And as for 1990, you don't even remember who was in the team."

Although the audience wants to ask only about 1974, Hölzenbein has a story about the Netherlands that he's determined to share. In 1966, he says, he came over to play in a youth tournament in The Hague. He and another German boy, who also later became an international, stayed with a local family. Twenty-five years later they were still in touch with the family. And it was during that very same tournament that Eintracht scouted Hölzenbein.

The audience is eager to get back to 1974, but Hölzenbein has other Dutch stories he wants to tell. In 1967 he returned to the Netherlands, this time with his girlfriend, the future Mrs. Hölzenbein, and he remembers that the hotel assigned them separate rooms. He had always thought that the Netherlands was so liberal.

Gradually, it's becoming apparent that neither player can understand why everyone in the hall is so interested in the World Cup final. "Now there's even someone writing a book about it!" marvels Rep.

Can Hölzenbein still remember July 7, 1974, or has it been driven out of his head by thirty years of talking about it? Can he still recall the moment when he saw Wim Jansen's raised leg advance toward him in the penalty area, or does he only know what he keeps saying about it and what he occasionally sees on television?

"I can't really remember it anymore," admits Hölzenbein. In his head, the World Cup final has been replaced by "the World Cup final."

So far this evening we have avoided mentioning the war. But it is the underlying reason we're gathered here. It is because of the war that Dutch fans care most about matches against Germany. The reverse is not true of German fans. In 1974, they weren't particularly interested in Holland. They could hardly treat every match against Holland, England, Scotland, Wales, Northern Ireland, the United States, France, Belgium, Denmark, Norway, Iceland, Poland, the Czech Republic, Serbia, Greece, Belorussia, Ukraine, Russia, Canada, Australia, or New Zealand as particularly significant.

I ask Rep whether he had particular feelings about Germans in 1974.

"That bike, eh?" he says.

He is referring to the Greatest Bike Theft in History: the commandeering of all Dutch bicycles by the German wartime occupiers. The dignitaries titter. Rep was probably joking.

"They should give us our bikes back," he continues. "But otherwise the war wasn't a big thing in my mind."

It was for certain other Dutch players, I say, men whose families had experienced the war very closely.

Rep says, "I think so. Because they really did want to beat Germany. After the final there were a few crying in the changing room."

But was the war never mentioned in the Dutch team's hotel in Hiltrup?

"Never," says Rep.

It's known that the Dutch midfielder Willem van Hanegem as a baby had lost his father, ten-year-old brother, and six other Van Hanegems during a British bombing of the family's home village of Breskens. Less well known is that the father of Ruud Krol, Holland's left-back in 1974, was one of the few Dutchmen who actually joined the Resistance during the war, as opposed to just talking about it afterward.

In 1999 I visited Kuki Krol in his little house in Amsterdam. He was a tiny man whose right foot was shrouded in an enormous boot. Only his big nose evoked his handsome son. From his settee, Krol Sr. sent me to inspect a buffet table on the other side of his living room. On the table stood a photograph of a dead young man. He had combed-back, Brillantined hair in the fashion of the early 1940s. In those days the dead man had worked in Krol Sr.'s shop.

Krol Sr. told me: "Some were lucky, but he wasn't. One day the German security police raided my shop. They came for me, but they found him. He was in the communist Resistance. They put him up against the wall, with his hands by his side—that was a technique of the time—and his bad luck was that that day he had three identity cards on him. He never came back. But they had come for me." At one point during the war Krol Sr. was hiding thirteen Jews in his corner apartment in Amsterdam.

Our conversation was awkward. Krol Sr. was an angry man. He had been good in the war but had been haunted by it forever afterward, and had never been rewarded for his goodness.

A couple of days after we met, he phoned me. He didn't want me to write about our conversation. He knew that he'd never managed to let go of the war, that he could only talk about it emotionally. He knew that sometimes that wasn't such a good idea.

He died in 2003, and now I'm publishing this fragment of our conversation. Kuki Krol was good in the war and spent the rest of his life paying for it.

The point is that his son Ruud (born in 1949) probably had more feelings about the war and the Germans than Rep did. But in 1974, Dutch people—players and civilians—rarely mentioned the war. It was still too early. Only in the 1980s and early 1990s did vocal anti-German feeling break out in the

Netherlands. In part, people were expressing a fear of the mighty new Germany of their own day, in soccer and outside.

From the mid-1990s, the anti-German feeling faded again. By the time of our evening in the Goethe-Institut, in 2004, hardly anyone in Holland is still afraid of the second-rate neighboring power with its stagnant economy. By now, the stereotypical German in the Dutch mind is no longer the fat Bavarian in the newest-model BMW but the unemployed skinhead on an East German streetcar.

After the debate, over beers at the Goethe-Institut, a German diplomat confirms that the Dutch have stopped hating Germans because they have stopped fearing them. There's certainly no hatred on display tonight. Trauma? It's great fun. A lot of Dutch people come up to Hölzenbein for a quick chat, though it's noticeable that most of them speak English to him, because few Dutch people speak German anymore.

Just before closing time we grab a table at a grand café: the Hölzenbeins, Rep, a Dutch friend of mine from childhood named Rutger, and me. It's Monday evening, and we're the only people in the café. (Rotterdam was bombed to pieces by the Germans on May 10, 1940, and afterward rebuilt with skyscrapers, so that nowadays there is often more space than people.) The bar staff, not knowing that two of us are demigods, agree to serve us only after lengthy entreaties. We order as many beers as possible. Rep and Hölzenbein chat about soccer in basic English and German, and only now do I see how differently players do it from normal people. It's a terrible realization: All those things you dream about (World Cup finals and so forth) aren't the things that actual players think about.

Rep says he doesn't have a single souvenir left from the World Cup of 1974. "I don't think so. Oh, yes, an Argentine shirt. I've got nothing from the World Cup '78. We didn't even swap—just went inside quick as a spear."

The players' syndrome explains why Hölzenbein was more interested in the World Cup of '54 than '74: In 1954 he was still a fan.

Give players the chance to chat without an interviewer, and they talk about the strangest things: Did you ever play with that guy? Strange bloke, wasn't he? Didn't I once play against you at a summer tournament in Abidjan?

Rep reminisces about a striker he played with at Valencia who was known as *El Lobo* (The Wolf), because he was also dangerous at night.

Hölzenbein asks if we know the former Dutch player John Pot.

"Cor Pot!" we correct him in chorus, referring to a journeyman defender turned journeyman coach.

"John Pot," says Hölzenbein decidedly. "Big, strong guy who used to play at the back for Fort Lauderdale."

"A darling of a man," adds Mrs. Hölzenbein.

"I've looked him up on the Internet, but found nothing," says Hölzenbein.

Later I Google John Pot and find only one reference: When George Best scored a brilliant goal for the San Jose Earthquakes against Fort Lauderdale on July 22, 1981, he beat (according to a reconstruction by the *Oakland Tribune*) Ray Hudson, Thomas Rongen, "Steve Ralbvsky, then John Pot and finally Ken Fogarty." Otherwise, it's as if John Pot never existed. I consulted several experts on Dutch soccer, but none had heard of him. A mystery is born.

Anyway, this is the kind of thing old players have in their heads: Where is John Pot? The fan who runs into a former player in a bar will ask him about his *Schwalbe*, or about the "Swimming Pool Affair" (a German tabloid story headlined "Cruyff, Champagne, Naked Girls, and a Cool Bath," which according to many Dutch fans cost Holland the World Cup final a few days later). But the typical former pro (and I'm not talking about Rep or Hölzenbein now) remembers his first goal for the first team, or the curvy housewife he met in a café on the night after the final, or the teammates who used to tease him, or the article in the local newspaper that hinted he was gay.

The history of soccer would read very differently if it were written by actual players. They would never organize a debate about a long-gone World Cup final, or if they did, it would focus on the postmatch banquet to which the wives weren't invited, and where Rep and Germany's Paul Breitner swapped suit jackets.

World champions or not, shortly after midnight we are kicked out of the café. On the street we say good-bye to my friend Rutger. Rep has been cadging cigarettes from him all night. Now the two grip hands like old pals, and Rutger shakes Hölzenbein's hand and kisses Mrs. Hölzenbein. Then Rutger turns to me and half-whispers, "You know, I'm never going to forget this."

I think Rep and Hölzenbein have had a nice time, too.

* The Internet has solved the mystery of John Pot. Since I wrote this article in 2004, various new references to him have appeared online. He seems to have been a

Dutchman, born in 1958, who never played professional soccer in his own country but featured in sixty-four games for Fort Lauderdale from 1980 through 1982. However, nothing else seems to be known about him.

Michael Essien
August 2005

The most surprising aspect of the Michael Essien saga, to his teammates, is that he has stopped smiling. A man of practically no words, the Ghanaian tends to sit beaming in a corner of a locker room when not bouncing around soccer fields so vigorously that you get tired just watching him.

Essien is upset because his club, Olympique Lyon, is blocking his transfer to Chelsea. Lyon want a fee of $54 million, which would make him the most expensive defensive midfielder in history. Chelsea, the world's richest club, has offered $35 million. Manchester United may also be interested. Meanwhile, Essien has gone on strike at Lyon. This tug-of-war is happening because the mute monster is the model player of our time.

His story is suitably globalized. Essien grew up in the steamy Ghanaian capital of Accra with four sisters. He spent his childhood dribbling around trees and sometimes crashing into them. He first appeared on television while helping Ghana's under-twelves thrash Benin, was later spotted by scouts at a tournament in New Zealand, and at seventeen got a trial with Manchester United. He showed up at Old Trafford with a fellow Ghanaian, whose bad behavior irritated United. The club didn't particularly like Essien, either, but offered him a spell with its Belgian farm team, Royal Antwerp.

Essien said no. He mooched around his agent's apartment in Monaco distraught, until the agent phoned Bastia in Corsica and persuaded them to take the boy. There Essien grew into a monster. He is less than six feet tall, but his body is nearly as broad as his smile. He says he never gets tired. Mind you, he also says his hobby is sleeping.

Bastia was delighted: Essien didn't even speak, which is exactly how soccer clubs like players. In 2003 it sold him to Lyon for €12 million. This May a Parisian court decided that part of that sum had been funneled to a

Corsican nationalist, terrorist and Bastia fan Charles Pieri, who had been jailed for ten years.

At Lyon Essien kept getting bigger, as if in a horror movie. "Physically, he's the most impressive person I've played with," says his teammate Sidney Govou. Another teammate nicknamed him the Bison. Essien himself remarks that he has yet to meet anyone who could knock him over.

An economist would note his multifactor productivity. The trend in sports is to measure more and more, and whichever variable Lyon chose, Essien was best on the team. He touched the ball more times than anyone else and had the most tackles, most completed passes, most interceptions of opponents' passes, and sometimes the most shots on goal, but despite his penchant for sawing opponents in half, he was rarely caught fouling. You could judge him without even watching him. Reading the stats was enough. He was voted France's best player of last season.

In short, Essien exemplified the growing physicality of most sports, from tennis to baseball. The average player now runs almost six miles a match, nearly three times more than thirty years ago. With everybody whizzing around, space shrinks. The center of midfield, where the ball is most often, has become like the line of scrimmage in American football: a "pit" where monsters like Essien roam, trampling the weedy playmakers who once ruled there.

The only playmakers still thriving in central midfield are the two-in-ones, men so physically strong that they double as monsters: Pavel Nedved, Michael Ballack, or Steven Gerrard. Weedy playmakers—Francesco Totti, Alessandro del Piero, and even Zinedine Zidane—struggle. The exemplary tale is that of Javier "the Rabbit" Saviola, Argentina's weedy playmaker in their 3–0 thrashing of Essien's Ghana in the World Youth Cup final of 2001. Saviola went straight to Barcelona for a salary of $4.4 million a year. Today, while everyone wants the Bison, Barcelona is quietly offloading the Rabbit onto their little neighbors Espanyol.

This autumn Essien may even help Ghana qualify for its first-ever World Cup. He needs to. Ghanaian fans often judge players by their willingness to "serve their country," and Essien, like most expatriate players, has been found wanting. The problem isn't that he emigrated. Ghanaians expect that. Whereas the country once exported cocoa, gold, and slaves, today it exports cocoa, gold, and workers. But fans don't like expat players showing up for an international match "in posh-posh cars," complaining that their plane tickets weren't waiting for them at the airport, and then resting on the pitch. Before a crucial qualifying match in South Africa in June, Essien had to insist, "We're ready to die for our country." Perhaps it was true, because Ghana won.

But he's miserable now. Lyon is testing the theory that Chelsea—funded by Roman Abramovich's billions—will pay any transfer fee. Chelsea is trying to prove them wrong.

In the few recorded instances of Essien speaking, he has mentioned his dream of joining Manchester United. But such sentiments seldom influence players, and today he would prefer Chelsea. Meanwhile, he wanders around shrouded in gloom and in his headphones, irritating his employer. "At that level of remuneration, a certain ethic should exist," says Jean-Michel Aulas, Lyon's chairman, expressing a peculiar moral philosophy.

At least the Zeitgeist is on Essien's side. As Damon Runyon wrote, "The race is not always to the swift, nor the battle to the strong, but that's the way to bet," and it's even more true now than when Runyon wrote it.

As I argue in my later article on Cesc Fabregas, the era of "monsters" ruling central midfield was short-lived. On the other hand, the era of Essien at Chelsea has been long-lived. Nine years after his arrival, he was still there, albeit not quite so monstrous anymore.

Fabio Cannavaro
July 2006

Holding the World Cup aloft is the highlight of a life, but the Italian captain Fabio Cannavaro was a world champion long before Sunday. Now he simply has the medal to prove it. The cherub carved from stone should also have been named player of the tournament, because he was the image not just of Italy but of this World Cup.

From soon after birth in Naples thirty-two years ago, Cannavaro cultivated a peculiarly Italian ambition: to be a defender. The man-marker is a peculiarly Italian profession, like gondolier or fashion designer. The most enjoyable thing in soccer, says Cannavaro, is marking: *"Marcare, marcare, marcare!"* He is scornful of strikers. They can play terribly and be praised for one goal, but defenders are hanged for one mistake. Cannavaro belongs to the Italian school that says the perfect match ends 0–0, because there were no errors.

Had he been born in Britain, he would probably never have found employment as a center-back: He is only five foot eight. To compensate, he built up his upper body and arms. A defender needs his arms, Cannavaro says, because he must constantly touch his striker, place him where he wants him to be. Cannavaro loves the details of his craft.

He understands his worth. Asked at Euro 2000 to name the best defenders there, he said, "After myself and Nesta, I think the Frenchman Thuram." But Cannavaro's sole mistake of that tournament allowed France's Sylvain Wiltord to score the equalizer in the final. France won.

On Sunday there could be no repeat. Going into the final, Cannavaro's defense had conceded once in six games, and that an unstoppable own goal. Cannavaro sets high standards for his men. When his colleague Marco Materazzi permitted a German shot in the semifinal, Cannavaro stood beneath the giant, lectured him, and then slapped him in the face. Cannavaro believes a defender does not permit shots—he throws out a limb to block them—or corners, free kicks, or even throw-ins.

Cannavaro was the tournament's best gymnast, ahead of Miroslav Klose. He routinely outjumps much taller men, or clears by overhead volley. So agile is he that he can defend side-on, forcing the striker into a particular direction, because he can always stretch to tackle. He can even break the rule that says defenders should not go to the ground. Cannavaro can, because he rises instantly. On Sunday he performed three sliding tackles on Florent Malouda in just over a second, possibly a world record.

His battles with Thierry Henry were everything a World Cup should be: the best against the best. Henry managed a shot, and once actually dribbled past Cannavaro, but was eventually substituted, drained and scoreless, like dozens of Cannavaro's opponents before him.

Cannavaro did not man-mark Henry. He and Materazzi had the flexibility to mark by zone. Cannavaro is both marker and libero: He probably had Malouda covered when Materazzi fouled him for France's penalty. For that, Materazzi may have taken a pounding worse than anything Zinedine Zidane did to him.

Cannavaro watched the penalty shoot-out without smiling, his massive tattooed arms folded, Andrea Pirlo hugging him from behind. Goals are not his business. He has scored one in one hundred internationals. Italians don't care. They admire defending. During Sunday's game their fans applauded him more than any other player. We should do likewise, because if you can't appreciate defending, this World Cup was rather empty.

It's a shame that Cannavaro consented to play in the World Cup in South Africa in 2010, aged thirty-six, thereby allowing himself to be humiliated in front of a global audience. It tarnished our memories of him. Somebody should have stopped him.

Dirk Kuyt
September 2006

I knew players like Dirk Kuyt even before he was born. As a kid I played against them in the dunes of his home village of Katwijk on the Dutch coast. I respected and feared the Kuyt type, but I never imagined Liverpool Football Club signing one. Yet last month the club bought the Dutchman for about $19 million. Today he hopes to start his first match for them, the Merseyside derby against Everton. The temptation is to say he won't be worth $19 million, but then Kuyt has always been, as President Bush might say, "misunderestimated."

On winter Saturday mornings around 1980, the year of Kuyt's birth, my soccer team would travel to Katwijk in the backseats of our dads' cars. Often our opponent would be Kuyt's future club, Quick Boys. As we passed Katwijk's churches, fast-food joints, and the bed-and-breakfasts with their German signs in the windows, sea gales would shake the car.

Quick Boys' locker rooms were always packed, because Katwijk's sailors and fishermen all played their soccer on Saturdays. Sundays were reserved for worshiping the Lord. Every local male seemed to play: Quick Boys currently have twenty men's teams, and fifteen teams in the under-nine age group alone. Telling the men from the boys was often tricky, because many Katwijk children—raised on fish, milk, and the west wind—were already as big as Kuyt is now.

Our opponents tended to be albinos like Kuyt and only had a handful of surnames between them, often Kuyt. They didn't bother much with ball control, perhaps because the wind and the Lord took charge of that, but in my memory we always lost. Sometimes we were watched by hundreds of spectators. And Quick Boys wasn't even the best club in Katwijk. Their rivals, FC Katwijk, later also became Dutch amateur champions. Having often watched the Quick Boys–Katwijk derby, Kuyt won't be overawed by Everton-Liverpool.

Amateur soccer was such a big deal in Katwijk that the local stars seldom bothered joining professional clubs. Yet at eighteen Kuyt signed for FC Utrecht. Nobody expected much of the potbellied sailor's son with Katwijkian ball control, but he almost instantly became a regular. In fact, the only thing that seemed to throw him at Utrecht was the godlessness of his new teammates. "In Katwijk certain things are taken for granted. I came to FC Utrecht and saw guys who lived with their partners, got a child, and only then got married," he marveled. The Lord only knows what he will make of the Premiership.

In 2003 a bigger Dutch club, Feyenoord, reluctantly shelled out $1.1 million for Kuyt. Few expected him to cope with the higher level, but his unforeseen rise continued: Within a year he was Feyenoord's best player. This was probably because Kuyt works harder at himself than does any other soccer player. He treats training sessions and matches as mere episodes in his packed working schedule. When not in the gym, or studying future opponents, he pays weekly visits to a mental coach, to a layer-on of hands, and to his personal physiotherapist.

None of this is intended to treat injuries. Kuyt never gets injured. He went five years and a month until this spring without missing a Dutch league match, eleven months longer than Frank Lampard's record streak in England. Rather, Kuyt hires healers to perfect an already superhuman body, much as Pamela Anderson got breast implants. He gives an example: "Recently my physio got special soles installed in my soccer cleats. Tests showed I don't stand completely straight on my feet, so that I can't move my neck fully. Since I've been wearing those soles, my neck is free again."

Besides injuries, Kuyt has also excluded loss of form. He is mentally so strong that he almost never plays badly. In each of the past four seasons, he scored at least twenty league goals.

Kuyt exudes the joy of a man in his prime whose every body part is in perfect working order. Most goalscorers save their energy for scoring. Kuyt gallops down wings and tackles on his goal line. A better defender than most defenders, he provides more assists than most wingers. His specialty is accelerating while receiving the ball, a horror for opponents.

Because he is never injured and always improving himself, he was able to advance inexorably from Quick Boys to Liverpool. This is an indictment of other soccer players. Kuyt's rise implies that his colleagues, even those who aren't drunks, are performing below their potential. If they all lived like Kuyt, professional soccer would be a better game.

"Doing your best isn't a chore, is it?" he asks. "I must thank God on my bare knees that I became a soccer player. And I do."

There is one thing Kuyt can't learn. No Katwijker will ever develop perfect ball control. "I don't have the technique of Robin van Persie," he once admitted, "but of all the Dutch talents I do have by far the best mentality." It has taken him far: Last month his deathly ill father, a tube emerging from his nose, presented him with the Dutch Player of the Year award at a gala evening.

But this summer's World Cup suggested that even Kuyt's mentality can't take him all the way. On his first venture onto international soccer's upper slopes, his running kept defenses busy, but in his only match as Holland's first-choice center-forward, against Portugal, he failed.

On August 15 Glenn Roeder, manager of Newcastle, one of countless clubs hoping to sign him, watched Ireland-Holland in Dublin. Holland's center-forward duly scored twice. Sadly, it wasn't Kuyt, but the twenty-three-year-old debutant Klaas-Jan Huntelaar, scorer of more than fifty goals last season. Huntelaar is the latest to overtake Kuyt in the hierarchy of Dutch center-forwards.

It's possible that Liverpool bought the wrong Dutch striker: that although Kuyt won't flop at Anfield, because he never flops, he won't quite conquer the place, either. However, Kuyt always proves doubters wrong. "My career is a straight line upwards," he notes. At the very least he will teach his teammates something about being an athlete.

Romario
March 2007

I t's often said he looks like the average Brazilian. Romario is coffee-colored, only five foot six (to be known as *O Baixinho* (Shorty) in Brazil is a pretty extreme condition) and not obviously an athlete. At forty-one he is segueing into middle age. His legs are bowed, his calves skinny. Only the vast thighs and torso give a clue to his trade. Romario is the most remarkable goalscorer still playing soccer. He claims to have scored 992 goals. When he gets his 1,000th he will retire, and a certain type of player will have gone extinct.

Of course, he will finish in Rio de Janeiro, at Vasco da Gama, the club where he began in 1985. Born in a Rio slum and raised in a slightly nicer slum, Romario is the supreme *Carioca*, or citizen of Rio, who expresses his patriotism partly by buying his native city's real estate. Outside Rio, his oddities are less appreciated. "In São Paulo," growls a Paulista, "he is regarded practically as an Argentinean." Romario is that characteristic Rio type, the *malandro*: an opportunist, a lover of fun, a rule breaker.

At twenty-two he left Rio to join PSV Eindhoven. A *malandro* and the Dutch workplace were not an ideal combination. Here was a man whose hobby was sleeping (fourteen hours a day); who said his teammates could not play soccer; who flew home to Rio when he felt like it, matches or not; who liked nightlife so much he was going "to keep going out until I am ninety years old." A PSV physiotherapist was made responsible for getting him out of bed each morning. On the pitch Romario rarely moved yet averaged nearly a goal a game.

He treated his European years as an exile, a strictly moneymaking exercise: "In Holland I work; I live in Rio." He failed to comprehend Dutch weather, or the natives' habit of turning up for appointments, or the way they expected great players to obey rules. The one Dutch phenomenon he appreciated was the tall blonde girls.

Yet he always scored, and eventually Barcelona signed him. Even at a giant club he remained blasé. Guus Hiddink, once his manager at PSV, remembers visiting Barcelona as coach of Valencia. Romario was about to kick off the match in front of one hundred spectators when he suddenly told the referee to hang on, jogged over to Valencia's bench, and kissed his old boss on both cheeks. Hiddink mimes the kisses. To Romario the match was just décor, with him the only character. In an increasingly corporate sport, his selfishness was almost heroic.

Brazilian greats are judged at World Cups. Partly due to his weird personality, Romario played only an hour at the Cup of 1990. He announced that the next tournament, 1994, would be "Romario's Cup." Brazil's coach, Carlos Alberto Parreira, who had previously banned him from the team, was persuaded to relent. "Romario came in a good mood," Parreira told me years later. "He wanted to be what every soccer player wants: world champion. Romario is very good in the team. He plays the drums, he tells jokes, he's not . . ."—Parreira tilted his nose in the air to show what Romario was not— "He's a happy man." That may be, yet Romario objected to sitting next to his striking partner, Bebeto, on the plane to the tournament, where his main sponsor was a beer brand.

"I can place the World Cup before the Brazilian as if it were a plate of food," said the boy from the *favela*. He did. The most functional of players, Romario used his genius only to score. "If it had been a European player, he would have put it in the far corner," observed Russia's goalkeeper Dmitri Kharin that World Cup. "But Romario is a Brazilian, and he put it in the near corner." His goal against Holland in the quarterfinal was finer still. A cross landed too far ahead of him, so he flicked himself three yards through the air and, while still dropping, virtually on top of the ball, hit a half-volley with the outside of his right boot into the inside corner of the net.

And that pretty much concluded his career in top-class soccer. He has spent the past thirteen years mostly in the decayed Brazilian league, with brief forays to places like Qatar, Adelaide, and Miami. One night I saw him playing for Flamengo in Rio's almost-empty Maracana stadium, built for 200,000. Most of the fans who had shown up spent the match running up and down the track, following the ball. In this sort of ambience, Romario sometimes paid his teammates' wages or forewent millions of dollars in unpaid salary. The match I saw he did nothing, except score.

By then, to his distress, he had missed the World Cup of 1998. He had been injured, and Brazil's coaches thought he was trouble. The decision possibly cost them the trophy.

Every now and then Romario would announce his retirement but did nothing about it. Then he realized he was approaching Pele's mark of 1,000 goals (Pele's 1,000th remains an epic moment of Brazilian history). Local journalists in Eindhoven got phone calls from Romario, still speaking his own inimitable brand of Dutch, and wanting to know how many goals he had scored in forgotten preseason warm-ups against village teams.

His quest offends soccer's collective ethos, and almost everyone disputes his count of 992. The Brazilian soccer magazine *Placar* gives him 891. Many Brazilians mock his pursuit of Pele (whom Romario once described as "mentally retarded"). But Romario deserves his moment. Goals are rarer now than they were in Pele's day: 12 were scored in Pele's two World Cup finals, none in Romario's one. A great striker nowadays might score 40 goals in a season twice in his career. Even *Placar's* count implies that Romario has been *averaging* that for twenty-two years.

That he got his goals mostly in Rio instead of for big money in Europe was his choice. "I'm difficult because I'm authentic," he said.

If you hear a player say that today, it's probably a Nike slogan.

*Romario is now Romario, MP. In October 2010, he was elected to Brazil's lower house of Congress for the Socialist Party. On election day he arrived in an armored BMW to cast his own vote and then visited the slum where he grew up. Romario has since become a left-wing critic of the World Cup in Brazil, calling FIFA's president, Sepp Blatter, "a thief"; FIFA's secretary-general, Jerôme Valcke, "a blackmailer"; and FIFA and Brazil's local organizing committee "corrupt entities." As in his playing days, he is his own man.

Gennaro Gattuso
April 2007

It was one of the images of last year's World Cup, though few people saw it: bearded Italian midfielder Gennaro "Rino" Gattuso cavorting around Berlin's Olympic Stadium in skimpy white underpants. Italy had won the final, and Gattuso was celebrating in his favorite manner. Horrified FIFA officials soon stopped him. But Gattuso had a right: It had been, for better or worse, a Gattusonian World Cup.

Underpants are seldom just underpants, and Gattuso's symbolized his transformation from peasant into king. For years his role in soccer teams was as servant to the stars. On Tuesday, when Milan visits Manchester United for the Champions League semifinal, he will be the team's spiritual leader. But more than that, the square-shaped Gattuso has become revered as an "antisuperstar": the antidote to everything glossy in modern soccer.

Central to the Gattuso myth are his simple origins. He comes from a small town in Calabria, one of Italy's poorest regions, where he played soccer on the beach with gas cans for goalposts. Many of Gattuso's relatives, like so many Calabrians, sought better lives abroad.

At nineteen, Gattuso did too. Whereas 85 percent of Italian men between the ages of eighteen and thirty-three live with their parents, he joined Rangers in Glasgow and fit right in. British players, he said, "tackle like men. In Italy, if you tackle a player they moan to the referee." Gattuso likes burying someone and then shaking his hand—though a Gattuso handshake can be scary, too.

While other Italian players in Glasgow went around in beautiful suits, he hung around in tracksuits with Scottish players, notes Gabriele Marcotti, coauthor of *The Italian Job* with Gianluca Vialli. Gattuso left Scotland after only a year, but with a souvenir: his future wife, Monica, whose father owned his favorite Glaswegian pizzeria. Gattuso has promised to rejoin Rangers while still in his prime, but then he has also said he will never leave Milan, and has flirted with Manchester United, so it's hard to know for sure.

At twenty-one he joined Milan. It seemed an odd match. If Milanese men are the best-dressed men in the world, and AC Milan players are the best-dressed men in Milan, as a quick visit to their training ground will ascertain, then what was Gattuso doing there? At five foot eight and 169 pounds, he is an unusually heavy player, and he calls himself "as ugly as debts." To quote an Italian saying: "Man descends from Gattuso." Furthermore, in a club famed for its passing, he received ironic applause at training whenever he completed a pass over five yards.

But he knew his place. "I'm just a stealer of balls," he says. Italians call his type a *mediano*, the guy whose job is to procure the ball for someone who can play—in Milan's case, the great Kaká. Here is a typical midmatch exchange between the two men:

Gattuso: "Go on, run."

Kaká: "I don't do defending."

Gattuso: "All right, then. Go up there and score."

But Gattuso reveres Kaká: "He is so perfect that sometimes I have to touch him to make sure he really exists." Indeed, Gattuso's most famous spat, the frantic bouncing up and down and shrieking at Christian Poulsen of Schalke, was prompted by Poulsen's taunting of Kaká. "He behaved like a child," Poulsen said afterward, but in fact Gattuso had behaved just like Rumpelstiltskin, the evil, bearded dwarf in the fairy tale.

Nonetheless, Gattuso improves Milan's brand. A peasant among aristocrats, he helps the club appear rooted. Certainly, he identifies with Milan, and with its owner, Silvio Berlusconi, to the extent that he chastised his then teammate Vikash Dhorasoo for reading the center-left daily *La Stampa*. "It's a communist rag," explained Gattuso, recommending instead one of Berlusconi's own papers.

Before last summer's World Cup, at an Italian squad meeting, Gattuso and others noted the team's reputation for petulance, diving, and arguing with referees. Gattuso said it had to stop.

During the tournament he policed Italian behavior. He also turned himself into a global brand. This was thanks only partly to his appearance with several teammates in—most appropriately—an underwear advertisement. Gattuso also helped marshal perhaps the best defense ever assembled. In the final, when Fabio Grosso cut out a French attack at the expense of a corner, something that would have won him applause in any other side, Gattuso beetled across to scold him: Italy didn't concede corners.

During the tournament Gattuso burnished his peasant's image. He displayed a preoccupation with toilets, saying that the night before the final, nervous, he had gone to the bathroom twenty times, while the night after, bursting with drink, his reported total hit twenty-eight. The tournament's venue being Germany, home to many Calabrian immigrants, including some of Gattuso's relatives, he frequently eulogized these people, "who worked so hard for years for five hundred euros a month." He seemed to be trying to identify with them. "This is the victory of a workers' team," he said after the final. "We have shown we have balls as big as houses" (just in case anyone had missed the underwear ads).

Gattuso became lionized as an "antigalactico." Even his beard seemed a throwback to an age when players were ordinary guys. In fact, Gattuso is far more glamorous than he admits. This Calabrian migrant is a globalized multimillionaire who recently adorned the cover of the Italian *Vanity Fair.* Many women adore him. Yes, he is a *mediano,* but in recent years *mediani* have staged a sort of peasants' revolt, upstaging the Kakás to become soccer's main men. Gattuso's rustic image, though it fits his personality, is also a carefully managed brand. A gifted speaker and no fool, he is his own best brand manager.

Still, he deserves the acclaim. The season after winning the World Cup is the hardest (we've all been there), and here is Gattuso, a step away from his third Champions League final in five seasons. Officials planning for next month's match in Athens had better pack some spare shorts.

According to Carlo Ancelotti's autobiography The Beautiful Games of an Ordinary Genius, *"Gattuso once ate a live snail at Milanello during a training session."*

Zlatan Ibrahimovic
April 2007

I went left; he went left. I went right; he went right. I went left again; he went to buy a hot dog." When Zlatan Ibrahimovic describes his moves in American street English, he sounds just like the basketball players on American inner-city playgrounds who are his soul mates. But whereas they usually remain mere neighborhood legends, the Swedish giant has become arguably the "winningest" player on earth.

Ibrahimovic, twenty-five, leads the playground legends who have conquered soccer as they once did basketball. His club, Inter Milan, is unbeaten this league season. Next Wednesday against Roma the club can seal the Italian championship. It would be Ibrahimovic's fourth league title in four years with three clubs—Ajax Amsterdam, Juventus, and Inter, as long as you overlook the irksome fact that Juve was stripped of its prizes for having fixed matches.

Ibrahimovic grew up in the Swedish harbor town of Malmö, among the ghetto flats of Rosengård, a neighborhood of immigrants. Son of a Croat mother and Bosnian father, he speaks Swedish and what he thinks he should call "Yugoslavian," though he isn't sure. School was not his thing. "I've been at this school thirty-three years," his former headmistress recalled, "and Zlatan is easily in the top five of most unruly pupils we have ever had. He was the number-one bad boy, a one-man show, a prototype of the kind of child that ends up in serious trouble."

While blond Swedes did homework, Ibrahimovic played soccer— sometimes for a neighborhood club, Balkan, but more often on the playground. In ghettos, whether the game is basketball or soccer, what counts is not the score but your moves. In basketball, "streetball" players invent feints and give them names like the "Chicken Fajita Wrap." The Harlem Globetrotters emerged from streetball. Zinedine Zidane's famous "Roulette" originated on a Marseille playground.

While other talented teenagers were being schooled at big clubs, Ibrahimovic was on the playground giving "no-look passes," a staple of both street soccer and street basketball. Eventually, he turned pro with Malmö. Niclas Kindvall, a teammate there, told me, "He gave passes at the wrong moment, took shots at the wrong moment. But he had it all." Ibrahimovic was never going to stay long at Malmö after foreign scouts saw him lob the ball over one defender and backheel it over another before scoring.

At nineteen, wearing the ghetto uniform of hooded top, woolly hat, and giant watch, he joined Ajax. There, however, he revealed his ignorance of what "streetballers" disparagingly call "field soccer." The sport rarely suits them. Dutch midfielder Edgar Davids once brought along to his club Juventus a Dutch-Arab kid who had humiliated him on an Amsterdam playground, but the kid took a dislike to field soccer and left almost immediately.

Ajax discovered that Ibrahimovic was slow, didn't know where to run, seldom bothered scoring, and despite being six foot three couldn't head. Fans began to wonder whether the club had signed the wrong Zlatan Ibrahimovic by mistake. The Amsterdam Arena persecuted him. He would loaf about yards offside, and a spectator would scream, "Come and sit up here, boy, and you'll see it!"

"I'd never thought about soccer before," Ibrahimovic admitted. "You want to sink through the ground when 50,000 people whistle at you." Sometimes after matches he locked himself in his apartment.

Ajax also struggled to take the ghetto out of the boy. Defenders who marked him had a nasty habit of breaking their noses. Teammates suffered, too. "He was sometimes unmanageable," says Ajax official David Endt. "Suspicion plays a big role with him. You see it in his game: that you won't be screwed by someone else, but you'll screw him." As the cliché went, Ibrahimovic was a Balkan, not a Swede. He became a vehicle for Swedes to debate immigration.

Yet his ghetto qualities also made him special. Most Swedish soccer players are anonymous worker bees. They follow "the law of Jante," a sort of Swedish code for living that ordains: "Don't think you're better than us." But Ibrahimovic had never learned Swedish codes. His style of soccer—the very fact that he had a style—existed to show up the fools facing him. "It's hard to compare him to another Swedish player in history," muses Malmö novelist Fredrik Ekelund. Sweden's former minister of culture Leif Pagrotsky says, "The reason he is so good is that he does things as a player that make him a bad boy: He expresses himself, doesn't obey the rules, doesn't listen." In Swedish terms, Ibrahimovic was *kaxig* (stubborn, proud) like his hero, Muhammad Ali. "I take the street to the field," he says.

Ibrahimovic baffled Swedes. When he took a penalty against San Marino even though the task had been assigned to someone else, it became a legendary moment of Swedish soccer. Later he briefly boycotted the national team. Yet Swedes, who love soccer but produced such an unlovely version of it, had been yearning for decades for a player like Ibrahimovic. He says, "During the World Cup in 2002 I was voted Man of the Match three times in Sweden, even though I hadn't played. The people love me."

Only in 2004 did the genius become a useful player. He began valuing goals above feints. He finally chose the right moments. In his words, "First the talent controlled me. Now I control the talent."

Juventus, the sport's most disciplined team, bought him and sent him to the gym. He gained twenty-two pounds. "Ibra" still caresses the ball under his soles, guiding it with every part of the foot, before deigning to score. However, notes Kindvall, "He has lost some of the abilities that made him a crowd pleaser. He used to do some incredible trick almost every game. I miss those things. But he has gained so much."

Inter would have won the title without Ibrahimovic's fifteen goals. Italy's next best team, Roma, trail by eighteen points and last Wednesday lost 7–1 to Manchester United. As Inter's Patrick Vieira commented, other Italian teams just weren't good enough this season. In streetball terms, Ibrahimovic "dissed" them all.

Paolo Maldini
May 2007

On a dark, snowy day in 1985, a scared sixteen-year-old made his debut for AC Milan. "Where do you want to play?" Milan's coach, Nils Liedholm, asked him. Amazed at being consulted, the kid said he preferred the right. He was right-footed at the time. He came on, didn't make any mistakes despite having sore feet from tight shoes, and has hardly missed a game since. In the Champions League final against Liverpool next Wednesday, a month before his thirty-seventh birthday, Paolo Maldini will probably win his fifth European Cup with Milan.

Maldini is brilliant, handsome, and nice. Nobody dislikes him. Even Tommaso Pellizzari, a fan of Inter Milan who wrote a book against AC Milan called *No Milan*, admits, "In twenty years of soccer, he never did something you remember as bad or ugly." Since many of us hope to achieve eternal perfection, the question is how Maldini does it.

It began with his father. Cesare Maldini had captained Milan himself, and his son seems to have constructed his life around seeking the old man's approval. "From the moment I first remember seeing a picture of him holding the European Cup," says Maldini, "I wanted to copy his success." Cesare, from Trieste, had the *grinta* (grit) that typifies players of that region, and so Paolo, who had more natural gifts than his father, developed *grinta*.

When Milan moved him to left-back in his teens, Maldini achieved through *grinta* and practice something almost unfeasible for anyone older than twelve: He made his left foot as good as his right. "He still surprises me every day with his quest to always improve and to look inside as well," says his father. Alberto Zaccheroni, who coached Maldini at Milan, recalls, "He plays the friendly game of the Thursday afternoon, against our youth team or an amateur side, as if it were the Champions League final."

In the Champions League semifinal against PSV Eindhoven earlier this month, Maldini threw his head in front of a Dutch striker winding up for a shot. He was kicked in the face and stretchered off. Within a minute or so, he had resumed work. To maintain this level of *grinta*, you have to believe in the institution for which you work. Hardly any players love their clubs—they leave that to fans—yet Maldini actually seems to, even though he supported Juventus as a boy. No doubt this love is connected to love of father: at seventy-three, Cesare still scouts for Milan. Paolo regularly turned down better offers from clubs like Manchester United and Chelsea, and once, when Milan pleaded financial trouble, accepted a pay cut of 30 percent. He talks often about the importance of playing in his city of birth and admits it distresses him that Milan signs so many foreigners.

Maldini has subordinated ego to club. This make him a walking reproach to players who seek status through anything but performance. Wayne Rooney, who often seeks macho confrontation, got a pat on the head from Maldini. Robbie Savage, a Welsh player who before a Wales-Italy match threw away a Maldini shirt on television, was not granted a response at all. Maldini seldom speaks, but when he does it keeps his teammates in line.

Yet none of this quite covers him. There is something supernatural about his body, as if he were a Greek god poorly disguised as a human. To remain a great player aged thirty-six—as hardly anyone in history has—you must always have taken perfect care of yourself.

Milan's training ground, Milanello, offers glimmers of an explanation. This sunny idyll on a hill above Lake Como comes alive a few minutes before ten each morning, when a parade of SUVs carrying multimillionaire players pushes past the armed guards. Maldini has made this commute for twenty years. Between training sessions, he sleeps in his Milanello bedroom. He says, "It's almost as though all your worries stop at the gates. This is the ideal manner to get the best out of you."

It would appear so, for Maldini is not alone at Milan. The back four likely to face Liverpool have an average age of thirty-three, with thirty-nine-year-old Billy Costacurta in reserve. This is because the "Milan Lab," the club's medical team, has discovered the secret of eternal youth. The lab is always testing players' muscles, brains, hearts, breathing, psyches, and so on, and then analyzing the data with computers. Whereas other teams still run laps together, each player at Milan follows his own customized regime. It works, particularly if you are a Greek god to start with. Adriano Galliani, Milan's vice president, reports, "Paolo's biological age is much lower than his actual age. The tests we have done now are better than three or four years ago."

As they say, it's partly a matter of how old you feel. Maldini believes that stress consumes energy. He tries to avoid it by not thinking about soccer outside work hours. He never reads the *Gazzetta dello Sport*, Italian soccer's daily pink bible, never appears on television or in gossip rags, and never talks about soccer with his wife and sons and seldom even with his dad. Almost a decade ago he stopped appearing as a disc jockey on radio. David Endt, an official at the Dutch club Ajax, cites Maldini to young players as the example of how to manage their lives. When Endt told Maldini this, Maldini replied that he felt honored. Not only that, he actually *looked* honored. This is another trick of the mind required to remain great: Despite knowing you are great, you have to feel humble. Everyone talks about this; few manage it.

If Maldini ever retires, the Milan Lab will presumably clone him.

In February 2009, when the forty-year-old Maldini played his last derby against Inter before retiring, the Inter fans held up a banner that said: "For 20 years our opponent, but in life always loyal." On the other hand, at his last-ever game a few months later, hard-core fans of his own club held up a banner that said, "On the field you were a never-ending champion but you lacked respect for those who made you rich." He had only played twenty-four years for Milan. If he did lack respect for certain people, you could sort of understand why.

Fernando Torres
August 2007

Last summer, for a couple of scorching days in Leipzig and Stuttgart, Spain was the best team in the World Cup. Briefly, there were thrilling scenes. In the famous Spanish phrase, "We played like never before, and lost as usual." But before they lost, the most thrilling sight of all was their blond kid up front, Fernando Torres.

Today Torres, twenty-three, kicks off the English soccer season with his new club, Liverpool, at Aston Villa. Whatever his precise transfer fee—perhaps $40 million—he is the most expensive Spaniard ever sold, and the most expensive player Liverpool has ever bought. However, his transfer is even more momentous than that implies. For years people eulogized Torres's loyalty to Atletico Madrid, the club he had joined at age eleven and supported for much longer. Despite being too good for Atletico, he stayed. He was feted as the last player as fan. His move proves that the two are in fact different species.

As the Torres legend goes, when he was four or five his grandfather began urging him to play for "Atleti." The old man dreamed of seeing Fernando wear the red and white in the first division. "Luckily he was able to see me play in the Calderón before he died," says Torres, "though not in the first division."

When Torres made his professional debut at seventeen, Atletico was suffering its "two years in hell" in the second division. The team of the Madrilene working classes is historically Spain's third-largest club, but it is dwarfed by its neighbor Real, habitually wastes money, and plays beside a gasworks on the dirty banks of the Manzanares River. Atletico is a biggish club that acts like a little one.

The local boy was immediately appointed Atletico's idol in residence. At nineteen he became club captain. Eventually, he practically became Atletico itself.

You can see why. Physically, Torres is acrobat, strongman, and sprinter in one. A mark of his quality is that he scores many different kinds of goals: dribbles, headers, lobs, and drives with both feet. In fact, the outside of his right foot is a source of weirdly brilliant lobs.

Torres has mastered perpetual motion. "He has a tremendous degree of fitness, a tremendous energy," Spain's coach, Luis Aragones, said last summer. Torres's three goals at the World Cup came in the last twenty minutes of matches, when exhausted defenders could no longer match his runs. However, noted Aragones, "We want to work on a couple of technical details."

Rafael Benitez, Liverpool's manager, confirmed immediately after forking out the record fee, "He needs to improve some things."

Partly because Torres does everything at top speed, his control is deficient. That explains why he scores less than he should: Excluding penalties, he averaged fewer than twelve league goals a season over the past four years.

Still, every summer some very big teams courted him. Every summer he stayed at Atletico. He seemed to think like a fan.

Yet this was a delusion. Torres himself, a thoughtful man, has explained it well: "When you're a supporter you think and dream about your club every day. You only see the good parts. When you cross the line and become a player, you see everything. That's not always pretty." Behind the curtain you see that a club is composed of venal humans muddling along. Everyone who ever gets on the inside of soccer feels this. A friend of mine, a Sunderland fan, says that when he became a journalist and stood in the tunnel beside the Sunderland players before a game, the illusion suddenly fell away for him. He never cared as much again.

Some players do remain fans on the side. Here's a scene from a Madrid hotel bar in 2002: Steve McManaman, then a player with Real, the world's biggest club, had just won a European game 3–0, but his thoughts were with the club he supported, Everton. "Macca" was working his cell phone to discuss Everton's sacking of their manager, Walter Smith. "I feel for him," sighed McManaman. "As a manager you're only as good as your material. They lost 3–0 at the weekend—three individual errors."

Yet the suggestion that McManaman should play for Everton just because he supported them would have struck him as absurd. Like anyone who ever worked to convert a raw talent, Macca had a career.

Torres does too. Given the choice between betraying his club and betraying his talent, he left Atletico. He returned from the ends of the earth (a Polynesian vacation) to talk to Liverpool. Yet even at his new club he still feels obliged to talk like a fan. He recounts how years ago some of his Madrilene friends got tattoos with Liverpool's slogan, "You'll never walk alone." Because of his job Torres couldn't get the tattoo, but his friends bought him an armband bearing the slogan.

In truth, a professional player always walks alone. Nonetheless, Torres represents a coup for Benitez. Spain's best players rarely emigrate. Like British players, they struggle with foreign languages in strange towns. Torres once said his game was not suited to England.

Benitez, a Spaniard himself, can reassure Spanish players that his Liverpool is a small corner of Spain. That's a sentiment that matters to professional players. Fandom does not.

When Torres joined Chelsea in 2011, he angered some Liverpool fans who had believed that he loved their club. With hindsight, his leaving it for a transfer fee of $79.5 million was the greatest service he could have rendered it.

Florent Malouda
August 2007

One freezing January in 2003 I trekked to Brittany to witness a French peculiarity: a village of 8,000 people with a soccer stadium that could fit twice as many. The village, Guingamp, which on the map occupied much the same spot as Asterix's cartoon village, somehow had a team in France's highest division. It even had a pair of promising players, called Didier Drogba and Florent Malouda.

That evening Guingamp was receiving Le Havre. Practically every villager walked to the stadium, evoking French wartime scenes of entire towns taking to the road. The crowd of 12,728 (approximately 13 of them from Le Havre) was impressive considering it was so cold that no sane human could have wanted to be outdoors. Malouda played terribly. Guingamp lost 1–2. It looked like a village team.

Tomorrow Malouda, now twenty-seven, should make his official debut for Chelsea alongside Drogba in the Community Shield match against Manchester United. This is the story of how a boy from the edge of the earth erased his personality to become the perfect professional.

Malouda grew up in French Guyana, on South America's northern tip, a skinny little brown kid nicknamed "Foufoup." He puttered about on his motorcycle, studied hard at school, always got home by seven thirty, and was already preparing for life as a professional player. His dad was a local coach, who after each match would be waiting beside the field with an analysis: "Florent, you gave twelve crosses, four of them bad. You keep the ball too long before shooting. Your four goals . . ."

Malouda arrived in mainland France at fifteen. A year later he was playing in the French second division. Rather like an MBA student, he had a career plan. "He was always a serious boy," explains his mother. "He left home knowing he would become a player in the French team." He joined Guingamp at twenty, Lyon at twenty-three, and at twenty-four made his debut for France.

One summer afternoon in 2005 I watched him train with the national team in the forest of Rambouillet. He was a new boy in a side with hierarchies as strict as the court of Louis XIV, but that day, during a dispute in a game of musical chairs, Malouda threw a mock karate kick at the king himself, Zinedine Zidane. Then the French split into sides for tennis soccer. Patrick Vieira, dauphin to Zidane, was made a team captain, and announced he had sold one of his players for twenty euros. Yet when a quarrel erupted over the score, Malouda took on Vieira. "Foufoup" understood hierarchies, but he also knew his own worth, and just how far he was permitted to go. The next summer he was France's best player for much of the World Cup final, yet accepted a lecture in the tunnel at halftime from his hierarchical superior, Thierry Henry.

By then he was the complete player. Malouda has no weaknesses. He can dribble, tackle, run, score, and cross with either foot. He can play in most positions. A stringy five foot ten, he looks as if he designed his own body to play professional soccer. Like most of Lyon's players, he is fit enough to play two games consecutively. (Instead of buying Malouda, Chelsea could have cut out the middleman and signed Lyon's brilliant fitness coach, Robert Duverne.)

Everybody in France admires Malouda. Last season he was voted the league's best player. Yet hardly anyone loves or hates him. He is the player as robot, a purveyor of statements like "What matters is the team." As he told the newspaper *L'Equipe*: "Since my arrival in metropolitan France, I've erased certain traits of my character to avoid being rejected by the system, to the point where I get reproached for nonchalance even though I'm an electric battery."

A French journalist explained to me the difference between Malouda and France's dopey working-class hero Franck Ribéry: "If Ribéry rode the Tour de France and were caught taking drugs, everyone would forgive him. With Malouda, everyone would say, 'You see? That explains it.'"

This summer Malouda's career plan indicated a move to a megaclub. Several showed an interest, including Real Madrid, but Malouda was determined to join Chelsea. He knew that Real absentmindedly buys dozens of players, who are often forgotten until they get discovered months later screaming inside closets. He also presumably knew that as a Stakhanovite athlete, he was made for Chelsea.

The only hitch was that the Londoners—for years soccer's biggest spenders—appeared almost out of cash. In 2005, when Chelsea paid Lyon $35 million for Michael Essien, they still followed the "reassuringly expensive" philosophy of shopping. This summer they spent weeks fishing behind sofas for bits of change, struggling to reach Lyon's minimum price of $27.7 million for Malouda. Lyon revealed that Chelsea's general manager, Peter Kenyon, even flew to Moscow to touch the club's multibillionaire owner, Roman Abramovich, for more cash.

Malouda will be worth it. That day in Guingamp, a club director told me, "From time to time we have a little fantasy: A Brazilian player comes, or Szarmach, the Pole who played three World Cups." With hindsight, having Malouda and Drogba on the village team wasn't a bad fantasy, either.

Michael Owen
September 2007

That first goal against Russia said a lot about Michael Owen. It looked so easy. England's John Terry and two large Russians jumped for a corner, missed it, and little Owen, who seemed to be coincidentally loitering by himself behind them, stopped the ball and placed it in the net off the inside of the post. It was his thirty-ninth goal for England. He added a fortieth that night.

It looks easy, yet hardly anyone else can do it: anticipating where the ball will land, finding space, and placing it like a golfer sinking a putt. The category of men who have scored as easily as Owen in international soccer for as many years is small: Today only Miroslav Klose, Ruud van Nistelrooy, and Thierry Henry can make a case.

Without Owen's gift, England was threatening to miss qualification for Euro 2008. With him back from injury, the English could win the title. In his years of injuries Owen has often been written off, but he himself may believe that at twenty-seven he is better than the unravaged eighteen-year-old who stunned the world at the World Cup of 1998. "You come into your peak in your late twenties," he told me when I met him five years ago. Whereas Owen 1.0 of 1998 was the product of nature, today's Owen—Owen 2.0, if you like—is the result of a career plan.

Owen grew up the son of a professional player in the Welsh town of Hawarden. He boxed a bit and was an obsessive golfer, team captain at the Hawarden Cricket Club, a good rugby player, and a decent sprinter who also enjoyed snooker and darts. There are British towns where the entire population put together plays less sport than Owen did, because they're too busy arguing in the pub about Manchester United. Owen has never read an entire book and only once seen an entire film: When he had a trial at Arsenal as a kid, the club took his group to the cinema, and out of courtesy Owen didn't leave. But he has no outside interests.

Whereas other gifted kids dream of becoming professional players, Owen always knew he would be one. Even as a small kid he played like a pro, running into space instead of chasing the ball and, when he shot, picking his spot instead of blasting. Long before turning pro, he was planning how he would behave when he got there. English players tend to divide into two social types. Players of the first type are so thoughtless and inarticulate that they would struggle in any profession but soccer: Think Paul Gascoigne, Lee Bowyer, Jonathan Woodgate. Then there is a minority type that thinks hard about the game: Gary Lineker, Gareth Southgate, or Tony Adams after giving up alcohol.

Owen told me that as a boy he watched Lineker and Alan Shearer "to get tips off playing, but also tips off how to conduct yourself off the pitch as well. If there was such a thing as someone copying exactly what they do and following in their footsteps, I don't think you'd go far wrong with players like that." His project—almost revolutionary in English soccer—involved not behaving like a half-wit.

It shows the instant you meet him. He enters the room—rapidly, of course—looks you in the eye, smiles, sticks out his hand, and says in his Welsh-Mersey lilt, "Hello, how are you?" An utterly banal sequence, except that few other English players could manage it. Owen may be the only England player with basic good manners.

Being both gifted and sensible, Owen progressed as rapidly as he moves. At seventeen, he made his Liverpool debut as a substitute, and when his team got a penalty, guess who was entrusted with it? At eighteen years and fifty-nine days, Owen became the youngest England player of the twentieth century.

This was weird. English soccer is run by the English working classes, who in their professions tend to follow the dictum that experience trumps talent. The best players traditionally had to prove their worth for years before being picked for England, after which they were given a berth on the team until years past their prime. In 1998, the notion of playing an eighteen-year-old in a World Cup therefore seemed heretical. England's manager, Glenn Hoddle, tried to dismiss Owen as "not a natural goalscorer," which raised the question of who on earth was. Owen began that World Cup on the bench beside another green youngster, a mere twenty-three-year-old named David Beckham.

Within a couple of games they were on the team. In St. Etienne, against Argentina, this produced an iconic moment of soccer history. A quarter of an hour into the game, somewhere in midfield, Beckham shoved the ball into Owen's feet, whereupon the small boy with the big head set off running. I still remember the scene in the press stand. I was sitting among the British journalists, men who regard a World Cup chiefly as an opportunity to consume fourteen pints a day on expenses. When England scores they never cheer, though people do jolt awake and shout, "'Oo gave the pass?"

But while Owen was running, the men around me wriggled their beer bellies out from behind their desks and began thumping their tables and screaming, "Go on, my son!" It worked, because Owen kept going. And then he put the ball into the top corner. An identical run of his earlier had produced an England goal from a penalty, and so in just sixteen minutes Owen had become one of the world's most dangerous strikers.

The goal registered not so much for its importance, or its technical accomplishment, as for the attitude it betrayed. World Cups are ruled by fear. Most players are on a mission not to screw up. Yet there was Owen, dribbling as if in his back garden in Hawarden. He had "balls," said Diego Maradona.

I asked Owen whether he hadn't been afraid to try that run. Didn't he think, as a teenager playing Argentina in the World Cup, "What am I doing here?"

"No," said Owen. "That was probably why you could succeed, and why a lot of youngsters burst onto the scene in any sport. It's because they don't have a fear factor."

He bought an entire street in Hawarden for his family to live on, while he and his girlfriend moved into a nearby mansion, Lower Soughton Hall. Meanwhile, he had become a hero who transcended the usual partisanship of soccer. When he ran into the stand chasing a ball in Southampton's little stadium soon after the World Cup, the opposition fans grasped at his legs as if he were a religious icon or a crate of beer. Later in 1998, I was in Valencia for a bad-tempered European tie during which two senior Liverpool players were sent off. When one of them abandoned the captain's armband on the turf, Owen was quickest to pick it up. Liverpool won 1–2, and after the final whistle the crowd berated the visitors and their own players. Owen, though, sensed what was coming. He dawdled until he was the last player left on the pitch, and then it came: his ovation. He applauded back.

The boy had balls and Road Runner legs, but he also had a brain. There are great instinctive players and great thinking players, but Owen is both. "Since I was a kid I've always watched players and tried to pick points," he told me. "But it's also important to try to use your strengths, because that's what got you there in the first place." Owen was born with pace and what he calls "an ability to know where the ball is going to be." But he also had the intelligence and application to work out how to improve his game. It's a rare combination.

You see his intelligence off the field, too. Many times after England matches I have stood in the "mixed zone," where journalists shout out questions to passing players. It's mostly a sad scene. Paul Scholes, who could barely talk, used to trudge by with head bowed—probably more out of shyness than rudeness. With other players, it was rudeness. David Platt used to stop to chat with selected journalists about horse racing. When David Beckham became captain, he always stopped for a word. "I just hit it and it went in" is his usual account of a goal, though Beckham's voice is so high-pitched that some words are audible only to certain breeds of dog.

Only Owen stops for a thoughtful analysis of his game. At the World Cup in Japan, he sometimes did so with a black garbage bag slung over his shoulder, so that he looked even more than usual like the boy next door. Owen seems immune to status. His partner is not a model but a girl he met in kindergarten, and life for him is not a series of confrontations in which you have to defeat all comers with your clothing, but a chance to play snooker, table tennis, or darts after training in your specially designed home. Or you could play golf. Whereas Beckham uses his clothes and hairstyles to draw the observer's eye, Owen, who is arguably equally good-looking, and has done much more for England, tends to make himself look neutral.

Quite soon Owen began picking up small injuries. In recent years they got bigger. Since 2004 he has had four operations, the most serious one after tearing his knee ligaments with nobody even near him against Sweden at the last World Cup. In the last two seasons he barely played for Newcastle, his club. British journalists who watched him in the Premier League noticed long ago that he had lost his teenager's pace. Too often they saw him disappoint against small sides. Many wrote off Owen.

That was to miss the two essential points about him. First, he has what you might call the opposite of nerves: The bigger the match, the better he plays. His goals generally come against teams like France, Argentina, Brazil, a hat trick against Germany, Brazil again, Argentina again, two late goals against Arsenal in an FA Cup final, saving England's qualification against Russia, and so on. That is why international soccer, not club soccer, is his natural milieu. Playing for Liverpool, Real Madrid, and Newcastle, Owen has never won a league title or a Champions League, and he probably never will. We will remember him for World Cups.

The other essential point about Owen is that being intelligent, he can improve even as he slows down. In 2002 I asked him whether the older Owen was better than the teenager. "Yeah, definitely," he said. "I've got a much better left foot than I had then. I can head the ball much better than I could then. I can drop off and hold the ball up much better than I did then. Results have proved that I have improved on them things." To borrow a phrase from the *Guardian* journalist David Lacey: From a scorer of great goals, he has matured into a great scorer of goals. "He may be the top goalscorer in the world," said England's previous manager, Sven-Göran Eriksson.

When Owen's body let him down again at the World Cup, he simply set to work at it. He paid for a helicopter to transport him between his mansion and Newcastle, where he spent his days doing exercises in the club's swimming pool and gym. He knew he owed the club that had risked $29 million on him in 2005. Given his absenteeism so far, that currently works out at more than $1 million a match.

His haul of three goals against Israel and Russia last month suggests Newcastle's investment is safe, even if he has already missed club matches with injuries this season. "Between my ears," Owen explained after his return for England, "I'm strong. There might be a lot of people with more skill than me, but there are not many who are mentally stronger. Whether it comes to long-term injuries, lack of form, or criticism, I have thicker skin than anyone."

Owen needs nine more goals to catch England's all-time leading scorer, Bobby Charlton, who got forty-nine. If he stays fit, he will. There is no longer any great mystery about that. The only mystery is whether he can emulate Charlton's feat of 1966 and finally carry England to their second-ever trophy.

With hindsight, both Owen and I were too optimistic about the benefits of maturity. My profile of him exemplifies the problem of interviewing soccer players: If you interview them, you have to quote what they say, and what they say often ends up driving the article. Owen said he had improved with age. At the time of the interview, in 2002, that view still seemed plausible, and so I made it the focus of the article. It turned out to be wrong.

Speaking to the "Guardian" in 2010, Owen admitted that he had passed his peak by the age of twenty-one because of his injuries. "At 18 to 20," he reminisced, "I was probably one of the quickest things around, at the peak of my powers. But what can you do?"

In March 2013, he announced that he was retiring, aged thirty-three, having played just seventy minutes for Stoke City that league season. He never had caught Charlton: he finished with forty goals for England, nine fewer than Charlton managed.

I have been reading a lot of sports books lately, as a reviewer for the Financial Times *and the British magazine the* New Statesman, *and in David Epstein's book* The Sports Gene, *I came across an interesting insight into speedy players like Owen. You would think that players with a lot of fast-twitch fibers would have an advantage in soccer, a sport that prizes pace. However, Danish physiologist Jesper Andersen found that in FC Copenhagen's development academy, the quickest players often don't even make it into professional soccer because they suffer chronic injuries as teenagers. Andersen told Epstein, "The guys that have the very fast muscles can't really tolerate as much training as the others. The guys with a lot of [fast-twitch fibers] that can contract their muscles very fast have much more risk of a hamstring injury, for instance."*

It seems that Owen was lucky even to make it into professional soccer and that his subsequent injuries were predictable. Other nippy strikers such as Robbie Fowler, Patrick Kluivert, and Fernando Torres also peaked before the age of twenty-four. In effect, their bodies doomed them.

Kaká
February 2008

The young man with the big smile sitting opposite me is the official "World Player of the Year." He looks more like an Edwardian poet. Willowy and fat-free, brown hair shiny as in a shampoo advertisement, with white middle-class skin that reveals he has never eaten a lousy meal in his life, Kaká could be the Brazilian Rupert Brooke.

His club, AC Milan, is the reigning European and world champion. Does he have moments on the field when he feels, "What I'm doing now is perfect"?

"Yes," replies Kaká, twenty-five, in his American-tinged English. "Sometimes, everything that I want to do, I can do. These are good games, a perfect game." When has he felt like that? "Ah, against Manchester, the semifinal of the Champions League. Both games, I could do everything that

I thought." Was there any particular moment of perfection? "The second goal in Old Trafford."

Phil, AC Milan's resident English teacher, sitting in on his pupil, recalls the scene: Kaká somehow contrives to get two of Manchester United's defenders to bump into each other and fall over. What's startling is Kaká's composure: He runs with his head up, seeing everything, and when the time comes he gently slots the ball past the keeper.

We are at Milanello, Milan's training ground in the Lombardian countryside near Lake Como, which may be the world's nicest office. The air is so clear here that at ten yards you can see the pores in a man's skin. The six training fields are so flat that you can lie on the ground and not see a single undulation. You sit in the bar, drinking perfect espressos for free, and every young man who passes, world champion or not, says, "*Buon giorno.*"

The players here are kept perfect by soccer's best medical team. Just in case the Milan Lab needed any more oomph, last week it took on Microsoft as a partner. Before meeting Kaká, I asked the lab's doctors about him. Jean Pierre Meersseman, head of the lab, shrugged: "What can you say? He's number one. Nobody is faster than him; nobody has the acceleration he has." Daniele Tognaccini, Milan's chief athletics coach, dubbed Kaká "the kilometers man." Though the Brazilian is a creator, he also covers more turf per match than any teammate except the worker Rino Gattuso.

Kaká has arrived only twenty minutes late for our meeting, which for a soccer player is early. He apologizes profusely for having missed me yesterday, has a stand-up read of the *Gazzetta dello Sport* newspaper, and then ponders the question of whether it's fun being Kaká. "It's a lot of pressure, responsibility. But these are good things: To have a big responsibility with Milan, it's good. I can manage this pressure." But when the season ends, can he finally exhale and relax? "I just relax when we win something. If we lose something, it's difficult to relax."

Kaká joined Milan in 2003. Uniquely in soccer, the team has barely changed since then. Have his colleagues here at Milanello become more than just colleagues? "Milan is a big family. In the year, I think, the same time I spend with my wife I spend here with my friends. The day before the game, we stay here in training camp. If we got sixty games in the whole season, there's another sixty days in camp, and every day training." The "feeling" between him and his fellow midfielders, he adds, "is abnormal. We've been playing together for five years, and now I know how Gattuso moves, Pirlo, Seedorf. We can play without seeing each other."

But is it hard to get motivated for sixty games a season? "Sometimes it's too much," Kaká agrees. "Every time we play in Champions League, we always have motivation and concentration. Champions League is always important because you have to win, every game. Championship—you have to win every game, but sometimes you don't have the motivation that you have against Inter, Juventus, Rome, and Champions League games." He is presumably referring to games in half-full stadiums in provincial Italian towns with hooligans throwing things.

Is that why Milan is only fifth in the Italian championship? "Errm, yeah, I think," he says with an embarrassed chuckle.

The question of motivation preoccupies Kaká. When he arrived at Milanello, he says, he noticed a curious quality about Milan's legendary defender Paolo Maldini: Every day, the guy wanted to win. "This surprised me," says Kaká. "For that I learn everything about Paolo. Why he's got this motivation, and the other players don't." It may explain why Maldini at thirty-nine is now in his twenty-third season on the first team.

Did Maldini tell him the secret? "No, I just observed him. He speaks *poco*—not very much."

Who are the talkers in Milan's locker room?

"The tookers?" Kaká is baffled, and Phil clarifies. "The talkers? Ahh, Ronaldo, Gattuso."

Kaká once thought of getting an MBA. Like many corporate types he motivates himself by setting himself objectives. But what objectives can he possibly have now that he has won everything? His habitual grin grows to cover the whole porcelain face. "I want to win everything again. World Cup, and Champions League, championship and Golden Ball, World FIFA Player of the Year, and . . ." He trails off, possibly because the list is endless. "These are the things I learned with Paolo. Always win."

*Two days after I published this article in the Financial Times, *I got a panicked e-mail from one of Milan's press officers. Where could he get a copy of the newspaper? They'd all be gone now, I said, and offered to e-mail him the article instead.*

No, he said, Kaká wanted the actual paper. The player was very keen to read the article in the Financial Times *itself. Milan's players spend endless hours before games*

*in training camp at Milanello, and Kaká likes to spend the time practicing his English.
What better study material than a profile of yourself?*

Cesc Fabregas
February 2008

A rsenal had won yet again, and Arsène Wenger, their manager, was loafing in the players' tunnel, relaxed, or as relaxed as Wenger ever gets. His prodigy, Cesc Fabregas, had scored again. An acquaintance of Wenger's, who also happened to be in the tunnel, asked why it was that Fabregas—always a wonderful passer and tackler—was now scoring too.

"I'll tell you a story about that," replied Wenger. "I told him this summer, 'The number on your back is 4 [traditionally the defensive midfielder's number]. So at Arsenal you'll be judged on your defensive positions, the tackles you make. Get that right, and the passes and goals will look after themselves."

From then on the boy began scoring. Wenger's point was that he had taken the pressure off Cesc's goals by telling him to worry about something else.

The manager paused, before adding his punch line: "Last year he missed thirteen [or however many it was] scoring opportunities." Wenger loves stats at least as much as he loves soccer.

Now his twenty-year-old Catalan is the complete player, who over the next three months will be central to deciding whether Arsenal wins the Premier League and Champions League. More than that, Fabregas represents a new shape of player: the little boy as leader.

Though Barcelona is a giant club, Catalonia hardly ever produces great players. There was excitement, therefore, when a fifteen-year-old urchin who had first watched Barça as a baby in his grandfather's arms was seen passing balls like a quarterback in the club's "Masia," or farmhouse, for young players.

Then Arsenal stole him. With hindsight that was inevitable. Like the old East German Stasi, Arsenal's scouting team sees everything. In 1999 I went to watch South Africa under-seventeens play Zimbabwe under-seventeens in a little Soweto stadium. It was a scary time and place, and a marginal match, but in the main stand were five other white men: Arsenal coaches who had landed at the Johannesburg airport that morning.

The Arsenal scout who spotted Fabregas was Francis Cagigao. The son of Spaniards who emigrated to London in the 1970s, Cagigao played for Arsenal in the FA Youth Cup final of 1988, but now scours Europe for Wenger.

Soon after Fabregas was spotted, he became Arsenal's youngest-ever debutant, at sixteen. Then he was Spain's youngest international in seventy years. It all seemed odd. The teenage Fabregas was built like a waif and stood barely five feet seven. "An unproven featherweight," wrote his then teammate Ashley Cole.

In those days, way back in 2005 or 2006, the central midfield in soccer was like the line of scrimmage in American football, a "pit" where monsters like Arsenal's Patrick Vieira (six foot three) roamed. The physical takeover of soccer, as in most sports from tennis to baseball, looked unstoppable.

Yet in just two years it has been reversed. The turning point occurred in Berlin just after half past six the night on June 30, 2006, during the match between Germany and Argentina at the last World Cup, when the Argentine coach, Jose Pekerman, sent on his big striker, Julio Ricardo Cruz (six foot two), instead of Cesc's old Masia playmate Lionel Messi (five foot six, thanks to growth hormones). Messi with his small turning circle would have twisted the giant German central defenders silly. But they ate up Cruz, and Germany knocked out Argentina. The era of the boy had begun.

At Arsenal, Fabregas has replaced Vieira in the central midfield. The Catalan, now about five foot nine but still built like a waif, has led a featherweight conquest of Europe's biggest clubs: Messi, Bojan, and Andrés Iniesta are at Barcelona; Robinho and Wesley Sneijder at Real Madrid; Carlos Tévez at Manchester United; Diego at Werder Bremen; Franck Ribéry at Bayern Munich; and Sergio Agüero at Atletico Madrid. All of them are five foot six. France's new playmaker Samir Nasri is five foot eight, but a waif like Fabregas. None of them is older than twenty-four.

It turns out that amid the galloping supermen of modern soccer, only little men slight enough to twist can find the remaining inches of space. That's why French coach Raynald Denoueix says clubs are now scouting shorties. Small is beautiful.

Robin van Persie, Arsenal's Dutch forward, explains this eloquently. "Cesc is slow," he told the Dutch magazine *Hard Gras.* "He's one of the slowest here. But he's still the quickest of us all. He always thinks two seconds ahead. I sometimes think, 'Why doesn't the opponent take the ball off him?' And there he comes, peep, with a very little feint. In training I catch up with him and think, 'Now I'll get you.' And with his toe he gives—peep—a very little pass for a one-two. That gets him another metre and a half. So irritating!"

A week before Arsenal and Milan drew 0–0 in the Champions League, Milan's Kaká told me that Cesc was "a new generation of player." "I mean," Kaká explained, "He's complete. He can defend, he can attack, he's got a good shot with his right, with his left. He can do everything. Modern player." Of course, Cesc's still a good seven years off his peak.

The ultimate triumph of the little men came at the World Cup of 2010. Spain's central midfield in overtime in the final consisted of Fabregas, Iniesta, and Xavi.

Nicolas Anelka
March 2008

A ccording to the etiquette for international players, being two hours late for a meeting with someone from outside soccer does not count as late. So the twenty or so photographers, wardrobe dressers, PR reps, and representatives of CNN, the world's worst television station, start to get antsy only when Nicolas Anelka's delay enters its third hour. We are waiting for the great man in a studio in North London, where he is to do a fashion shoot for his new clothing line and explain how the most expensive player in history aims to spend what should finally be the peak years of his career.

Everyone sits around exchanging bored sports-and-film gossip and eating cake. Eventually, the CNN crew has to leave. They arrange for a PR woman who happens to be around to do the interview instead. Such are the rigors of world-class reporting.

Anelka arrives four hours late, without apologies. The rumor is that he had some physiotherapy at Chelsea, but nobody has bothered telling us.

He is ushered into the wardrobe room to don his first outfit. And as soon as he starts to undress, you understand why he feels he has the right to waste the afternoon of twenty London yuppies: What a body! Sprinters' legs, the upper torso of a basketball player, on top a thin and fragile shaven head, and the whole coated the color of milk chocolate. No fat; just fast-twitch muscle. Anelka strips down to a tiny pair of briefs, watched closely by a Swedish PR woman, a gay fashion worker, and *Player* magazine. What is his waist size? Thirty-four inches, the same as *Player* magazine's, even though Anelka at six foot one is four and a half inches taller.

Over the next hour, while Anelka poses in various outfits, and gets dressed and undressed again, he explains why he has had such a weird career, and whether in the next two years, perhaps playing a new position, he can redeem it and convert himself from one of the great players of our time into one of the great achievers.

But first, that body.

Do you appreciate how lucky you are to have been born with that?

"No," says Anelka, in a thin, reedy voice that you sometimes have to strain to hear. "When I started soccer, when I came to Clairefontaine, the best [soccer] school in France, I was small and—how do you say?" he holds his thumb and forefinger very narrowly apart. Despite a decade in English soccer, Anelka can hardly speak an English sentence without an error.

Weak?

"Yeah."

Stick-thin?

"Yeah. And my brothers, they are smaller than me. And they are older than me. So I don't know how I became like that, but I think it's because I work every day. It's not like I was already strong and tall."

Anelka was born twenty-nine years ago in Versailles, the son of a civil servant from the French Antilles. He grew up a few miles from Louis XIV's palace, in one of France's *banlieues*, or immigrant ghettos. This is of course the standard origin for top French players. In fact, Patrick Vieira and Thierry Henry grew up near Anelka in poor *banlieues* in the same generally rich region west of Paris.

In 1998 the three youngsters were part of a group of friends who laughed together, listened to music in the evenings, and generally kept each other company in the French squad at Clairefontaine, as they waited to see which of them would make the final cut for the World Cup. Anelka was only nineteen but already France's most gifted center-forward. "I remember he didn't need to work as hard as others," Vieira records in his autobiography. The day Anelka was cut from France's squad, he packed and left at once.

Anelka is famously a loner, but when I asked him if it was possible to have friends in soccer, he said, "I have some friends in soccer. It is people I know from maybe ten years."

Players from your generation, like Thierry Henry?

"I think so, because I know them since I was kid, so I think it's more simple."

He has said elsewhere that he has lost his presoccer friends from his youth in the *banlieue*—not because he changed, he insists, but because they began to regard him differently when he became a star.

Anelka was only seventeen when Arsenal's manager, Arsène Wenger, poached him from Paris St. Germain's youth team for just under $800,000. And the sad fact is that although he left Highbury at twenty, he arguably had the best years of his career there. The teenage Anelka had the pace of an Olympic sprinter, plus technique. Playing in front of Dennis Bergkamp's passes helped too. He has never since beaten his seventeen league goals of the 1998–1999 season when Arsenal won the English double. After he scored twice for France against England at Wembley in early 1999, French captain Didier Deschamps remarked, "Now we have our Ronaldo." (Few people then gave much thought to Henry, a fragile winger sitting on Juventus's bench.)

France, who had won the World Cup in 1998 without a striker, was now complete. You could hardly wait for all the World Cups Anelka would play. To date, he has played zero.

In the summer of 1999, Anelka made the decision that changed his career: He left Arsenal for Real Madrid, for $35 million. Wenger has called Anelka the best natural finisher he had worked with and said that his departure was his biggest regret as a manager. Vieira's verdict: "He made a big mistake in leaving."

Couldn't you have learned more by staying with Wenger, soccer's most respected shaper of young players?

"No. I think I can learn myself. You know, soccer is not about one coach. It's about . . ." But just as Anelka is about to explain what soccer is about, he is interrupted by photographers shouting instructions on posing. The flashes pop. Anelka continues, "He's a good manager. Sometimes you make your decision, and you make your decision. And that's it." Anelka is not the type to admit any sort of dependence on anyone in soccer.

So which coach taught you the most?

"I think I had good relations with Kevin Keegan [who coached Anelka at Manchester City]. It was very easy for him to teach me things in training because he used to play soccer, he used to be one of the best, and he used to play up front like me, so I always had a great time with him." This may be the first instance in recorded history that anyone has claimed to have learned more from Keegan than from Wenger.

We return to the wardrobe, where the dresser and a couple of minders fuss over the half-naked Anelka in English and French: "That looks really good." "Rapper style." "Hanging off." "Too short." "They're slim fits." Anelka is concentrating so hard on the clothes that he cannot answer any questions until we exit the wardrobe area.

You came onto the scene at Arsenal already apparently complete. What have you learned since as a player?

"I think you learn confidence on the pitch. When you first start, you don't know anything about playing soccer. Ten years later, because you've played so many games, you know what to do and how to do it. You are not afraid anymore to try things, not like when you used to be very young. I think it's special, because only people who have played soccer can speak about it. Even if I tried to speak about it, it's difficult to make people understand. You need to trust you, more than anything, because if you don't have confidence in you on the pitch, even if you are the best player in the world, you won't do anything."

Do you always have this confidence?

"Sometimes it's difficult because you know sometimes you will have a bad game. You are not confident every game."

On Anelka's first day at Real Madrid, as he tells it, nobody bothered to introduce him to anyone in the locker room. It wasn't a great start. He says that Samuel Eto'o and Geremi—fellow black young Francophones—had a friendly word with him, to say, "Watch out. Some senior players have already gone to the president to ask why you've been signed when Fernando Morientes is already here."

It ended up being quite a season. That March of 2000, Anelka boycotted a practice to protest how Real's coach Vicente del Bosque was using him.

Everyone said his older brothers—who managed him as the only product of the family business—had put him up to it. The consensus in the British media was that Anelka was "mad." They rechristened him "Le Sulk." Real, already fed up with the expensive kid, gave him a forty-five-day ban. It became the most Anelka-esque episode of Anelka's career.

I went to Madrid during the ban to have a look. Anelka was celebrating his twenty-first birthday. He played golf and tennis, hung out with his brothers and the neighborhood pets, went to Real for punishment training, but was sent home for not calling in advance, and then served birthday cake and Coca-Cola to the hordes of journalists waiting outside his house.

A club spokesman had told the journalists, "If we had known all this before, we wouldn't have signed him. To have done otherwise would be masochistic." Del Bosque said: "This is not a school."

In fact, Real, like most soccer teams, was rather like an old-fashioned British boarding school. You could see this even as Madrid took the field in a Champions League game against Dynamo Kiev while Anelka was spending another evening at home.

The team was led onto the pitch by the trio of Raul, Fernando Hierro, and Fernando Redondo. Raul (good at games) was the most popular boy in the class. Hierro was the school captain: He had been around forever, was challenged by no one, and so had become a bit of a bully. Redondo was their pal. Roberto Carlos, Steve McManaman, and Fernando Morientes tagged along, good enough and sociable enough to have gained acceptance. But Anelka, as so often in soccer, was the strange, quiet boy who got bullied.

As Henry says, "In soccer they never stop telling you that you're nothing without the others. But in fact you're always by yourself. Nico has understood that."

Eventually, Anelka decided to try to block out the negative in Madrid and concentrate on the positive. That season Real had two teams: a weak one in the league and an unbeatable one in the Champions League. In the final in Paris, with Anelka in the side, Madrid hammered Valencia 3–0. As a photographer instructs him to smile, he recalls, "I think it's something special when you play a final in France, in Paris. How do you say? Good memory." Is there a moment he remembers in particular? "When you take the trophy."

A few weeks later, at Euro 2000, Anelka became a European champion with France too, though he didn't play in the final against Italy. At only twenty-one, he had already won almost everything. But in the eight years since, he has added just one more prize: a Turkish league title with Fenerbahce. Imagine what Anelka's career might have been like if he had stayed with Wenger, or had turned up to practice at Real. But after that season he had to get out of Madrid. Anelka had played for two big clubs, and left both in bad odor. After that, he would barely get another chance in top-flight soccer.

Was it hard to do your growing up in public?

"It was very difficult, but people don't think about it. I think they don't want to think about it. They just want to see someone's success. But it's difficult when you're playing in big clubs and you are very young. You never know what's happening inside the club, or inside your life. And they expect you to be good all the time. It's hard to be good all the time. I don't think people realize: It's a nice game, it's nice to watch, but"—and for once Anelka laughs—"it's not an easy game."

The incomprehension of outsiders is perhaps the dominant theme of Anelka's conversation.

Paris St. Germain paid Real $30.2 million to bring the local boy home. The aim was to build a team around Anelka for the black and brown kids from the *banlieues* who populated the Auteuil end of the stadium (not so much for the Boulogne end, who are chiefly white skinheads).

PSG's president when Anelka joined was Laurent Perpère. He told me that Anelka didn't speak. "You never knew what he wanted," said Perpère. He remarked that in this the player strangely resembled Ronaldinho, who joined PSG in 2002 and also failed there. "He always smiled, but you never knew what he wanted. He was always in another world."

PSG's coach, Luis Fernandez, didn't hold with kids being stars. Perpère explains, "He thought there should be only one star in Paris, and that was Luis Fernandez." In the end, Fernandez and Anelka got involved in some sort of fisticuffs at a training session in October 2001. Anelka said, "Luis comes from the *banlieue*, like me. So we're used to shouting matches. We always reconcile afterwards." But PSG quickly loaned Anelka to Liverpool. He would have liked to stay there, and Steven Gerrard was a great admirer, but Liverpool wouldn't keep him. And so the parade continued, through Manchester City, Fenerbahce, Bolton, and now Chelsea.

At which club were you happiest?

"I think I was happy everywhere I played. There was no regret."

But why has a great player like you not always played for great clubs?

"I think it was more about my character than my football," says Anelka, as we trek back from photo shoot to wardrobe yet again. "A lot of people were speaking about me, but not on the football pitch, maybe outside. That's why some of the doors was closed. But I kept working." It annoyed people, he has said, to see a twenty-three-year-old driving a Ferrari. The critics forget the sacrifices he had made, leaving home as a child to join the academy in Clairefontaine where the boys were told that only four of the twenty-two of them would make it. "And at the start, I wasn't one of those four."

Is your personality perhaps not suited to soccer?

"I think it suits soccer, because if I didn't have any personality, I wouldn't be here today and play for the big clubs. So—maybe it was too strong." Anelka allows himself a smile.

Is that why your sporting heroes are strong personalities, like Maradona, Cantona, and Mike Tyson?

"There's something special about them because they're very good at what they're doing, and at the same they do what they want. They have extreme personality. I play football, and I try to be myself. But people say I have a strong personality. I don't say anything. People say that. I have the luck to have—not the same personality, but a strong personality. They are a great example for me."

The second theme of Anelka's conversation is beginning to emerge: Life is a morality play in which he is in the right. Anelka is one of the few northern European players (as opposed to Brazilians or Africans) with faith. While at Arsenal, he converted to Islam. Later he changed his name to Abdul-Salam Bilal. His faith was a reason he later chose to play in Turkey. Other leading players, including Franck Ribéry and Robin van Persie, who both married Muslim women, are also among the few European converts to Islam.

Within the game, the austere religion is a sort of antidote to locker-room lad culture. In British locker rooms in particular, the ultimate term of praise for a teammate is *one of the lads.* You get to be one of the lads through shopping, drinking, and sex, whenever possible in the company of other lads. Islam appeals to the likes of Van Persie, who need to be saved from laddism. But

Anelka has no gift for lad culture, because he is not clubby, anything but "one of the lads." His only laddish aspect is his dress. Islam is his shield from having to pretend to be a lad.

His social problems cost him on the French team as well. The future Ronaldo missed a total of four years of international soccer because of rows with France's coaches and his own walkouts. He didn't want to play for Roger Lemerre, because whereas Lemerre addressed all the other players with the familiar *tu*, he sometimes used the more formal *vous* with Anelka. Later he once refused to show up for Jacques Santini. "Santini," reveals Anelka between wardrobe changes, "is not a good manager anyway."

Raymond Domenech wouldn't take him to the World Cup of 2006, even though Lilian Thuram went to try to talk the coach into it, bringing a mute Zinedine Zidane with him to add weight to his argument. Domenech picked Djibril Cissé instead, who isn't even a poor man's Anelka. Even when Cissé broke his leg just before the World Cup, Domenech still wouldn't pick Anelka. Anelka says that when he's with the French squad nowadays, he watches and speaks only when appropriate. You might almost think he had a difficult relationship with his own country. His two famous brothers have emigrated: One stayed on in Madrid, and the other runs a bar on Miami Beach.

Will you return to France after your career?

"I have already my flat in Paris. Of course I will come back to Paris because it's my city, and France is my country."

Thierry Henry obsessively watches soccer on television, even games in the French second division. Anelka once said he never watches soccer.

Still not?

"Sometimes, when I have the chance to watch. If I have to choose I won't watch any games, because, errr, I do it every day. Soccer is a beautiful game, but it's also work that I have to do every day. It's not like when you are kids and you play soccer just like a hobby. When I'm off the pitch, I try to think about something else."

Has soccer often made you unhappy?

"No. Even in difficult time, I had people around me, and my family, and even in difficult time we were happy, because when you know you didn't do anything, nothing can happen to you because you are not as bad as people try to make people believe. And when you believe in God, you know the reverse will come, because you didn't do anything wrong."

In interviews Anelka often asserts his own happiness, perhaps to show that the world can't touch him.

At twenty-nine, he is now late-phase Anelka. The next two or three years are the most crucial of his career. They can turn him into more than just a story of "what might have been." This January, nearly six years after he left Liverpool, he finally returned to a big club: Chelsea, which paid $30 million to bring him from Bolton. Avram Grant, the club's manager, admitted, "He had a bad reputation ten years ago, but I could say the same about any one of us."

Do you know the significance of the figure of £85 million? (It's the total amount that has now been paid for him in transfer fees, spread over nine transfers, more than for any other player ever.)

"Yeah."

Does that sum make you proud?

"No. I don't care about records, because first of all I don't look at the money they spend on me. If you want to look at the money, it's people outside."

So what does make you proud in your career?

"Work. I had a lot of—how do you say?—difficult times, but even in difficult times I kept my head . . ." He tilts his head upward. "How do you say? Up? And I think I'm happy about where I am today and what I did."

What do you mean by "difficult time"?

"When people try to make story about my character and everything. When people try to say things about me that was wrong. It was difficult, when you know you didn't do anything."

Have you been waiting years to rejoin a big club?

"I think so, because I played in the beginning of my career in big clubs, and I knew I have the quality to play in the big clubs. I stayed focused. I wanted to come back in a big club. And I did it. Now I'm twenty-nine. I don't need to move again. Because I have a club who can give me Champions League; it can give me a title every year."

He knows that this is his last chance. Nobody doubts his gifts. However, he has gone through seven thin years, and his scoring record lags the best. Anelka averages one goal every three league games over his career and one every four games for France. Peers like Michael Owen and Thierry Henry average one goal every two league games, and Ruud van Nistelrooy does better. Admittedly, Anelka has played for worse clubs than they did, but that is part of his problem.

The photo shoot is finally over, and we sit down at a table in a quiet room. *You're twenty-nine now. You must be a man in a hurry.*

"A hurry for what?"

To achieve everything now.

"No. I live my life like I have to live it."

So you're not a man who's set yourself goals like winning a big prize with France, because you've been unlucky with the French team. Or winning the—

"I won already almost everything in my career. I think something missing like a World Cup and—I think, yeah, that's it."

How would you describe yourself as a player, as a striker?

"Mmmm. I'm a striker, but I can play in midfield. I like to play with the ball, I like to participate on the pitch, so I'm not the same striker I was ten years ago. I like football; I like to touch the ball. I'm not thinking like a striker, who wants to only score goals. I like to pass the ball; I like to create. So I can describe me now like a nine and a half. Not like a nine, or not like ten."

So you could see yourself dropping back a little?

"I did it already. I did it when I was playing in Turkey, and I loved my time there, my position."

To celebrate the end of the interview, Anelka cuts himself a small slice of sponge cake.

*To see how Anelka's international career ended, read the profile of Raymond Domenech in Part II.

Didier Drogba
May 2008

Didier Drogba never wanted to play for Chelsea. He writes in his new autobiography, published in French this week, that when Chelsea bought him for $44 million in 2004, "It just wasn't the team I wanted to join."* But Mar-

---

* Didier Drogba, *C'était pas gagné* (Paris: Editions Prolongations, 2008).

seille wanted to sell him, and his agent said he'd be stupid to turn down the salary. Then Drogba hoped he'd fail his medical exam at Chelsea. "I was disgusted to sign for Chelsea," he admits.

This makes bizarre reading before Drogba's farewell match for the club, Wednesday's Champions League final against Manchester United in Moscow. The Ivorian center-forward has won two English titles with Chelsea, yet the autobiography describes a man who's never been ecstatic to be there. No wonder *C'était pas gagné* will only appear in English in August, when Drogba will have safely emigrated. But the book's strangest passages concern Drogba's unconsummated love affair with Chelsea's previous manager, José Mourinho.

The central event of Drogba's life is his exile from the Ivory Coast at age five. In the book is a photograph of a child standing between a baggage cart and two worried parents at the Abidjan airport. He was moving to France to live with an uncle, a professional player. The six-hour flight, alone with his favorite toy, passed in a blur of tears and tissues.

He was right to be scared. His uncle constantly changed clubs, and each year Drogba found himself in a new school, usually the only black boy in class. Later, he, his parents, and five siblings lived in a room of just over one hundred square feet in a Parisian suburb.

At twenty-three he was still "almost a substitute of a substitute" with Le Mans in France's second division. Three years later he gets to Chelsea, but the move echoes his childhood exile. In London the sun sets before four o'clock, and at Chelsea he feels like the new boy. "I had the impression, at first, of not being accepted by the English [players]," he recalls. In the locker room, Englishmen John Terry and Frank Lampard sit together, and the Africans have their corner. Gradually, Drogba concludes that this is natural: "A black goes to a black, a Portuguese to a Portuguese, an Englishman to an Englishman."

Then he starts playing brilliantly. He becomes famous, especially in the Ivory Coast, where some babies are christened "Didier-Drogba." In his country's civil war, he says he becomes "an icon of reconciliation."

Yet he's constantly thinking of leaving Chelsea. He stays because of Mourinho. When Drogba writes about him, the book's tone shifts from merely overwrought to cheap romantic novel. The two first meet when Drogba's Marseille plays Mourinho's Porto in 2003. At halftime Mourinho asks him,

"Do you have a brother or cousin in Ivory Coast, because I don't have the money to bring you to Porto?" Mourinho's "charming smile" and "mastery of French" seduce Drogba. It is love at first sight.

At Chelsea, they are finally together. Mourinho assembles his players and tells them, "You have never won anything. I have just won the Champions League with Porto." The handsome Portuguese is a great professional who gives his players pages of notes on every opposing team, even tiny Scunthorpe. Moreover, he's psychic. "On the bench I've heard him describe what would happen in an almost surgical way," writes Drogba. "Sometimes this was almost disquieting. As if he could see the future."

Late in last year's FA Cup final, an exhausted Drogba hears Mourinho calling to him from the bench: "Continue. You'll score. Stay concentrated." Banal as this may sound to nonbelievers, Drogba is inspired. He scores. Like a horse whisperer with horses, Mourinho knows how to talk to players. Afterward, Drogba hunts him down in the stadium's catacombs, and they cry in each other's arms.

When Mourinho is sacked, the two are tragically parted. But Drogba is "intimately convinced" they will meet again. He adds, "With his gift of divination, he must know the date precisely." However, Mourinho, in his pretentious preface to the book, merely guesses at it: "When we're old, Drogba retired from soccer and me rolling around in a wheelchair? Whatever, Didier will always be in my heart." Cue sunset over fields of swaying corn.

Mourinho's successor, Avram Grant, is treated rather differently. In fact, he isn't treated at all. Whereas Drogba analyzes all his other coaches, he doesn't even mention Grant.

This summer Drogba will leave Chelsea, either to follow the man of his dreams, or to join his beloved AC Milan. The *Sun* has serialized Drogba's account of a visit to Milan, where he miraculously "happens to run into Adriano Galliani, Milan's vice-president." (I too am forever happening to run into Galliani while in Milan.) Drogba tells Galliani he'll join Milan "whenever you want." Mourinho hears of the rendezvous and is furious. He and Drogba don't speak for two weeks. Then they suddenly joke about it, look into each other's eyes, and laugh. "Our only moment of misunderstanding is erased," writes Drogba.

Lost amid the fuss is the truly remarkable aspect of the Milanese visit. Drogba had to see his dentist in Paris, so of course he chartered a private plane. When the dentist cancels, Drogba flies to Milan to party instead. Here, at last, is the solution to global warming: Ban professional soccer.

I was wrong. Drogba didn't follow Mourinho to Italy after all. In hindsight, I overestimated the role of friendship—or even love—in soccer. Players do what's best for their own careers. The people they meet along the way are secondary.

Franck Ribéry
July 2008

His shorts look too long for him, as if he's a player from the 1950s, or he's wearing his dad's gear. He has the scarred face of a losing featherweight boxer. Like Charlie Chaplin, Franck Ribéry (five foot six) is the little man personified. He is also one of the most exciting soccer players alive. He's the reason for some of us Parisians to trek out to the ghetto of Saint-Denis on freezing nights to watch France in the Stade de France, even despite Raymond Domenech and the sense of watching an over-thirty-fives team whose players don't like each other anymore. He is the reason Bayern Munich might just win the Champions League this season. (The Bundesliga title is taken for granted.)

When Ribéry recovers from the torn ligaments that mercifully liberated him from France's European championship shortly before it ended in tears, we will have our new model player back: the peasant as hero. His unlikely rise is a story of the French north and its underclass transplanted to a villa outside Munich.

Central to the Ribéry myth are his origins. He comes from Boulogne-sur-Mer, a poor town on the Channel coast facing England, where he grew up in a largely immigrant *quartier* with unemployment rates of up to 60 percent. "As a kid I spent all my time with Muslims," Ribéry has said. One of them became his wife, who converted him to Islam. His Muslim name is Bilal, after Islam's first black convert. Claude Boli, a French historian who specializes in black sportsmen, says that Ribéry's religion and his humble origins make him as much of an outsider in mainstream France as are his black and brown teammates on the national team.

The North is not where the French dream is. Its place in the French imagination is nicely captured by the new comedy *Bienvenue chez les Ch'tis*, which this spring became the highest-grossing French film ever. It features a postmaster who is transferred from Provence—where the French dream is—to a rainy town in the North where people eat fries and drink and hang around the cobblestoned streets. The Ch'tis are revealed as lovable after all.

Ribéry is a Ch'ti. "Ti Franck" speaks the Ch'ti dialect with Flemish influences and was once an unemployed Boulogne dropout hanging around the streets. His status as one of life's victims is made visual by the scar that runs across the right side of his face and his forehead, legacy of the time when, aged two, he flew through his dad's car's windshield. Ribéry bears his stigmata with pride. "In a certain way this accident helped me," he has said. "As a child it motivated me. God gave me this difference. The scars are part of me, and people will just have to take me the way I am."

The one thing the young Ribéry could do reasonably well was play soccer. "Since I was very small I haven't stopped running," he says. "It's a quality that not many professional soccer players have." He got into Lille's soccer academy, but was soon kicked out for failing at school. Later he earned €150 a month playing for his hometown team.

"I've had difficult moments," he admits. He was offered a chance at Alès in southern France, drove there overnight, played a game in the heat of the next afternoon with blisters on his feet, and got a small contract. Then Alès went bankrupt, leaving Ribéry overdrawn at the bank. One of his many agents has said that Ribéry then was incapable of even filling in a form for social security. The teenager briefly worked on a building site with his dad. "I really didn't think about the French team then, but I did about turning pro," he says. Finally, Brest, in France's third division, offered him a giant contract: €2500 a month!

He got better fast, but had dubious agents with a taste for financially iffy clubs. After a brief stint with Galatasaray in Turkey, he joined Olympique Marseille. There, in late 2005, the contours of today's unique player started to emerge through the northern fog. Ribéry is a rare soccer player who can dribble the ball a few yards forward in almost any situation. He crouches over the thing, guarding it like a miser, knowing just how far he can take it before pushing a pass into a hole nobody else had seen. Bernard Lacombe, director of soccer at France's eternal champions Olympique Lyon, and owner of one of the best pairs of eyes in the game, explains that on the pitch Ribéry does everything different from everyone else.

Ribéry was the great Zinedine Zidane reborn as a small crab. But he also had something "Zizou" never had: He was a perpetual-motion machine, chopping the air with his little hands as he ran. He moved even as he received the ball, which, as Thierry Henry notes, made him "a nightmare for defenders." He dribbled like a Brazilian, passed like a Dutchman, and ran like a Brit.

In the spring of 2006, Ribéry was the antihero the French public was waiting for. The French were growing bored with their globalized multimillionaire players who had hogged the spots in *les Bleus* for a decade. The team felt like an exclusive gentlemen's club. The public embraced the little Ch'ti who hung out with his Ch'ti relatives rather than with fellow celebrities. He seemed more fan than player: Indeed, in July 1998, when several of the French players who flopped at Euro 2008 were already on the pitch winning the World Cup, little Ribéry was celebrating on the streets. When he posed in *France Football* magazine recently for a photo with some of the magazine's readers, he looked as ordinary as they did, if perhaps smaller and uglier. The one hint of his stardom was his finely honed goatee. Much of the public also approved of the fact that he was white, unlike all other French forward players to have emerged since 1998.

Finally, two weeks before the World Cup began, he made his debut for France against Mexico. Barely a minute after coming on as a sub, to cheers from the crowd, he already stood out by the simple measure of running into space and calling for the ball, something the other *Bleus* seemed too old and blasé to do. A newspaper poll showed that 69 percent of the French wanted him on the World Cup squad. France's coach, Raymond Domenech, responded with a grin: "Sixty-nine—I like this number." Eventually, Ribéry was picked. "The coach put my name in twenty-third and last position," he notes. Watching the news at home on the sofa, he burst into tears and fell into the arms of his sick dad. It was like a scene from *Bienvenue chez les Ch'tis*. He would be the public's representative in *les Bleus*.

Zidane, whom Ribéry had always followed as a fan, adopted him as a sort of nephew. Ribéry soon got used to eating meals with the great man, and even began to joke with him. At Bayern too, Ribéry loves the puerile gags that characterize soccer locker rooms. From the start with *les Bleus*, he told *L'Equipe*, the palace gazette of French soccer, "I wasn't alone in my corner. I joked, I teased everyone, they teased me."

Still, he admits that before France's first match of the World Cup, a deadly dull 0–0 draw with Switzerland, "I was stressed. I suddenly realized that this was the World Cup." Zidane had told him to ration his energy in the heat, but Ribéry forgot and ran himself into the ground. In one early game, there was the sight of Henry wagging an index finger as he lectured the new kid wearing the schlemiel's number 22. That was the hierarchy then. Ribéry admits that at first on the field he would sometimes just stand there watching Zidane like a fan.

But during the World Cup, Ribéry seemed not merely to play better each game but actually to become a better player. At first, he often played with his head looking down at the ball. Turning his back on a defender, he would sometimes block his own view forward. But by the second round, when he scored a solo goal against Spain, he was a real international. Offers poured in, from Arsenal, Real Madrid, almost every big club in Europe. The world's 1 billion Muslims liked his public prayers before matches. He almost won France the World Cup, too, but late in the final against Italy—only forty-three days after his debut for France—his shot rolled just past the post. "If I had scored . . . ," he mused in *France Football*. "Ah! If I had scored, my friend. I still haven't got over this match."

He returned home confused by his new status. He still invariably described himself as "simple." But from a cheery ugly little Ch'ti nobody had ever heard of, he had been transformed into a cheery ugly little Ch'ti who was the national hero. Sometimes his new status helped: He persuaded the small northern club Calais to sign his younger brother, François. (The boys' father, also François, clearly didn't have much imagination when it came to names.) Third-division Calais seemed the sort of ambience where Franck himself would look more at home than at the Stade de France.

But being famous wasn't always easy. When he ate an ice cream cone on the beach with his family, the photograph made the newspapers. The popular French *Guignols* satirical TV program unveiled a Ribéry puppet that said dumb things in a weird accent. The real Ribéry appeared on France's 8:00 p.m. national television news to announce that he would leave Marseille for a giant club. Marseille's fans were angry, and someone threatened him in his own home. He decided to stay at Marseille for another year.

On the field, though, he became ever more dominant. In September 2006, not three months after the World Cup final, France met Italy again in a qualifier for Euro 2008. France won 3–1, largely thanks to Ribéry. When the Italian Gennaro Gattuso finally caught him after another wild chase, he tapped him on the neck and said, "You've given me a hard time." From a world champion, that was respect.

There are two types of attacking players. The one type—the passer, Zidane—wants the ball in his feet so that he can pass it. The other type—the runner, Henry—runs deep so that the passer can give it to him in space. Ribéry, uniquely, was both types in one.

And he has body, too. The night before the kickoff of Euro 2008, two great European coaches were having a chat at a sponsor's evening in Basel. The subject, of course, was kilometers. "How many kilometers a game do your fullbacks run?" one coach asked the other. "And your central midfielders?"

Yet when the coaches began talking about individual players, they didn't praise kilometer-eating supermen like Dirk Kuyt or Gianluca Zambrotta. Instead, they rhapsodized about little Ribéry. They particularly admired his strength. One of the coaches, who had worked with Ribéry, said, "He once picked up one of our doctors, a guy of 100 kilos, and put him in a washbasin. The doctor didn't want to go, and fought back, but he couldn't do anything."

Last summer Bayern paid $34 million for Ribéry. Though he arrived in Munich with barely a word of German, he wore Lederhosen when required ("It was a bit strange suddenly to walk around in a costume like that") and made practical jokes from the start. "I've met my match here in a player like Lukas Podolski," he concedes. "With him it's always fun. It's true that I put toothpaste on his doorknob and salt in his glass. And I once hid his soccer boots. I also stuck his locker closed with plasters so that he couldn't open it and get changed. So he was late for practice several times." Because most soccer players are like children, these antics have lightened the atmosphere at a club where players traditionally hate each other.

In his first German season, Ribéry won the German double and was voted the Bundesliga's Player of the Year. Starting from the wing, he ran games. Mark van Bommel, his teammate at Bayern, says that soon Ribéry will be the best in the world. English clubs occasionally try to sign him. No wonder that when Ribéry hurt his ankle in France's last game of Euro 2008 against Italy, Bayern got a bit emotional. The club's eternal general manager, Uli Hoeness, said Bayern was "incredibly annoyed with the French doctors," who had made "twenty-five different diagnoses" of Ribéry's injury. Given that these were the people who had missed Lilian Thuram's heart condition for the fourteen years he played for the national team, Bayern should count themselves lucky the docs didn't amputate Ribéry's arm by accident.

To get away from it all after work, he goes home to a villa in the countryside outside Munich. "I do need a bit of peace," he says.

You can imagine. An ordinary joe who has stumbled into a world of glamour, as if he had won a lottery to become a star player, is now supposed to win the Champions League. This season millions of spiritual Ribérys with scarred faces in living rooms around Europe will be cheering him on.

After Ribéry's various embarrassing sex scandals, failures with France, and tens of millions of euros in earnings, French fans no longer consider him an ordinary joe.

Michael Ballack, Ronaldo, Andriy Shevchenko, and Francesco Totti
September 2008

On September 22, 1976, a great soccer player was born in Rio. "Do you know who Ronaldo was named after?" his father asked a visiting reporter years later. "After the doctor who closed off his mother's tubes after his birth. Ha, ha. Doctor Ronaldo, his name was."

That birth kicked off the most fertile week in soccer history. Four days after Ronaldo, little Michael Ballack was born in Görlitz in the German Democratic Republic, Francesco Totti followed in Rome on September 27, 1976, and the quartet was completed when Andriy Shevchenko came to earth in the Ukrainian village of Dvirkivschyna on September 29.

There was probably something in the water that summer. On July 1, 1976, Ruud van Nistelrooy and Patrick Kluivert had both been born in the Netherlands. Whatever the secret, as the quartet turns thirty-two and sees the finishing line ahead, it's a chance to sketch a sort of composite career of the modern soccer star.

The first point to emerge is that origins barely matter. In modern soccer it's irrelevant whether you come from a village evacuated after the Chernobyl disaster (like Shevchenko), a Roman family so traditional that your mother was forever ironing your soccer uniform (Totti), or Dr. Salvador-Allende-Strasse 168, Karl-Marx-Stadt in East Germany (Ballack).

All four grew up dreaming of greatness. Totti wanted to be a gas station attendant and Ronaldo a singer, Shevchenko boxed, and Ballack was identified by the GDR as a future speed skater. Only Ronaldo was a teen prodigy at soccer: At seventeen he sat on Brazil's bench at the 1994 World Cup final, reputedly shaking with nerves for fear he'd be sent on. The first thing he bought with his new wealth was braces. His buckteeth had plagued his youth.

The other three reached the top later. None featured at the Youth World Cup of 1995. The Player of the Tournament, a Brazilian named Caio, was hardly heard of again.

Ballack took longest to become a star. At twenty-two he still wasn't a regular in the German Bundesliga. His long stretch in anonymity may be why he is the only member of this quartet never to have married a model or showgirl. Instead, he met a pretty waitress at the Café Am Markt in Kaiserslautern. Meanwhile, Ronaldo has worked his way through a legion of blondes collectively known as the Ronaldinhas.

This is the first generation of globalized soccer players. Whereas the first former Soviet players to move west flopped, Shevchenko left Dynamo Kiev for Milan and adapted instantly. He had merely gone from a partly capitalist country with a strong mafia where the common man had nothing to a partly capitalist country with a strong mafia where the common man went about dressed from head to toe in Armani. He married an American model.

All four gave their children cosmopolitan names. Shevchenko named one son Jordan, after Michael Jordan; Ballack's boys are Louis, Emilio, and Jordi; and Ronaldo's boy is Ronald, because the player and his then wife enjoyed eating at McDonald's. Even Totti, the eternal Roman, called his daughter Chanel.

By their late twenties, these players were living a merciless succession of great moments—even if Ballack's involved just missing the great prizes. Time at the top moves too fast to allow much time to savor. In Yokohama in 2002, not an hour after Ronaldo had scored twice to win the World Cup final, a Brazilian journalist told him, "We are not interested in the past, only in the future." Didn't Ronaldo want to win Olympic gold? What about the next World Cup?

"I don't want to feel any pressure now about the future," Ronaldo answered in his quiet way. "I don't want anything except to celebrate. Thank you very much." He had finally learned the one essential skill for life at the top: saying no.

All these players devised a way of dealing with stress. Totti stayed forever with AS Roma, where he is loved even when he doesn't perform every week. Shevchenko has just rejoined Milan, the best club at cosseting players. Ronaldo prioritized World Cups, often dropping out of club soccer for months on end. And by the time Ballack reached the top, he was mature enough to cope with the pressure. All four seem to have managed to remain decent people.

We can now chart each man's peak. Ronaldo's was in 2002, Shevchenko's in 2004 when he was voted European Player of the Year, Totti's in 2006 when he won the World Cup, while Ballack almost won everything this summer. It shows that the further forward you play, the more dependent you are on acceleration, and the earlier you peak. Ballack, the only pure midfielder of the quartet, has lasted best.

The journey ends prematurely. Gradually, injuries take a cumulative toll. Totti and Ballack are now struggling to return to fitness. Shevchenko hopes to score his first goal of the season before his birthday. Ronaldo is recuperating on a Rio beach from yet another horrible knee injury, but cannot yet say good-bye: "I feel such a passion for soccer that I'm ready for any sacrifice to come back." He hints at joining Manchester City.

However, the Brazilian weekly *Veja* recently photographed him sprawled potbellied on a yacht, smoking and drinking beer. In one way or another, this is how it ends.

Xavi
April 2009

Every December in Paris, some glamour boy is awarded the "Golden Ball" for European Player of the Year. There should be a parallel ceremony in a back room, where Europe's most underappreciated player is given a scuffed plastic sippy cup. The award would long have been hogged by Claude Makelele, a ball winner so unobtrusive that Real Madrid flogged him to Chelsea in 2003 rather than give him a pay rise. Real hasn't reached the semi-finals of the Champions League since. "Why put another layer of gold paint on the Bentley," asked Makelele's friend Zinedine Zidane after Real bought David Beckham that summer, "when you are losing the entire engine?"

Paul Scholes of Manchester United succeeded Makelele as the European player with the highest performance-to-attention ratio. However, Scholes lost the sippy cup when every pundit on earth began pointing out how under-appreciated he was. Now the sippy cup goes to Xavi Hernández Creus, who as the central midfielder of Barcelona and Spain drives on both of the world's best soccer teams. More than that: As Chelsea will notice when they meet Barcelona in the forthcoming semifinals of the Champions League, Xavi incarnates Barcelonan soccer.

This is only partly because he is a local boy, who still used to ride the subway to the stadium when he made his debut for Barcelona a decade ago. More significantly, Xavi was raised practically from birth to be Barcelona's version of a quarterback—or, as they call it in the Nou Camp stadium, a "number four."

The "four" buzzes around central midfield distributing passes like a quarterback. It's a role created by Johan Cruijff, the Dutchman who updated seventies "total football," as it became known, for Barcelona. Soon after Cruijff began managing Barça in 1988, he spotted a reedy kid named "Pep" Guardiola toiling unnoticed in the youth teams and anointed him a "four." Guardiola became a legendary "four." Today he manages Barcelona.

One day in the late 1990s a tiny "four" named Xavi, too timid to speak, showed up at training and began passing like Guardiola. Boudewijn Zenden, then playing for Barça, told me, "We said, 'It's the same kind of player!' They had this education where you just open up a can of number fours. It's hard to say, but Xavi's a more complete player than Guardiola." Guardiola himself agreed, telling Xavi, "You're going to push me out the door." Though Xavi is undeniably more mobile than Guardiola, and has eyes in the back of his head, these are not judgments he easily accepts. He recalls, "I'd watch older players and think, 'With him there, I'm screwed.'"

Xavi didn't seem to want to become a Catalan hero like Guardiola. He didn't do the things that get players headlines, like squabbling or being transferred or scoring a lot of goals. He never spoke much. At five foot six on a good day, he was no superhero. All he did was hit passes, left to right, up and down, like someone filling in a crossword puzzle at top speed. Just as the legendary Chelsea defender Ron "Chopper" Harris incarnated the foul, Xavi incarnates the pass.

Cruijff had taught Barça a style straight out of a Graham Greene novel: Everything hinged on finding the third man. Everyone had to be in motion so that the man on the ball could always choose between two players to pass to. No wonder Barcelona kept producing "fours." After Xavi came the even littler Andrés Iniesta, and then Cesc Fabregas, currently in exile at Arsenal, who says with Xavian modesty, "Xavi is several classes better than me."

At Euro 2008, Xavi, Iniesta, and Cesc were all on the field weaving triangles together. In the final, they made the Germans chase the ball as if in a training exercise. Spain is now unbeaten in thirty-one games. They had another undefeated run of twenty-five games before falling to Makelele's France at the World Cup of 2006. Plainly, they have been the best national team on earth for five years now. Moreover, Barcelona is the most glorious club side on earth. If Xavi isn't careful, people will soon notice him. Luckily for him, Barça's forwards get most of the credit, and as he always tells everyone, he's not half as good as Iniesta anyway.

By now I think people have noticed Xavi.

Johan Cruijff
May 2009

When a teenage waif named "Jopie" Cruijff began training with Ajax's first team, many of the senior players had already known him for years. Cruijff had grown up a few hundred yards down the road from the club's little stadium, in Amsterdam-East. He had been hanging around the locker room with the first team since he was four. Nonetheless, he surprised his new teammates. It wasn't just his brilliance they noticed; it was his mouth. Even while on the ball, the kid never stopped lecturing, telling senior internationals where to run. Maddeningly, he generally turned out to be right.

Jopie Cruijff would become more than just a great soccer player. Unlike Pele and Maradona, he also became a great thinker about soccer. It's as if he were the lightbulb and Edison all at once. It's impossible to identify one man who "invented" British soccer, or Brazilian soccer. They just accreted over time. However, Cruijff—together with Rinus Michels, his coach at Ajax—invented Dutch soccer. The game played today by Holland and Barcelona is a modified version of what the two men came up with in Amsterdam in the mid-1960s. Only now are the Dutch finally liberating themselves from Cruijff's style and, above all, from his bizarre personality.

Johan Cruijff (his real name, although foreigners prefer "Cruyff") was born on April 25, 1947. His father, Manus, a grocer, supplied Ajax with fruit. Cruijff practically grew up at the club. He learned his excellent English—which is probably more correct than his Dutch or Spanish—from eating warm English lunches at the homes of Ajax's English managers of the 1950s, Keith Spurgeon and Vic Buckingham. "I didn't have a very long education," he told me when I interviewed him in Barcelona in 2000, "so I learned everything in practice. English too."

He was just a kid when Manus boasted that one day he would be worth 100,000 guilders. Manus's death when Cruijff was twelve was probably the formative event of his life. Decades later, he'd still sometimes sit up at night in the family kitchen in Barcelona chatting to his father's spirit. A fatherless boy in a locker room full of men, Cruijff always had to be tougher than anyone else. He was. There are reports of him cheating at Monopoly to beat his own beloved children.

On Cruijff's debut, Ajax lost 3–1 at a club called GVAV. The newspaper reports mostly misspelled his name. After that the seventeen-year-old didn't play any more away games for a while. His mother, who cleaned Ajax's locker rooms, ruled that he could play only home games, as they were supposedly safer. Ajax in those days was a little semiprofessional outfit, merely the neighborhood team of Amsterdam-East. But two months after Cruijff's debut, on January 22, 1965, a gym teacher for deaf children named Rinus Michels drove his secondhand Skoda through the gates of De Meer to start work as a coach. Michels had a crazy idea: He was going to turn Ajax into a top international club. The teenage waif he encountered was equally ambitious. Within six years they had done it.

The style that they invented is now known as "total football." "We never called it that. That came from outside, from the English," Ajax's outside-right Sjaak Swart told me. It was a game of rapid one-touch passing and players endlessly swapping positions in search of space. Every player had to think like a playmaker. Even the keeper was regarded as the man who started attacks, a sort of outfield player who happened to wear gloves. Wingers and overlapping fullbacks kept the field wide. Cruijff could go where he liked, conducting the orchestra with constant improvisation. The world first noticed in 1966, when Ajax beat Liverpool 5–1 on a night so shrouded with mist that hardly anyone saw the game.

Cruijff and Michels were lucky, of course. By some demographic fluke, half the young men in Amsterdam-East seemed to be world-class soccer players. A slow bohemian smoker named Piet Keizer became a fabulous outside-left. Kuki Krol, an Amsterdam Resistance hero, produced a willowy defender named Ruud. And one of the few Jews in the neighborhood to survive the war, a man named Swart, used to take his son Sjakie to Ajax on the back of his bike.

But Cruijff was the most original player in all of Amsterdam-East. His great Dutch biographer, Nico Scheepmaker, would later remark that whereas other great players were merely two-footed, Cruijff was "four-footed": Hardly anyone had kicked with the outside of his feet before Cruijff did. Cruijff was also astonishingly quick for a chain smoker—"If they time normally with me, they're always just too late," was one of his early bon mots—but he preferred to emphasize his quickness of thought. Speed, he explained, was mostly a matter of knowing when to start running.

To Cruijff, soccer was "a game you play with your head." He was a man who came from Mars and said, "This is how people have always done it, but they were wrong." He rethought everything from scratch, without caring about tradition. Perhaps his greatest goal ever was a case in point. Ajax was playing a friendly against an amateur side, and there were no television cameras, but what seems to have happened is that Cruijff was advancing alone on the goal when the keeper came out to confront him. Cruijff turned and began running back with the ball toward his own half. The keeper pursued him until the halfway line, where he realized that Cruijff no longer had the ball. At some point he had backheeled it into the net without breaking stride.

Cruijff took responsibility not only for his own performance, but for everybody else's too. He was forever pointing, a coach on the field. Michels had told him, "If a teammate makes a mistake, you should have prevented that mistake." Frank Rijkaard, later a teammate of Cruijff's and opponent of Maradona's, said that Maradona could win a match by himself, but didn't have Cruijff's gift of changing the team's tactics to win it.

As a leader, Cruijff was a child of his time. Like his contemporary Franz Beckenbauer, or the students in the streets of Paris in 1968, he was a postwar baby boomer impatient to seize power. The boomers wanted to reinvent the world. They didn't do deference. Before Cruijff, Dutch soccer players had knocked on the chairman's door to hear what they would be paid. Cruijff shocked Ajax by bringing his father-in-law, Cor Coster, in with him to do his pay talks.

Cruijff drove everybody at Ajax crazy. He never stopped talking, in that working-class Amsterdam accent, with his very own grammar, his penchant for apparently random words ("Them on the right is goat's cheese"), and the shrugs of shoulders that sealed arguments. He once said about his playing career, talking about himself in the second person as usual, "That was the worst thing, that you always saw everything better. It meant that you were always talking, always correcting."

His personality was so outsized that Michels hired not one but two psychologists to understand him. Cruijff, always open to new thinking in soccer, was happy to talk to them. One shrink, Dolf Grunwald, blamed everything on Cruijff's father fixation. "Really [Cruijff] denies all authority because he—subconsciously—compares everyone to his F. [Father]. . . . If he can stop seeing in Michels the man who is not as good as his f. [father], we'll have moved on a lot." (Grunwald died in 2004, but Dutch author Menno de Galan obtained his notes.)

Grunwald said that when teammates attacked Cruijff, he became "more nervous and talkative." But when Cruijff felt accepted, he calmed down. "Then his attitude changes too: soft voice, sits down, hangs or lies, talks less, somewhat damp eyes."

After Grunwald fell out of favor with Michels, Cruijff was sent to Ajax's other shrink, Roelf Zeven, where he lay on the sofa and talked incessantly about his father-in-law, Coster. Here was the missing link in Freud's work: the father-in-law fixation.

All the talking may have helped. From 1971 to 1973, Cruijff's Ajax won three straight European Cups. A neighborhood team from a country that had never done anything in soccer before, whose stadium would have been small for the English second division, and whose players earned no more than successful shopkeepers had reinvented soccer.

Then Ajax blew itself up. Cruijff's departure was instigated by the player power that he himself had created. In 1973 the players gathered in a countryside hotel to elect their captain. The majority voted for Keizer, against the incumbent Cruijff. He fled to Barcelona, whereupon Ajax's team collapsed. Cruijff himself would never win another international prize as a player.

The transfer fee Barcelona paid for Cruijff was so big—5 million guilders—that the Spanish state wouldn't countenance it. Finally, Barça got him into Spain by officially registering him as a piece of agricultural machinery. Cruijff scored twice on his debut, and that season, 1973–1974, Barcelona won its first title in fourteen years. Immediately afterward he rushed off to the World Cup in West Germany.

The Dutch team that summer was largely his creation. It was Cruijff, the captain, who had told midfielder Arie Haan that he would play the tournament as libero. ("Are you crazy?" Haan had replied. It proved to be a brilliant idea.) It was Cruijff who had groomed Holland's striker, Johnny Rep, as a youngster at Ajax, sometimes screaming at the bench during games, "Rep must warm up!"

The tournament wasn't Cruijff's best month in soccer, but it was the month that most people saw him and the style he had invented. For many foreigners, the Cruijff they know is the Cruijff of his only World Cup.

Cruijff notionally spent the tournament at center-forward, but he was always everywhere. Sometimes he'd sprint down the left wing and cross with the outside of his right foot. Sometimes he'd drop into midfield and leave opposing center-backs marking air. Sometimes he'd drop back just to scream instructions. Arsène Wenger tells the story of Cruijff telling two of Holland's midfielders to swap positions and then returning fifteen minutes later to tell them to swap again. To Wenger, this showed how hard it was to replicate the fluidity of "total football" if you didn't have Cruijff himself.

Holland hammered Brazil in the semis, but after that everything went wrong. Several days before the final, the West German tabloid *Bild* published a story headlined "Cruyff, Champagne, Naked Girls, and a Cool Bath." It claimed that several Dutch players had held a nocturnal party with half-clad *Mädchen* in their hotel pool. Cruijff spent much of the night before the final on the phone to his wife, Danny, promising her the article was a lie. It was a terrible moment for a man who had spent his adult life building the secure family he had lost at age twelve; Cruijff was no George Best. That phone call, says his brother Henny, is why he played "like a dishrag" in the final. None of it would have happened if their father hadn't died so early, added Henny.

Admittedly, Cruijff wasn't a dishrag in the first minute of the final. Dropping back to libero he picked up the ball, ran across half the pitch, and got himself fouled just outside the German area. Referee Jack Taylor, an English butcher, wrongly gave Holland a penalty. But thereafter, Cruijff mostly hung around in his own half, allowing Berti "the Terrier" Vogts to mark him out of the game. In fact, Vogts had more scoring chances than Cruijff did. Holland lost 2–1. At the reception afterward, Cruijff buttonholed the Dutch queen Juliana and asked her to cut taxes.

Cruijff's next four years at Barcelona were mostly depressing. He got kicked a lot, won no big prizes, and suffered from stress. "If you're not enjoying [soccer], you can't bear the pressure," he said later. In 1978, at only thirty-one, he retired. He refused even to play in the World Cup in Argentina. Many foreigners wrongly believe he was boycotting the Argentine military regime. Rather, haunted by the "swimming pool incident" of 1974, Cruijff stayed home for "family reasons."

A Dutch television broadcaster tried to change his mind with a campaign called "Pull Cruijff Over the Line" (with a theme song by "Father Abraham" of Smurf-song fame). Cruijff briefly mused about playing on the condition that he could take his wife. Nothing came of it. And so David Winner argues in *Brilliant Orange* that the "swimming pool incident" determined the outcome of two World Cups: 1974 and 1978, which Holland again lost in the final.

In October 1978 Cruijff played his farewell match: a friendly with Ajax against Bayern Munich, which Ajax lost 0–8. And that would have been the end of Cruijff the player, but for a pig farm. In Barcelona, Cruijff and his wife, Danny, had met a French Russian opportunist named Michel Basilevitch. "The most handsome man in the world," Danny Cruijff called him. Basilevitch, who drove a leased Rolls-Royce, persuaded them to put the bulk of their money in a pig farm. The Cruijffs lost millions of dollars. Next thing anyone knew, Cruijff had returned to soccer, in the United States, with the Los Angeles Aztecs and later the Washington Diplomats.

Though he loved money with the passion of a man who had grown up without it, he hadn't come just for the cash. He enjoyed the anonymity of the United States—he could go shopping without being bothered—and he fell in love with soccer again. As ever, there were irritations. In Washington, he drove his British coach, Gordon Bradley, and his British teammates crazy with his fancy ideas about soccer. Once, after Bradley had given a team talk and left the locker room, Cruijff got up, wiped the blackboard clean, and said, "Of course, we're going to do it completely differently." One of the British players, Bobby Stokes, said that when the "Dips" bought Cruijff they should also have bought a year's worth of cotton wool to block the other players' ears. At one point Cruijff grew so despairing of his teammates that he announced he would limit himself to only scoring goals, and did.

The American years provided perhaps the most characteristic Cruijff story: Cruijff and the Florida bus driver. Pieter van Os, in his Dutch book on Cruijff's American years, interviewed several eyewitnesses to construct a full account. What seems to have happened is that just after the Dips landed in Florida for a training camp, the bus driver got them lost. Cruijff had never been to the place before. However, he immediately went to the front of the bus and, standing beside the driver, dictated the correct route. Apparently, he often used to direct taxi drivers in cities he didn't know. Maddeningly, he usually turned out to be right.

When Cruijff returned to Ajax in 1981, the Dutch were skeptical. The Calvinist Holland of the time distrusted anyone who thought he was special. Cruijff had never been very popular in his own country, where he was known as "Nose" or the "Money Wolf." By now he was thirty-four, with a broken body. Surely, he was just coming back for the money, right?

He made his Second Coming in an Ajax-Haarlem game. Early in the first half, he turned two defenders and lobbed the keeper, who was barely off his line. For the next three years, Dutch stadiums sold out wherever Cruijff played, as people flocked to see him one last time. He gave us thirty-yard passes with the outside of his foot that put teammates in front of the keeper so unexpectedly that sometimes the television cameras couldn't keep up.

But what he did on the field was only the half of it. The older Cruijff was the most interesting speaker on soccer I have ever heard. "Until I was thirty I did everything on feeling," Cruijff said. "After thirty I began to understand why I did the things I did." In 1981 I was twelve, living in Holland, and for the rest of my teens I imbibed everything he said about soccer. It was as if you could read a lucid conversation with Einstein in the paper every day or two.

Cruijff said things you could use at any level of soccer: don't give a square ball, because if it's intercepted the opposition has immediately beaten two men, you and the player you were passing to. Don't pass to a teammate's feet, but pass it a yard in front of him, so he has to run onto the ball, which ups the pace of the game. If you're having a bad game, just do simple things. Trap the ball and pass it to your nearest teammate. Do this a few times, and the feeling that you're doing things right will restore your confidence. His wisdoms directly or indirectly improved almost every player in Holland. "That's logical"—the phrase he used to clinch arguments—became a Dutch cliché.

Cruijff had opinions on everything. He advised golfer Ian Woosnam on his swing. He said the traffic lights in Amsterdam were in the wrong places, which gave him the right to ignore them. His old teammate Willem van Hanegem recalls Cruijff teaching him how to insert coins into a soft-drink machine. Van Hanegem had been wrestling with the machine until Cruijff told him to use "a short, dry throw." Maddeningly, the method worked.

The aging Cruijff won two straight league titles with Ajax. When he was thirty-six, and Ajax wouldn't pay him enough, he switched to its arch-rival, Feyenoord, and won the title again in his final season as a player. As Scheepmaker said: Statistically, buying Cruijff didn't guarantee you a championship, but it certainly made it immensely more likely. When Cruijff was substituted during his last match, Scheepmaker folded up his desk in the press box and rose to applaud a man who, he said, had made his life richer than it would have been without him.

Unfortunately, the only time I ever met Cruijff, he ended up hating me. I had interviewed him in his Barcelona mansion in spring 2000, and things had gone quite well. As per agreement, I wrote about it in the Observer *ahead of Euro 2000. The newspaper had paid him for it. Initially, the* Observer *and Cruijff had also agreed that he would write a series of columns during Euro 2000 (with me as ghostwriter), but that deal fell through, as deals with Cruijff often do.*

A few months after Euro 2000, I wrote a starstuck account in a Dutch magazine about my meeting with the great man. The cover of the magazine was a photograph of me holding a drawing of Cruijff beneath the words, "Johan and Me."

Cruijff was furious. He said I should have paid him again before writing about the meeting a second time. Suddenly, two attacks on me appeared in the Dutch press. In brief, they said I was a plagiarist who wrote about other people's extramarital affairs and had accused Cruijff of fraud.

I don't know if anyone has ever had a more upsetting experience with his childhood hero. If so, I can't bear to hear it.

Andrés Iniesta
May 2009

It rarely happens, but sometimes a player stops to savor the moment. On Wednesday night Andrés Iniesta was twenty-five years old, in Rome, at his peak, and part of a Barcelona team that was passing rings around Manchester United. This was as good as it gets. So for a second during yet another attack he just rolled the ball around under his foot, as if tickling its belly. In Rome, Iniesta showed his sport the way forward.

Iniesta, his teammate Xavi, and Barcelona's coach, Josep Guardiola, possibly don't share DNA, but in soccer terms they are brothers. The first brother, Guardiola, emerged twenty years ago as the definitive Barça playmaker: effectively the side's quarterback, who launched almost every attack with a perfect pass. The second brother, little Xavi, was better. Finally, almost a decade ago, a tiny white-faced teenager showed up at Barça's training. Guardiola studied Iniesta for a bit, turned to Xavi, and said, "You've seen that? You'll push me towards the exit, but that guy will send us both into retirement."

It took a while. In 2006, when Barcelona last won the Champions League, Iniesta appeared only as a substitute. But inside the club, everyone knew he was coming. Last year I asked Barcelona's then coach, Frank Rijkaard, to name the player with the perfect personality for top-class soccer. Rijkaard hemmed and hawed, but finally, in triumph, shouted out the right answer: "Andrés—Andrés Iniesta! He's always there in training, always tries, and is just a wonderful soccer player."

Iniesta's magical year began in Vienna last June 30. In the final of Euro 2008, his Spanish team passed rings around Germany. Vienna prefigured Rome. Both times, Iniesta, Xavi, and their buddies seemed to be playing piggy-in-the-middle against Europe's second-best team. Germany and United chased ball in the heat. It wasn't fair.

Barcelona has to play like that. "Without the ball we are a horrible team," says Guardiola. "So we need the ball." Barça is too little—perhaps the shortest great team since the 1950s—to win the ball by tackling. The unofficial minimum height for top-class soccer is about five feet eight, and Xavi, Iniesta, and Lionel Messi are below it. The minimum for central defenders is about six feet, and Carles Puyol is below that. So Barça defends either by closing off space through perfect positioning or by keeping the ball. Johan Cruijff, Dutch father of the Barcelona style, teaches, "If we have the ball, they can't score."

Modern soccer is supposed to be manlier. Managers talk about "heart," "grit," "bottle," and mileage covered. What Iniesta showed in Rome is that these are secondary virtues. Soccer is a dance in space. When everyone is charging around closing the gaps, you need the technique of Iniesta to find tiny openings. In Rome, he barely mislaid a pass. Sometimes he'd float past United players, his yellow boots barely marking the grass. Occasionally he hit little lobs, a sign that he knew this was his night.

We know how good United is. That's the measure of how good Barça was in Rome. In games at this level, some very respected players get found out. It happened to United's Ji-Sung Park, Anderson, and Michael Carrick, but also to Wayne Rooney. Excellent with his right foot, he is helpless with his left. Barcelona covered his one foot.

When it was over, Barça's players celebrated with Barça's fans behind the goal. But as we looked from players to fans and back again, already it was impossible to say which was which. Iniesta is a Barça fan. On Wednesday he was one of seven starting players raised in Barcelona's academy, the Masia.

Had he popped into the VIP buffet elsewhere in the Stadio Olimpico, he'd have seen a portent. Eusebio, Portugal's star of the 1960s, was hanging around alone in a blazer. Every few seconds, someone would come up to hug him, or just express awe, and Eusebio would smile. He must do this one hundred times a week. A year ago, you couldn't have imagined Iniesta in old age receiving such honors. You can now. In Rome Rooney called him "the best player in the world at the moment." Iniesta's next target: the World Cup 2010.

Watching Iniesta during overtime of the World Cup final in Johannesburg, I was reminded again of the Champions League final. In Johannesburg Iniesta had been kicked to pieces by Mark van Bommel all game, but when Van Bommel went into defense to replace John Heitinga (who had been sent off), Iniesta was suddenly free. From that moment on he ran the game and, fittingly, scored the winner. In the space of three years, from June 2008 through May 2011, he won three Spanish titles, two Champions Leagues, the European Championship, and the World Cup. Not bad for a man so modest and ordinary looking that when a woman in a Barcelona café mistook him for a waiter, he dutifully went to the kitchen and got her order.

Eric Cantona
August 2009

Eric Cantona had just won his first league title in England, with Leeds United, in 1992. British television reporter Elton Welsby, desperate to get him to talk, ventured into baby French: *"Magnifique, Eric!"* Cantona replied, "Oh, do you speak French?" *"Non,"* admitted Welsby. And that was the end of that.

The mostly silent player—so well known, yet so little understood—continues to exert fascination twelve years after his retirement. At Old Trafford, where Cantona won four titles in five seasons with Manchester United, fans still sing "Oooh Aaah Cantona." As Philippe Auclair reports in his new *Cantona: The Rebel Who Would Be King*: "In 2008, a poll conducted in 185 countries by the Premiership's sponsor Barclays found him to be this competition's 'All-Time Favourite Player.'"* This summer, two new symptoms of Cantomania have appeared: Auclair's biography follows shortly after Ken Loach's movie *Looking for Eric*, in which Cantona (played by himself) steps out of a life-size poster to befriend a Mancunian postman.

Cantona wasn't the best player the Premier League has ever seen. He was a tad slow, never won an international prize, and dazzled the Premiership when it was still a backwater. Yet he lives on in fans' minds in larger-than-life-size format. Perhaps we now have enough distance to understand why. Both Auclair's and Loach's works, despite their flaws, help explain what made Cantona such a seminal figure for Manchester United, for English soccer, and indeed for English life in the 1990s. Cantona was an immigrant who landed at just the right moment.

---

* Philippe Auclair, *Cantona: The Rebel Who Would Be King* (London: Pan Macmillan, 2009).

The man who arrived in England in January 1992 had been a glorious failure in France. At twenty-five, he had already played for six clubs. He had also already briefly retired from soccer, after walking up to every member of the French league's disciplinary committee, repeating the word *idiot*, and then walking out of the room. He collected red cards. Yet England needed him.

In the early 1990s it was a shabby country deep in recession. It was also quite isolated. At this time, just before Eurostar trains and budget airlines connected Britain to the rest of Europe, the mysterious European Continent was a world away. Cantona brought it close. Loach's beautifully made, moving, and occasionally sentimental film is set in present-day Manchester, and whenever Cantona appears on-screen he provides a visual shock in the gloomy city: such a handsome figure amid the mostly pasty and overweight local soccer fans. When he arrived in 1992, that shock was even more pronounced.

English soccer then was as shabby as the country. Auclair describes the game of that era as "a drab, sometimes vicious affair." The author, incidentally, is not only a French journalist but also a well-known indie musician who sings under the name Louis Philippe. He became very big in Japan, and now lives in London, though for three years he trekked all around Britain and France interviewing more than two hundred people for this comprehensive, fair, if at times pretentious tome. Auclair also forced himself to watch "hours upon hours" of Cantona's English matches on tape, which reminded him how bad they were. English teams of the time mostly featured "hard-tackling box-to-box one-footed midfielders" and giant center-halves and center-forwards who couldn't play soccer, all rolling around in the mud. The British mistrust of what was then known as "continental flair" was such that even after Cantona in his first six months in England had helped Leeds win the title, Leeds's manager, Howard Wilkinson, sold him to Manchester United for just $2.15 million. When United's manager, Alex Ferguson, told his assistant, Bryan Kidd, the price, Kidd gasped: "Has he lost a leg or something?" Wilkinson's own son cried when Cantona went.

Crucially, Cantona had the physique to cope with the frenzy of English soccer. "People don't realize how huge he was," says Auclair. But Cantona could not merely rise above the frenzy; he could transform it into order. It had been years since England had seen a player like him, who seemed to know where everyone on the pitch was at any moment, who could position himself almost unmarked "between the lines" of the opposition's defense and midfield, and who could put the ball where he intended to with the speed and spin he wanted to. While giants galumphed around him, he found time. Ferguson told Auclair that Cantona became one of those players who "teach you something you didn't know about soccer, and can't be learned, because you had no idea it existed before they did it." English soccer has seen players like that since: Dennis Bergkamp, Gianfranco Zola, Thierry Henry, Cristiano Ronaldo. But back in the early 1990s Cantona alone could play this sort of soccer consistently. He was the player Ferguson had been searching for. The manager had already realized that United—without a league title since 1967—needed to abandon the traditional British style. Cantona showed him (and rising youngsters like Ryan Giggs and David Beckham) how.

In Ferguson's words, he was "the perfect player, in the perfect club, at the perfect moment." Partly this was Ferguson's doing. The success at United of a player who had left in bad odor almost everywhere else may be the manager's biggest triumph, as big as any Champions League trophy. Ferguson quickly understood that the key to Cantona's fairly simple personality was always to take his side, no matter how wrong he was. The strategy paid off.

But the Frenchman made his impact on English soccer as much off the field as on it. He was a different man from other players. Almost any other player describes himself as a "professional." The key to Cantona is that he saw himself as an artist. That is obviously part of his appeal to Loach, the reason the director made Cantona effectively the cocreator of *Looking for Eric*. Cantona, by playing himself, seems to be using the film to tell us something about who he is.

Cantona knows something about the arts. He has painted, exhibited photographs, produced plays, and read poems (and almost signed for one French club after its president gave him a Joan Miró painting), but he also saw his soccer as a form of art. Auclair, who actually is an artist, points out that Cantona has a naive view of artists. To the player, the "artist" is simply someone who expresses himself with absolute freedom.

Still, the point is that as a self-proclaimed "artist," Cantona saw his job as performing. The professional merely tries to win matches. Cantona always wanted to give something to the fans. It bothered him that in France, the small crowds were generally cold and critical. But English fans, so numerous, noisy, and close to the pitch, responded to him. He performed for them. "In just two months in England I feel more at home than I ever did in France," he said. "Now that I have mastered the perils of driving on the wrong side of the road, I can cope with everything."

A professional would have ignored Matthew Simmons, the fan who abused Cantona from the stands at Crystal Palace in 1995, because to the professional, fans are incidental, but Cantona leaped into the stands and karate-kicked Simmons. To Cantona, that too was part of being an artist. Self-expression might mean a pass flicked off the outside of the boot over a defense. It might mean learning to play the trumpet (badly) during his nine-month ban for kicking Simmons. Or it could mean violence on an impulse. Auclair works hard to defend him against English xenophobes, but on the evidence of his book, Cantona's career is a litany of spontaneous violence: punching teammates, leaping into the crowd to slug people even before Simmons, taking on almost a whole team of opponents after a match, judo-kicking an opponent, breaking a television reporter's rib, and so on.

For Manchester United's fans, the violence was part of his appeal. The club's history—and that of Ferguson himself—divides into pre-Cantona and post-Cantona eras. It wasn't merely that Cantona taught United "continental" soccer. He also changed the club's identity. Perhaps the seminal moment was the press conference he gave after his leap at Simmons. Faced with a roomful of journalists who were expecting him to say he was sorry for what was then being portrayed as the most dastardly act in British life since Hitler's Blitz, he said only (the accompanying commentary is by Auclair): "When the seagulls [a sip of water] follow a trawler [leaning back, smiling, pausing again], it's because they think [another pause] sardines [and another] will be thrown into the [slight hesitation] sea [a smile and a quick nod]. Thank you very much." The journalists guffawed. The artist had branched out into performance poetry. As the credits roll at the end of Loach's film, footage of the speech is shown: it's the quintessential Cantona moment, the artist confronting the world.

What most United fans—and Ferguson—loved about the speech was its lack of contrition. So much of Cantona's appeal was that he did whatever he wanted, no matter what the world thought. He was happy to reject the world, and to reject old friends at the merest suspicion of disloyalty. This, of course, has since become Ferguson's stance: If you're not with Manchester United, you're against us, and we don't care anyway. No wonder the manager, who is still close to his former player, now tells anecdotes of Cantona's physical assaults as if they were charming jokes. He admired the violence.

Auclair told me, "It chimes in with Cantona's own perception of the world, which is totally black-and-white: Either you are with me and you are my greatest friend, or you are my enemy. It's more calculated in the case of Alex, whereas Cantona, I think, had serious behavioral problems. He was one of the elements that helped Ferguson build that particular side of Manchester United."

The Cantona of Loach's film, too, is a talisman who protects the postman and other United fans against a hostile world. It's fitting that in the climactic scene, dozens of United fans, all wearing Cantona masks, including Cantona himself, take apart a villain's mansion to help their mates. Violence in the service of justice is part of Cantona's—and Ferguson's—ethic.

However, after the Simmons incident, Cantona quietly changed. He resolved to ditch expression through violence. While coaching kids as part of his punishment, he told one boy, "If you're going to get a yellow card, walk away and don't argue with the referee." Cantona mostly stuck to that ethic himself while winning his last two titles with United.

He never won anything grander. He should have been France's center-forward when they became world champions in 1998, but when he understood that his role would be subordinate to Zinedine Zidane's and Youri Djorkaeff's, he pulled out. That's why, as Auclair says, the enduring fascination with him is entirely English. Cantona is not part of the legend of French soccer. In fact, had he played in the 1998 World Cup, and gotten in Zidane's way, or caused renewed fractures within the squad, the French legend of 1998 might never have happened.

By then he had retired anyway. He quit suddenly in 1997, aged only thirty. Admittedly, he had got fatter, even double-chinned, but once again he was rejecting the world's largesse while it was still being offered. Cantona was being fabulously himself. So alluring are the spoils of soccer that it's hard to think of another player strong enough to walk away while still at the top. Cantona had thought he would return to soccer later, but he could never quite be bothered. He wouldn't have had the same impact again in England anyway, because by the late 1990s brilliant "artists" were flooding the Premier League.

Auclair describes Cantona's retirement from soccer as a death. In fact, his own account makes clear that it wasn't. Afterward, Cantona successfully reinvented himself. Though he once said he "would love to be poor," he has been an efficient point man for Nike, as well as popularizing beach soccer, and has become an artist of sorts. It's not that he has a gift for any other art form besides soccer. "He's a decentish actor," Auclair grudgingly admits. Indeed, Cantona's halting diction in Loach's film suggests why he so rarely spoke to the world: That wasn't his forte. Yet it still looks like a pretty good life: money plus a rung (however low) in the artistic pantheon. It's more than most former players manage.

Cantona lives on, in Britain at least, as the man who took English soccer from an English era to a continental one, and as the man who together with Ferguson and the club's then marketing manager, Edward Freedman, forged Manchester United's modern identity. The Premier League has seen better players, but nobody as transformative.

That final scene of Loach's film was horribly imitated in October 2010, when a gang of balaclava-clad United fans descended on Wayne Rooney's house, threatening to kill him for the crime of saying he would leave United.

In 2011 Cantona became director of soccer at the relaunched New York Cosmos, but he continues to attain greater postplaying fame as an actor in films and TV movies.

Thierry Henry
December 2009

I live in Paris (lucky). I always watch France at the Stade de France (not so lucky in recent years). I was there the night Thierry Henry's handball against Ireland got France to the World Cup. Lining up at the train station afterward, crushed in amid furious Irish and apologetic French fans, you could see France would be carrying two leaden legacies to the World Cup. The first would be the handball. The second would be Thierry Henry himself. The Henry problem has nothing to do with the handball. Rather, after fifteen years as a professional, the thirty-two-year-old is now almost completely worn-out. France's coach, Raymond Domenech, must be wondering how to avoid picking his captain for South Africa.

This is hard because Henry was once the world's best striker. At Euro 2004, after he had scored a casual double against Switzerland, I asked Swiss keeper Jörg Stiehl what made the Frenchman special. Stiehl explained that when most players shoot, they are so busy watching the ball and their opponents that they can barely see the goal. They hardly aim. But Henry retained perfect ball control even while sprinting past defenders. "He has time to look up and see where you are," said Stiehl. That's why Henry seldom needed to shoot hard. He just rolled the ball beyond the keeper's reach.

He was still the world's best striker in 2006, when the highlight of the World Cup was his duel in the final with the world's best defender, Fabio Cannavaro. Henry would have appreciated the encounter even though he lost, because unlike many players, he loved soccer. In his Arsenal years he'd sometimes sit at home in Hampstead watching French third-division matches, having fun identifying the players who should be playing higher. In Arsenal's locker room he'd quiz his teammates about obscure soccer trivia.

The death knell came in 2007, when he was twenty-nine and Arsène Wenger sold him. The moment Wenger sells a star is like the moment the surgeon invites the patient into his office for a private chat. That's the moment you know it's all over. Wenger excels at selling players for a fortune the instant they pass the top of their personal hill.

One morning in the spring of 2008, a few months after the sale, Henry sat in Barcelona's trophy room explaining to some Spanish television reporters that he was playing badly because he was missing his daughter in London. He's still playing badly, but it's not because of his daughter. I saw Henry live several times this year in the Stade de France and for Barcelona, and he now moves like somebody's dad with back problems. Six days after

France-Ireland, Barcelona's decision makers watching Henry stumble around against Inter Milan will have reminded themselves to buy a new striker—possibly as early as this winter. Already Henry rarely starts for Barça.

Physical decline is all the crueler if your body was once perfect. Someone like Zinedine Zidane, never much of an athlete to begin with, could age with more grace. No wonder that after the furor over the handball Henry admitted to having considered retirement. Knowing when to stop is the hardest thing in sport, and he has stuck around at the top level a season too long. The old Henry wouldn't have needed the handball. He would have eaten Ireland up over the two games.

This should have been the moment to write a fawning sporting obituary, assigning Henry's place in soccer's pantheon. He's not up with the gods—Pele, Maradona, Cruijff, Zidane—as he might have been, had David Trezeguet's penalty been three inches lower and France won the last World Cup. However, he belongs in the second row, alongside Michel Platini, George Best, and his own hero, Marco van Basten.

Unfortunately, it's no time for obits. Henry still has one last World Cup to play. Domenech is too loathed at home to dare risk dropping his most powerful player. Yet he should. Henry damages France. The team has better forwards: young Karim Benzema and Nicolas Anelka, already thirty but with all his faculties still intact. France has better ballplayers: Franck Ribéry (who covets Henry's spot on the left wing) and the rising playmaker Yoann Gourcuff. Henry slows down France's attacks.

Above all, the self-absorbed, domineering captain cows his teammates and coach. Against Ireland, a fearful Domenech left in the terrible Henry and substituted Gourcuff instead. You hope someone—possibly some of France's world champions of 1998—can persuade Henry that he was too great a player to allow himself the closing humiliation of a fourth World Cup.

With hindsight, "humiliation" was too weak a word. Luckily for Henry, he experienced most of France's World Cup from the bench. A few weeks later, soon after he had begun playing for the New York Red Bulls, the local Fox 5 television station offered him the coronation of a live interview. One early question must have surprised him, "So you just won the World Cup, right?"

Henry handled it gracefully. "No, not just. I did. The last one we didn't." While he talked, his "handball goal" against Ireland was endlessly replayed on the screen behind his head. Still, it was a nice example of an interview in which the player comes across as more measured and intelligent than his interviewer.

Lionel Messi
May 2010

Opinions differ as to who first put Leo Messi on a soccer field. His dad says the boy's grandma forced the coach, Don Salvador Ricardo Aparicio, to let the tiny five-year-old play with his older brothers. Aparicio's own version was that he only had ten players and, spotting the tyke kicking a ball against a wall, asked Messi's mother, "Will you lend him to me?"

Opinions converge on what happened next. Messi's mom dressed him in the team's uniform. The first ball came to his right foot, but nothing happened. Then a ball fell to his left. "He came out dribbling as if he'd played all his life," "Apa" later recalled.

A stray foreigner witnessing the moment in the fading Argentine river town Rosario, birthplace of Che Guevara, a place that time forgot, might have gasped. Argentines didn't. They recognized Messi at once: He was the *pibe*, "the boy," they had been waiting for.

Usually the main suspense before a World Cup concerns who will win it. This year, people are just as eager to know whether in South Africa we will see the full Messi. If he can match some of the moments he has given us with Barcelona, but in soccer's ultimate setting—well, the game doesn't get better than that. This World Cup is in large part about Messi. But to understand him, you have to understand his Argentine football ancestry.

It was sociologist Eduardo Archetti who explained the *pibe* to me, one day in Buenos Aires in 2000. The *pibe*, Archetti said, is a figure that Argentine soccer fans have had in their minds at least since the 1920s. The *pibe* learns his soccer on the *potrero*, a bumpy urban space, where only those who can dribble can keep the ball. He plays the creative game that Argentines call *la nuestra*, "ours," a style that they say comes from a child's imagination. In 1928 journalist Borocotó proposed in the great Buenos Aires soccer magazine *El Grafico* that Argentina build a monument in "any walk-way" to the inventor of dribbling. The statue, Borocotó wrote, would depict "a *pibe* with a dirty face, a mane of hair rebelling against the comb; with intelligent, roving, trickster and persuasive eyes and a sparkling gaze that seem to hint at a picaresque laugh that does not quite manage to form on his mouth, full of small teeth that might be worn down through eating 'yesterday's bread.'"

You may recognize the description. Indeed, when Maradona came along fifty years later, Argentine soccer fans had been expecting him. A tango, "El sueño del pibe" (Dream of the *pibe*), had been written about him in 1943. In the song, which Maradona has sung in public, a young *pibe* likens himself to bygone legends:

Dearest Mamita,
I will earn money,
I will be a Baldonedo,
A Martino, a Boyé

And the song ends with the *pibe*'s dream:

He took the ball, serene in his action
Ran past everybody to the keeper
And with a firm shot he became the shooter.

The song anticipates not just Maradona's great goal against England in 1986 but England's revenge by little eighteen-year-old Michael Owen in 1998 (Argentines nodded sadly and said, "The English have found themselves a *pibe*") as well as many of Messi's goals.

The point is that to Argentines, Maradona and Messi are quintessentially Argentine. A soccer fan whom Archetti interviewed in the late 1990s told him, "Now our problem is that we have had Maradona, and we will always expect to get another one." The fan himself knew the expectation was absurd, but he had it. Roberto "El Negro" Fontanarrosa, the legendary Argentine cartoonist, novelist, and Rosario soccer fan, believed something similar. "Maradona could never have come from Belgium," he told me.

Archetti, incidentally, had said that Argentine heroes are expected to die young, and sadly, that's just what happened to both him and Fontanarrosa. Archetti died of cancer in Norway in June 2005, four weeks before Messi won Argentina the Youth World Cup in Holland. Poor Fontanarrosa went in 2007. At least he lived long enough to see Messi. He must have recognized the *pibe* at once.

Messi may be quintessentially Argentine, but crucially, he left Argentina in adolescence. It was all because he had an extreme version of the *pibe* physique: at age thirteen, he was only four foot six. To reach a normal height, he would need hormone treatments costing about nine hundred dollars a month. His poor steelworker father begged help from the club Messi had joined, Newell's Old Boys. "The Lepers," traditionally run by incompetents, decided not to spend their shrinking resources on the tiny kid.

What saved Messi's career was his family's origin in Catalonia. A cousin there persuaded Barça to look at him. In a trial match Messi scored five goals. The club agreed to pay for Messi's treatments. The family left Rosario, crying, on what was Messi's first plane journey, and landed in a European city of which they knew so little that they were surprised to find it was on the sea. Every night in Barcelona, the *pibe* injected the hormones into his feet. So short initially that when he sat on the team bench his feet didn't touch the ground, he grew to five foot six, just big enough to be a player.

I first saw him at that Youth World Cup of 2005. In the final Argentina beat Nigeria 2–1, with two penalties from Messi. My main memory is his second penalty. Some penalty takers wait for the keeper to dive, before choosing the other corner. But Messi just needed the keeper to shift his balance fractionally onto his right leg, before choosing the other corner. My neighbor in the stands was the world's leading expert on youth soccer, the ancient, birdlike Dutchman Piet de Visser, a scout for Chelsea, and late in the game he inevitably exclaimed, "Maradona!"

The same thought had struck Maradona. "I've seen the guy who is going to inherit my place in Argentinean soccer," he announced on his television talk show, *La Noche del Diez*. "Messi seems to have an extra gear, a sixth speed. The ball remains on the upper part of his foot, like it's glued to it. He feels the ball: That's what makes him different."

But the overwhelming sensation when you watch Messi is still this: He's a child. The nerd with the flowerpot hairdo looks like a kid who has won a competition to spend a day with Barça. His physique seems to mock all the man monsters and fitness rooms and "food supplements" of modern sport. When Messi receives a ball and doesn't bother touching it, but just sets off running and lets it trot alongside him, he looks like a boy out with his pet dog. He dribbles with steps three-quarters the length of a normal pace, allowing him to change direction faster than any opponent. And being a child, he has superior balance to the men around him. That explains a characteristic Messi trait: how often he wins the "second ball." Often he'll get tackled, the ball will spin loose, the tacklers will be off balance, and Messi, who has instantly regained his full height, picks up the ball. That's how he scored two of his four goals against Arsenal in April.

Put simply: he's a *pibe* from the *potrero*. "He expresses very well the collective dream of Argentine soccer," says Jorge Valdano, the Argentine player–turned–technical director of Real Madrid and poet of the game.

Yet Messi is also more than a *pibe*. Thanks to his growth problem, the most gifted player on earth entered the best soccer academy on earth, Barcelona's Masia. The Masia saved him from becoming a second Maradona. Like many players of his era, Maradona had lived like a rock star. But Barcelona had learned from Maradona, and later from Ronaldinho. Each had joined Barça as the world's best youngster. Both had fallen for temptation: Maradona for cocaine, Ronaldinho for drink.

Temptation found Messi too. After he broke into Barcelona's first team, Ronaldinho began taking him out on the town. Finally, Josep Guardiola, then coach of Barça's second team, told him: "You've two options. Either you keep on partying, and you'll be out of here in days. Or you start eating properly, quit the alcohol, go to bed early, and come to practice on time. Only then might you become the best in the world."

Barça models itself on a family, and it made sure Messi became not a rock star but an obedient son. Albert Capellas, youth coordinator at the Masia, which is housed in an ancient farmhouse next to the Nou Camp, says: "Messi and [Andrés] Iniesta don't live here anymore, but this is their home. They come to eat, and if they have a problem they come to us, as they would to their mother and father. For us they are not stars. It's Leo, it's Bojan, it's Andrés. We say, "You are a good man. Don't lose your values."

On the field, too, Barcelona molded the *pibe* into a good boy. Frank Rijkaard, the Barcelona coach who gave Messi his debut, told me in 2008, "I've seen games where for ninety minutes it looked as if he was playing one against eleven, and he kept getting kicked, but we only won 1–0, or it was 0–0, or we lost 1–0. He's a fantastic dribbler, but he was making leaps forward by seeking variation in his game: One time you dribble, another time you give the ball back and go deep. He was becoming more effective by doing less." Maradona could dribble, pass, and score, but thanks largely to Barcelona, Messi also mastered soccer's other main craft: tackling. He is the complete player.

You might say the *pibe* became a European. It was an education Maradona never had. At twenty-two, Messi's age today, Maradona was still playing in Argentina. In any case, Messi's personality is more conducive to a long and consistent career than Maradona's was. A man with nothing to say, he lacks Maradona's wild poetry. "I don't go out much. I enjoy being alone at home," he says in two sentences never spoken by Maradona. Messi may not have all Maradona's good qualities, but he lacks the bad ones.

Yet, Argentineans ask, why doesn't he play well for Argentina? When he's with Barça, the only man who can stop him is Inter Milan's *pibe*-crushing coach, José Mourinho. When he's with Argentina, just pulling on the blue-and-white shirt seems to do the trick. Perhaps Argentina suffers from a plethora of *pibes*. At times the team resembles Snow White and the Seven Dwarfs. Messi doesn't combine well with Carlos Tévez, Sergio Agüero, or Pablo Aimar (all five foot six), certainly not when coached by Maradona (five foot four).

Some Argentines believe the émigré doesn't love his country enough. This enrages Messi, who as a teenager refused to play for Spain's youth teams. (If he had, and was going to this World Cup with *La Roja*, FIFA might as well have handed Spain the trophy at the opening ceremony.) Messi says, "Nothing gets me more upset than for you to tell me I'm not Argentine. What do you know about my feelings?" His Swedish teammate Zlatan Ibrahimovic has commented dryly that if the Argentines don't want Messi, they can give him to Sweden.

Messi's fellow *pibe* Maradona will probably try to resolve the matter by setting the boy free in South Africa. Like Maradona at the World Cup of 1986, Messi could then roam the pitch like a happy child. If all goes well, the Argentines will be able to rewrite that 1943 tango.

It turned out in South Africa that there is a way to stop Messi, and Maradona himself stumbled upon it. All you need to do is ensure that the boy keeps getting the ball fifty yards from the opponents' goal. Then the opposition can form a nine-man screen to stop him from getting through. The Germans did.

In 1986 Maradona won Argentina a World Cup by himself. Having lost one almost by himself in 2010, he and the nation have now called it quits.

David Beckham
October 2010

Davrid Beckham jogged up to take one of the last free kicks of his international career. The French fans sitting near the corner flag in Paris's Stade de France rose and whistled him, mocking England's iconic player. Then they got out their cameras. As "Becks" took the kick, a thousand flashes popped.

Since Beckham won the Spanish title with Real Madrid in 2007, his career has passed through a long twilight. He'll probably never play for England again. He still occasionally turns out for the L.A. Galaxy, but not many people notice anymore. He is increasingly prone to fouling younger, faster opponents. Deepening grooves mark the onset of middle age in that perfect face. Yet as the player fades, Beckham the brand is simply entering a new phase. It's time to disentangle what soccer's most powerful individual brand means to different people, and where Beckham and his brand managers can take it after he retires.

Beckham has three main constituencies. The first are the people inside soccer. To his teammates—and to Real Madrid fans who had expected another lazy *galactico*—Beckham was an "honest professional." To them he wasn't a showoff on a billboard, but the sweet, quiet, and slightly dim boy in the corner of the locker room.

At Manchester United, Beckham had absorbed Alex Ferguson's dictum that everything you achieve is thanks to the team and that afterward you shower and get on the bus and keep your head down. When Beckham tries to describe himself, he usually gropes for the word *professional*. Criticized in public by his teammate Landon Donovan at the Galaxy in 2009, he hit back with the harshest slur he could think of: "It's unprofessional in my eyes. In soccer players' eyes throughout the world, it would be unprofessional to speak out about your teammates, especially in the press and not to your face." Not once in seventeen years in soccer, he added, "have I been criticized for my professionalism."

Beckham's second constituency, the English nation, has been the least kind to him. Few British heroes are as popular at home as they are abroad. The basic reason is that the British can place each one of their compatriots precisely on the national class ladder. Just as Winston Churchill was unmistakably upper class, Beckham was clearly Essex Man, and so each was distrusted by members of other classes. To quote the musical *My Fair Lady*: "An Englishman's way of speaking absolutely classifies him, / The moment he talks he makes some other Englishman despise him."

Beckham's one inelegant feature is his voice, that high-pitched, nasal monotone. Whenever he appeared after an England game to convert soccer into clichés, something of the magic drained. Beckham became a vehicle for the British to mock their new cult of vapid celebrity. To most adult English people, there was something tacky and absurd about him. Typically, when a pair of his boots was auctioned for charity in 2000, they were bought by a man dressed as a ferret to publicize a new Web site.

Even Beckham's own class treated him with suspicion. Many in the working classes felt that Beckham had deserted his roots—hence the peculiar enmity he attracted from fans of West Ham, his local club in childhood.

Worse, in a country that prefers its heroes flawed, his physical perfection counted against him. That's why Beckham's first appearance in the national melodrama had to be as villain. After getting sent off against Argentina in 1998, he took more abuse than any English player before him. Things got so bad that a placard outside a Nottingham church proclaimed, "God forgives even David Beckham."

His third constituency—the rest of the world—was the most grateful, and it's here that Beckham will best be able to build in coming decades. The Beckham brand is strongest abroad, because foreigners experience him without the irritating soundtrack. At the World Cup of 2006, after England's dull victory over Trinidad, I was hanging around the "mixed zone," the place where journalists shout questions at passing players listening to iPods. Everyone was hanging around pointlessly. Suddenly, there was a stampede, and I was knocked over by a sprinting Asian cameramen. I looked up from the floor: Beckham had arrived. "And for that you knocked me over?" I wanted to ask the cameraman. Beckham wasn't going to say anything worthwhile. But then foreigners barely noticed what Beckham said. To them, he is simply beauty, fame, and wealth incarnate, an Andy Warhol painting come to life.

Like Marilyn Monroe or Charlie Chaplin, Beckham works best as a silent brand. Fittingly, his first autobiography was essentially a picture book. It's this visual brand that has been carefully managed from the start. Typically, Beckham's first meeting with his future wife seems to have been orchestrated to boost both their brands. Beckham was lucky that just as his career was starting, he met a brand manager as gifted as Simon Fuller, the future creator of *American Idol*. Fuller supported Manchester United. In the mid-1990s, when he was managing artists, he suggested to his client Victoria Adams that she go and watch Beckham play. Jimmy Burns writes in his *When Beckham Went to Spain:* "Victoria subsequently related . . . that Fuller's ambition at the time had been to have her dump her then boyfriend Stuart in favour of someone famous, like a footballer."

It worked. The Beckhams produced three sons, bearers of the Beckham brand. Over the years, it was above all Mrs. Beckham and Fuller who turned a very good right-half into a great brand. They understood that Beckham speaks through his body. It became a work of art in progress, the creation of hairdressers, tattooists, soccer managers, couturiers, and his wife, who all redesigned him endlessly as if he were a doll.

Once his appeal was discovered, it was marketed. In soccer, it has long been thought best practice to shield yourself from the media. Beckham, however, went on promotional tours of the United States and Asia. The inspiration seemed to come from his wife: In soccer you are expected to let your feet speak for you, but in pop music, where you are your image, life is ceaseless self-promotion.

The farther away people are from England and from soccer, the louder the Beckham brand seems to speak to them. Chinese women created Beckham shrines on their office desks. There was a Buddhist Beckham shrine in Thailand and a chocolate "Bekkamu" statue in Tokyo. Many of these admirers know him not so much from soccer as from his advertisements. The ads are so potent that one selling Castrol oil was blacked out in Teheran in 2003, on the orders of the city's then mayor, Mahmoud Ahmadinejad, while Iran also banned television commercials showing Beckham's bare legs. (The Iranian ads, incidentally, skirted the borders of truth in advertising. "Makes your bike go like Beckham" was the tagline. Did that mean "Quite slowly"?)

Beckham has sold everything from sunglasses to chocolate. He is the place where high fashion and soccer meet, the sweet spot that companies like Nike and Adidas are seeking. And it is not simply that he sells products—the products sell him, too. A Beckham ad for hair cream or jeans is also an ad for Beckham. He initially conquered America in a similarly oblique way. When a small independent British film went into production, it got permission to use his name in its title. *Bend It Like Beckham* finally appeared in 2002 and became a surprise hit in the United States. Later Fuller sent the man himself to play there.

So strong did Beckham's brand become that over time he helped brand his own country. I first noticed this during the World Cup of 2002 in Japan. Arriving in a provincial airport, I was met by a tournament volunteer, a middle-age Japanese woman who was helping us clueless foreigners find our way around. Hearing I was from England, she said, "England players, all so handsome!"

"What?" I asked. "Paul Scholes? Nicky Butt?" (A friend to whom I told this story later that day continued, "David Seaman, Emile Heskey, Danny Mills?")

"David Beckham, so handsome," the woman said. To her, he represented the nation. The St. George's Cross, once chiefly associated with tubby soccer hooligans, came to be identified with England's handsome captain and began appearing on fashion items worldwide. His Order of the British Empire is a tiny recognition of his marketing efforts for Britain.

Beckham never seemed quite able to comprehend the reach of his brand. "You just can't think about it," he would tell friends. He could grasp it only narcissistically: His wife reported him dancing around the house chanting, "I'm a gay icon!"

He grew into the most powerful individual brand that soccer ever produced, but the game itself never made enough of him. Partly that's because inside soccer, the collective always takes precedence over the individual. Ferguson, for instance, admired the honest professional Beckham, but he distrusted the Beckham brand. He hated the way the media sometimes made it seem that United's squad consisted of just one player. It outraged Ferguson that internal incidents, such as the boot he kicked into Beckham's face in 2003, made the newspapers. (Beckham didn't leak the stories. His wife's PR people did, in the interests of her ceaseless self-promotion.)

United's commercial executives wanted to use Beckham's brand to sell the club abroad. They understood that United gained its tens of millions of foreign fans largely thanks to its trio of "pop stars": George Best, Eric Cantona, and Beckham. But brands meant nothing to Ferguson. When Beckham's form finally faltered in 2003, the manager pounced. He benched Beckham and then packed him and his brand off to Madrid.

In part, soccer clubs were simply too incompetent to use Beckham's brand. On the June day that Real agreed to buy him, after weeks of negotiations, it emerged that the club had prepared no replica shirts bearing his name. "It's a bit tricky because we don't know what number Beckham will get—and we may not know for quite some time," a club spokesman said. Yet he also claimed that Real had received more than 2 million inquiries for Beckham shirts.

It was a repeat of the earlier signing of the Brazilian Ronaldo. Then, too, the club had prepared no shirts, and so counterfeiters printed fake "Ronaldo 9" shirts to meet demand. When Real finally got its act together, it had to give Ronaldo the number 10 in order to create demand for its own replicas. With Beckham, again, counterfeiters probably pocketed most of the early profits. When Real finally named his number, two weeks after signing him, it was the manifestly unsexy 23. (Michael Jordan's old number meant nothing to most soccer fans.) And so most of the value of the Beckham brand has accrued to companies outside soccer.

Now the brand will have to transition to a new existence after soccer. In England, late-career Beckham is becoming a "national treasure." This happens to the most famous Britons when they grow older, and, as it were, exit the game. It's a sad fate: an upscale version of redundancy. The Queen Mother was the ultimate national treasure, but other examples include Tony Benn, Ronnie Biggs, and even Churchill in the 1950s. Beckham is next. The biggest stains on his brand (the red card in St. Etienne, the affair with Rebecca Loos) appear largely forgotten in Britain.

Beckham's brand managers now need to recast their property for a career after soccer. The man's inarticulateness precludes a future as coach or pundit. And so his best postcareer models are not the well-spoken Johan Cruijff or Franz Beckenbauer, let alone the undirected Diego Maradona, but Pele. The Brazilian has never had anything to say, either. He thrives as a smiling doll who travels the world shaking hands for global corporations.

Beckham can do that better. As a professional, managed by professionals like Fuller, he won't toss away his brand. His Hollywood friends will teach him to preserve the patina of youth even in middle age. Companies outside soccer will find better uses for him than his clubs ever did. The mockers won't be rid of Beckham for decades yet.

Wayne Rooney
October 2010

One day in 2004, Wayne Rooney was doing what he usually does when he isn't playing soccer: watching television. At the time he was breaking with Everton, the club his clan had always supported. Sky TV was reading out text messages from viewers who called him a rat, a greedy traitor, and so on. Watching at home, Rooney grew fed up. He texted the program himself: "I left because the club was doing my head in—Wayne Rooney."

At first Sky assumed the text was fake. "Would the people pretending to be Wayne Rooney stop sending text messages?" asked the presenter. Later, though, the presenter said something like, "We know Wayne Rooney is watching—and we are watching him."

At this, Rooney became paranoid. It was dark outside. He had already been receiving death threats from disgruntled Everton fans. Was someone stalking him with a secret camera?

It was a scene that captured many of the difficulties of being Wayne Rooney. On the upside, he is the most accomplished English player since Bobby Charlton. On the downside, everyone wants a piece of him: fans, the media, his agent, Manchester United, and United's manager, Alex Ferguson. In fact, due to his peculiar historical circumstances—a great English player living in contemporary England—Rooney may be the most grabbed-for player ever.

The latest battle for Wayne Rooney, this month, transfixed much of the nation. First, Rooney suddenly let it be known that he was leaving United, the club where everyone had assumed he would play forever. Fans and Ferguson expressed surprise. Again, as in 2004, he was called a greedy traitor. Again, he got death threats. Then, equally suddenly, Rooney signed a new and improved five-year contract with United worth an estimated $280,000 a week. Once again, everyone was surprised.

It's hard to know what Rooney thinks, because he rarely speaks in public, and has never been heard to say an interesting sentence in his life. Yet from his seat in front of his television, watching the world talk about him, he must marvel at how everyone gets him wrong. None of the people who want a piece of Rooney—not even Ferguson—seems to understand what it's like to be him.

There are two types of English player, those from the working class and those from the underclass, and Rooney is the latter. Born in 1985, he was raised in the poor Liverpool neighborhood of Croxteth, initially in a one-bedroom council house that later became a drug rehabilitation center. His father (also Wayne) was an intermittently employed casual laborer. His mother worked as a lunch lady and stayed in the job, earning "about £287 a month" by Rooney's estimate, even after her son grew rich.

They were a tight-knit Catholic family, part of the Irish diaspora that had crossed the sea to Liverpool over the previous two hundred years. Eight branches of the Rooney clan lived in Croxteth. Every summer they would rent a bus and head off en masse for the vacation camp Butlins. Rooney grew up knowing not only his cousins but also his future wife, Coleen, and her extended family, too.

He never dreamed of becoming a professional player; he always knew he was going to become one. At nine, he joined Everton's academy. Soon afterward, in a boys match against Manchester United, he scored with an overhead kick from ten or fifteen yards. Initially, there was silence, but after a few seconds even the parents of the opposing team broke into applause. That doesn't often happen in serious children's soccer.

Rooney spent much of his childhood kicking the ball against the wall of his grandmother's house. He sometimes pretended to be a Ninja Turtle, and at school showed an interest in the life of Jesus but not in much else. He left education at sixteen with no certificates—a rare feat in today's Britain—and almost immediately broke into Everton's first team.

Seventeen years and 111 days old, he became the youngest man ever to play for England. Afterward, a friend drove him back to Croxteth (Rooney didn't yet have a driver's license), where he spent the evening eating potato chips, drinking Coke, and kicking a ball around with his pals, who wanted to know what Beckham was really like.

English soccer wasn't supposed to work like that. Traditionally, players were picked for their country only once they had served their time and established themselves as "honest pros." As in most British working-class occupations, seniority mattered. But Rooney broke all the rules. At one early training session with England, the boy dribbled past several players and then, as was his habit, lobbed the keeper. Initially, there was silence. Then his fellow internationals spontaneously broke into applause.

Like every new celebrity in modern Britain, Rooney became the object of hype. At first, he was very popular. He was treated as the authentic masculine counterweight to Beckham's constructed effeminate beauty. There are two types of British player: ugly ones like Rooney, Paul Gascoigne, and Nobby Stiles and pretty ones like Beckham and Michael Owen. The British public usually prefers the ugly ones.

And English fans had been waiting decades for Rooney to arrive. Not only did he score goals, but he was that rare thing in English soccer: a player who sees space. Soccer is best understood as a dance for space. The team that can open spaces when it attacks, and close down spaces when it defends, generally wins. There are two kinds of passers: ones like Beckham, who pass the ball straight to a teammate, and ones like Lionel Messi, who pass into empty space. Rooney finds space. It's partly because he has perfect control of the ball, which means that he never has to look down at it and instead can run with his head up looking for space.

The few previous Englishmen who could see space—chiefly Gascoigne and several so-called mavericks in the 1970s—ruined themselves with alcohol and various other vices. Rooney hasn't. He has been England's main man since he was eighteen. The country's need for him often segues into dependence. Among the many groups who want their piece of him, England's fans often appear the most desperate.

Rooney was never surprised or confused by his own rapid rise. He liked playing for England at seventeen. It was good soccer, and he knew he was good enough. Before kickoff, while experienced internationals would sit around the locker room like bags of nerves, he would be banging a ball against the wall as if he were back home in Croxteth. He couldn't wait to go out and play. "I have never gone around pinching myself, saying this is unbelievable, isn't it amazing what I'm doing," he says in his autobiography, a revealing document despite being aimed at nine-year-olds. "Of course it's fantastic playing for Man Utd, brilliant playing for England, but my main thought when I turn out for either of them is the same—I deserve it." On the soccer field Rooney is happy because he controls events. Off the field, by contrast, other people often control him.

He first noticed this when the tabloids revealed his taste for prostitutes. Like every public figure in the UK, Rooney has forfeited his private life. He became a way for Britons to mock the supposed habits of members of the underclass or, in British slang, "chavs." Rooney rose during the country's boom years, when even some of the poorest Britons had discretionary cash, and Coleen's shopping habits and tan were scrutinized for "chav" markers. The clan's parties were written about with breathless derision. Rooney says that the worst thing about being a professional player is "press intrusion into your private life." Eventually, he learned to keep secrets from close friends and relatives, in case they inadvertently let something slip and it got into the tabloids. "Every time I got in the car, I was looking in the mirror to see if I was followed," he says in his autobiography. His recent loss of form may be connected to new tabloid stories about his dealings with prostitutes.

Rooney spends his leisure time watching television partly because players need to rest, partly because he has few other interests, but partly also because despite having a bodyguard, he cannot leave his house without being hassled. "It's difficult to do 'ordinary' things, like going to the pub or even Asda [a supermarket]," he admits. "There's always someone who claims he's an Everton fan and wants to insult me, or someone who hates Manchester Utd and wants to have a go." So Rooney has become a multimillionaire semicaptive. Had he been a great Spanish or German player, life would have been easier.

Then his managers wanted control, too. David Moyes, his manager at Everton, tried to protect the boy in the man's milieu. Rooney didn't want to be protected. He was perfectly happy in the milieu. He felt that Moyes was jealous of him and upset not to have been invited to his eighteenth birthday party. More important, even at eighteen, Rooney knew he was too good for Everton. So—despite the clan's links to the club—he left for Manchester United.

United's fans became another group who wanted their piece of Rooney. Like many of Everton's fans in 2004, they were enraged to discover this month that he would contemplate leaving their club. On the field Rooney, his face reddened with effort, doing the defensive running that the most gifted players sometimes disdain, gives the impression of devotion to the cause. He looks like the British fan's ideal: a fan in a jersey. Surely, he would want to stay at United forever. If he didn't, he must just be greedy.

This dichotomy drawn by fans and media—you're either loyal or greedy—misunderstands how players think. The word players use to describe themselves is *professionals*. Professionals—whether they are players, academics, or bankers—don't choose between love and money. They pursue success in their *careers* (another favorite players' word). If they can get success, then money will follow.

A player knows his club will dump him if he isn't good enough, and so he will dump the club if it isn't good enough. Rooney was good, and so he left Everton for United. Players regard clubs not as magical entities but as employers. Like most professionals, they will move if they can find a better job. The better job isn't necessarily a better-paid one. Rooney could reportedly have earned more than $280,000 a week at Manchester City, and if he had put himself on the market, Real Madrid might have offered him more too. But United's total package—the chance of prizes, the familiar surroundings, plus pay—seems to have appealed most. This is careerism rather than greed.

By convention, players always talk as if only the team's performance matters. Of course, they don't think that way. Rooney knows exactly how many goals he scored in each season of his career and has set himself the target of always bettering the previous year's tally. Even when United finished without prizes in 2006, Rooney judged it "a decent season for me." He never seems to have adopted the view of life that Ferguson tries to inculcate in his players: United against the world. Rather, Rooney is a careerist.

Players hardly ever come out as careerists. That's because the game is pervaded with the rhetoric of lifelong love for club: Players are always trying to keep fans happy by kissing their club's badge or talking about how they have supported the club since childhood. Yet probably no professional player is "loyal" in the sense that fans use the word. Pundits sometimes rhapsodize about the old days, when players often spent their entire careers at one club, but that was because clubs could then simply forbid them to move. No longer.

Contrary to popular opinion, Rooney is not especially selfish. He's just typical of his profession. Nowadays he is often contrasted with teammates like Paul Scholes, Ryan Giggs, and Gary Neville, who have supposedly stayed "loyal" to United all their careers. But it would be more accurate to say that these men have a happy employer-employee relationship with United. Had United benched Giggs for a while in his prime, he would surely have been out the door fast. Instead, United was the perfect workplace for him. It didn't suit Rooney as well.

Alex Ferguson is a paternalist employer: He tries to create father-son relationships with his players. That's why he doesn't mind that at sixty-eight he is generationally out of touch with them. When Cristiano Ronaldo was trying to leave United for Real Madrid in 2008, Ferguson persistently talked about "the boy" as if he were his child. He said, "If it was your son, you'd give him the best advice possible on his career. Now, I honestly believe that could be the worst thing he could do—go to Real Madrid." Some players enjoy this type of working relationship. Giggs, whose own father abandoned the family, has thrived under Ferguson for twenty years. But it's not the relationship Rooney wants.

When he threatened to leave United, he, like Ronaldo, was treated as a thankless child. "Since the minute he's come to the club, we've always been a harbor for him," Ferguson complained. "Anytime he has been in trouble, we have done nothing but help him. I was even prepared to give him financial advice, many times. I don't know how many times we have helped him in terms of his private life and other matters."

Ferguson sees intervening in Rooney's private life as central to his remit. Like many English fans, the manager has in his head the "Gazza" narrative: Great British talent falls prey to temptations and forfeits his career. (This month alone, Gascoigne has admitted drunk driving and been arrested for suspected possession of Class A drugs.) Ferguson always thought that Gascoigne's career might have been saved if he had joined United. Rooney, another talent from the underclass, is often likened to Gascoigne. Indeed, Rooney's nickname inside the game is "Wazza" (partly because *wazz* is British slang for "urination").

British talents have traditionally needed a father figure. But Rooney doesn't. In fact, he barely seems to need a manager at all. His thoughts on his first meeting with Ferguson show his typical lack of interest in and insight into people from outside his clan: "I was surprised by how tall Sir Alex Ferguson was."

Rooney has his own father, and uncles, and if he has a second father, it's his agent. In autobiographies of modern players, the agent typically emerges as a rare close friend made in adulthood: Everyone else the player meets wants a piece of him, and the agent, though he also wants a piece, acts as the gatekeeper. Paul Stretford won a ferocious battle among agents for control of Rooney, has represented him all his career, and also represents Coleen in her work on television and as an all-purpose celebrity.

This month's battle for Rooney's signature was in part a battle between two wannabe father figures. When Stretford threatened that Rooney would leave United, he was obviously bargaining for a better contract, but he was also showing Ferguson how weak the manager's grip on the player is.

Afterward, Ferguson tried to cast the new contract as an errant son returning to the fold. He said, "I think Wayne now understands what a great club Manchester United is." Rooney was made to apologize to his teammates and to Ferguson.

Yet the affair showed that United need Rooney more than he needs them. True, it would be hard for Rooney to move to another English club: Uncomprehending fans would make his life a misery. And he seems poorly equipped to move to Spain. Rooney once scored 0 percent on a Spanish exam at school, and Spain is far from his clan. Still, he does have an unlimited choice of willing employers.

United, by contrast, is short of superstars. They have several aging players who will need replacing at great expense soon: Giggs, Scholes, Neville, Rio Ferdinand, and Edwin van der Sar. The talent in the club's pipeline tends to disappoint: United has produced no great youth player since Beckham's generation emerged fifteen years ago. The club's frugal owners, the Glazer family, limit spending on new players. Without Rooney, United looks a little thin.

It's the story of Rooney's life: Other people want a piece of him. That isn't always fun. This spring United kept playing him exhausted and hurt. By the time the World Cup came around, he was empty. He played poorly for England, and the nation's fans—who weren't getting their piece of him—booed him. After one game he shouted into a nearby television camera (and if you're Rooney, there is always a nearby television camera), "Nice to see your own fans booing you. If that's what loyal support is, for fuck's sake."

Rooney knows that fans, managers, media, and agents love him only because they need him. Their "loyalty" quickly turns into anger, intrusion, exploitation, or mockery. He has no intention of being "loyal" in return. That means that sooner or later, this month's spat with United will probably be repeated.

Frank Lampard
October 2010

One of the delights of soccer is watching Frank Lampard prepare to shoot. He stands almost perfectly upright, and raises his head for a good look at the goal. The right arm is held out for balance, the left arm is flung out for power, and the inside of the right foot strikes the ball just off center, so that its swerve will confuse the keeper. Lampard kicks only as hard as he needs to. Rarely do you see him trouble the crowd in the second tier. In short, he could be a photograph in a training manual. "He scored between twenty and twenty-five every year," reminisces Guus Hiddink, who briefly coached him at Chelsea.

Lampard is not far off from being the perfect player. He's possibly Chelsea's fittest player and one of the quickest, and he can tackle and pass and get everywhere. But like most players he will be remembered chiefly for what he did with his national team, and so he will be remembered above all as a failure. Lampard belongs to England's "golden generation," which was supposed to win trophies but never got past the quarterfinals of any major tournament. He is the symbol of his generation: an apparently brilliant failure.

The question is why his generation failed. You could call it the Frank Lampard question. Some argue that the players simply weren't that good. Others—English fans in particular—diagnose a "lack of spirit." As Jonathan Wilson notes in his *Anatomy of England*, that's been the standard domestic critique of English players through the ages. For some players, "the triple lion badge of England could be three old tabby cats," lamented the *Daily Express* in 1966, and at many World Cups since.

Hiddink has a different explanation. The Dutchman got to know Lampard during his happy stint as Chelsea's caretaker-manager in 2009. As someone who almost became England's manager in 2006, Hiddink watched the player with particular interest on television during the South African World Cup. Over a late-night men's dinner in Amsterdam, and in a five-star hotel lobby (Hiddink's natural habitat) in Istanbul, the chatty Dutchman tried to answer the Frank Lampard question: What does Lampard lack?

When Hiddink arrived at Chelsea in February 2009, he immediately began looking for interpersonal conflicts in the team. That's what he always does. At Chelsea, he didn't find any. Hiddink told Didier Drogba to stop dropping back into midfield, explaining that Drogba lacked the technique to prosper there, and Drogba agreed. Being Dutch, Hiddink kept a close watch on the German Michael Ballack, but even Ballack never gave him any trouble.

As for Lampard, Hiddink somewhat inadvertently tested him by substituting him in a game against Barcelona. When the board with Lampard's number was held up, someone else on the bench murmured, "Be careful. Lampard never gets taken off." Indeed, Chelsea's staff had always struggled to persuade Lampard that he ever needed any rest. That night, the player did take a moment to clock that he really was being substituted. But then he trotted straight to the bench and never mentioned the matter afterward. He was the perfect pro.

Yet that wasn't good enough for Hiddink. The Dutchman has never been a workaholic, he is a habitué of the golf course, and his jowly face over his ritual drink of cappuccino reveals a man who enjoys the good life. Perhaps his own tastes equipped him to spot Lampard's flaw: The player's problem was precisely that he did too much.

"Frank is a box-to-box player, as they call it in England," Hiddink reflected in the hotel lobby in Istanbul. English players, Hiddink said, need to be set limits: "'This is your area and this is your task.' If you don't do that, Frank has so much energy, so much drive, that he often does too much. In my early days at Chelsea too, he'd come back to his own defense, collect the ball, worm himself forward through the midfield, and then he'd actually score quite often, I must say," Hiddink chuckled fondly, "in his energy-eating style."

Of course, being everywhere is precisely what Lampard had been brought up to do. In his autobiography, *Totally Frank*, he explains that his father, the former West Ham defender Frank Lampard Sr., had always told him "to make things happen." That meant he had to have the ball. When Lampard joined Chelsea, his dad advised him, "Shout for the ball every time you're near it and make things happen. Only then will people say that Frank Lampard won that game or this game for us." Lampard agreed. He aims, he explains, to be "someone who was involved in all aspects of the play, from defending to making the final pass, as well as hitting the back of the net regularly." Surely, any manager would want a player like that. "If you can demonstrate these qualities then you become indispensable," Lampard believes.

But that's not what Hiddink wanted. He'd often sit down with Lampard at Chelsea's training ground and say, "Surely, we should be able to build up towards you, so that you can more easily get through a season of sixty games, and not be completely finished every four weeks. With Essien and Jon Obi and Ballack behind you, we should be capable of limiting you to your zone." And Lampard would reply: "Oh, yes. Yes, yes. I never really thought about that." Hiddink chuckles fondly again at the memory.

Hiddink wasn't just worried about saving Lampard's energy, about leaving him power for the crucial moments in a game when you need it most. He also saw that Lampard, by going everywhere, was slowing down Chelsea's attacks. The ball moves forward faster when a midfielder doesn't come to fetch it. Hiddink felt that Lampard at Chelsea, like his box-to-box twin, Steven Gerrard with England, was taking too much responsibility for moving the game along. At the World Cup in South Africa, Hiddink said, you'd see Gerrard collecting the ball in England's defense and then running twenty yards with it. Gerrard was working as hard as he could, showing spirit. However, the effect of his work was to slow England's attacks. His running gave the opposition's defense time to move into position.

Other teams—most notably Arsenal, Germany, and increasingly also Brazil—like to strike the moment the opposition loses the ball. In basketball, this is known as the moment of "turnover." When the ball is turned over from one team to the other, the team that has lost it is fractionally out of position. That's when you need to move play forward in three quick passes. But England's galloping midfielders do that too rarely. That's one reason England has gotten so little use out of Michael Owen—the ultimate "turnover" striker—since his hat trick in Munich in 2001. Nor has England found much purpose for the nippy counterattackers Theo Walcott and Aaron Lennon, beyond Walcott's hat trick in Croatia in 2008. England just doesn't open spaces for its speedsters with three swift passes. The image of England in the matches it loses is either hefty center-backs punting the ball upfield or Gerrard lumbering forward with it.

Most good coaches surely know that Lampard and Gerrard do too much. The first time Rafael Benitez met Gerrard, he told him, "I've watched your games on video. Your problem is you run around too much." Jamie Carragher, present in the room, recalls that he "stared at Stevie and could see the deflation." After all, running around is precisely what Gerrard has always been praised for. English fans love it. A month after the World Cup of 2010,

I attended a meeting of the LondonEnglandFans supporters' club, and the fans themselves briefly debated whether they shared any blame for England's failure in South Africa. One woman noted that when England was passing the ball around at the back, fans would shout, "Get it forward!" or "Get stuck in!" They tended to like players who ran around a lot. So do the fearsome tabloids. Lampard and Gerrard are responding to English cues. At the *moment suprême*, they will tend to forget the words of Hiddink and Benitez (and presumably Fabio Capello) and do too much.

Yet Lampard and Gerrard perform better with Chelsea and Liverpool than they do with England. I asked Hiddink why that might be. He raised the issue of "coaching" on the field. At big clubs, great players coach wayward colleagues: "Drop back!" "Take it easy," or simply, "Stop running around so much and stay in your zone." At Chelsea or Liverpool, experienced continental players reinforce the coach's message in real time. But watching England labor in South Africa, Hiddink had noticed almost none of that. He said, "If you look at [Gareth] Barry, he could have played more intelligently. He ends up swimming because he's not coaching in midfield, and so is forced into playing left-back or right-back. You don't see that internal coordination in the English team. The center of your team, defensive midfield and central defense, is really the nerve center. England wasn't sending out any impulses saying, 'This is how we must do it.' You can see if coaching is happening, and there was none or almost none."

Hiddink thought he knew why that didn't happen. Players like Lampard and Gerrard had become demigods in their own country, he pointed out. "At a certain point players get a status—sometimes rightly, sometimes forced—that creates a sort of screen around them. Others think, 'Oh, I can't touch him or make demands on someone who's such a big name in England.'" The demigods themselves might want to be coached, Hiddink said, but their teammates don't dare. And so the demigods are allowed to run around too much.

Lampard's flaw—and the golden generation's—isn't a lack of spirit. It's an excess of it.

The Autobiographies of Jamie Carragher, Ashley Cole, Steven Gerrard, Frank Lampard, and Wayne Rooney
October 2010

Frank Lampard emerges naked from the showers after a training session with Chelsea. Suddenly, his new manager, José Mourinho, pops up and looks him meaningfully in the eye. "All right, boss?" asks Lampard

"You are the best player in the world," replies Mourinho.

The naked player doesn't know quite what to say.

"You," continues Mourinho, "are the best player in the world. But now you need to prove it and win trophies. You understand?"

Now Lampard is thrilled or, as he recalls in his autobiography, "walking on air." He calls his mother to tell her what Mourinho said.

"Yes," she replies, "I already knew you were the best in the world."

For the next couple of days, says Lampard, "I felt ten feet tall and trained harder than ever. Everything I tried came off." Mourinho had actually lifted him.

It's one of the odder scenes in this collection of autobiographies by five leading members of England's golden generation.* Players' autobiographies are a much-derided genre—"Is there a more debased literary currency?" asks the game's chief historian, David Goldblatt—and certainly there was something bizarre about HarperCollins paying Wayne Rooney $9 million for his story in five volumes, only one fewer than Winston Churchill's complete history of World War II. "Hopefully there will be a lot of things to read about," said Rooney, signing his contract in tracksuit bottoms and a hood.

Yet the strange thing is: There *are* a lot of things to read about in these books. Even though most of them didn't sell and are already out of print, taken together they illuminate what it is like to be a leading English player today.

---

* Jamie Carragher, *Carra: My Autobiography* (London: Corgi, 2009); Ashley Cole, *My Defence: Winning, Losing, Scandals, and the Drama of Germany, 2006* (London: Headline, 2006); Steven Gerrard, *Gerrard: My Autobiography* (London: Bantam Books, 2007); Frank Lampard, *Totally Frank* (London: HarperSport, 2006); Wayne Rooney with Hunter Davies, *My Story So Far* (London: HarperSport, 2006).

Of course, some of the books are worse than others. You close Ashley Cole's *My Defence* feeling dirty and stupid for having read it, your main emotion surprise that his agent let him write it. Rooney's book reads a bit like an essay that a child has been forced to write in elementary school. Even with family photographs and school reports, he can barely get up to book length. The experience must have been a comedown for his ghostwriter, Hunter Davies, a former biographer of the Beatles (he got to sit in on Lennon and McCartney's composing sessions) and of Wordsworth (a sort of eighteenth-century forebear of Rooney's). Yet even Cole's and Rooney's books reveal a lot about their subjects, sometimes inadvertently. Lampard's book is the dullest and smuggest of the five, yet that fact too seems to be a true reflection of the man as well as of his ghostwriter.

All these five players already have very clear public images, shaped by the tabloid newspapers that they despise (yet read). This is their chance to reach us without their words getting distorted. That must have been why they wrote these books. Only Rooney presumably did it for the money; the others can scarcely have been paid enough even to feed a journalist.

Lampard, Gerrard, and Carragher are positively eager to speak to us. It's questionable how many people need five hundred pages of Jamie Carragher, but his is the best of these books. In part, *Carra* is a reflection on the whole genre. "I've read most players' autobiographies," he claims. "I had a fair idea in my mind what makes a good read." Lampard is keen to demonstrate that he was in the right in every dispute of his career, and Gerrard's effort was actually named Sports Book of the Year in the British Book Awards. These three men gave us more pages than their publishers probably wanted. In other words, players' autobiographies aren't all empty. The very fact that agents, lawyers, and club media officers will have taken a red pencil to every line helps the players speak. They can trust this medium. Usually, the most we get from them is thirty seconds of platitudes after a match. These books are the deepest public statements that they will make during their careers.

Reading them, you get to know these players rather as they seem to get to know each other during long weeks in team hotels abroad before England gets eliminated. "I suppose that's the upside of boredom," Cole reflects. "It makes you talk more and get to know each other better. I came away from Germany knowing more about Stevie Gerrard, Wazza and Lamps than I ever did." These books help you understand the stages of a player's life, from boyhood to media victim. And they even make you feel slightly sorry for these men (though perhaps not for Cole).

STAGE 1: BOYHOOD

"I was nearly called Adrian" are the first words of Rooney's projected five volumes. "That was what my father wanted. A bit posh, I suppose, and doesn't quite sound like me. In the end, though, my mum talked my Dad out of it."

All these books are keen to establish the author's social origins at once: as a member of a tight-knit, loving working-class family. The message is that however much the player earns per week, he remains anchored and authentic. Early on in each book, each writer offers a long paean to his family. "I'm looking for my Mum in the jubilant crowd" is how Cole opens his story, while Lampard tells us he has inherited "my Mum's perception, humanity and sensitivity," and "my Dad's ambition, hard work and vision." Gerrard, like Rooney, has happy memories of childhood summer vacations at Butlins with the extended family.

You inevitably suspect pretense, yet it makes sense that the players should feel this way. After all, childhood in the family home was about the only time in their lives that they were not treated as celebrities. Only then did people relate naturally to them. Almost everyone they meet afterward has ulterior motives for the relationship. No wonder the players feel nostalgic for childhood. "Family means everything to me, all together, sitting around and laughing, under one roof," says Gerrard. "However crazy my life became with Liverpool and England, I wanted that protective wall of my family around me."

Reading about their origins is strangely repetitive in another way, too: The five of them between them come from just two regions, Liverpool and East London. (The Northeast seems to have had its day as a source of English talent.) Cole's first club, Senrab in the East End of London, also produced Ledley King, Lee Bowyer, John Terry, and Bobby Zamora; Lampard played for Senrab's local rival, Heath Park, in greener Essex suburbia. Another future member of the golden generation soon shows up, too. When Lampard is thirteen or fourteen and playing for West Ham, he is sent to the training pitch to "watch a young boy play because he was so good. We were told he was the best prospect to come to the club in years." Joe Cole was ten at the time.

By that sort of age, the players are spending much of their time among future professionals. Lampard has been doing so since birth: his father is Frank Lampard Sr., the West Ham stalwart, his uncle is Harry Redknapp, and his elder cousin is the future England international Jamie Redknapp. Lampard grows up playing keep-away with Jamie in Uncle Harry's garden and going to the local park for fierce private training sessions with his dad, who also scouts Rio Ferdinand for West Ham. (Ferdinand and the other children in his neighborhood are most impressed when Lampard Sr. pulls up at his family apartment in poor Peckham in a black Mercedes.) Sometimes Bobby Moore drops by the Lampard home for tea, biscuits, and a chat about soccer. "It never occurred to me," Lampard says, "that the man who had lifted the World Cup as captain of England was sitting on my couch."

The other players break into this world not much later. At eight, Gerrard is already training at Liverpool with Jason Koumas and a brilliant goalscorer named Michael Owen, who soon becomes a close friend. Cole and Rooney join the respective academies of Arsenal and Everton at nine, though all these five players seem to have played most of their early soccer informally with friends; you can't get to the 10,000 hours of practice required to achieve mastery if you rely on the academy. Lampard is underwhelmed by West Ham's famous academy anyway, even if around this time it also produced Michael Carrick, Jermain Defoe, and Glen Johnson, the supporting cast of the golden generation.

By their teens, the five authors are already on a career track. The schoolboy Gerrard is courted by Alex Ferguson ("top man," adds Gerrard), and letters from other clubs keep landing on the family doormat. A crucial staging post—their equivalent of university entrance exams—is trying to get into the then national academy at Lilleshall. Gerrard is rejected. "Me! Captain of Liverpool Boys! Rated by Liverpool!" He admits that the brush-off hurts to this day. Lampard doesn't get in, either, but curiously their contemporary Carragher does. Pretty soon, Carragher makes his debut for England schoolboys playing up front ("A shy striker called Emile Heskey [sat] on the bench"). Of course, Carra scores, "the Italian keeper Gianluigi Buffon having no answer to my lethal finishing."

With all this going on, school cannot matter much. The five are not necessarily stupid—well, Carragher, Lampard, and Gerrard aren't. Rather, as budding stars they are taught to view anything outside soccer as a distraction. That's why players are seldom complete human beings. The only one of the five who seems to show any interest in his education is Lampard, who (almost uniquely among England players since World War I) attends private school. One of several kids "from 'new money'" at exclusive Brentwood in Essex, he plays soccer matches at schools like Eton. However, he is keen to emphasize to the reader that he was pretty nifty with a book, too. Aged sixteen he gets a very impressive ten General Certificates of Secondary Education, including, famously, a starred A in Latin, before Lampard Sr. tells him to leave school to concentrate on soccer.

None of the four others need much encouraging. Life away from soccer doesn't seem a natural home for any of them: Gerrard, for instance, "never had many mates" at secondary school but did at Liverpool FC. He passes nine General Certificates of Secondary Education, yet spends his last school exam pondering "exactly how I would burn my uniform." Most of Rooney's school reports (perhaps the best thing in his book, and one unarguable benefit of the New Labour government's famous "targets") describe him as a popular and sociable child. However, his results are disappointing, even in the one subject where you would think he'd do quite well. At eleven, he gets a B for phys ed, with the comment, "wayne is a very agile sportsman who's worked hard throughout the year. he needs to maintain this level of work next year." What does it take to get an A in PE?

Rooney leaves school and becomes a star. (He makes his debut for Everton at sixteen years and ten months, yet is disappointed that the club waited so long.) The other four leave school and become apprentices. "Only now do I realize that it was one of the happiest times of my career, a life without the constant pressure I would come to know later," says Lampard. Gerrard feels much the same way. He particularly likes the practical jokes of the locker room. The boys at Liverpool cut off bits of each others' socks, punish each other for wearing unfashionable clothes, hit each other with towels, and lock up the club podiatrist for three hours. It's all hilarious (especially when the furious podiatrist leaves his job), except sometimes when it isn't. Gerrard writes: "If someone couldn't take the banter or a prank, arguments would erupt. Rucks were part of my daily life. If I ruined someone's trainers and they weren't happy, I reacted. Pushing and shouting broke out. 'Can't you fucking well take a joke?' I'd scream at Greggo or Wrighty . . ."

Practical jokes are an aspect of soccer life that just doesn't translate well when explained to outsiders. Gerrard cannot seem to see what these rituals are for. Benignly, they bond the group members to each other and to the institution. Less benignly, they establish who is top dog, who can bully whom, and who is protected by his lapdogs. The role of Michael Owen amid all this is interesting: "All the banter and wind-ups often had Michael bang in the middle of it. He was clever about it, though. Michael hated getting caught. He was just focused on reaching the top. Greggo and Boggo were different." Where are Greggo, Boggo, and Wrighty now?

STAGE 2: YOUNG PROFESSIONAL

Their professional debut isn't some sort of Hollywood moment. They had seen it coming for years, much as an upper-middle-class boy knows he will go to college. After Rooney makes his debut for Everton, he and his mates get fries and gravy from the local fast-food joint and then kick a ball around on the street. Rooney is not in awe of his new adult teammates, who after taking one look at him have nicknamed him "Dog," though he cannot think why.

All five make their debuts in the utterly familiar environments of their home clubs, though none of the others is quite as much at home as Lampard. When he stands on the touchline at eighteen, ready to go on against Coventry, Uncle Harry, West Ham's manager, puts his arms around him and Coventry's waiting substitute, thirty-eight-year-old Gordon Strachan, and tells Strachan, "Go easy on him!" Frank Sr., West Ham's assistant manager, smiles from the dugout.

Perhaps the most confusing thing about life on the first team is that suddenly there are foreigners. The players had spent their youth entirely among English people. "My mind was closed to other cultures back then," Lampard admits. "I was very much a home boy whose interests and tastes didn't venture much beyond the boundaries of London and where I grew up." The foreigners are scary. The teenage Gerrard is worried when Liverpool appoints a French manager: "On first impressions, Gérard seemed a nice guy. But I was shitting myself because of the language. I didn't know how good his English was. . . . I was just terrified of this French set-up. I wanted it to be English, to be people I knew and understood." Later Gerrard is similarly anxious about England's plans to appoint a foreign manager. To this day, he retains an instinctive suspicion of foreign players and their supposed propensity to cheat. "Piss off to Spain or Italy, where they niggle, dive or pull shirts," he writes.

Given these stereotypes, it's no wonder that each nationality tends to stick together in a club. When Lampard arrives at Chelsea, the club's training ground consists of six small dressing rooms. Lampard joins the "English section," whose members are Terry, Jody Morris, and for some reason Eidur Gudjohnsen. Beyond that, Lampard recalls, "there was an Italian room, a French room and the rest of the world. It was a terrible set-up for a soccer club and didn't help at all in building and promoting the team spirit." Lampard spends the next few years working chiefly with foreigners, but their foreignness never quite wears off. When he acquires a Spanish girlfriend, who later becomes the mother of his children, it is something "I just never imagined in a million years."

At this stage in his ascent, the player has another scary encounter with a new force: the tabloids. A ritual of the modern top-class player's career is an early hazing by the *News of the World*. Especially if you are a talented Englishman playing in England, your almost unlimited access to sex is balanced by having to perform it in front of the nation. At Liverpool's Christmas party in 1998, a young Carragher, dressed in a Quasimodo costume, is photographed "working my way through a variety of angles" with a stripper. On the eve of publication, "I waited at a garage until midnight for the first edition of the Sunday papers."

Carragher doesn't get caught that way again. Any leading player in Britain soon becomes a sort of part-time professor of media studies. There is nothing very new about this. Arthur Hopcraft wrote in *The Football Man* more than four decades ago, "The Football League, in wintry discontent in 1968, called upon all League clubs to deny Press facilities to any representative of *The People*, after the newspaper had published a series on the drinking capacity and bedroom manners of one of Stockport County's players."

The *News of the World* excels at this sort of thing. It gets hold of a video of Lampard, Ferdinand, and Kieron Dyer cavorting with an array of girls in the Cypriot resort Ayia Napa and exposes Ashley Cole, then at Arsenal, for being illegally "tapped up" by Chelsea. Rooney's taste for prostitutes goes public. The stories upset the players, so much so that Cole writes his book in a (very unconvincing) attempt to deny the allegations. Cole actually seems more upset by a later suggestion in the *News of the World* that he is gay. I personally have never wavered from my conviction that Cole is the most heterosexual man on earth, and had not previously realized that anyone had ever dared suggest otherwise. Yet after wading through page after page of his denials of this long-forgotten story, even I had to start to thinking that he was protesting too much.

The tabloids bring unhappiness and paranoia into these players' lives. But on the upside, in the new world there is money (an irrelevance, the players insist) and girls (even more of them than the players were used to). When Gerrard recalls a night on the town with the phrase "I was out trying to pull a few birds," the plural gives away the confidence of the rising player. ───

STAGE 3: BREAK WITH BOYHOOD CLUB

While Arsenal's "Invincibles" finish the league season unbeaten in 2003–2004 and are dancing on the pitch at the end, Ashley Cole thinks (or so he tells us), "I want to stay on at Arsenal and break David O'Leary's 555 league appearances. Even beat John Lukic as the oldest player, running out until I am 40. . . . I felt like I was in the land of make-believe when I walked through the famous Marble Hall to sign up for Arsenal aged nine. Now I'm touching the dream." He loves this club, he swears.

The break with their boyhood club is a central drama of most of these books. All the players break except Gerrard, and even he came very close to going to Chelsea. Each player describes his break in detail, and what emerges from their accounts, cumulatively, is that it's wrongheaded of fans to expect any player to think like a fan. True, all these players were once fans. But once they become players, they join a different species.

They do still remember how fans feel. When Rooney and Carragher were born, their fathers were both devoted Everton supporters. In fact, though Rooney escaped being named after Adrian Heath, James Lee Duncan Carragher was named after Evertonians Gordon Lee and Duncan McKenzie.

(Gerrard's dad supported Liverpool, but the young Gerrard regularly went to Goodison Park, too, and he admits that the childhood pictures of himself in an Everton uniform are genuine.)

Rooney first went to Goodison as a six-month-old in diapers—probably a fraction too young to break into the reserves—and at age nine wrote a letter to the club's center-forward, Duncan Ferguson, telling him he shouldn't be in prison. "In all the photos of when I am little, I seem to be wearing an Everton strip of some sort," notes Rooney. He even wears his Everton uniform to his tryouts with Liverpool, at nine; Carragher does the same when he starts playing five-a-sides at Liverpool's School of Excellence.

Rooney isn't wearing Everton colors to be defiant. It's just what he wears after school. Liverpool likes the look of him nonetheless and asks him back the next week. But in the meantime, Everton offers him schoolboy forms. Rooney signs for the club he loves. However, he admits, "Had Liverpool asked me to sign first and not have another trial, then I'm sure I would have signed for them and been a 'Red.'" In other words, even at nine he is not thinking as a fan. Fandom is just a small part of his identity. Like the other four authors, he relates to soccer as a player. Later, after joining Man U, Rooney will talk about how he hates Liverpool, and maybe he did, as a fan, but he didn't hate them as a player.

Carragher, despite regarding himself as "the biggest Blue in Bootle," does join Liverpool. Quite simply, he explains, the club's youth academy is better than Everton's. Other Everton fans like Robbie Fowler and Steve McManaman make the same choice. Still, Carragher's feelings for Everton do take a while to die. When he's first named as a sub for Liverpool's first team, in 1996, he is warming up on the field at halftime when the latest scores from other grounds are read out over the loudspeaker. Everton is beating Newcastle 2–0. Carragher spots his dad in the stands eating a meat pie and gives him the thumbs-up. His dad, despite being an Evertonian, is furious at his son's stupidity. Luckily, the Liverpool fans at the away end don't spot the gesture.

The players do have some genuine fans' emotions. However, these emotions are much weaker than the players' desire to make it as a player. Each of these books comes out and says at some point that players are motivated by ambition, not loyalty. Discussing Nick Barmby's move from Everton to Liverpool, Gerrard says, "The argument that raged about his move was stupid.

Barmby had to leave Goodison for Anfield. He wanted success. End of debate." The player might support one club or another, but that is an irrelevance.

The problem is that the fans don't see things that way. As Carragher notes, "Fans will never accept that a Liverpool player may want to leave for professional reasons. They cling on to the far-fetched notion that their favourite players wouldn't even think of playing anywhere else." Being a loyal supporter is a shibboleth of English soccer, the game's equivalent of motherhood and apple pie. Players are always being encouraged to talk as if they are fans first. That's why Cole in his book still goes on about his love for Arsenal. "My heart and soul was tied to Arsenal with a fisherman's knot. I don't think even Houdini could have unraveled it," he says. Fans hear these claims and are tempted to believe them. Then, when the player leaves—in Cole's case because Arsenal were offering him only $100,000 a week—the fans feel betrayed. In other words, the players get tripped up by their own attempts at PR. Then the fans berate them for leaving, and that turns the players against the fans, who just don't understand.

Carragher's final emotional break with Everton comes on January 24, 1999. He has just returned from Old Trafford, where Liverpool had been leading Manchester United 0–1 in an FA Cup tie only to concede twice in the last two minutes. Carragher goes straight to his local pub in Bootle "to drown my sorrows, hoping I'd see a few sympathetic mates." But, he says, "Perhaps I should have known better. As I walked through the door, there was laughter. Friends, people I'd grown up and traveled around Europe with following Everton, didn't think twice about treating me like any other 'dirty' Kopite."

He turns around and walks out. His old friends don't understand. They are relating to him as soccer fans. "Now I wasn't a fan, but someone who'd been toiling for his team only to see the biggest win of his career stolen in the worst way possible." That's when his patience with Everton snaps. He spends much of a long, honest, and erudite chapter on Everton castigating the club's fans. However, he remains such an instinctive fan that he later transfers his loyalties to Liverpool. He writes *Carra* as part of his ongoing debate with fellow Liverpool fans. Liverpool being a surprisingly small town, he knows many of them personally. After he retires, he plans to sit in the stands among them. Still, he admits, if Liverpool benched him, he would leave the club. Even he is always a player first.

Lampard, Rooney, and Cole enter their first clubs as fans, but they swiftly become employees. As Cole asks, "What do they say about not getting too close to the club you support because you learn too much and it ruins the mystery essential to blind hero-worship?" When Rooney signs his first professional contract at Everton, he is aghast to find that "over a hundred press people and twelve different camera crews" have been invited to witness the moment. He sips water straight from a bottle on the table, and Moyes beside him whispers, "Use the fucking glass!" Rooney soon starts going off Moyes, and off Everton.

Lampard as a teenager at West Ham gets weekly abuse from thousands of fans, after his uncle and father lose popularity. When the eighteen-year-old is carried off badly hurt on a stretcher at Villa Park, some West Ham supporters in the away section cheer. Lampard dreads driving to his home ground on match days. "There wasn't a single time that I left Upton Park after being slagged off or jeered by some of the supporters that I didn't take their anger home with me," he admits. "These punters had so many hang-ups about me that I began to wonder if the torrents of abuse I received were actually some amateur attempt at collective therapy."

That his father played more than seven hundred games for West Ham doesn't give the fans pause. Lampard devotes pages and pages to this long-gone time. "It's important to me that people understand just how deeply I feel about what happened," he writes. He says he has no feelings for his boyhood club anymore.

Professional soccer is an uglier working environment than most of us ever experience, let alone in our teens. Fans might say that players are paid enough to put up with this sort of thing, but that's a peculiar kind of morality. Even rich people can hurt. Lampard says, "I am actually quite sensitive, that's how I am."

Reading these books, you understand why players are so ready to break with their boyhood clubs. If only they would ditch the hypocrisy. "I'll always be an Arsenal fan, even if I'm not an Arsenal player," Cole claims to be thinking as he applauds his fellow supporters one last time after the lost Champions League final of 2006.

Much as one sees why players leave, it's worth dwelling on Cole's long account of why he joined Chelsea, because the story is unintentionally hilarious. First comes the famous phone call from his agent, Jonathan, telling Cole that Arsenal is offering him a mere £55,000 a week. By now this passage is a classic of soccer literature, but age cannot wither it: "When I heard Jonathan repeat the figure of £55k, I nearly swerved off the road. 'He is taking the piss Jonathan!' I yelled down the phone."

In fact there is a strikingly similar passage in *Carra*, when Rafa Benitez tells the millionaire Carragher in 2005 that he won't be getting a pay rise: "I was speechless. Rarely, if ever, have I been left feeling in such a state of numb shock." Yet in Carragher's book this is a passing incident, whereas in Cole's the insulting offer is the centerpiece of the book. Indeed, it's the main reason why Cole wrote the book: "I just hope the fans understand where I've come from, the reasons for leaving and the reasons for doing this book. I'm not asking for sympathy—just an awareness of what's gone on, how I didn't want to leave, and how I feel the board messed things up. Not me."

"I'm not the deepest of thinkers," Cole admits at one point, and he genuinely seems to believe that once readers know the full facts of the case, they will see that he has no interest at all in money and was in the right on every point in the saga. The book is too easy to parody, largely because Cole has no ability to observe himself from the outside. At one point, he and Arsenal's David Dein have yet another discussion about a new contract. At the end they shake hands, and Dein asks him to keep the conversation under his hat. Cole writes, "The most effective contract I can ever enter into is the unwritten one where I look someone in the eye and give my word." He pledges: "Mr Dein, I won't be telling anyone." But later the negotiations take a bad turn, and so Cole recounts the conversation (including his monastic vow) in the book.

No criticism of Cole is ever justified. Though he writes the book after leaving Arsenal, anyone who ever doubted his loyalty to Arsenal takes a lashing. When former player Peter Beagrie has the temerity to criticize him on television for not stopping a Swedish header at the World Cup, Cole notes Beagrie's former clubs ("Manchester City, Bradford City and Scunthorpe United") and the size of his head. Score settling takes up much of *My Defence*. People who do not either cross Cole or praise him barely figure in the book.

He also spends many pages explaining (in bizarrely overwrought language) that Chelsea didn't illegally "tap him up." However, my conclusion on reading Cole's own account is that they did. That in fact is exactly what the FA Premier League's tribunal found. In any case, who cares? If you want to write a courtroom thriller, there needs to be something at stake. Here the issue was a player trying to move from a big club to an even bigger one. Cole ended up with a fine of $135,000. I wept bitter tears. It isn't true that all soccer players have IQs of 63. However, jointly with Bat Ye'or's mad *Eurabia*, *Ashley Cole: My Defence* is the worst book I have ever read.

STAGE 4: STARDOM

What's it really like to be a famous player? As usual, it's Carragher who captures it best. In May 2001 Liverpool completes their "Treble" of cups by beating Alaves 5–4 in overtime in the UEFA Cup final. Carragher describes the scene in the locker room afterward: "Mentally, physically and emotionally we were too drained to celebrate. I threw off my kit, kicked off my boots, dipped myself into a bath that was bigger than a swimming pool and stared blankly at my teammates. . . . The pace with which each triumph had overlapped the next meant none of us had had a chance to pause to absorb the scale of our accomplishment. . . . We were too exhausted and bewildered to appreciate the view."

The serial reader of these autobiographies soon grasps that being a multimillionaire professional player is often not much fun. The players can't get up to much because of hassle from fans, tabloids, and their clubs' dietitians. The nation follows their every move: Even Carragher receives an offer to sell his wedding pictures to *Hello!* magazine.

All this encourages isolation. In any case, players are discouraged from developing interests outside soccer. It just drains energy. And so they end up spending a lot of time sitting around. Rooney, whose only hobby is sleeping, takes up betting on sports out of sheer boredom. A typical player's summer vacation is Dubai in midsummer, but as Rooney says, all hotel rooms eventually come to seem the same. He doesn't seem very interested in anything beyond soccer: "I suppose I'm laid back. I don't get bothered, either way, by what people do or say. All I care about in life is being out there, playing soccer—and of course Coleen. That's about it really."

The players are encouraged to marry young, in the hope that this will keep them at home, but it doesn't always work out. All five players issue paeans to their wives or girlfriends that echo the ones they gave their parents, but at least two of said wives or girlfriends are now ex-wives or ex-girlfriends. Thankfully, Gerrard and Carragher largely spare us the details of their private lives. They only want to talk about soccer. Their books are the truer for it.

Not everyone is so circumspect. The reader's heart sinks when Cole reveals that he is about to propose marriage to Cheryl. Their chosen venue is Highclere Castle, and we feel their pain when Jordan and Peter Andre stage their own celebs' wedding there shortly before the Coles' big day. Cole still recalls Cheryl's reaction verbatim: "no way! Right Ashley, we're changing venues!" Astonishingly, Cole also reprints his wedding speech in full.

Much of the fun the players have is on the team bus (Rooney and his United teammates play Shit Head, a simplified version of poker) or at the training ground (Gerrard and Peter Crouch at Liverpool play a game called Bare Arse, in which one player shoots at another player's bare arse). Every player believes that his own club has a unique team spirit.

There is the odd interesting personal revelation: It turns out that Rooney likes to sleep with a television set, a light, and a vacuum cleaner or hair dryer all switched on.

But what you really want from these books is insights into life on the field. Of course, Rooney and Cole are unable to deliver any. Here is Cole's analysis of "that skilled live-wire Cristiano Ronaldo": "His skills are slicker than his hair, and any defender has to be on top of his game to stand a chance of keeping tabs on him." And here is Rooney's: "Ronaldo is a great lad and loves to have a laugh."

Luckily, Gerrard does provide the odd glimpse of soccer and players. He gives a wonderful account of the years spent unlearning his English love of the tackle. "For most professionals," he explains, "tackling is a technique. For me it's an adrenalin rush. . . . [T]he sight of the other team with the ball makes me sick." When he tackles, he doesn't hold back: "I can't." And so, in his early years as a pro, he keeps hurting people in training and getting sent off in matches. Gerrard recounts his catalog of victims with some pride. Eventually, he learns to take it easy and to tackle with one foot instead of two. This is a rare detailed account of the mechanics of soccer.

Occasionally, too, Gerrard captures another player in a vignette. Here he is, in the penalty area and poised to fire in a loose ball against Arsenal in the FA Cup final of 2001: "I swung my foot back and then brought it in and down. No contact. The ball had gone. Michael [Owen] had pounced in front of me. Half-volley, full impact, past David Seaman, 1–1. I was still going through with my redundant shot when Michael sprinted away, making for Liverpool's fans."

The scene nails what made the young Owen special. Gerrard manages the same for the referee Pierluigi Collina: "Jesus, he scared me. 'Gerrard!' he'd shout if I crossed the line into what he considered unacceptable, and he'd wave that long, bony finger at me in admonishment. Shit, I'll be good. Collina's bulging eyes were terrifying."

Carragher, who watches soccer obsessively on television, comes up with a surprising admission: Even he would have picked Ferdinand and Terry for England ahead of himself. "I was too similar to Terry. He's a better version of me."

If there had been more expert analyses of their craft, getting through the books would have been less of a slog.

STAGE 5: ELIMINATION WITH ENGLAND

In the spring of 2000, Gerrard gets his first experience of England's locker room. The occasion is only a friendly against Ukraine, but you wouldn't know it: "As kick-off approached, the players talked louder and louder. . . . Battle-cries began. Each player was made to feel that nothing else in his life would ever matter as much as this. Club affiliations and expectations were irrelevant."

Shouts come from all corners of the locker room. "This is England!" "Our country!" "Don't miss a tackle!" Fucking deliver!" Alan Shearer and Tony Adams stand in the middle of the room, Shearer screaming and Adams walking up to each teammate in turn to ask, "Are you fucking ready for this?" Gerrard looks Adams straight back in the eye and says, "You bet I'm fucking well ready." In fact, he is "so hyped up I almost couldn't tie my laces. Fucking let me at Ukraine. Where are they?" He has never experienced anything like this at Anfield.

The golden generation will forever be associated with failure amid hysteria. Yet reading these five players' accounts of international soccer, you see that they also have an artisan's interest in their time with England. To them, playing for their country means close encounters with the best practitioners of their particular craft.

For most of the five, the international debut is a source of anxiety. Lampard is lucky. Not many of us get to make our England debuts playing in midfield besides our beloved elder cousin, who guides us "through every step and pass." During the game, Lampard even briefly thinks back to the old days in Jamie Redknapp's garden, when the two of them would kick balls at Grandpa's birdcage.

Gerrard is so nervous before his first meal with England's squad that he doesn't dare go into the dining room. Happily, Jamie Redknapp (who emerges from these books as a thoroughly good egg) rounds up the other Liverpool players, and they all walk in together. Then they introduce Gerrard to his new teammates. Shaking hands with the United players, he discovers that they don't have horns.

The quality of training startles Gerrard. The other players pass the ball around much too fast for him. Shearer hits every ball into the top corner. And when Gerrard first runs into a Beckham cross in training, "It was a goal before I touched it. Honestly. Beckham puts his crosses in just the right place; it is in fact harder to miss." Whenever England gets knocked out of yet another tournament, the players get depicted as buffoons, but if you have actually played with them, you probably can't see it like that.

Internationals know that a newcomer in their world needs help, and so almost everyone rallies round—sometimes even the opposition. When Gerrard comes on as a sub against Germany at Euro 2000, and hits a few passes, Germany's Didi Hamann, his teammate at Liverpool, runs past and says, "Keep doing what you are doing." When the ball goes out of play, Gerrard turns to his opponent and confides, "I am shitting myself here, mate." Hamann replies, "Relax Stevie. Just do what you do normally." Of course, that doesn't stop Gerrard taking him down shortly afterward with "a full-whack tackle," then shouting, "Fucking get up, Didi!" and later complaining to journalists that Hamann had "squealed like a girl."

Only one of the five authors is unfazed by his international debut. Admittedly, Rooney is surprised to be called up at seventeen years and three months: When Moyes first tells him, he assumes it's for England under-twenty-ones. Yet once the misunderstanding is cleared up, Rooney goes out for a kickabout on the street with his friends. When he finally arrives at England's hotel in St. Albans, he is so tired from the long drive that he sleeps for hours and has to be shaken awake for the team meeting.

Gerrard's overcharged emotional tone contrasts with Rooney's blithe emptiness throughout their two books, but nowhere more so than on the topic of England. Before Rooney's first game in a big tournament, England-France at Euro 2004, he politely waits for Sven-Göran Eriksson to deliver his team talk and then tells the other players, "Just give me the ball. I will do it."

Rooney's self-belief is all his own. Yet most of our five players seem to share the national view that England is destined to win a tournament. After qualifying for the World Cup of 2002, Gerrard immediately thinks "of England in 1966, and how special it would be to bring the trophy home."

Self-belief peaks in 2006. Most of these books first appeared that spring, in a bid to benefit from the national hype, while Rooney got his $9 million from HarperCollins partly with an eye to his writing a Churchillian account of winning the pot. After the World Cup some of the books were reissued, with updates that try to explain the unexpected failure in Germany.

On the way to glory, the players endure long days in their hotel in Baden-Baden. At least the games room is brilliant and equipped with its own comment book. Cole recalls, "Stevie Gerrard cracked us all up when he scribbled 'What a pile of shite.'" Oh, happy days.

Then they meet Portugal. "We were better than them. Miles better," Cole reflects before the game. As the players wait to go out onto the pitch, Rooney and Cristiano Ronaldo chat in the tunnel. The subject: Quinton Fortune. Manchester United's South African reserve is supposedly leaving Old Trafford. Ronaldo asks Rooney whether he knows where Fortune is off to. Rooney doesn't. Nor does Ronaldo. Then they wish each other good luck.

All five memoirs agree on one point: Rooney did not stomp on Ricardo Carvalho's genitals. Well, certainly not intentionally. The sending off was all Ronaldo's fault. And so the game comes down to a penalty shoot-out—a climactic scene in all these books, like the shoot-out at the end of a western. All our heroes bar Rooney are there, as if Eriksson had deliberately selected his writers to take the penalties.

"Of course you can't help but think about Southgate, Batty, Pearce, Beckham and Waddle and all those penalty nightmare misses of old," admits Cole, who is due to take England's fifth kick. "It lurks in your mind somewhere, adding more pressure and a little bit of fear."

First, Lampard's shot is saved. Owen Hargreaves scores, and then it's Gerrard's turn. "I broke away from the safety of my friends in the centre-circle. Suddenly I was alone. . . . The journey was only forty yards, but it felt like forty miles." Following Eriksson's advice, he counts the steps on his walk so as not to think about the pressure. Nonetheless, his shot is saved too. "For months, now, it had played on my mind that I would have to take a penalty in the world cup," he explains. "I knew we would come up against a shootout in Germany. My nerve, and my accuracy, just went. Shit."

Next comes Carragher. As he later discovers, he has been chosen to take for the wrong reason. Eriksson's assistant Tord Grip will explain afterward: "He took one really well for Liverpool in the Champions League final." But Carragher notes that although he has watched the DVD of the Istanbul match "a thousand times," he has never yet spotted himself taking a penalty. "It's frightening to think England's assistant manager could be so ill-informed," he comments. It's hardly as if a penalty shoot-out in the World Cup were an unforeseen event that nobody could have planned for. How did the Swedes keep themselves busy in the six months before the tournament?

Nonetheless, Carragher places the ball on the spot—and scores! Unfortunately, the referee hasn't blown his whistle yet. Carragher has to retake, and this time the keeper saves. Inevitably, Ronaldo scores, and England is eliminated again, before Cole gets his turn.

A nation mourns, but not Carragher. Sitting on the team bus waiting to leave the stadium, he receives a text message that says, "Fuck it. It's only England." Those are Carragher's thoughts exactly. Of course he is upset, but: "Whenever I returned home from disappointing England experiences one unshakeable overriding thought pushed itself to the forefront of my mind, no matter how much the rest of the nation mourned: 'At least it wasn't Liverpool,' I'd repeat to myself, over and over. I confess. Defeats while wearing an England shirt never hurt me in the same way as losing with my club."

He thinks this is a typically Liverpudlian point of view. He recalls the fans on Liverpool's Kop stand singing, "We're not English, we're Scouse."

As he says, "I'm sure there are a whole range of social reasons for this. During the 1970s and 1980s, Merseysiders became increasingly alienated from the rest of the country. The 'us' and 'them' syndrome developed, and it's still going strong. . . . There's no affinity with the national team." To Carragher, Wembley 1966 doesn't mean England winning the World Cup. It means Everton winning the FA Cup. In 1986, ten minutes after Maradona's Argentina had beaten England, "I was outside playing with my mates copying the handball goal." As a boy he traveled around Europe following Everton, yet it would never have occurred to him to go to Wembley to watch England. It must be different for Londoners, he says. These are honest thoughts, the sort you don't tend to read in the tabloids in the months before a World Cup.

Rooney gets over the disappointment fast too. In the locker room after the game, Eriksson tells him not to worry about his red card. "But I hadn't," Rooney tells us. "It was already history." On the team bus to the airport, he sits next to Cole, tells him he is sorry, and says (according to Cole, anyway) that he will knock out Ronaldo the next time he sees him unless the Portuguese says he's sorry. Yet Rooney doesn't seem angry, more "let down" by Ronaldo. Then, according to Cole, "Wazza got out his mobile and tapped out a text to his Man United team-mate. By the look on his face, he was doing it through gritted teeth but he sent it. He texted something like: 'Well done Ron!' like he was being sarcastic or something, 'All the best in the next round.'" Some English fans might have spent the next few years blaming Ronaldo, but Rooney gets on with his career.

Even after getting knocked out, Cole still believes the pretournament hype: "On our day, without doubt, we're better than them, France, Germany and Italy. The world cup had our name written all over it, and it should have been our time. We should have won it. But we didn't play well enough."

So the reality of poor performances matters less than the greater truth of English superiority. Let's leave it to a wiser man to provide the final judgment. "The real reason behind England's short stay in Germany is simple," writes Gerrard. "We were just not as good as we think we are." It was "stupid" of him and the other players to go around "constantly claiming we could win the world cup." It mustn't happen again, he says. "In future tournaments, we must learn to be humble."

Unfortunately, it didn't quite work out like that in South Africa. The golden generation is on its way out, and most of its books now fill the warehouses of secondhand Internet bookstores, waiting to be pulped.

Edwin van der Sar
March 2011

One April afternoon in 1991, Ajax Amsterdam's goalkeeper, a hulking bear called Stanley Menzo, limped off injured. When his replacement bounded on, you wanted to laugh. The twenty-year-old Edwin van der Sar was big-eared, rail-thin, and dressed entirely in purple, with tiny shorts. By way of warming up, he literally skipped around the penalty area. He looked like a particularly campy gymnast. Then he began to keep, and never stopped. Twenty years later, as Manchester United's keeper prepares to retire at the end of the season, he has redefined goalkeeping.

The pre-Sarian goalkeeper—who still lives on in some of the more primitive regions of Britain—was a hulking bear who kept goal because he couldn't play soccer. He could barely kick a ball in the right direction. He got applauded for spectacular saves. He lived up to the old adage that "goalkeepers are crazy." He had a longer career than outfield players, but still tended to get out of the game in his midthirties before he began to look silly. Managers rarely paid him much attention unless he let a ball through his legs. But Van der Sar has changed what we expect from goalkeepers.

I've followed him for twenty years. We're just a year apart in age, and he grew up five miles from me in the Netherlands. He looks just like the villagers we used to play against on windy Saturdays in the bulb fields, near the North Sea: At six foot seven, he isn't far off average height for the region, and his long, pale, gloomy face, that of a Calvinist pastor circa 1872, is typical too. As a boy he liked playing soccer—as opposed to keeping goal—but never dreamed of turning pro.

Still, his coach at his amateur club spotted his potential. In 1988 Ajax summoned him to play an evening trial match for their second team. The stadium was empty, except for a gaggle of the keeper's friends who positioned themselves at one end with a banner that said, "Van der Sar in Oranje." He'd end up playing a record 130 matches for Oranje, the Dutch national team.

When Ajax signed him, his old amateur coach got a finder's fee of 1,500 guilders (then about $800) in an envelope. That was the going rate for a young goalkeeper. But quite soon, it became clear that Van der Sar was the goalkeeper that Holland had been looking for since the late 1960s. When Johan Cruijff and Rinus Michels first dreamed up the country's distinctive style of "total football," Cruijff had a vision of the perfect goalkeeper: an out-field player in gloves. It had always bothered Cruijff that the typical goal-keeper just stopped balls. It was a waste of a player, Cruijff thought. The goalkeeper should start attacks, passing like an outfield player. Wouldn't it be perfect, he mused, if you could combine with eleven men rather than ten, and it just happened that one of them could save a ball when necessary?

Van der Sar was that outfield player in gloves, total football's missing link. (David Winner, author of *Brilliant Orange*, the book about the Dutch game, muses that perhaps Holland should have taken the seven-year-old Van der Sar to the World Cup of 1978 instead of the hopeless goalie Jan Jong-bloed, who ended up conceding three goals in the final.) Van der Sar, two-footed, adept at the one-touch pass, given to dribbling past opposing strikers when the mood took him, could have been a professional outfield player and perhaps more than that. At the World Cup of 1994, he played in the outfield in Holland's training sessions in Florida and looked to be one of the better performers. Cruijff would later call him "Ajax's best attacker."

The start of his career coincided with one of soccer's rare rule changes: After 1992, goalkeepers could no longer pick up passes from their teammates. That made a keeper's foot skills more important even than Cruijff had imag-ined. Van der Sar pointed the way for his profession.

But he was a new model keeper in other ways, too. Traditionally, keepers got praised for their saves. Van der Sar tried *not* to make saves. He organized his defense so that he wouldn't need to make them. Every save meant that something had gone wrong beforehand. He read the game so well, positioned himself so perfectly, that strikers seemed to shoot straight at him. You rarely noticed Van der Sar—he was quite a boring keeper—but he rarely let in goals, either. On the other hand, when he had to make a save, he generally did.

When other keepers discuss him, the point they return to is that he seldom errs. In Cruijff's phrase, he is "very complete"—equally happy whether catching crosses, making reflex saves, or standing up in a one-on-one against the forward and forcing the guy to shoot at him.

He also had the perfect keeper's temperament. The Dutch call him an *ijskonijn*, an "ice rabbit." Van der Sar never seems to enter the emotional state of losing oneself that is characteristic of soccer. This goalkeeper isn't crazy. Even after great victories, he has fought off teammates who grabbed him too boisterously during the celebrations. He says, "I sometimes see nice, quiet boys go nuts on the pitch. Then I think: they can say I'm a 'dead one,' but I don't think those guys are 100 per cent." Van der Sar rebuffs the emotion around him with a chilled irony that usually falls short of being actually funny.

Last, there was his shape: perfect for the modern game. The big, burly English keeper, who could fight his way through a crowded penalty area to a cross (think Arsenal's David Seaman), was going out of fashion by the 1990s. Even in England referees were no longer letting forwards push and foul the way they used to. In the new genteel game, Seamans were redundant. The new model keeper had to be both a giant and a gymnast—a rare combination. Van der Sar has it, as does the era's other preeminent keeper, Gianluigi Buffon.

His first career went brilliantly. Keepers are meant to start slowly, but by age twenty-four he had become Holland's automatic number one and had won the Champions League of 1995 with what was practically an Ajax boys team. (It's a tribute to that side's youth and love of soccer that sixteen years later, four of its members still play professionally: Van der Sar, Clarence Seedorf at Milan, Nwankwo Kanu at Portsmouth, and Jari Litmanen for Finland and now in training with the Finnish champions HJK Helsinki, while Edgar Davids is currently on trial with Sheffield Wednesday.)

In 1999, generally considered the world's best goalkeeper, Van der Sar agreed to move from Ajax to Juventus. The story goes that as he waited in the Amsterdam airport to fly down to Italy to sign, his phone rang. It was Alex Ferguson. Did Van der Sar fancy joining Manchester United? The keeper apologized: He'd already said yes to Juventus. For years afterward, as United went through substandard keeper after keeper, Ferguson would regret having called Van der Sar a day late.

Van der Sar probably regretted it, too. His years at Juventus were his worst. For the only time in his career, he lost confidence and committed what the Italians called *papere*—keeper's errors. The Italian media dubbed him Van der Gol, for "goal." Juventus asked him to have his eyes tested. In 2001 they packed him off to little Fulham in London.

In Dublin on September 1, 2001, I was present at the nadir of Van der Sar's career. Holland lost 1–0 to Ireland and missed qualifying for the next year's World Cup. After the final whistle, Van der Sar strode off in what, by his standards, was a state of high emotion. He passed a small table that stood beside the field. It looked doomed. Van der Sar lifted a long leg to administer the coup de grâce. But then, instead of shattering the table, he lifted his leg an inch higher and merely flicked a plastic cup off the tabletop. That was Van der Sar: the ice rabbit with perfect footwork.

His best then seemed behind him. Fulham had assured him it was bound for glory, but the money dried up, and the former world's best goalkeeper ended up spending four years at a West London neighborhood club. Manchester United and Arsenal seemed content soldiering on with substandard keepers. Whereas in the Netherlands a goalkeeper was expected to be an outfield player and in Italy an infallible shot stopper, in England little seemed expected of him at all.

Most soccer managers undervalue and misunderstand goalkeepers. When the sports economist Bernd Frick studied salaries in Germany's Bundesliga, he found that keepers earned less than outfield players, despite mostly being older. They also command lower transfer fees: The British record for a keeper is a mere $18 million, paid by Sunderland for Craig Gordon in 2007. Perhaps the main reason is managerial ignorance. Even great managers like Ferguson or Arsenal's Arsène Wenger view keeping as an alien craft, like flower arranging. Since they barely understand what keepers do, they are loath to pay much for them.

Finally, in 2005, Ferguson risked shelling out $3.5 million on Van der Sar. The keeper was pleased and surprised. At thirty-four, he had thought his career was winding down. He was looking forward to returning to the dunes by the North Sea, where he'd play center-forward for his old amateur club. "Scoring goals is the most fun," he says.

In fact, his career was restarting. At United he won three straight league titles, and, early one morning in Moscow in 2008, the keeper you barely noticed finally became the hero. The Champions League final between United and Chelsea went to a penalty shoot-out. Van der Sar had a bad record in shoot-outs: With him in goal, Holland had exited Euro 96, Euro 2000, and the World Cup of 1998 on penalties. If he'd mastered this one particular keeping art as he has all others, the Dutch would probably have won another trophy.

Chelsea had spotted Van der Sar's fatal flaw: On penalties, he dives too often to his right. Chelsea's first six kickers shot to his left. He didn't save a shot. In fact, by this point he'd deserved to lose the shoot-out. However, the legendary slip by Chelsea's captain John Terry saved United.

Then, after six penalties, Van der Sar figured out what was happening. As Nicolas Anelka prepared to take Chelsea's seventh, the keeper pointed a giant glove to his own left. (This is where prose as a medium fails. I urge you to watch the shoot-out on YouTube.) "That's where you're all putting it, isn't it?" Van der Sar was saying. Anelka froze. The keeper had found him out. Reduced to a bag of nerves, he hit a gentle shot at midheight to the keeper's right. Van der Sar, smiling as he dived, stopped it. "That one, all-decisive save is yet to come," he had said years before. Here it was. Later that morning, records United's unofficial historian Jim White, the ice rabbit breakfasted on two small packets of Cocoa Puffs and a banana.

Van der Sar had never imagined being so good so old. He kept expecting to decay. Surely, his eyesight must be going. It wasn't. "Everybody doubts themselves," he said recently after a mistake at Liverpool. "Every writer doubts themselves, every artist doubts himself and every soccer player does. That is what certain players thrive on." (Note the reference to writers. After Roy Keane's departure, Van der Sar became the only member of United's reading circle.)

Van der Sar has peaked later than he had ever imagined, later than anyone had thought goalkeepers could. Yet that makes sense and will help change the conventional wisdom about goalkeepers' careers. Soccer's ideal generally is old heads on young legs, but that's particularly true for keepers. Joop Hiele, Van der Sar's former keeping coach, once explained, "Goalkeeping is registering the situation, recognizing it and finding the solution. The more often you do it, the easier it gets." An older keeper is so familiar with the structure of attacks that he has time to organize his defense. Younger keepers can't. All they have is their talent. And when they make mistakes, they start doubting themselves. That's exactly what happened to United's young American Tim Howard, the club's last failed keeper before Van der Sar.

Other old players get sick of soccer, but not Van der Sar. He mused recently, "There was a point last year when it was four degrees and the rain was pouring down. Ben Foster [then United's deputy keeper] asked me whether I still wanted to do it in such rubbish weather. I said I loved it."

He might have continued for even longer but for the brain hemorrhage that felled his wife around Christmas 2009. She seems to have recovered well, but she needs regular treatment in the Netherlands. Asked when he decided to retire, he says, "Let's just say that it was playing on my mind from the moment Annemarie had her stroke." Van der Sar feels it's time for him to become a house husband for a while—preferably after pocketing the treble of league, Champions League, and FA Cup.

Anyway, he couldn't go on forever (could he?). "He made the point himself: It is pointless trying to be Superman into your forties," reports Ferguson. In the showers at work one day, Wayne Rooney lobbied the Dutchman to continue, but to no avail. It was left to another teammate, Rio Ferdinand, to deliver the encomium. "To be honest," the center-back told United's official magazine, "he's changed my thinking when it comes to goalkeepers. If I ever become a manager, then I'll be looking for my goalkeeper to exhibit as many of Edwin's traits as possible." And so says everyone in the game.

Robert Enke
October 2011

Review of *A Life Too Short: The Tragedy of Robert Enke*, by Ronald Reng (Yellow Jersey Press, translated from the German by Shaun Whiteside)

On November 10, 2009, the German goalkeeper Robert Enke kissed his baby daughter, said good-bye to his wife, and left the house. He said he would be back about 6:30 p.m., after training at his club, Hannover.

When he didn't return, his wife called his goalkeeping coach, Jörg Sievers. What time might she expect her husband back after training? "The line fell silent," writes Ronald Reng. "At last Sievers said, carefully, 'There was no training today.'" Enke had driven around for eight hours and then laid down on the railway line in front of the regional express train from Bremen. He was a depressive, something he had kept secret in soccer.

Enke had often talked to a friend, the German journalist-cum-novelist Reng, about writing a book together. Now Reng has written it alone, beautifully. He is one of the few good writers to have penetrated the innards of soccer. Enke's wife gave him Enke's diaries and the poems Enke wrote on his cell phone. In fact, writes Reng, "I have deliberately excluded passages [from the diaries] that I see as too revealing." Not many biographers do that. The upshot is a book not just about Enke, suicide, and depression, but about the stress that pervades most soccer players' lives.

The East German–born Enke rose fast. At age twenty he was keeping in the Bundesliga, Germany's top division. Soon afterward he joined Benfica in Lisbon. With hindsight it's ominous that he fled home in panic straight after signing the contract, but soon he was thriving in Portugal. When Reng first met him, over lunch in Lisbon, he saw "a professional sportsman inspired by the idea that he has to climb ever further, ever higher." They became friends, and Reng slips himself judiciously into the book as a minor character.

Enke climbed as high as Barcelona. However, he would play just one game for the Catalan club, a cup match against the third-division side Novelda. Stricken with fear, he let in three soft goals, and Barcelona lost. His captain blamed him at the postmatch press conference. It triggered a depression. Enke fled to Istanbul, where again he played only one match, a howler, before fleeing Turkey. Then this excellent keeper briefly became unemployed. He recovered his equilibrium only at quieter, smaller clubs, first Tenerife, and then Hannover, his last club.

Enke was a depressive and therefore an exception, but his fears were fairly typical for a soccer player. Soccer, after all, is usually told as the simplest story: victory or defeat, success or failure, hero or villain. The usual player's career is a series of dislocations (transfers) punctuated by public humiliations.

However, the humiliations are worse for goalkeepers, as the amateur keeper Reng knows. Because their mistakes often decide matches, keepers live in anxiety yet rarely mention it. Their profession requires that they present themselves as stoics, as safe pairs of hands. Anyone who "can't take the pressure" is viewed as suspect. Indeed, soccer's preferred pedagogic mode is the application of pressure. Frans Hoek, Barcelona's goalkeeping coach when Enke was at the club, would scream at his keepers, in his heavy Dutch accent, "Esto noooo!" Not that! Hoek remembers telling Enke, "You're too nice. Soccer's a hard world. As a player you sometimes have to be brutal." Enke wasn't the only player who was often happier as a substitute than when he had to perform.

Several keepers confess their fears to Reng. René Adler, who that autumn of 2009 had looked like Enke's main rival for the German goalkeeping jersey at the next year's World Cup, recalls how Enke, a friend, had advised him not to join a big club until he felt ready. Ignore the world's pressure to move upward, Enke had said. Enjoy how well you are doing now. This was heresy in a game where everyone—players, fans, and media—takes it for granted that it's better to play for a big club than a small one ("It's a dream come true"), better to be a starter than a reserve. Adler told Reng, "Among Bundesliga professionals you're always showing off about how strong you are. It was really good to talk to someone about the anxieties."

Enke suffered great anxieties from his battle with Adler for the German shirt. However, we'll never know whether it was that, or a belated reaction to the death in 2006 of his two-year-old daughter, Lara (born with heart problems), or something else apparently trivial that sent him into depression again in the summer of 2009. "If you could just have my head for half an hour, you'd know why I go mad," he once told his wife. Hoping to play at the World Cup of 2010, he felt unable to come out as a depressive. Reng suspects that is why Enke wanted to write a book. It was to have been his testimony.

A Life Too Short is at times almost unbearably painful, but it is the mature work of a writer who has gone far beyond sensationalism. It allows you to go back and read soccer differently. All English fans recall the soft American shot that England's goalkeeper Robert Green muffed in the country's first game at the last World Cup. Green was promptly dropped. I now wonder whether he subconsciously intended to miss the ball, because he wanted to be dropped and escape the anxiety.

Robin van Persie and Rafael van der Vaart
November 2011

You never know a player as deeply as when you follow his whole career, start to finish. I still remember Rafael van der Vaart as an eighteen-year-old backheeling a goal while diving forward for Ajax Amsterdam in the Dutch league's big match against Feyenoord. And I've seen video of a raven-haired eleven-year-old Van Persie swerving past the keeper in a kids' match in Rotterdam.

I grew up in Holland, support the Dutch, and have waited years for these two to become the players we always knew they could be. Van Persie at Arsenal has done that and more; Van der Vaart down the road at Tottenham has merely become the best incomplete soccer player on earth.

The great Dutch quartet of Van der Vaart, Van Persie, Wesley Sneijder, and Arjen Robben were all born within sixteen months of each other in 1983 and 1984. Each of the four has headed the pack at different times in their careers, but the early leader was Van der Vaart. Born in a caravan park near Amsterdam, to a Dutch father and Spanish mother, he entered the great Ajax academy at age ten. Ajax turned the street player into a "functional" professional player.

That knocked some of the fun out of him, he has admitted, but it also meant that when he made Ajax's first team at age seventeen, he had almost no more growing up left to do. Like Clarence Seedorf or Patrick Kluivert before him, Van der Vaart arrived almost complete. He hardly ever did a trick for the trick's sake. He could shoot hard with almost no backlift, hitting the desired bit of the net as accurately as a darts player throwing a triple twenty. In other words, he was pretty much the player then that he is today. When

Van der Vaart was eighteen, Ruud Gullit said he wasn't "talented" anymore—he was already a star. Even when people called him the next Cruijff or Van Basten or Zidane, it didn't seem to go to his head.

Meanwhile, Van Persie down in Rotterdam was still a sulky adolescent. Raised by his single father, a sculptor who works with garbage and old paper, Van Persie seems to have channeled his hyperactivity into going around town with a ball. He'd even dribble into stores. He'd kick around obsessively with mostly immigrant kids, and to this day his Dutch (now deteriorating after seven years in England) retains a peculiar Moroccan immigrant accent. Through constant use he perfected his left foot, though not what he used to call his "chocolate" right one.

Feyenoord, never the best-run club on earth, seemed to resent the uppity kid with a 1950s quiff and more talent than the senior players. "I am better than the others," he said once. Van Persie would do things such as arrive an hour late for a game because he hadn't realized the clocks had changed or steal a free kick from the club's specialist, Pierre van Hooijdonk, and miss it. Looking back recently in a revelatory documentary for Dutch TV, he told his journalistic confidant, Henk Spaan, "I wasn't good enough myself then." He was merely a talent, obsessed with individual skill. He did help Feyenoord win the UEFA Cup of 2002 as an outside-left, but even in the final he kept receiving passes motionlessly and then trying to trick his way past experienced defenders. Before long, he admits, Feyenoord had "more or less written me off." In 2004 the club packed him off to Arsenal with good riddance.

Shortly afterward Van der Vaart left Ajax for Hamburg. In three years in Germany he would make an excellent impression, though not as good as his stunning wife, Sylvie, who overcame breast cancer and to this day frequently features as a celebrity on German TV shows.

Van Persie arrived in London unready for the top. He and his young Dutch Moroccan wife struggled to settle, and early on he made news chiefly for antics such as overturning his BMW and then fleeing the scene. Luckily for Van Persie, Arsenal employed an older Dutchman named Dennis Bergkamp. "Everything was right about that man," Van Persie says in Spaan's documentary. "The way he behaved, for a start. He was number 10, I was number 11, so I was sitting next to my idol every day. And I still kept him on a pedestal."

One day Van Persie was sitting in the hot tub at Arsenal's training ground, watching Bergkamp do a passing exercise outside with a fifteen-year-old, a sixteen-year-old, and a fitness coach. Van Persie stayed in the water for forty-five minutes, his skin wrinkling, as he waited for Bergkamp to hit just one imperfect pass. Bergkamp never did. Van Persie reflected, "I can pass well too; I can play soccer well too. But this man was so driven, so focused, that I thought, 'I have to make a big step to get to that level.' From that moment I began doing every exercise at 100 percent. If I made one mistake, I was angry, because I wanted to be Bergkamp."

It wasn't only Bergkamp. When Van Persie joined Arsenal, "the Invincibles"—then on a run of forty-nine unbeaten league games—were perhaps the best team in the Premier League's history. They set the bar high for a young man. Sol Campbell told him to keep getting into the penalty area, to make it his domain, because defenders didn't like that. When Van Persie noticed he hadn't been doing it enough, he'd write an essay to remind himself.

In that company he had everything to prove. Sometimes in those early seasons he'd deliberately go for the goal himself rather than pass. He needed to prove his own worth to the team. Those goals gave him not so much joy, he says, as relief.

Gradually, he began to outstrip Van der Vaart. The little number 10 had waited years for Manchester United or Barcelona (favorite club of his Spanish relatives) to come knocking. In the end he went to Real Madrid instead, but joined the long list of stars whom Madrid buys in a fit of absentmindedness and then locks up in a cupboard and forgets. Sometimes Van der Vaart found himself watching from the stands. One evening in Holland's locker room, Van Persie told him that he'd put in a good word for him at Arsenal. "Would you? That would be great!" exulted Van der Vaart. But Arsenal never bit. Arsène Wenger considers the midfielder "heavy on his legs."

All the big clubs decided against Van der Vaart, and one can understand why. Whereas Van Persie for years was immature but potentially perfect, Van der Vaart had limits. When you see his roly-poly father, you know the son has to battle his weight to survive in top-class soccer. He rarely tackles, has little pace, and has only one foot (albeit a brilliant one). The great Dutch coach Guus Hiddink says that if you play Van der Vaart, all your other midfielders have to work harder to compensate for his physical shortcomings. A coach needs to ask himself whether the player is worth it.

For both Van der Vaart and Van Persie, last year's World Cup was very nearly their crowning moment. But Holland lost to Spain in the final (with Van der Vaart's Spanish relatives cheering on the Dutch), and both players personally had bad tournaments. "I wasn't playing at my best. However hard I find it to accept, it's true," Van Persie admitted to Spaan. Both he and Van der Vaart suffered from the presence of their teammate Wesley Sneijder. Van Persie cordially loathes Sneijder, whom he privately calls "the smurf," and in South Africa Sneijder rarely rewarded Van Persie's runs with passes. Van der Vaart likes Sneijder, but few coaches will play two undersize slow coaches in central midfield. The only slot usually went to Sneijder.

A few weeks after the World Cup, Spurs's chairman, Daniel Levy, told his manager, Harry Redknapp, "I've got a present for you." Redknapp thought it might be a car. Instead, he discovered to his delight that his chairman had nabbed Van der Vaart for just $12.5 million. The transfer happened so fast that the player never even returned to Madrid to say good-bye. He didn't mind. He loved the old training ground at Spurs Lodge, with its rundown wooden benches and the showers that barely worked. He loved relaxed English preparations. "Man, it's beautiful," he told a Dutch magazine. "In the evening you're playing Champions League against Inter Milan, and at 5:00 p.m. you're still home. You tell your wife, 'Well, darling, I'm off to play Inter. See you later,' and then you hammer the European champions."

Above all, he loved the spaces that English opponents left him. Born without pace, Van der Vaart has developed a gift for positioning himself between the opposition's back four and midfield. Just below the top level, he has found a team that can live with his incompleteness. Even Luka Modric plays in his service. No wonder he recently scored six goals in five consecutive league games.

Even that pales beside Van Persie's twenty-nine league goals so far this calendar year. The tally is particularly remarkable given that the Rotterdammer spent his early career as a number 10 or winger. Wenger converted him, as he'd previously converted Henry, though he struggled to discourage Van Persie from trying to be an all-rounder. "I want you to work less," Wenger told him. Van Persie's job was to be only to finish moves.

"I'm not a born striker," he has admitted. But gradually, he has perfected his shot: take a half step to steady himself, focus, and then fire with total conviction. Simultaneously, he remains an excellent creator. In Opta's statistical rankings for last season, Van Persie was not merely the player in the Premier League with the most shots from open play; he was also ranked eighth for "chance creation," just two spots behind Van der Vaart. It's a rare double gift.

Van Persie has coped surprisingly well with the recent loss of his two best providers, Cesc Fabregas and Samir Nasri. The little Frenchman was a friend who must have reminded Van Persie of his teenage companions in Rotterdam, the North African immigrant kids who adored tricks on the ball. But Fabregas was Van Persie's lifeline. Sometimes Van Persie might get the headlines for a beautiful volleyed goal—but often it would have been Fabregas's pass that made the decision for him, that practically forced him into just that volley.

Of course, after Fabregas left, Van Persie thought of leaving Arsenal, too. But he loves his new house in Hampstead (the formerly bohemian North London neighborhood now invaded by investment bankers and soccer players), his family is settled there, and he wanted to be Arsenal's captain and locker-room leader for a full season. After all, he'd worked years to gain status at the club. "It's important to him to know that he's valued," says Spaan. "Deep down he may still be an insecure figure. He is growing with his own importance." In this new Arsenal side you often see Van Persie talking to teammates during games. He knows that this is his peak, that right now, this autumn, free of injuries, not recovering from a big tournament, he is the best center-forward on earth. He must suspect that this is as good as it gets.

He currently leads the great Dutch quartet. Van der Vaart never made it at the top, Sneijder is seventeenth in Serie A with a fading Inter, and the chronically injured Robben may never quite come back.

But Van Persie's graying temples are an omen of the end. The final audit will probably record both his and Van der Vaart's careers as brilliantly anticlimactic. Van der Vaart never won the league after leaving Holland; Van Persie hasn't won a prize since Arsenal's FA Cup of 2005. It could all have been so different if Iker Casillas hadn't got his studs to Robben's breakaway

shot in the World Cup final. As it is, Van Persie and Van der Vaart will probably leave us only with memories.

*I was wrong about Van Persie: his career did get better after he left Arsenal at
age twenty-nine for Manchester United in 2012. He had probably mulled over the
same scenario that I predicted in this article: that if he stayed at Arsenal, his career
risked being anticlimactic.*

*I inadvertently played a tiny role in his transfer to United. One day in the summer
of 2012, I was having a Chinese lunch in London with John Foot, a professor of Italian
history and expert on Italian soccer (he wrote the excellent "Calcio"). Over dumplings,
Foot mentioned his estimate that more than twenty Italian clubs were being investigated
for match fixing.*

*Just around that time, Van Persie was reportedly talking to Juventus. I mentioned
to a friend of Van Persie's that if the striker joined Juventus, he might quite unknow-
ingly find himself playing a lot of games against clubs that had thrown the match by
arrangement with gamblers. The friend told Van Persie's agent. The agent was shocked
by the figure of twenty suspect clubs. Soon afterward, Van Persie signed for United instead of Juventus. As Wenger later said, that move sealed the destination of the English
title in 2012–2013. Foot, an Arsenal fan, still wonders whether he should have kept
his mouth shut that lunchtime.*

Hope Solo
August 2012

The American soccer goalkeeper Hope Solo could win her second straight
Olympic gold today. But even if the U.S. women beat Japan in the final
at a packed Wembley, it would be almost a detail in Solo's life. She already
possesses every element for legend: a superhero's name, dysfunctional family,
triumph over adversity, controversy, beauty, celebrity, oh, and athletic genius.
Sunil Gulati, president of the U.S. Soccer Federation, admits, "She has transcended women's soccer."

Solo, thirty-one, was conceived on a conjugal visit by her mother to her
father in jail. She was born in Richland, Washington, the town created to

produce plutonium for atom bombs. Its plutonium filled the bomb dropped sixty-seven years ago today on Nagasaki, Japan, notes Solo in her forthcoming autobiography. She adds, "In my hometown, that incineration is still celebrated. The logo of my high school is the nuclear mushroom cloud." The school teams were called the Richland High Bombers, and fans would cheer, "Nuke 'em, nuke 'em, nuke 'em till they glow!" Perhaps unnecessarily, Solo explains, "We don't do politically correct in Richland."

Solo's mother tested plutonium samples. Solo's beloved father, Jeffrey Solo (possibly not his actual surname), coached his daughter in sports. He also had at least two families simultaneously. Bizarrely, both his partners were called Judy Lynn Solo. He was a versatile criminal, often in jail. He once kidnapped Solo and her brother until armed police surrounded him when he tried to cash a check. It was an unusual childhood for a female American soccer star; Solo's teammates mostly come from comfortable homes.

Solo's father eventually became homeless. When she ran into him in a Seattle park one day, they reconnected. Shortly before he could come and watch her at the World Cup of 2007, he died of a heart attack.

A natural athlete who played as a forward in high school, Solo first kept goal for the United States at age eighteen. But she entered national consciousness during that 2007 World Cup, when she was benched before the semifinal against Brazil. Veteran keeper Briana Scurry played, and the United States lost 4–0. Afterward, Solo said, "There's no doubt in my mind I would have made those saves" and dismissed Scurry's past trophies as irrelevant.

To some, Solo's outspokenness made her a role model for strong women. However, her apparent disloyalty outraged her American teammates. Solo by name, solo by nature, was their view. "They ostracized her for a while," says her agent, Richard Motzkin. Solo flew home from the World Cup alone. Eventually, says Motzkin, "everyone was able to move on." Still, old sores may explain why Solo's autobiography will appear only after these Games. Already it's selling briskly. Gulati says, "How many soccer players in the U.S. write books that presell well? One, ever."

In 2008 Solo won Olympic gold. She also lifted the veil from goings-on in the Olympic Village, admitting to having smuggled an unnamed celebrity into her room. Soon she became a celebrity herself. Her smoldering looks help: "Marry Me Hope, I'm Solo," said one fan's banner. She has appeared on the TV show *Dancing with the Stars*. But Motzkin says Solo is less extroverted than she seems: "The whole notion of 'celebrity' still is something Hope is not entirely comfortable with."

Even so, she can hardly stay offstage. Shortly before the Olympics, she was warned for testing positive for drugs. She blamed a medicine prescribed for "premenstrual purposes." Days into the Games, after the NBC-TV pundit Brandi Chastain mildly criticized an American defender, Solo tweeted that Chastain should "get more educated" and told her, "The game has changed from a decade ago." Chastain has been an icon since removing her shirt to celebrate victory in the 1999 World Cup final, and many in American soccer considered Solo's jibes disrespectful and distracting. But they know there is no way to keep her quiet.

Zlatan Ibrahimovic
March 2013

The best soccer player's autobiography of recent years is probably *I Am Zlatan Ibrahimovic*. In it, the Swedish striker recounts his rise from an ethnic ghetto in Malmö to greatness. Zlatan (as he is usually known) is currently banging in goals for Paris St. Germain.

Zlatan has a Bosnian father and Croatian mother. They married to get the dad a Swedish resident's permit and soon separated. Zlatan's book, ghostwritten by David Lagercrantz, is an immigrant's tale. In fact, having sold seven hundred thousand copies in Sweden alone and been published in fifteen countries, it's probably the best-selling European immigrant's tale since Zadie Smith's *White Teeth* (2000). The book was also short-listed for Sweden's prestigious literary award the August Prize. Once you get past the obligatory snicker prompted by the phrase "soccer player's autobiography," you can see that Zlatan's book strangely resembles an earlier immigrant's tale, *Portnoy's Complaint* (1967), Philip Roth's classic novel about growing up Jewish in 1930s and '40s Newark, New Jersey.

Each man's story illuminates the other. Moreover, each illuminates the increasingly typical yet rarely heard immigrant experience. (Portnoy himself isn't an immigrant, but his parents were the first in their families to grow up in the United States, and they still feel themselves outsiders in American life.) Most of the talk about immigrants nowadays comes from politicians pontificating about them. These books are wonderful firsthand accounts of what it's like to grow up in an immigrant family. Though Zlatan and Roth are separated by an ocean and four decades, the overlaps are remarkable.

Zlatan's book is a confessional autobiography, Roth's a fictionalized confessional autobiography. Roth's narrator, Alex Portnoy, is, like Roth, a Newark boy born in 1933. (Roth, who recently announced that he had given up writing, turned eighty on March 19.) Both Zlatan and Portnoy are angry prodigies looking back on the ghetto from early maturity—Zlatan narrates age twenty-eight, Portnoy age thirty-three. And both books, in large part, are odes to the native blonde girl.

Like many children of immigrants, Portnoy and Zlatan grew up segregated from the native mainstream. Portnoy explains (the novel is told as a long session with his mute shrink, Dr. Spielvogel), "In my cousin Marcia's graduating class from Weequahic High, out of the two hundred and fifty students, there were only eleven *goyim* and one colored. Go beat that, said Uncle Hymie." In short, the dominant American caste of the day—white Gentiles— was almost wholly absent from Newark. As for Zlatan's concrete ghetto of Rosengård, in Malmö, "It was crawling with Somalis, Turks, Yugo's, Poles and north Africans, but there were no native Swedes."

These are experiences that few natives can comprehend. The first thing Zlatan told Lagercrantz was that he wanted his book to be ten times better than "the one about the Swedish king," but the player soon spotted a problem: his excellent ghostwriter "came from a completely different world from mine." Zlatan's Rosengård was as far removed from mainstream Sweden as Portnoy's Newark from mainstream America. "Swedish TV didn't exist for us," writes Zlatan. "We lived in a very different world from the Swedes. I was twenty when I saw my first Swedish film, and I had no idea who the Swedish heroes and sports stars were." Instead, he and his father used to watch videos of American boxers such as Muhammad Ali and George Foreman or the films of Bruce Lee and Jackie Chan.

Similarly, Portnoy, recalling his family's Thanksgiving meals, wonders, "Why then can't I believe I am eating my dinner in America, that America is where *I* am, instead of some other place to which I will one day travel . . . "

Both men's parents know almost nothing of the social norms outside their ghetto. In this incomprehensible new country, the first generation almost cannot succeed. Zlatan's father is a hard-drinking janitor, Portnoy's an underpaid insurance agent. Portnoy's parents possess just three bound books, not including schoolbooks. Zlatan says his parents never asked things such as, "'Do you need help with your homework?', or 'Can I explain anything in Swedish history to you?' None of that. Beer tins, Yugo-music, empty fridges and the Balkan war, that's what we had at home."

Home is a place of emotional frenzy. Ferocious arguments with parents are the norm. When Portnoy is six or seven, his mother threatens him with a knife when he won't eat his dinner ("Only *why?* What can she possibly be thinking *in her brain?*"), and she regularly threatens to banish him from their apartment forever. Zlatan's mother beats him with a ladle and actually does banish his half sister from their apartment forever. "We bear grudges and we exaggerate," Zlatan explains.

Like many immigrants, Portnoy and Zlatan grow up under the shadow of a disaster happening in the old country. For Portnoy, it's the Holocaust; for Zlatan, it's the Balkan war. Both boys sense mostly unspoken anxiety. Zlatan writes, "The war was something strange. I was never allowed to hear about it. I was protected. . . . I didn't understand why my mother and my sisters went around dressed in black. It was totally incomprehensible, it was like a fashion trend." But he does know that his father's Bosnian village was massacred and ethnically cleansed by Serbs.

Early in *Portnoy's Complaint*, 1941 is mentioned as the quasi-innocent date when Portnoy's family moves from Jersey City to Newark. Later, however, his sister reminds him where he would be had he been born in Europe: "gassed, or shot, or incinerated, or butchered, or buried alive."

Portnoy is an intellectual prodigy, just as Zlatan is a sporting one, but neither man's parents have the nous to guide his life path. Like many ghetto children, both boys are caught between an old country and a new one, in neither of which they belong. No wonder they grow up angry. "That extended period of rage that goes by the name of adolescence," muses Portnoy. He expresses his anger with words, Zlatan with words and violence. "I was aggressive," Zlatan writes. "I pulled down trousers and held boys tight." As his former headmistress once told a journalist, "I've been at this school 33 years, and Zlatan is easily in the top five of most unruly pupils we've ever had. He was the number one bad boy, a one-man show, a prototype of a child that ends up in serious trouble."

Driven by adrenaline, both Portnoy and Zlatan become serial transgressors. Portnoy, famously, is a compulsive masturbator, and Zlatan is a bicycle thief. After hearing that he is to join the first team of the local professional club, Malmö FF, he recounts, "I think I went outside and nicked a bicycle again, and I felt like the coolest guy in town."

Both men hide their crimes from their parents. Zlatan throws away a letter from the police before his father sees it; Portnoy locks the bathroom door. But whereas Zlatan embraces his inner bad boy with pride, Portnoy cannot: "Shame and shame and shame and shame—every place I turn something else to be ashamed of." Portnoy fantasizes about newspaper headlines exposing him to the world as a bad boy: "ASST HUMAN OPPY COMMISH FOUND HEADLESS IN GO-GO GIRL'S APT!" and the like. In Zlatan's case, the media actually do frequently expose him. Even when he returns to the Swedish national team's hotel an hour late after a quiet drink in Stockholm, it's front-page news. He complains he can't buy a carton of milk without the story making the newspaper.

Both men spend their youth feeling awkward, unsure of how to behave. They are at ease in only one place: the sports field. Portnoy's game is baseball, where he masters every mannerism of the center fielder, so that he *looks* like a pro even though he's not very good. He asks Spielvogel, "It's true, is it not?—incredible, but apparently true—there are people who feel in life the ease, the self-assurance, the simple and essential affiliation with what is going on, that I used to feel as the center fielder for the Seabees?" The novel's famous ode—"Oh, to be a center fielder"—helps elucidate why, in both the United States and Europe, so many of the best athletes come from ethnic ghettos.

The ease and self-assurance envied by Zlatan and Portnoy belong—in their immigrant minds, at least—to the dominant native caste. The polite, restrained white Anglo-Saxon Protestant American ruling class of Portnoy's childhood is scarcely distinguishable from the polite, restrained native Protestant Swedes of Zlatan's. Indeed, in Roth's later novels, "Swede" will become the ultimate marker of untroubled gentility: in *The Professor of Desire* (1977), the Jewish main character lives in a ménage à trois with two Swedish girls, and in *American Pastoral* (1997), the Jewish main character is known as "the Swede" because of his blond Gentile ease. Portnoy and Zlatan feel looked down on and excluded by this caste. Fittingly, to this day the committee of Swedes that awards the Nobel Prize for Literature still denies Roth the final token of acceptance. (Portnoy would argue that they couldn't possibly comprehend Jewish angst.)

Both Zlatan and Portnoy yearn with wonder for that incomprehensible being: the blonde native girl who, miraculously, feels at home in the place where she lives. To attain her would be to conquer this alien society. But she seems unattainable. Zlatan recalls "being at the Borgar School in Malmö and seeing chicks in Ralph Lauren polo shirts and practically wetting my trousers when I wanted to ask them out." Thirteen-year-old Portnoy skates around a frozen local lake behind gaggles of Gentile girls and marvels, "The *shikses*, ah, the *shikses*. . . . How do they get so gorgeous, so healthy, so *blond*?" He dreams of skating up and introducing himself as a *goy* named Alvin Peterson. ("I have to speak absolutely perfect English. Not a word of Jew in it.") But he is sure his big nose will expose his origins. Similarly, Zlatan (equally anxious about his own big nose) admits that hard as he tried in adolescence to dress like a posh Swede, he always ended up looking "Rosengård from top to toe."

Both men first encounter the dominant native class at age seventeen: Portnoy goes to Ohio for college; Zlatan becomes a professional soccer player. Gradually, through the medium of blonde native girls, they start to integrate. During Portnoy's freshman year at college, he spends Thanksgiving in Iowa with the family of his Gentile college girlfriend. Unused to WASP etiquette, he is astounded when her father greets him before breakfast with the words, "Good morning." It's a phrase never heard in the Portnoy household. "At breakfast at home I am in fact known to the other boarders as 'Mr Sourball' and 'The Crab.'"

Compare Zlatan's wonder at his future wife, the perfect Swedish blonde Helena: "She came from a model family from Lindesberg, one of those families where they say, 'Darling, would you please pass me the milk?', whereas we at table mostly just hurled death threats at each other." To Helena, Zlatan is "a miserable Yugo, with a fast car and a gold watch, . . . who played his music too loud." She teaches him about fish knives and forks and how to drink a glass of good wine. (It turns out you don't down it in one gulp like milk.) Portnoy briefly shacks up with a posh WASP who "knew how to eat her dessert using two pieces of silverware (a piece of cake you could pick up in your hands, and you should have seen her manipulate it with that fork and that spoon—like a Chinese with his chopsticks!)."

Gradually, success, native blondes, and painfully acquired table manners raise Portnoy and Zlatan from the ghetto. Portnoy becomes "Assistant Commissioner for The City of New York Commission on Human Opportunity," and Zlatan becomes the best-ever Swedish soccer player.

Their parents follow their sons' ascent with awe. Soon after Zlatan turns pro with Malmö, he notices a graying man watching a training session from far away beneath some trees. His father—who had never bothered to watch him play when Zlatan was a kid—has finally shown up. Zlatan recalls, "'Look,' I wanted to shout, 'Look! Look closely! Your son is a wonderful soccer player.'" Soon, Zlatan writes, his father's house "became a sort of museum of my career. He cut out every article, every little news item, and he still does." And here is Zlatan's twin across the water, Portnoy: "Whenever my name now appears in a news story in the *Times*, they bombard every living relative with a copy of the clipping. Half my father's retirement pay goes down the drain in postage, and my mother is on the phone for days at a stretch and has to be fed intravenously."

The parents can enjoy the success only vicariously, because it's difficult for the prodigal son to introduce them into polite society. When Zlatan flies his family to Dubai on vacation, Zlatan's mother bops his brother Aleksandar on the head with her shoe in business class at six in the morning, and a brawl erupts. Helena doesn't know where to look.

Zlatan buys the exact pink suburban house in Malmö that he had fantasized about as a ghetto teenager. He even wins the Jerring Prize, in which the Swedish public elects its favorite sportsman (usually some blond skier). The bad boy is moved to tears: no previous award had touched him as much. "Maybe I understood it as a sign . . . that I was truly accepted, not just as a soccer player, but as a person, despite all my outbursts and my background." He hasn't merely become a great athlete. He has accomplished something just as difficult: he has become a Swede.

No wonder both men live the ideology of integration and antidiscrimination: it has enabled their own personal journeys. Assistant commissioner Portnoy fights for the rights of others to leave their ghetto. As he informs an Israeli girl, "Who do you think got the banks to begin to recruit Negroes and Puerto Ricans for jobs in this city? . . . To do that simple thing? This *pig*, lady—Portnoy!"

Zlatan, too, crusades against segregation. When he joins Inter Milan, he is disgusted by the setup he finds in the locker room: Brazilian players sit in one corner, Argentineans are in another, and everyone else has their corner, too. Zlatan understands people sitting with their friends—that happens at all clubs—but "here they did it on the basis of nationality. That was so primitive!" He tells the club's president, Massimo Moratti, that the national cliques must go. These attacks on segregation are about the only views on society Zlatan expresses in his book.

Success doesn't quite mean a happy ending, though. Ghetto scars never go away. Portnoy ends his novel still very much in therapy with Spielvogel. Zlatan, playing for the great FC Barcelona, feels snubbed by Barça's cold, courteous (almost Swedish) coach, Josep Guardiola. Guardiola is a Catalan running a Catalan institution; Zlatan is the outsider. When Guardiola stops talking to him, Zlatan again feels "like that separate, difficult boy from the ethnic neighborhood who didn't really belong. . . . It was just like in the juniors at Malmö FF." After he finally throws an old-fashioned Portnoyesque tantrum at Guardiola, his fate at Barcelona is sealed.

Just as a generation of novelists told the story of Jewish America, and music the story of black America, the arts are now creating a narrative for the European immigrant experience. Zlatan was given a podium because he is a brilliant athlete—but there must be countless other second-generation kids sitting in their childhood bedrooms around the Continent, aching to tell their versions.

Lionel Messi
June 2013

This week a blot appeared on Lionel Messi's résumé. A Spanish financial crimes prosecutor lodged a legal filing accusing him and his father of committing tax fraud worth more than $5 million. The Messis deny it. Is Messi the latest global brand—after Apple, Starbucks, Google, Amazon, and Bayern

Munich's president, Uli Hoeness—to have his reputation sullied by alleged tax evasion?

Almost all great athletes nowadays grow up shielded from normal life. They are encouraged to concentrate on sport, while the entourage—a mix of family and longtime confidants—runs everything else. The entourage finds advisers to handle money. These advisers are often chosen more for their charm and proximity than their expertise. Messi's father said of the tax allegations, "It is all a mistake. You have to speak about this to the tax experts and lawyers who need to clear it up. I don't understand what is going on. I don't manage these matters. I am resident in Argentina."

The court filing says the Messis hid "significant income" from his image rights by channeling earnings through tax havens such as Uruguay and Belize. According to the filing, Messi and his father displayed "total opaqueness" toward the Spanish authorities.

Whatever the truth, one difference stands out between Messi and someone like Hoeness: The German is a savvy businessman who understood the benefits of a Swiss bank account. Messi is a soccer player only. Not much seems to go on in that little head. He has never been heard to say an interesting sentence. He is an uncharismatic introvert, whose home life with girlfriend and baby son bores the public. Messi is interesting only as a player.

He sees the field better even than spectators high in the stands. Dribbling with three-quarter steps, he can change direction faster than any opponent. Being tiny, he has superior balance to bigger opponents. And unlike some great dribblers, he is focused on the goal. In 2012 he scored a record (and almost inconceivable) ninety-one goals in sixty-nine games. He has been voted European Player of the Year four years running, another record. He has won two European Champions Leagues and five Spanish titles with Barcelona. When he met the new soccer-loving Argentine pope Francis in April, it was unclear who was more in awe of whom.

More than that, Messi makes the world happier. On the field he resembles a child at play. When he receives a ball and doesn't touch it, but sets off running and lets it trot alongside him, he looks like a boy out with his dog. The world's second-best player, Cristiano Ronaldo, perennially scowls, but Messi either looks blank or smiles. There is nothing cynical about his play. He seldom fouls, refuses to be substituted even in pettifogging games, and continues chasing around long after victory is sealed—which is how he got to ninety-one goals. We live in the age of Messi, and perhaps the best way of spending these years is to watch every match he plays.

Messi proves his quality in public every week. That sets him apart within the global elite. A constant background noise during these years of crisis has been the tumbling of reputations. People at the top repeatedly turn out to be frauds: bank traders register huge "profits" that end up destroying their banks, chief executives appear on magazine covers one moment and in the dock the next, and celebrated athletes get busted for drugs. (No drug could help anyone dribble like Messi.) David Cameron might not have become British prime minister if his rich parents hadn't sent him to Eton, and Hollywood's PR machine can turn an ordinary actor into a "star," but Messi is a rare member of the 1 percent who indisputably got there on merit. Others have feet of clay; he has feet of gold. Consequently, few complain about his earnings, which *Forbes* estimates at $41.3 million this year. His wealth is generally considered deserved.

Still, even Messi has things to prove this coming year. Barcelona— Europe's preeminent team in the Messi era—was humiliated by Bayern Munich in the Champions League semifinal this spring. Messi's challenge now is to return Barça to the top.

However, he has the most to prove in his own country. Although he has hung onto his Rosario accent, he is not beloved among Argentines, who often dismiss him as spiritually Spanish. He has been accused of not singing the national anthem. Despite those ninety-one goals, he finished third in the voting for best Argentine sportsman of 2012. He has won nothing yet with Argentina's full national team (though he led a youth side to Olympic gold in 2008). Some say he shines for Barcelona thanks chiefly to his brilliant teammates—most of whom, playing for Spain, became European and world champions without him.

By convention, great players prove themselves at World Cups. If Messi leads Argentina to glory in Brazil next year, most people would agree he is the best ever. No tax scandal would diminish that.

George Best
September 2013

Review of Duncan Hamilton, *Immortal: The Approved Biography of George Best* (Century)

After George Best began drinking at Manchester United in the late 1960s, the club's manager, Matt Busby, used to call him into his office. "He talked quietly to me," Best would recall. "He screamed at me. He suspended me. He fined me. He put an arm around me. He did everything humanly possible." But Busby—who like many Britons of the time didn't understand alcoholism—failed. Best, probably the most gifted British soccer player ever, went from social drinker to alcoholic.

Today a club would arrange counseling, but Busby allowed Best to drift away. Perhaps, the manager said later, it was because his earlier United team had died in the Munich air crash of 1958. In Busby's words, "I had lost the other lads. That maybe made me more lenient with those who came afterwards." Or perhaps Busby was soft on Best for the same reason most people were. As Busby's son Sandy asked Best at the old man's funeral in 1994, "You know he loved you?"

One tantalizing question hangs over Duncan Hamilton's diligent, highly readable biography: could better handling have saved Best from alcoholism? Hamilton, twice winner of Britain's William Hill award for sports book of the year, suggests an answer.

Best was born in 1946 into an apparently functional Presbyterian family in Belfast. His father was an iron turner in the shipyards, his mother then still a teetotal housewife. The boy was shy, polite, and intelligent (Hamilton says his IQ was nearly 150). Joining United at age fifteen, he boarded with a suburban Manchester landlady called Mrs. Fullaway, who would become a British legend herself. "He's a grand lad," she says in one of Best's first newspaper profiles. "He doesn't smoke or drink and eats everything up I serve him." In the profile, Best says he has no time for women and doesn't dance.

Yet his talent and his beauty changed everything. More like the rising sixties pop stars than the gray fifties soccer players, Best considered himself an entertainer: "I think I'd let people down if I didn't put on a show." A narcissistic performer, he would lie awake before games, visualizing brilliant solo feats. His hero wasn't so much a soccer player but Zorro, the masked swordsman of the Hollywood movies who outwitted and mocked his enemies.

Soon Best was wearing his hair long and buying new outfits every day. Mrs. Fullaway's house drew flocks of women (Best said he once slept with seven within twenty-four hours) and reporters. At first he loved the attention. To satisfy requests from fans, United's apprentices were commandeered to stuff locks of his hair into envelopes. But gradually the attention got out of control. "An amazing number of people," said Best, "walk up to you while you're trying to take a pee and want to shake hands with you." He had become one of the first modern celebrities.

His career peaked in May 1968, the month of youth, when United beat Benfica to win the European Cup. Best scored, but to his disgust he didn't give the brilliant solo display he had visualized. Afterward, he said, "I went out and got drunk."

Though only twenty-two, he would never win another medal. He'd expected United to rule Europe for years, but instead they declined around him. Almost compulsively competitive, he couldn't handle losing. Meanwhile, his once-dreary hometown was collapsing into sectarian conflict, and people wouldn't leave him alone. Having begun drinking to mask his shyness, he ended up drinking to escape. His career faded with the 1960s.

He became Britain's most public alcoholic, yet few could see what was happening to him. The mainstream British belief then was that drunkenness was funny. Even Best himself, in later after-dinner speeches, tended to treat the whole thing as a joke: "In 1969 I gave up women and alcohol. It was the worst twenty minutes of my life." You close the book feeling that a crazy adult life and lack of any guidance made him an alcoholic.

After leaving United in tears in 1974, he had cameo spells with various small clubs. Occasionally, the old brilliance resurfaced. In 1980, in an indoor game in San Jose, California, I saw him stamp on the ball to send it over his opponent's head.

By then he had endured his mother's death from alcoholism, for which he blamed himself. Later came bankruptcy, prison, divorces, and a liver transplant. A keen reader in later years, he treated the disasters philosophically. Surviving so long was a sort of success, he said.

He died in 2005 at age fifty-nine and was given practically a state funeral in Belfast, which named its airport after him. Almost no other symbol unites Northern Ireland's Protestants and Catholics.

Immortal strips away the myth to show the human Best. Hamilton is a guarantee of quality, but not in this case of brilliance. Approved and helped by Best's sister Barbara, Hamilton catalogs the drinking, yet never quite gets inside the alcoholic's head. It's as Best suspected: nobody could understand what it was like to be him.

Eusébio
January 2014

No great footballer grew up further from great football than Eusébio, the Portuguese forward who died of a heart attack on Sunday, January 5, 2014, aged 71. Born in 1942 in the Portuguese colony of Mozambique, he spent his youth playing barefoot on dirt fields. His closest contact with the game in the motherland was listening to Benfica's matches on a crackling radio. Yet he became Portugal's most famous footballer, used as a national symbol by the country's fascist government.

Eusébio da Silva Ferreira was one of eight children of a white railway mechanic from Angola and a black mother. Blessed with a boxer's torso and a sprinter's legs, he ran 100 meters in 11 seconds while still a teenager. He played unpaid for the local Sporting club.

A chance conversation in a Lisbon barbershop in 1960 changed his life: a Brazilian coach, whose team had toured Mozambique, rhapsodised about the youngster to Benfica's coach Bela Guttmann. Guttmann flew to Mozambique and signed Eusébio for a pittance. Eusébio would always remember a newspaper photograph of his widowed mother sitting at a table with her arms around a pile of money.

Benfica flew him to Lisbon. But Sporting Lisbon—for whose Mozambican franchise Eusébio had played—claimed him too. He spent months in the Algarve waiting for the quarrel to subside. In his first big game for Benfica in 1961, a friendly against Pele's Santos, he scored three goals as a substitute. "Who's that guy?" Pele asked.

Within two weeks of joining Benfica, Eusébio was playing for Portugal. In May 1962, he ended his first professional season by scoring twice as Benfica beat Real Madrid 5–3 in the European Cup final. After the match, Real's great Alfredo Di Stéfano gave him his shirt—a symbolic handing over of the mantle.

Eusébio lost his other three European finals, but he won eleven Portuguese titles with Benfica and always transfixed fans. A twenty-first-century athlete in a much slower era of football, he achieved precision at top speed. He smacked the heavy leather balls of the day so hard that keepers just prayed for survival. In 1965 he was voted European Footballer of the Year.

Little of his career was shown on TV, and the one month when he registered worldwide was his only World Cup—in England in 1966. His nine goals for Portugal made him the tournament's leading scorer. His four that beat North Korea after Portugal had trailed 3–0 represented "one of the best individual performances you'll ever see," said England's Bobby Charlton. Portugal's ensuing semifinal against England was scheduled for Goodison Park in Liverpool, where the Portuguese had played twice and felt at home. However, England's Football Association belatedly arranged a switch of venue to Wembley in London, a bigger stadium and England's base. The Portuguese had to take a train down the evening before the game. Why was the match moved? "We were poor and small. England was rich and powerful," Eusébio told the journalist Gabriele Marcotti. England's 2–1 victory left him forever feeling cheated, convinced that Portugal would have won in Liverpool. Famously, he cried on the field. "I looked at the sky and said, 'Lord what have I done to deserve this?' and that's when the tears came."

Yet he could also be magnanimous in defeat. In the 1968 European Cup final against Manchester United, again at Wembley, he blasted a cannonball at United's keeper Alex Stepney, who somehow caught it. Eusébio repeatedly patted Stepney on the back, tried to shake his hand, and when rebuffed, gave him the thumbs-up.

Several richer foreign clubs tried to sign him from Benfica. However, the Portuguese dictator António Salazar wouldn't let him leave, and to ensure he stayed, even made him do three years' military service in the anti-aircraft artillery. For Salazar, Eusébio was the ideal symbol of the Portuguese empire: a determinedly apolitical sportsman whose magnificent body seemed to incarnate the natural treasures of the colonies. Salazar, Eusébio said long after the dictator's death, "was my slave master, just as he was the slave master of the entire country." However, he hadn't spoken out during his career. He had feared jail, he later explained.

Mozambique's armed struggle for independence raged during his prime. Eusébio never backed it. Even his nickname, "The Black Panther," discomfited him with its echo of the radical American Black Panther movement. Eventually he reconciled his two homelands, telling the British sociologist Gary Armstrong: "I represented Africa and Portugal."

In 1975 he moved to North America, to earn about four times more than at Benfica. He began with the Boston Minutemen, helped Toronto Metros-Croatia become North American champions in 1976, and wound down his career with the now long-forgotten Las Vegas Quicksilvers and New Jersey Americans. After six operations on the same knee, he retired in 1979. He had scored 733 goals in 745 professional matches. In later years he limped, slept into the afternoons, and overdid the whisky. Yet he remained beloved in Lisbon. He hoped his funeral procession would pause by his statue outside Benfica's Stadium of Light, before entering the stadium. Portugal's government has declared three national days of mourning.

PART II:

Managers and General Managers

Glenn Hoddle and Tony Blair
June 1998

A re Glenn Hoddle, England's soccer coach, and Tony Blair, the British prime minister, in any way related?

The evidence is piling up. Hoddle, a devout Christian and keen singer, spent a formative spell in France with Monaco before getting his first big break as a team manager with Chelsea. Two years ago he became the youngest ever England coach, replacing the scandal-hit Terry Venables.

Hoddle made Paul Gascoigne the key member of his team, but the moment Gazza stepped out of line he dropped him from the World Cup squad. Now Hoddle is the undisputed boss of the England side.

Blair, a devout Christian and keen singer, spent a formative spell in France as a Paris bartender before joining the Labour Party in Chelsea. Last year he became the youngest British prime minister in two centuries, replacing the scandal-hit Tory government. He made Gordon Brown the key member of his cabinet, but the moment Brown stepped out of line, complaining that the prime minister's job should have been his, Blair's aides leaked to the press that Brown had "psychological flaws." Brown remains minister of finance, but Blair sets the agenda.

Few of the similarities between the two men are coincidental. The mood in British soccer and politics in recent years has been uncannily alike. Blair and Hoddle have come to power on the same wave.

What unites them is that they are outsiders: Blair within the Labour Party and Hoddle in English soccer. Labour was wary of Blair because he was not a member of the tribe. He had not worked in the mines, at sea, or in the railways; he had soft hands and was married to a lawyer. It was said that he did not know "The Red Flag," Labour's unofficial anthem, by heart.

Nor does he belong to any particular British class or region. He was born in Scotland but soon moved to England, and his father, who had been adopted by a working-class family, rose in the world. Blair went to private school and, in a school election at the age of twelve, briefly stood as a Conservative candidate.

Hoddle was not a member of the soccer tribe. He grew up in Harlow, Essex, an antiseptic, anonymous New Town, not the traditional working-class background of most players.

He became even more isolated within the game when, on a soccer trip to Bethlehem, he found God. After that he would not swear or do anything to excess, which made many other players regard him with suspicion. Furthermore, he stood out in English soccer as an artist among battlers.

As outsiders, Blair and Hoddle would not normally have risen to the top. However, their luck was that the more traditional leaders had failed. Labour, led by members of the party tribe, had lost four general elections in a row, and in desperation turned to Blair. Soon afterward the UK did too, after years of sleaze and decay. English soccer had been decaying too, though Venables, who took charge in 1994, had improved things. But image remained his problem, and so the Football Association turned to Hoddle.

These two outsiders were not interested in tradition. Blair knew the UK had won World War II and that it had long been a sovereign state, just as Hoddle knew that England had won the World Cup in 1966—he had run through Harlow that day waving a banner. But neither man thought these memories should determine policy. Blair, for instance, decided to treat European monetary union as an economic issue alone. Hoddle deserted England's traditional long-ball game.

Both also deserted the romantic schools that had helped shape them. Blair, who joined a far-left Labour Party, has been cruel to the Left in power. Hoddle, once the star of a Tottenham side that played romantic soccer, has turned out a dull but competent England team.

What these two men care about is not history but achievement. Blair wants to make the UK a modern economy; Hoddle wants to win the World Cup. This means keeping up with best practices around the world. Blair has borrowed key policies, such as welfare-to-work, from the United States, while Hoddle draws more from continental Europe. When England held Italy to a 0–0 draw in Rome last October, it was much commented on that his team played like an Italian side.

Success and failure become apparent much more quickly in soccer than in politics. If Hoddle's England does well in the World Cup, it will be seen as an omen for Blair's UK. Yet Blair would do well to resist crawling over any England success, as he has in the past, because this alienates the public. Instead, he should congratulate his long-lost brother quietly.

Daniel Passarella
December 2001

Sometime in the late 1980s Inter Milan were losing an away match by several goals when in the last minute they were awarded a meaningless penalty. The fearsome Argentine center-back Daniel Passarella began galloping forward to take it, but before he could get there, Alessandro Altobelli, reasoning, like any striker, that a goal is a goal, stepped up and hit the ball into the net.

Back in the locker room Passarella threw a fit. "It's always the same!" he screamed. "At 0–0 no one dares take a penalty, but when it doesn't matter anymore they all do." Grabbing his genitals, he added, "You are cowards! You have no balls, no cojones."

This went on for some time. Most of the Inter players were used to Passarella and paid no attention, but after a while Altobelli could take no more. He strode up to the Argentine and asked, "You talking about me?" Passarella knocked him out with a single punch, stripped, and wandered off to find the showers.

A few minutes later Altobelli came to. He stared about him enraged and then, spotting the fruit bowl customary in Italian locker rooms of the era, grabbed a little knife meant for peeling oranges. In the shower stalls he found a naked Passarella calmly shampooing his hair. "Come on then!" Passarella cooed at his knife-wielding colleague.

Altobelli didn't know what to do. He didn't really want to stab his teammate to death like Norman Bates in *Psycho*. He would probably have been fined, or even transfer listed. So he just stood in front of Passarella waving the knife for a while until, to his relief, other players dragged him away, and he could pretend this was happening against his will. All the while Passarella continued soaping his hair.

"Passarella," concluded the former player who told me the story, "was a thug, a murderer." That may sound harsh, but Passarella himself might take it as praise. As coach of River Plate, Argentina, Uruguay, and now Parma, he has prided himself on ferocity, toughness, discipline. He sometimes seems to believe he works in the army rather than the entertainment industry.

The past few years have been unkind to "El Kaiser." Argentina, the team he took to the quarterfinals of the last World Cup, has blossomed since his departure. Uruguay unexpectedly qualified for the World Cup nine months after he resigned as its manager. In November he took over Parma, proclaiming, in his thick Argentine accent, that he had the players to "finish in the top four" of Serie A. The team is now sixteenth in the table after four consecutive league defeats. Sunday's match at Atalanta could be his last.

Sacking a manager after a month in the job would normally be silly, but in this case it would simply correct the error of having hired him in the first place. The Passarella mode of management does not work, and had he not been a great player ("the best defender I have ever seen," judges Diego Maradona), Parma would never even have considered him.

Passarella is the victim of a youth spent in the Argentina of military dictators: of Juan Perón, who had served in the Italian army under Mussolini, and thugs like Jorge Videla, who had electrodes attached to the genitals of dissenters and made thousands of people "disappear." Passarella, short-haired *"gran Capitán"* of the Argentine team that won the 1978 World Cup for the generals, was their poster boy, their soldier on the pitch.

The generals lost office after the Falklands War, but Passarella completed a glorious playing career in Italy, socking Altobelli, head-butting an opposing side's physiotherapist, kicking a ballboy who was slow to return the ball. Later, as manager of Argentina, he revived all the generals' prejudices, saying he wouldn't pick homosexuals or players with earrings or long hair. The latter edict, unfortunately, ruled out Gabriel Batistuta and Fernando Redondo.

Batistuta had a haircut in order to play in the last World Cup, but Passarella's rule remains too silly for words. What, Maradona asks, about Mario

Kempes, Argentina's chief goalscorer in 1978, "who had a mane down to his waist?"

It sums up Passarella's problem as a manager: He can only work with some players some of the time. If you are short-haired, obedient, and respond well to being shouted at, you can work with him. If you aren't and don't, you can't. Senior players tend not to tolerate being bullied, which is why Passarella has always preferred working with youngsters.

Passarella, I was told by Mauricio Macri, president of Boca Juniors, "rules through fear." You won't find this childish and outdated method advocated in any management textbook. Few people perform consistently for a boss who scares them. Passarella's style is unvarying: exhortation coupled with bullying. "I'm trying to teach my players that we need courage, heart, and pride," he said last week.

But most players need different treatment at different times: Sometimes they need to be relaxed, sometimes to be listened to. Great soccer managers, like great fathers, know how to mix fear and love.

Maradona, in his frank and often hilarious memoir, notes another problem: If you demand total discipline you have to be totally disciplined yourself. But he recalls Passarella "smearing shit on the door-handles at the training camp, to amuse himself and his mates." That really will not do.

In December 2013, Passarella stepped down as president of River Plate. Under his rule in 2011, the famous club was demoted for the first time in its 110-year history. Happily, the team soon returned to Argentina's top division, but once again, the Passarella motivational methods did not seem to have paid off.

Arsène Wenger
May 2003

With the ironic courtesy the French do so well, Arsène Wenger fields half-witted questions from the British sporting press. Occasionally, the corners of his lips turn up and he ventures a joke: "You always feel sorry, you see. Even for Chelsea." Otherwise, the Arsenal manager's comportment retains its inhuman perfection: Never a hair out of place, and rarely a clause, either.

Wenger's work is almost as perfect. Admittedly, Arsenal has just surrendered the Premiership to Manchester United, but on Saturday afternoon it should dismiss Southampton to pick up a second FA Cup running. Though no bigger than several other English clubs, Arsenal constantly ranks among the country's two best teams. Nick Hornby, author of *Fever Pitch*, a memoir of supporting the club, says that whereas United wins prizes because it is a giant institution, Arsenal does so only because Wenger is its manager. The Frenchman is a standing reproach to almost every other manager in sport. Few have such a hinterland of knowledge, and no one else has used it so well.

Wenger's path began in the village of Duttlenheim, in Alsace, where his parents ran a restaurant. Growing up near the German border helped make him a cosmopolitan. He learned the Alsatian dialect and later German and English.

Though already planning a life in soccer, Wenger went to college to study economics. The litany of British soccer is that you must leave school at sixteen to dedicate yourself to the game, but the degree helped set him apart from other managers. Whereas some spend to show their status, he understands the value of money. He famously signed three great Frenchmen, Thierry Henry, Patrick Vieira, and Robert Pires, for less than the $35 million for which he sold the troubled Nicolas Anelka.

Wenger can buy players cheaply partly because he makes them himself. He learned this running Monaco's soccer academy, where his products included Lilian Thuram and Emmanuel Petit, who went on to win the 1998 World Cup with France. Later, as manager of Monaco's first team, he shaped George Weah so profoundly that when the Liberian was voted World Player of the Year in 1995, he gave the award to Wenger.

Many great players feel that sort of bond with Wenger. They respect him because he respects them—unusual in the hierarchical world of soccer. When the authors of a French book asked Thuram to nominate a mentor for a joint interview, there was only one possible choice. "It's always he who guides me, who inspires me," said Thuram of Wenger.

Wenger had turned the midfielder Thuram into a defender, just as he turned the defender Petit into a midfielder and the winger Henry into a center-forward. He took Henry, Vieira, and Anelka from reserve benches or youth teams to soccer's zenith. "Arsène has always analyzed the game of every player so as to bring him to reflection and progress," says Thuram. "He remains a *formateur*, an educator. Coaches sometimes forget that they are there to shape."

In fact, they usually forget this. Most sportsmen never realize their potential for want of a *formateur* like Wenger. A student of autobiographies, Wenger believes that greatness ensues only when a talent meets someone "who taps him on the shoulder and says, 'I believe in you!'"

After Monaco, Wenger went to Japan to coach and have his mind broadened. The Japanese dedication to detail spurred his progress to perfectionism. "You feel you have more chance of winning if you concentrate every part of your energy on how to win," he said. "If you lose a day by not concentrating on it, you feel guilty." It is a terrible realization that hits people in all fields and stops them from ever relaxing again. Wenger went from *Homo universalis* (by sporting standards) to monomaniac.

Arriving at Arsenal in 1996, he was effectively an unknown foreign chief executive with a funny accent taking over a high-profile traditional company in decline with many entrenched senior figures. His success was total.

Wenger used all the tools. Previously, the prematch meal at Arsenal had consisted of baked beans with Coca-Cola. "Some players went on to the pitch burping," Dennis Bergkamp reminisced. Not under Wenger. He also applied statistics—a common tool in American sports but never in soccer—to work out, for instance, when in a match particular players tended to tire and require substitution.

He introduced the doctrine of continuous improvement. In September, he was ridiculed for saying Arsenal could go through the season unbeaten, but he was only being a perfectionist. Losing the title this year hurt terribly. "The job of coach," as he defines it, "consists of many efforts to have, from time to time, a supersatisfaction, but, above all, many disappointments that you must surmount to return."

Of the million or so Britons who call themselves Arsenal fans, approximately none appears unhappy with Wenger. Besides transforming their club, the Alsatian has created several great players and changed British soccer management. The game needs more economists-turned–youth coaches.

Guus Hiddink
March 2006

I t's what glossy magazines call a "dream home." The nineteenth-century mansion on the Amstel River in Amsterdam is still being renovated, but Guus Hiddink and his girlfriend plan to move in soon. The world's most sought-after soccer coach has never been a workaholic, and as a fifty-nine-year-old multimillionaire he's had enough of driving to practice every morning. Now he intends to live Amsterdam's bohemian, arty life. Only the job of England's manager might entice him away.

For months Hiddink has been linked with every big coaching job in soccer. Last week he said he was quitting PSV Eindhoven, the provincial Dutch club where he has spent much of his career. This summer he will coach Australia at the World Cup, and afterward take over another national team. We will soon discover whether it is Russia, as the oligarch Roman Abramovich hopes, or England.

Hiddink is one of six sons of a village schoolteacher from the Achterhoek, or "Back Corner," of the eastern Netherlands. The Back Corner is wooded and quiet, and on visits home from stints in Madrid or Seoul, Hiddink enjoyed tootling along its back roads on his Harley-Davidson Fatboy. "Pom-pom-pom-pom-pom." He puffs out his cheeks to mimic the motor's roar.

Growing up among brothers—two of whom also became professional players—prepared him for a life among sportsmen. "I learned to share, listen, and communicate," he has said. Hiddink is a man at ease with other men. He has the gift for the right friendly gesture, grabbing your shoulders from behind by way of greeting, happy to talk but also to sit listening while others tell stories. He is a large, soothing presence.

He grew up milking cows, plowing behind two horses, and dreaming of becoming a farmer. But Dutch agriculture was already dying, and he went into soccer instead. At nineteen he became assistant coach of the Back Corner's semiprofessional club, De Graafschap. The head coach spotted in training sessions that his young assistant could play a bit, and so Hiddink made an unusual career move: from coach to player. The handsome, round-faced, wavy-haired playmaker was too lazy and slow for the top, but he did play with George Best on the San Jose Earthquakes. "I was his roommate," says Hiddink, enjoying what to him is a quirky American word, and he mimics himself fielding the phone calls from Best's groupies: "George is not here. George is sleeping."

In 1984 Hiddink became PSV's assistant coach. He waited three years for the head coach to be sacked, took his job, and a year later was holding aloft the European Cup. Hiddink, then sporting a Groucho Marx mustache, was a collegiate manager. He had less status than some of his players, but that didn't matter because he has what he calls "a small ego." He smoked cigarettes with his stars, swapping jokes and listening to their ideas as if they were brothers. In the Dutch tradition, Hiddink respects player power.

Later, when coaching in Turkey and Spain, he arrived at a defining insight. He decided he would ignore the circus around soccer: death threats, newspaper headlines, or what the club's vice president supposedly said to the center-forward's mistress. "Mister, let it go," urged his assistant at Valencia. "Limit yourself to soccer." Since then, Hiddink has.

In 1998 he led Holland to the World Cup semifinals. In 2002, more surprisingly, he repeated the trick with South Korea. Hiddink taught the formerly obedient Korean players to think for themselves on the pitch. He is now doing the same with Australia, and would do so with England. Hiddink always wants autonomous, thinking "Dutch" players: a center-back who knows when to push into midfield, a striker who drops a few yards.

In Korea Hiddink achieved a status possibly unprecedented for a soccer manager. The country had craved global recognition, and he delivered it. His autobiography in Korean reportedly sold more than 160,000 copies in the first month of publication. Altogether in 2002, thirty-seven books with Hiddink's name in the title appeared in Korean, most of them in the self-help genre. In the Back Corner, Korean tour buses made pilgrimages to the Hiddink ancestral home. After the World Cup, the man himself dropped in on his octogenarian parents. "Well, it wasn't bad," admitted his father. "Coffee?"

Hiddink returned to PSV and last year took the club to within minutes of another Champions League final. In his spare time he coached Australia to their first World Cup since 1974. But meanwhile the Dutch tax police were after him. Hiddink had claimed to be living in Belgium, where taxes are lower, but the taxmen disputed this. According to Hiddink, they tapped his phone calls to find out where he spent his nights. These days the answering machine of his cell phone warns, in German, "Careful, the enemy is listening." This German phrase from World War II appears to be Hiddink's way of accusing the taxmen of Gestapo practices. Their interrogations helped persuade him to leave the Dutch labor market.

Russia has offered him a nice gig: a fantastic salary to live beside the Amstel and occasionally pop to Moscow on a private jet provided by Abramovich. But the job lacks the magic of being England's manager. Hiddink would relish England's three biggest challenges. He has the psychological expertise to inspire tired multimillionaires. He loves dealing with difficult characters: Wayne Rooney would be a cinch for him. And he would improve the thinking of a team that has everything but intellect. Hiddink has a better résumé than any English candidate for the job, and better English than the other foreign candidates.

London too offers a bohemian, arty life. His girlfriend would be an hour from her beloved Amsterdam. But Hiddink isn't sure whether he wants the job. He dreads the British tabloids crawling all over his family. In any case, the Football Association may choose an Englishman instead of the best man. It could be another case of British newspapers plus British fear of immigrant labor damaging British national life.

Sven-Göran Eriksson
May 2006

What if England had to go to the World Cup without Wayne Rooney? Sven-Göran Eriksson, England's manager, gave his trademark weak smile. The Swede is often depicted as being entirely without charisma, but in fact he has the gentle charm of a family doctor. We were sitting in his little office in London's Soho Square: two desks shoved together, a table to chat at, and a sign on the wall saying, "Talk low, talk slow, and don't say too much," which may be the Eriksson family motto. It was two weeks before Christmas. Rooney was healthy. His broken foot at Euro 2004 had probably sealed England's elimination, but there was no reason to think that would happen again.

"It should be very good to have Plan B and Plan C," Eriksson replied, "but the fact is very simple: We have only one Wayne Rooney, and as he played in Portugal, that was fantastic. As long as he was on the pitch, we kept the ball very well up front. We couldn't find another one. But who finds two Wayne Rooneys?"

Now Rooney has a broken foot again and may miss the entire World Cup, Eriksson's last tournament managing England. "I think we will win it this time," the Swede said this month. Whether Eriksson's last shot at eternity comes off or not, we can already assess his legacy. We have discovered his one outstanding quality. We know his impact on English soccer, and on British life. And we have some indications even for the coming World Cup.

The Eriksson era began during a sumptuous dinner one night in Rome in 2000 when he took a call from Britain on his cell phone. He chatted for a couple of minutes in English, then turned to his assistant at Lazio Roma, Tord Grip: "What do you say to being my assistant manager with England?" A Swedish friend dining with them shouted, "Never England! That's bad food, ugly women, and terrible weather." But Eriksson and Grip were already discussing which players to pick.

To Eriksson, England didn't mean ugly women at all (quite the contrary). It didn't merely mean $6.6 million in salary. It meant memories of the Saturday afternoons of his youth in the backwoods town of Torsby watching English soccer on television, supporting Liverpool.

In January 2001 Eriksson became England's fourth manager in four years. The country's soccer was in the midst of an identity crisis. The traditional English game—muscular, not very clever, long balls hoofed forward by big men on muddy pitches—had failed. England needed to adopt the intelligent passing soccer of continental European teams. Yet no English manager seemed capable of this. For the first time ever, England hired a foreigner.

Not everyone was delighted. To quote the *Sun*: "What a climb-down. What an admission of decline. What a humiliation. What a terrible, pathetic, self-inflicted indictment. What an awful mess." The newspaper organized a protest, which prompted comedian Jeremy Hardy to comment, "I don't know why everyone's making such a fuss about a foreign manager when it's having all those English players in the team which is the problem."

Eriksson set about teaching those English players to think autonomously, as continental ones do. In his early days on the job he would call them in one by one for chats before a match. After explaining the opposition's tactics in the player's zone of the field, he would ask, "What would you do?" The player would generally look blank and say, "I dunno. You're the boss, Boss."

In England, the manager had traditionally done any thinking that was required. But gradually Eriksson's players began doing some, too. This was quite a turnabout in a team—captained by David Beckham—that is rich in everything but intellect.

But the change in England's players had little to do with Eriksson. He is not a revolutionary, but merely a symptom of a foreign revolution that began in English soccer a decade ago when Frenchman Arsène Wenger became manager of Arsenal. None of Eriksson's first-choice eleven now plays his club soccer under an English manager. Eriksson believes that traditional English soccer no longer exists. "No one is playing it like that today in the Premier League," he remarked in Soho Square. He said it might still be possible to speak of "northern European soccer. Maybe." He has also noted that traditional drinking habits are disappearing from the English game.

On September 1, 2001, Eriksson's decreasingly English team beat Germany 5–1 in Munich. This was before everyone began hammering Germany, and it remains the zenith of his reign. But he entered the postmatch press conference unsmiling, said that the score line flattered England, and added that the most important thing was that the German coach's father recovered from the heart attack he had suffered that night.

This was wonderful psychology. Eriksson knew he would get credit for the victory anyway. By sidestepping the credit, he bought the chance to sidestep blame when England lost. But it also said something about him. In the words of the English poem, he can meet with triumph and disaster and treat those two impostors just the same.

He had learned this long before coming to England, during a career that has been an education in managing hysteria. His curriculum vitae is packed with "bubble clubs": Benfica, Fiorentina, and Lazio, run by megalomaniacal chairmen, covered by sensationalist newspapers, followed by unrealistic fans. Bubble clubs have a tendency to go bankrupt.

The soothing tedium of Eriksson's manner was the perfect antidote to these environments. When he was named England's manager, I was excited because a year earlier I had interviewed him in Rome. I had gold in my notebook! But turning to the relevant pages, I saw I had barely made a note. Eriksson had spoken fluently for nearly fifteen minutes while saying nothing. The second time I met him, at lunch with a small group in Zurich, we all hoped to get him chatting. Instead, he spent the meal politely questioning a Chinese journalist about Chinese soccer. His mediocre English—so rare for a Swede—also tends to neutralize inquiries. The sadness of the British media is that it is forever trying to extract words from Eriksson and Beckham, one of whom hardly says anything, while the other has nothing to say.

Only in his last months in England has Eriksson become more forthcoming. In Soho Square I asked him how he judged his own record on the job: quarterfinal of the World Cup 2002 in Japan and quarterfinal of Euro 2004 in Portugal.

"Ooohhh," he began. "If you had asked me the day before I took the job, of reaching the semifinal in Japan [sadly, it really was only the quarterfinal], I think the whole nation would have been happy with that." It's true that when he took over, England looked unlikely even to qualify for the World Cup. "If you asked the nation today, they wouldn't be happy with the quarterfinal. It has to be more, I suppose. It was okay in Japan, I think. We met Brazil, and we were not fit enough second half to compete with them, even if we had eleven against ten men. I was not happy with Portugal, to go out in the quarterfinal." He said the problem both times was that his players were tired after long seasons. Luckily, though, they would have an extra week of rest before this World Cup.

But surely one week couldn't be the only thing that has kept England out of the semis. "The last two times? I would say so." The only thing? "If you're not fit enough. . . . [I]n Japan, we never scored one goal the second half. So I think the main reason is that."

It's probably true that the English Premiership is physically more demanding than any other league. Yet Eriksson was refusing to acknowledge a pattern. The three games England has lost under him in major tournaments, against Brazil in 2002 and against France and Portugal in 2004, all followed the same sequence: the Englilsh start well and score in the first half, then retreat to their own penalty area where they tackle bravely and hoof the ball away blindly for the rest of the game in hope of a backs-to-the-wall triumph reminiscent of Dunkirk in 1940. But their opponents, allowed to have the ball and camp around England's goal almost without interruption, eventually score. Even England's victory over Argentina in 2002 mostly followed this pattern, except that the Argentines didn't score.

It seems a curious method, given that England now has excellent players capable of keeping possession. Has Eriksson failed to eradicate an ancient reflex of English soccer? "Well, it's nothing we try to do, but sometimes we are tired. We can't keep the ball, and then it ends up there." He added, "I think we were a little bit unlucky. France—how could we lose that game? Two stupid goals in two minutes, was it? And against Portugal, we could have won that game, except we didn't."

This summer will be different, he promises. "We are much better now than we were two years ago, four years ago." He points to *France Football* magazine's authoritative poll for European Player of 2005: second and third places went to two Englishmen, Frank Lampard and Steven Gerrard, while John Terry also made the top ten. "I don't know when England [last] had three in the top 10. And we had [Jamie] Carragher [at] number 20."

On the other hand, Rooney has broken his foot, and England's best goalscorer, Michael Owen, has only just recovered after five months out with a broken foot. Owen insists he is now fit, but he once told me, talking about his performance at Euro 2000: "I had just come back from injury, so I wasn't playing at my best. Sometimes they say it's as long as you've been injured, that's how long it takes until you're firing again. So if that was the case, I obviously wasn't playing to my best ability in Euro 2000."

This bodes ill. Indeed, during my interview with Eriksson, his World Cup wall chart dropped off his office wall: splat. Some of Eriksson's more credulous predecessors might have resigned there and then. The Swede merely chuckled.

He may not win the World Cup, but he has already left a mark on this country. It's mostly to do with the way he speaks. Unlike most of his predecessors, Eriksson doesn't use rhetoric drawn from the two world wars: no talk of hand grenades, trench warfare, players bloodying their shirts for England. Until this month, he never spoke as if England had a manifest destiny to win trophies. He doesn't believe that England should play its own brand of soccer. In short, he has quietly buried England's exceptionalism in soccer.

In one department he has been revolutionary. English soccer, like many English working-class professions, always observed the rule that experience trumped quality. That was why apprentice players cleaned the professionals' boots. Players were selected for England only after years of professional service, and then kept their places until years past their prime.

But Eriksson made Rooney England's youngest debutant ever. Now he is taking an even younger man to Germany: Theo Walcott, who has never appeared in a Premiership match and will be the youngest player on any squad at the World Cup. Picking Walcott was probably wrong, but it is brave.

In a small way Eriksson has changed British society, too. He showed that a foreigner could do "the second most important job in the country"—to quote the title of a book about England managers—without destroying the national essence. Britain is now dotted with foreign chief executives and sports managers, but Eriksson is the most visible example of the British economy's globalization. Even though he hasn't done a brilliant job, and despite the FA's pledge in 2000 that he would have an English successor, he as a foreigner has been sufficiently acceptable to most English fans that the man initially chosen to succeed him was a Brazilian, Luiz Felipe Scolari.

Scolari refused the job, fazed by English hysteria. But nothing ever shook Eriksson. The tabloids have devoured him for his foreignness, his love affairs, his defeats, and his flirts with better offers. All through it he has remained polite and bland. "I can't change the English press," he explains. "I suppose? I don't think so. But I know for sure they will not change me. Yes. Absolutely sure." In any case, he added, he didn't read newspapers. "And in fact if I buy them, I buy them for the Sudoku. I like that."

If he never wins a prize, his crowning moment will remain the press conference the night in Lisbon in 2004 that England lost to Portugal. Several hundred hard-bitten soccer journalists crowded into a sweaty hall to quiz the loser. He told them, "I'm really sorry about it. Once again I thought we had a good chance to reach the final here." It was bland as ever, yet in the circumstances simply to remain tedious was dignified, even heroic. When he finished, the journalists applauded. It wasn't because they thought he was a good coach. They just thought he was a good man.

José Mourinho
January 2007

This is the end game. José Mourinho may be paranoid, but now they really are out to get him. Behind closed doors men are scheming to oust Chelsea's coach. Juventus's manager, Didier Deschamps, admits he was approached to replace Mourinho, but says he won't. As a conspiracy theorist, Mourinho must feel vindicated. The intrigues around him accord with the way he interprets the world.

Mourinho was raised in Portugal under a regime that no longer exists in Europe: a fascist dictatorship. As a boy he lived on the estate of his great-uncle Mario Ascensao Ledo, sardine magnate and onetime president of Vitoria Setubal soccer club. The child Mourinho played soccer with a servant and attended private schools, thus escaping the miserable education then reserved for most Portuguese. He learned the languages—initially French, English, and Spanish—that made his career. Mourinho first rose in soccer as a translator, and his linguistic gifts helped attract Chelsea.

In 1974, when he was eleven years old, Portugal's Carnation Revolution brought down fascism. Most of his family's businesses were expropriated, and the estate was lost. Elsewhere, the childhood realm of Mourinho's future wife, Tami, was also being shattered. In what is now Angola, where her parents were Portuguese settlers, guerrillas fought colonial rule. Her father joined the Portuguese army and was shot and left disabled. When Portugal's new rulers surrendered the colonies in 1975, the family went as refugees to Lisbon, feeling betrayed.

Portugal's revolution was the last in western Europe. Most of us on this side of the Continent can no longer imagine hidden forces overturning our lives. Mourinho can.

Experiences like his and Tami's—common in poor countries—tend to produce conspiracy theorists. Intellectually, there are two sorts of countries: ones where people tend not to believe in conspiracy theories (most of western Europe) and ones where they do (poor countries). Thus, many Iraqis believe that Saddam Hussein is still alive, his execution staged; many Arabs assume the Jews were behind the September 11 attacks; and many Africans think Western scientists concocted AIDS in laboratories.

A peculiarity of Portuguese conspiracy theories is the centrality of soccer. This may be inevitable in a country whose two best-selling dailies are sports newspapers. Eusebio, the greatest Portuguese player ever, has explained that the English arranged Portugal's elimination from the World Cup of 1966 by moving the England-Portugal semifinal from Liverpool to London. Today many Portuguese assume that their team's exits from Euro 2000 and the World Cup of 2002 were fixed.

Just as Texas is the home of UFO sightings, so Portugal's second city of Porto nurtures soccer conspiracy theories. Porto's setting is enchanting: the mountains, the Douro River, the vineyards where port wine is made, the Atlantic. But the city's main buildings are mostly concrete monstrosities. Under fascism, the state spent on Lisbon instead. What bothered Porto almost as much were the perceived plots against its soccer. There are sometimes as many as nine top-division clubs playing in a thirty-mile radius of the city, perhaps the highest density in Europe, but the biggest is FC Porto, the club where Mourinho made his reputation. A story from 1940 has the fascist secret police arresting two Hungarian players of Porto as spies; one was later executed. Many locals still assume that Portuguese soccer is rigged against them.

In 2004 Mourinho took this mental heritage to England, where he found conspiracies everywhere. Here is a sample of his allegations, which English people are conditioned to dismiss as wacko:

- Arsenal controls the Premiership's fixture list and rigs it to give Chelsea a tough schedule. ("Is José Mourinho the only one who can look at the fixtures and find something very strange?")
- Sky Television broadcast Michael Essien's knee-high tackle on Liverpool's Didi Hamann hundreds of times, because it hates Chelsea and wanted Essien suspended. In fact, all of England

hates Chelsea. "When we lose there will be a holiday in the country."

- A hidden hand placed Chelsea in a strong group in this season's Champions League, forcing them to pile up yellow cards.
- "Something is happening with the English press in relation to Frank Lampard." Because Lampard is an excellent player, the press is scheming to undermine him.

Mourinho talks like this partly in order to unite his players against the world—and most players are dumb enough to fall for it—but he also appears to believe it.

British newspapers love his conspiracy theories. Rather than report an encounter between two brilliant teams, we cover Mourinho. This is partly due to British soccer's hierarchies. Players are not trusted to speak, and so the manager is the voice and face of the club. Mourinho's Armani cashmere coat became Chelsea's de facto crest. He is the English game's dominant personality, as malign as he is brilliant.

Now Chelsea's owner, Roman Abramovich, appears to be getting sick of him. The problem is not Mourinho's results. Match for match, he remains probably the most successful soccer coach ever. All the talk of Chelsea trailing Manchester United by six points in the league is a mere snapshot. Come May, Mourinho may well have clocked up his third title in three years. Meanwhile, Chelsea remains in the Champions League and in both domestic cups. Rather, his problem is his persona. His bad image in England—due to his team's workmanlike soccer, and to his paranoia—has clung to Chelsea.

Now others within the club are intriguing against Mourinho. The characteristic form of business in rich countries is the corporation. It is meant to provide transparency, reducing the scope for conspiracy theories. But Chelsea is a different animal. The club's power structures are rarely visible. Several men around Abramovich are each building an empire: his Russian advisers; Pino Zahavi, the Israeli agent; Chelsea's chief executive, Peter Kenyon; the sporting director, Frank Arnesen; and Mourinho. They never all sit down together for formal meetings. Private chats drive events. In this environment, a hidden hand can suddenly take away your realm. Mourinho understands how that works.

Glenn Hoddle
April 2008

Ehhhmmmmm," says Glenn Hoddle. After a monologue about the World Cup of 1998, the tournament that will always remain the highlight of his career, he falls silent. "The only problem is that you've done enough here to write a book. Ha, ha, ha, ha, ha, ha," he laughs loudly. "I've got to say, we've touched on things there that I haven't spoken about."

"You mean like visualization?" I ask.

"Yeah, a lot of that stuff. It's not been done with a reporter, as such. And even touching the England stuff as in depth as that."

That's what a journalist likes to hear. But it's too late. If we had had this interview ten years earlier, I could have sold it somewhere for a bag of money. Sadly, not many people care about Glenn Hoddle anymore. Before the interview a friend tells me, "At least you can find out whether he's nuts or not." The name Hoddle now chiefly evokes images of the born-again England manager who brought in faith healer Eileen Drewery to cure injured players and who was sure that England was going to win the World Cup of 1998 until it didn't. Where does Hoddle work now? Still at Wolves? No, nowhere anymore.

He is the Robert F. Kennedy of English soccer. American liberals sometimes lie awake at night wondering what would have happened if Bobby hadn't been shot dead by Sirhan Sirhan in the Ambassador Hotel in Los Angeles on June 5, 1968. Then he would have beaten Richard Nixon in the presidential elections later that year, and the United States would have pulled out of Vietnam, and. . . . But if you think like that you go mad. Similarly, you can't think about what would have happened if English soccer had chosen the Hoddle path. It's just that sometimes you can't help but wonder. And Hoddle can't either.

Like most people I had almost forgotten Glenn Hoddle, when one wet afternoon on a Parisian side street I answered my cell phone, and it was him. A week later we were sitting down at a table in the "Polo Bar" of a hotel in

Ascot. It's a posh place, walking distance from the racecourse. Fake Greek statues dot the cold lawn outside the window.

At first glance I don't recognize Hoddle because he's gone gray, but he still looks like a sportsman with his bodywarmer and red shirt, and those famous long legs folded beneath the table. We order cappuccinos, and he shows me the brochure for the soccer academy that he's trying to set up in Montecastillo in Spain: a second-chance academy for teenagers who have been cut by English clubs. He thinks he can get "15 to 20 percent" of the kids back into professional soccer. He says, "I'm excited. It's my company. [I have] freedom, with no chairman, chief executive, board of directors, referee making a silly decision—a minute to go, ruins your week—[or] a set of fans on [my] back. I've turned down six or seven jobs to keep this going. This is very, very, very much like a soccer club, in a way. And if we get onto the golf and the property side, with the Glenn Hoddle Academy, that could open doors for a second one pretty quickly." And Hoddle laughs at himself. "*He says, still trying to raise the money for the first.*"

He got the idea for the academy as a rising young manager at Swindon and Chelsea, when he kept having to tell seventeen- and eighteen-year-olds, "Sorry, but you're not good enough at the moment." He'd always tell the player, "Prove us wrong. I'd love to see you in a few years' time." But he didn't hear from many of them again.

"It was horrible having to do it," he says. "First experience of doing it to six eighteen-year-olds, when four of them broke down in the office and cried, I thought, 'Well, this isn't very nice. I thought soccer management was going to be a bit different to this.'" He decided then that when he had finished working as a manager, he would start the academy. John Syer, the sports psychologist who worked with Hoddle for years, once told me, "Glenn hides it well, but he has a heart of gold."

Still, it must have been hard for Hoddle the young manager to empathize with failures. Nobody had ever doubted that the boy from Harlow would make it. Hoddle says, "I was one that they were ready to sign on. I left school and went straight to an apprentice. Even though, when I look back at some of the clips, seventeen when I played: I was like a beanpole. Strong wind, and I'd have fallen over. But you have to have aggression. My first thing I ever did on a soccer pitch, I came on at seventeen against Norwich. Big Duncan Forbes was the center-half for Norwich. I broke his nose!" Hoddle bursts out laughing. "I ran for a ball, and it was right above him, and I was so excited, as a kid going on at White Hart Lane, I just jumped, and I was so determined to win this ball"—as he tells the story you know he can see that ball hanging in the air again—"and I caught him, and his nose went, 'Tffuuummmm.' Poor Duncan probably broke his nose about half a dozen times. It was my first minute of being on, and Spurs fans must have thought, 'Ooh, we've got a real Dave McKay here!'"

Yet even then Hoddle was developing his distinguishing quality: "That was me real gift, I thought: my vision to see a picture." He had learned it from Jimmy Greaves. When Hoddle was a fourteen-year-old schoolboy at Spurs in 1972, the worn-out old alcoholic had returned to train with his former club. Greaves had been granted a testimonial against Feyenoord to make some money. Hoddle says: "We played in a tight gym upstairs. It was ten a side, really tight, and he was in and around the goal all the time, and the one thing I saw was, before that ball was coming to him, he was forever looking 'round his shoulders. It was amazin'. 'Cause that was what he lived off, goalscoring: the ability to be looking and looking and looking, and he knows the ball is going to come, from where that girl is"—Hoddle points to a waitress at the other end of the Polo Bar—"and now it's being passed and he'd go 'Tcchoom'; he'd turn and pop it into the net before you even know it. And you'd think, 'Shit.' As that ball was coming he had that instant picture, where the goal was and where the defenders were. So he could swivel and hit it first time. It was such a tight game, it was amazin'. Okay, credit, I picked it up. Some people could have watched it and not seen it. But I learned off that."

In 1986 I moved with my parents from the Dutch town of Leiden to North London. On Saturdays I'd sometimes take the W3 bus from Alexandra Palace to Spurs. You went for Ossie Ardiles and Chris Waddle, but mostly for Hoddle. He could put the ball on your big toe with either foot.

I remember this when Hoddle says he sometimes tells his son Jamie, a promising cricketer, "J, when you go over that white line, you have to become an actor sometimes; you have to go into a different person. When you come off, you haven't got to be aggressive."

I tell him I'm surprised: I remember Hoddle as a player who seemed to bring his own personality onto the pitch. He seemed to have a calm about him.

"Hmmm," says Hoddle. "It's interesting you saw a calm. I always looked at me when I watched videos, and I think it was: I used to make myself look as if I had more time than other people. I think David Beckham's got that. Sometimes McEnroe looked like he had so much time when he's playing shots. I also think the ball changes shape when certain players are in possession of it. It becomes an attachment of their body, when with others it's not." He pauses, then: "That's something I was gifted. I think I had that from a very, very early age." (This is the closest he will come during our conversation to invoking God.) "I had that ability to not be under pressure until I was absolutely being kicked. Whereas some people can be put under pressure from ten yards. You start to close them and they start panicking." He laughs. "I didn't realize until later on in my life that I was actually visualizing for a split-second when I hit passes, and when I hit shots." Hoddle stands up, and on the Polo Bar's patterned carpet he assumes the pose that every English fan over the age of thirty-five still has in his head: Glenn Hoddle with his arms spread wide, about to hit a long pass. "So if I saw Tony Galvin," he explains, "on the left wing, and I saw the fullback, and Tony was there"—and twenty-five years later, Hoddle can still point them both out, somewhere in the air of the Polo Bar—"as I drop my head down to hit the ball, I can see him. Even now, to this day. I can see Tony Galvin, and I can see where I've got to hit the ball, over that fullback's head, and I know Tony'll be there." It makes him laugh: "I'm just visualizing seeing Tony. I know where he is; the tunnel's on that side. I know exactly where I am. I can see it!"

Nonetheless, Hoddle's Tottenham never won the title. He was something of an amusing irrelevance in English soccer. Because he was slim, and had beautiful long legs, and didn't charge around like a homicidal maniac, he was nicknamed Glenda. He played fifty-three times for England, but in most of those games he was expected to charge around like a maniac.

How often did he play in his own position? "Probably once, actually. It was Hungary away, qualifier. I played behind two strikers. I think I scored two and made one, or I scored one and made the two. That was the only time I played that way. They sort of played the midfield three behind me and let me go in just behind Trevor Francis and Paul Mariner."

I feed him an easy one: Does he agree with the view that England never put the trust in him that France put in his contemporary Michel Platini? "Absolutely. And I think if you cast your mind back to the eighties, particularly in this country, a creative player—it was so difficult. You had muddy pitches. You had rules where you could kick people; you could pull their shirts back. You could stop the creative player and not get booked.

"Your Wimbledons and your Watfords—that's the reason why those long-ball teams had some success. They'd wait for the back four to squeeze up to two yards from the halfway line, so you were playing in a 60-by-40 box, all the time, on, normally, mud. So for the creative players in them days"—and Hoddle's voice goes hushed with horror—"you're talking about a different game completely than now. And we had our head in the sand, we really did, about how the game could be played. Now it's completely different. And with the back-pass rule, the game is opened, spread out, on beautiful pitches."

"It was an ambition of mine to move abroad," he says. He had offers from Schalke, Cologne, and PSV Eindhoven, and very nearly went to Napoli, but in the end he chose Arsène Wenger's Monaco. In England, Hoddle the player never played more than a cameo role.

But when he became a manager he was going to change everything. In Rotterdam in October 1993 Ronald Koeman (who by then should already have been sent off) curled a free kick over the English wall. England lost to Holland and didn't qualify for the World Cup of 1994. The manager, Graham Taylor, was sacked. Long-ball soccer was discarded. At last, England was going to be turned into a European soccer country.

Initially, the task was given to Terry Venables, because in 1994 Hoddle was only thirty-six years old. Yet he was already player-manager of Swindon and had the team playing attractive continental soccer. Then he moved to Chelsea, and in 1996, at thirty-eight, he became England's youngest manager ever. He was given the opportunity he had never had as a player: to set English soccer on a new path. And one October night in 1997, he succeeded.

When I ask him which match during his tenure as England's manager made him proudest, he says, "Definitely Rome away. Italy." England had to draw in Rome to qualify directly for the World Cup. "Italy had won seventeen matches out of seventeen," says Hoddle. "Not even a draw."

He fielded eight defensive players. England put on the most disciplined performance most of their fans could remember, even if that sounds like damning with faint praise. Still, a couple of minutes from time it almost went wrong. Hoddle says:

> I don't know if you remember, 'cause I remember it like it was yesterday, because it was the only time in soccer where I actually physically felt my heart *jump*. Wrighty [Ian Wright] hit the post. Teddy [Sheringham] came in and—should have scored, maybe. Hit the target, got blocked, I think. And they came down the left-hand side, right in front of our bench. And they put a cross in, and Vieri backed away, had a header back across the goal. I remember Dave Seaman not moving.
>
> We weren't behind the header, we were watching it come back across, so I can't see whether it's going in the net. I came out in such a sweat. I really thought the ball had gone in the net.

After the game, when an elated Hoddle had confided his anxieties to Seaman, the keeper had told him, "It wasn't a problem; it was going wide." The way Hoddle tells it, you know Seaman had no idea where the ball was. Hoddle shakes with laughter.

The game ended 0–0 and has gone down in English legend as "The Italian Job." That evening, England had become Italy. Hoddle had created a modern team that had learned from other countries. The future of English soccer had arrived.

Several other England managers have attempted an "Italian Job" since, but usually in vain. The moment against Croatia at Wembley in November 2007 when six English defenders neglected to mark a single Croatian striker was more typical.

In Hoddle's mind there was a moment when his career turned, when it was decided that he'd be spending this winter's afternoon in the Polo Bar with me, and not on a throne somewhere. It was a moment at the World Cup in 1998, which felt like the moment when Vieri's header flew toward Seaman's top corner.

The moment: "When Sol Campbell scored and it was disallowed."

The match: England-Argentina in St. Etienne. Eighteen-year-old Michael Owen scored his solo goal. At halftime the score was 2–2. Sitting in the press stand, I looked up for the first time and saw Scottish journalist Patrick Barclay eating his hand. Barclay looked at me and raised a meaningful eyebrow: I also had at least five fingers in my mouth, he meant to say. Neither of us could understand it, because neither of us supported England.

Shortly after halftime Beckham kicked Diego Simeone softly, almost in slow motion, and was sent off. And shortly before the final whistle, in a full Argentine penalty area, with the scores still tied, Campbell headed the ball into the net. Hoddle says: "We thought we'd done it with ten men. And then to see five of your players celebrating by the corner flag, and Argentina coming down the right wing, and you've only got five outfield players!" Hoddle always knows which wing it was because he can still see it happening. "And I can remember Gary Neville sliding in at the far post just as the fella was gonna hit it. And he toes it away for a corner. And we're trying to get all the players back in. Amazin'. Amazin'."

When the match went to penalties, Paul Ince and David Batty missed their kicks. Not only had England not practiced penalties, but Batty had never taken one in his life.

"Did you enjoy those nights, those moments?" I ask.

"They're fantastic nights, they are," says Hoddle. "That's why you do the jobs. You don't remember how much money you earned. They're the things that you remember."

But surely St. Etienne is a bad memory?

"Well, was it? It was a titanic effort. We went down to ten men with a complete second half, almost, and extra time, against a top, top team. It weren't against Switzerland. And we nearly pulled it off. We should have done, if the referee had done his job right. David should never have been sent off. And Sol Campbell's goal—well, still to this day I can't understand why he's disallowed it." (Here is where Hoddle's visualization skills fail him. Beckham kicked Simeone, and just before Campbell headed home, Alan Shearer elbowed the Argentine keeper.)

I quote another retired player, who said that the moments that you're all sitting broken in the locker room together, heads down, are also special moments. The solidarity of the shared pain is something to treasure. You just don't realize it at the time.

Hoddle is talking quietly now. His high has passed. "They are. Unfortunately, they're not the one you think it's going to be. What I always wonder, if we'd have beaten them with ten men, as we'd come close to doing, what would have happened? You know, you can have a 'media momentum' sometimes, which is a bit false, but I think maybe the momentum of that match would have took us—well, I don't know where it could have took us."

Back in 1998 Hoddle had known for certain: If it hadn't been for Beckham's red card, he would have won the World Cup. In his extremely badly written *Glenn Hoddle: My 1998 World Cup Story* he says, "I couldn't get away from my belief that we'd have won the world cup if we'd have beaten Argentina, and no-one on this earth will ever change my opinion that if we'd had eleven men on the pitch we'd have won that game." That England would then have still needed to beat Holland, Brazil, and France was a detail. In the final words of his book: "I'll always believe it should have been me. It should have been England."

I put it to him that he still isn't finished with that World Cup. He replied, "You know what: I've never looked at the game. Sorry, I looked at the game after, when we went back in the summer, but I never studied the game. It would be interesting to look at that game now, really look it as a bit of a performance, rather than be involved in it as we were."

Eight months after St. Etienne his career at the highest level ended. In an interview with the *Times*, Hoddle was quoted as saying that handicapped people were paying for sins in former lives. This was widely felt to be (1) a nutty idea and (2), in Tony Blair's new PC Britain, unkind to handicapped people.

Now Hoddle reflects, "My emotion would be just purely frustration. Because it was a story that wasn't true, not my beliefs—not how it was put anyway. And I had people that weren't strong enough to stay with me, under such a stupid thing." He means the FA officials who seized the opportunity to get rid of an unpopular manager. "My record stands up against anyone, really, in international soccer, so, errrm—"

That's an interesting view. After all, some people in international soccer have won the World Cup. Hoddle reached only the round of sixteen. "Stands up against anyone in international soccer?" I repeat.

"Well, no, just if you look at the stats, the record is one of the better England manager's records, if you like. And it wasn't for soccer reasons that they sacked me."

He's right on both counts. Hoddle's England won 61 percent of its twenty-eight matches outright. On the day we speak, in February 2008, that is better than any other England manager in history. The next best performers—Alf Ramsey, Ron Greenwood, Sven-Göran Eriksson, and all the prewar selection committees combined—are grouped a fraction behind him at about 60 percent.

Hoddle's also right to say that his career finished strictly because of his stupid opinions about something outside soccer. And now he's drinking cappuccino in the Polo Bar.

Was it a trauma?

"What? The ahm . . ."

The sacking.

While Hoddle thinks about that, Sky Television and an Elvis-like singer fill the background. "I've got to say it was a massive disappointment, because I knew what perhaps we could have done on the pitch." And he talks about his fantastic players, "your Shearers, your Inces, your Sheringhams, your— Owen, he was just a puppy. Your Tony Adamses, your Campbells, your Nevilles. Young Beckham. Scholes—'the jewel in my crown,' I called him. Stuart Pearce. Players that had real, real pride in their work."

While he was still managing them, Hoddle sometimes seemed to look down on his players, viewing them as less intelligent and less skillful than he had been himself. He once told Beckham, when they were practicing volleys in practice, that he didn't have "the skill" for it. Now, though, he remembers the players as partners in his greatest adventure.

Hoddle never got a top job again. In English soccer, an alcoholic wife beater can be "one of the lads," whereas a somewhat arrogant man who finds God on a visit to Bethlehem is a dangerous lunatic. Hoddle didn't swear, didn't drink much, and didn't have many friends. For most of his career he had never needed any. But after England, he could only get work at Southampton and Tottenham, and later a division lower at Wolves. He resigned in Wolverhampton in July 2006 and hasn't worked at a club since. The day we meet, he still is only fifty years old.

When he launches into a critique of England's current 4–4–2—too rigid, too few overlapping players who move forward one line, very different from when he was in charge—I ask whether it's frustrating still to be thinking like a top-level coach but not to be working as one. "Yeah," says Hoddle, "that's a good question, and I'm thinking that myself now, as I'm talking to you. But, but—strange that, because you must have read my mind." He chuckles, trying to turn it into a joke.

Hoddle has kept thinking all those years. He quotes Pele: "The wonderful thing about soccer is that we're all learning, and there's something else to find out about the game." Back when he wrote his *World Cup Story*, he still thought that he made only one mistake at his World Cup. He should have taken Eileen Drewery to France to heal England's injuries.

By now, though, Hoddle has had a decade to stew on that tournament, and he doesn't say anything to me about either Eileen or reincarnation. If you're an intelligent person with half-baked ideas, and a whole country makes fun of them, then you learn from the experience even if you never get a chance to repeat it.

In the Polo Bar Hoddle says he should have taken a sports psychologist to the World Cup. He used one at his clubs. "At first players hated it," he admits. "It's all so difficult." But just imagine, he goes on, if Scholes, who was too shy ever to speak, had said of a teammate during a group discussion, "To be honest, I've always thought he's one of the best center-halves I've ever played against." Then the player would think, "*Oh bloody hell*, didn't realize—hang on a minute." It would have given the man a charge of confidence. But Hoddle's England didn't have psychologists or group discussions.

Would visualization and sports psychology have helped get rid of England's historic penalty trauma? "I think it definitely would. There's certain techniques that you can do."

That's new, too. After England was eliminated, Hoddle said that you couldn't practice penalties. Now he tells me, "Nine times out of ten if you miss a penalty in shoot-outs, it's between the walk between the halfway line and the placing of the ball. So it's in your mind where you've missed it. I can tell, I think nine times out of ten, if a player's gonna miss it. With how he reacts, what his eyes are doing, when he gets the ball on the spot. But it does help if you're like Brazil and you can get a left foot, right foot, left foot, right foot, and hit the top corner." He laughs curtly. "You don't see a goalkeeper dive in the top corner. So whether you work on that visualization, it's quite handy to have those abilities. We had one left-footed player in the whole squad: Graeme Le Saux."

When he starts his academy, Hoddle wants to teach the teenagers to visualize:

Sometimes I sensed where people were, actually. Behind me or something. If I can just help these young players a little bit, to play with your head up and see the picture. Some people play with their head down, and some people play with a picture.

I used to do a thing with players, I'd say, "I want you to keep that ball up, but look at me." And it's really hard. They'd get to two, and they'd drop it. Three. But suddenly, if you keep practicing, you can get to ten. You don't have to look at the ball to be in control of it.

I say, "I can see that the academy makes sense. But you were the most successful young manager in England. Then you got the big job. In terms of soccer, you did it quite well. Now you'd normally be at your managerial peak, but you're no longer a manager. Isn't that strange?" He answers, "Yes. If I'm honest, I thought I'd be doing it [the academy] when I'm about sixty-five." And he laughs at himself again.

Suddenly, it turns out that we have been sitting here for nearly two hours. The short English winter's afternoon is nearly over. Hoddle has to go. He's taking his son to a sports psychologist. "We've done visualization with him. That's worked really well."

But it could all have been so different.

The Glenn Hoddle Academy in Montecastillo closed in 2011, and another effort in Dubai folded, too. But in October 2013 he was appointed to the FA Commission, advising the English Football Association on how to improve the England team.

The main thing I took away from meeting Hoddle is how normal and reasonable he seemed. It helped me understand how years of tabloid coverage turns almost every England manager into a caricature of himself. I had expected to meet a ridiculous person.

Diego Maradona
September 2008

Of course Argentina shouldn't have let Diego Maradona coach its soccer team. He won't last long in the post. He has enough trouble getting out of bed, let alone showing up in Glasgow for Scotland-Argentina on November 19. The fat cigar smoker and former cocaine addict with the geriatric's heart may not even be around for the next World Cup. But all this misses the point. A national team doesn't exist only to win. It also represents the nation. And nobody in soccer incarnates his country and its fans like Maradona does. That is part of his genius. Here are some scenes from his life, and from two recent films about him, which explain why Argentina had to give him the job.

Mexico City, 1986: After his two legendary goals have knocked England out of the World Cup, Maradona and his teammates sit joking in the locker room. The striker Jorge Valdano teases him: While Maradona was dribbling past six Englishmen, Valdano was running alongside him calling for the ball. Why didn't Maradona pass? Yes, replies Maradona, I was watching you, and kept meaning to pass, but the English kept getting in the way, and suddenly I'd beaten them all, so I just scored.

Valdano is awed: "While you scored this goal you were also watching me? Old man, you insult me. It isn't possible." And the midfielder Hector Enrique calls from the showers: "Lots of praise for the goal. But after that pass I gave him, if he hadn't scored, he should have been killed!" Everyone laughs. As Maradona notes, Enrique had shoved the ball into his feet in their own half.

It is a characteristic Maradona scene: Though he towered over his teammates, he always felt one with the team. When I asked Valdano if he liked Maradona, he replied, "I *love* Maradona. I'm from the country of Maradona."

Buenos Aires, 2004: Maradona lies in intensive care, his heart failing. Argentines gather outside the hospital doors. They expect him to die young. That is what Argentine heroes do: Eva Perón, Che Guevara, Carlos Gardel, the singer Rodrigo. In the Catholic tradition, the heroes die to redeem the country's sins.

Like Evita, Maradona is a sort of Argentine folk saint. In Carlos Sorín's 2006 movie *The Road to San Diego*, an illiterate woodcutter decides that a fallen tree in the forest resembles a cheering Maradona. He crafts the thing into a statue of Maradona and carries it across Argentina. Some people he meets laugh at him, noting that the statue looks nothing like Maradona, but many grasp its religious status. "Santa Maradona," as a Brazilian truck driver remarks.

In Emir Kusturica's new documentary *Maradona by Kusturica*, crowds form around Maradona wherever he goes, as if he were an icon in a Catholic procession. It looks exhausting, but Maradona understands the iconography. In his interviews with Kusturica, he wears an outsize silver cross and explains how God saved him in intensive care.

Qatar, 2005: Maradona and Pele appear at the launch of something or other. Afterward, writes James Montague in his book *When Friday Comes*, the Qatari crowd rushes the stage. Everybody ignores Pele. Montague says, "All I can see in the melee is the top of Diego's unkempt Afro, buried in a sea of adoring fans." Agustín Pichot, Argentina's former rugby captain and Maradona's friend, explains that people love Maradona because he is "authentic." We feel we know him. He is flawed like us.

That's partly because Maradona *looks* like an ordinary person. Never has a great athlete looked less like a great athlete. In Sorín's film, set in poor, provincial Argentina, we see rural people with withered faces on rickety buses—a cheap prostitute, a blind lottery-ticket seller—who recognize themselves in the tubby, little former slum dweller. Maradona is their link to greatness.

Germany, World Cup, 2006: Maradona is here as a fan. He sits in the stands wearing an Argentine replica shirt, jumping rhythmically with the other Argentine supporters. Pele or Franz Beckenbauer couldn't have done it. But Maradona embodies Argentina.

Cinemas, 2008: Kusturica's film is agitprop for Fidel Castro, Hugo Chávez, and Emir Kusturica. Yet it also captures a truth about Maradona and Argentina: The player avenges the country's frustrations about its place in the world. The film includes a cartoon version of Maradona's goal versus England, in which he dribbles past Margaret Thatcher (who gets herself decapitated), a handbag-wielding Queen Elizabeth, a horned Tony Blair who bites

Maradona's ankle before dropping into the underworld, and a pistol-toting George W. Bush.

Kusturica calls the goal "one of those rare moments that a country heavily in debt to the IMF triumphed over one of the rulers of the world." That, surely, is too much honor for England. However, Maradona and many Argentines experienced the goal as just that. If you want to understand why Latin America is going left-wing, look at Maradona. He incarnates Chávezian resentment.

In Kusturica's final scene, two musicians (one of them the great Manu Chao) stand on the street playing a song: "If I were Maradona. . . ." Suddenly, Maradona is standing beside them, listening. Behind his huge sunglasses, he starts to weep. He knows how the fans feel. He is one himself. The Argentine team has always belonged to him.

Josep Guardiola
March 2009

A year ago, one of Barcelona's countless vice presidents mused over lunch at the Nou Camp stadium that perhaps Josep "Pep" Guardiola should be the club's next coach. It seemed a weird idea. Guardiola was then thirty-seven and had never managed a professional soccer club, let alone the biggest on earth.

True, replied the veep, but Guardiola was a Catalan, and "Barça" longed to have a Catalan coach. After all, she added, when the Catalan Victor Valdés was given a chance as Barcelona's keeper, he wasn't yet a world beater, but he had learned on the job.

I never wrote about the conversation because I assumed she was fantasizing. But months later Guardiola got the job. He then transformed last season's jaded and hedonistic Barça team into what the great Italian coach Arrigo Sacchi calls "the most beautiful soccer cause of recent years." Next month Guardiola's lot meet Bayern Munich in the quarterfinals of the Champions League. Perhaps only Barça can stop an English side from winning the trophy again.

Guardiola's inspired appointment offers two lessons to any company: how to choose a boss and how the boss should choose his team. The key point about Guardiola is that he has been identified with Barcelona almost from birth. He comes from Santpedor, a village so Catalan that many locals spoke the forbidden regional language throughout General Franco's dictatorship. At thirteen he entered the "Masía," the "farmhouse" for young players next to Barcelona's stadium. Most of his life since has been spent in the square kilometer of the Nou Camp. As Jimmy Burns writes in *Barça: A People's Passion*, locals still remember Guardiola as a skinny fifteen-year-old ballboy illegally running onto the pitch and hugging a player during a European semifinal in 1986. They remember him as a skinny playmaker, standing on the balcony of the Generalitat building in 1992, holding aloft the European Cup, and saying in Catalan, *"Ja la teniu aquí"* (Here you have it). The phrase gave many in the crowd gooseflesh, because it deliberately echoed the legendary *"Ja soc aquí"* (Here I am) of the Catalan president Josep Tarradellas when he returned from decades of French exile to Barcelona as an old man, after Franco died.

In other words, Guardiola, a reader of Catalan poetry, is such a perfect Catalan hero that he's practically a character from a nineteenth-century nationalist poem himself. Cynics mockingly call him "the Myth." Most Barça fans always hoped that the Myth would return one day as the skinny coach, though perhaps not quite as soon as this.

This background matters because it helps Guardiola govern with the grain of the club culture. As Joan Laporta, Barça's president, told a business partner, "I was looking for somebody who understood the Barça way, and nobody understands it better than he does." The Barça way is the attacking, quick-passing soccer down the wings that the Dutchman Johan Cruijff introduced to the club. In Guardiola's phrase, Cruijff painted the chapel, and subsequent coaches must merely restore and improve it.

The local media and fans agree. By governing with the grain—by *being* the grain himself—Guardiola wins instant acceptance in this club of tireless warring factions. It's like the company that dares appoint an unknown from the ranks as CEO because everyone likes him and he understands the company.

Contrast this with a "star" CEO or coach from outside who tries to overturn the corporate culture: José Mourinho, for instance, won prizes at Chelsea but was never entirely accepted there, largely because his defensive tactics offended English soccer culture. The moment Chelsea stopped winning, Mourinho had to leave.

Star players obey Guardiola because they know they have no chance of forcing him out. They stick to the three-page "Code of Good Conduct" he wrote before the season, stick to their zones on the field, and when the great striker Samuel Eto'o dares talk back at practice, he is banished to the showers in seconds. Barcelona's players are so good that as long as they serve the collective, they will win prizes.

And that's the main management lesson from Guardiola's work: He kept his best players. A year ago everyone expected Barcelona to sell the difficult, underperforming Eto'o and Thierry Henry. But Guardiola knew that soccer's scarcest resource is talent. It would have been easier to buy lesser, more dutiful players. Instead, he dared persevere with class. He melded Eto'o, Henry, and Lionel Messi into soccer's most thrilling attack.

Only one step remains in Guardiola's career path: to displace Sant Jordi as the skinny patron saint of Catalonia.

José Mourinho
April 2010

In 1996, José Mourinho suddenly became a powerful man. At only thirty-three, the unknown Portuguese had come to Barcelona chiefly to translate for the English manager, Bobby Robson. However, he fast became more than a translator. Mourinho took a duplex in the beach town of Sitges, near Robson's house, and often talked soccer with him over dinner, recounts Mourinho's biographer Patrick Barclay. Robson let Mourinho write dazzling scouting reports. And Mourinho had one great advantage over his boss: He spoke Spanish. When Robson talked to players, or gave press conferences, Mourinho interpreted. Many felt he sometimes added thoughts of his own.

Barcelona gave Mourinho's coaching career liftoff. Yet when soccer's winningest coach returns to town with Inter Milan for Wednesday's semifinal of the Champions League, he doesn't come as an old friend. To the contrary: Mourinho has become the anti-Barcelona, the man who stands for everything that Barça is not. He now helps define the club's identity.

That's new, because when he worked at Barcelona, few locals had heard of him. Even the club's president knew him only as *el traductor* (the translator). Only Barcelona's coaches and players understood his importance. Mourinho charmed the then captain, Pep Guardiola, and persuaded everyone that he knew soccer. He was even allowed to coach the team in some friendlies. Barça was arguably the first side he ever managed.

In 2000 he drove out of Sitges almost unnoticed to coach in Portugal. Four years later, Barça fans watching Porto win the Champions League noticed a vaguely familiar face on their television screens: *El traductor* had become champion of Europe. They also noticed that he had rejected Barcelona's etiquette. Barça's motto is "more than a club": Everyone in the institution is expected to make himself subservient to it. But at the press conference, after Porto's victory, Mourinho talked mainly about himself. He, too, seemed to consider himself "more than a club." Whereas Barcelona prizes elegant humility, Mourinho is shouty.

As a tactician, too, he was the anti-Barcelona. The club's creed is "beautiful soccer." Mourinho's was "It's not important how we play." His genius lay in finding and exploiting his opponent's flaws. As he said, "If you have a Ferrari and I have a small car, to beat you in a race I have to break your wheel or put sugar in your tank."

When he returned to Barcelona as coach of Chelsea in 2005, he proclaimed that he had already won as many European Cups as Barcelona had in its history. To show how well he knew Barcelona's Ferrari, the day before the match he announced Barça's lineup. He beat Barcelona—chiefly because he had spotted that Barça's then left-back, Gio van Bronckhorst, couldn't tackle—and enraged the city. Sociologists like to say that groups define themselves by contrast to some imaginary Other. For Barcelona, Mourinho had become the Other.

When Chelsea visited again in 2006, Barcelona fans pounded on their team bus and jeered, "*Traductor!*" As in all dysfunctional relationships, Mourinho and Barcelona know just how to hurt each other: He regularly beats Barça, and Barça pretends not to respect him.

In truth the club feared Mourinho. In 2008 two club officials visited him in Portugal to canvass him about becoming head coach. He would have loved it: the world's best players, and the ultimate revenge. But Barça finally decided he wasn't the right man. Instead, it appointed his old friend Guardiola. Seeing Guardiola now, Mourinho must reflect on how easy the star player's path to the coaching summit was compared to his own.

Before their two teams met in Milan last week, Mourinho put more sugar in Barça's tank. Inter's playmaker Wesley Sneijder says, "His team talk lasted over two hours, spread across two days. He emphasized Barcelona's strong points, and wanted us to use those to knock them out." Inter clogged the central defense, frustrating Barcelona. Afterward, when Barcelona's players grumbled about the referee, Mourinho chastised, "They should say that Inter was stronger, and that's it." He loves it when Barcelona's moral superiority slips.

For decades Real Madrid functioned as Barcelona's imaginary Other. Now one little man has usurped Real's role. On Wednesday, Mourinho should take those cries of *"Traductor!"* as a covert tribute.

Arsène Wenger
April 2010

In 2004 Arsène Wenger was looking for a defensive midfielder who could one day replace Patrick Vieira at Arsenal. The manager wanted a runner. So he ordered a search through modern soccer's computerized databases for the defensive midfielders who covered the most ground per match. The search produced an obscure name: Mathieu Flamini, a rookie at Olympique Marseille, was covering eight and a half miles on average in the handful of professional matches he had played. He didn't even have a professional contract yet. Wenger went to watch Flamini, saw that he could play soccer, and signed him.

Flamini spent four years mostly on the Arsenal first team and in his last season ran more miles per game than anyone else in the Premier League. He then refused to renew his contract and joined Milan.

The story sums up Wenger's genius in evaluating players—and his lack of funds to keep them. Currently, after Arsenal's 4–1 thrashing by Barcelona in the Champions League, Wenger is being viewed with pity. His Arsenal team hasn't won a prize for five years. Critics berate him for refusing to spend the money he has on big transfers. Yet the critics are wrong. Perhaps no soccer manager does more with what money he has than Wenger. No wonder that Billy Beane, general manager of the Oakland A's baseball team, and the man who brought novel *Moneyball* methods of evaluating players to baseball, himself probably the most admired executive in sport, calls the Frenchman "undoubtedly the sports executive whom I admire most." Wenger remains a model of how to value players.

A key to Wenger's career is something he did outside soccer: studying economics at the University of Strasbourg in his native France. That helped teach him both the precise value of money—to him, $25 million is not simply "a lot"—and the importance of data. Most managers in hidebound, anti-intellectual soccer don't understand either point well. But value for money and respect for data are Wenger's abiding reference points when he looks for players.

Caring about data, Wenger pioneered the use of stats to assess players. More than twenty years ago at Monaco he worked with a computer program called "Top Score," developed by a friend. It assigned points for any act a player performed on the pitch. "Most players who got high scores went on to have successful careers," said Wenger. Few managers rely so much on statistics. Wenger got rid of Gilberto Silva when the data showed that the Brazilian was taking a split second longer to pass the ball on than he had the season before. He often uses stats to back up a hunch he already has about a player. Perhaps, he half-jokes, he doesn't have enough confidence in his own judgment.

One hunch concerned a young Liberian playing in Cameroon named George Weah. Wenger—who monitored half the leagues on earth years before everyone else did—kept getting intriguing reports about Weah. However, the reports would add that the guy was a rough diamond. Finally, Wenger sent a Monaco colleague to West Africa to watch him. The colleague phoned back after the match, "The bad news is, Weah broke an arm. The good news: He played anyway."

At that, Wenger took the gamble and bought him. After signing his contract, Weah sat at the table with his head in his hands. Wenger said, "George, cheer up, you've just signed for Monaco." Weah replied, "Yes, boss, but nobody gives me any money." It turned out he didn't have a penny. So Wenger pulled five hundred French francs out of his wallet—then about ninety dollars— and handed it to Weah. Wenger, a funny man away from press conferences, likes to joke about the size of Weah's "signing bonus." The Liberian exemplifies Wenger's knack of getting quality cheap.

In the old days it was easy. When Wenger joined Arsenal in 1996, other Premier League managers were still barely scouting abroad. Nobody else seems to have realized that Milan's reserve Vieira and Juventus's reserve Thierry Henry were great players. Spotting that didn't require mystical insight—Vieira convinced Arsenal's fans of the same fact inside forty-five minutes in his debut against Sheffield Wednesday—but none of Wenger's British rivals seemed even to know Vieira.

However, over time Wenger lost some advantages, because others copied him. They too began using stats and scouting abroad. And Manchester United had an advantage over him: more money.

This season Arsenal is believed to have the fourth-highest wage bill in England. Chelsea pays the most, then the two Manchester clubs. Logically, Arsenal should finish fourth. Instead, it is third. That's impressive.

Beane, at the Oakland A's, knows all about working with a small budget. He told me, "If you have less than your competitors, you can't do things in the way that they do it or you are destined to fall behind them. If we did things exactly like the Yankees, we are destined to finish exactly where our payroll says we should. If Arsenal want a striker and Man U want a striker and Chelsea want a striker, well, Arsenal will get the third-best striker." In other words, the critics who urge Wenger to pursue expensive big names like his rivals do are wrong. Wenger knows it's pointless for Arsenal to chase stars.

Those who think that for some bizarre psychological reason he doesn't want stars—especially goalscoring or muscular stars—are wrong. He loves them. He's tried to buy many of them, too. Sitting in his office at the Emirates Stadium after a match early this season, he mused to guests about the period when he was weighing up an unknown striker at Le Mans called Didier

Drogba. Wenger decided not to take the risk. Imagine Drogba at today's sweet-passing Arsenal, he added; he'd score a hat trick every game.

Or, he went on, there was the time he flew the teenage Cristiano Ronaldo to London. The boy, still unknown at Sporting Lisbon, was shown around the Highbury stadium, was given an Arsenal shirt with his name on the back, and agreed to join Arsenal. But before he did, Manchester United played Sporting in a friendly. The kid so awed United's defenders that on the plane home they urged Ferguson to buy him. Sporting said it had already agreed to sell him to Arsenal, Wenger recalls. United offered nearly $20 million, a multiple of Arsenal's price. United got him. But Wenger told his guests in the office, "Next time you see him you ask him—he still has that Arsenal shirt."

And after the sixteen-year-old Wayne Rooney netted from thirty yards for Everton against Wenger's Arsenal in 2003, Wenger said he thought the boy was the best English player he'd seen since coming to the country. But very soon after, bigger clubs were chasing Rooney.

The point is: Wenger knows he cannot have established stars. He knows that if City offers Emmanuel Adebayor and Kolo Touré much higher salaries than they get at Arsenal, the players will leave. Arsenal could have gotten stars by going hopelessly into debt, as "bubble clubs" like Lazio Roma, Valencia, Rangers, and Celtic have done, but this economist refuses to bankrupt his employer. Over time, Wenger spends more modestly on transfers than less successful clubs like Liverpool, Newcastle, even Tottenham, let alone Real Madrid. From 1998 to 2007, Wenger's net spending on transfers (i.e., his purchases minus his sales) was £39 million. Ferguson's was £123 million. (I owe these calculations to Len Williamson.) Yet Arsenal remained competitive with Man United in this period, while also building the expensive Emirates Stadium, which will raise the club's revenues in the long run. Beane compares Wenger to the legendary American investor Warren Buffett: "He runs his club like he is going to own the club for a hundred years." And he adds, "Wenger seems to understand that you are only as strong as your business. People don't want to hear that the business is running good. Until the business starts to go awry."

However, running a good business isn't enough for Wenger. When he worked in Japan and saw how painstakingly Japanese girls arranged flowers, or cleaners picked up bits of paper, he became a perfectionist. He still wants

Arsenal to win everything. Now that other managers have copied his old tricks, he needs to find new methods to differentiate himself from his rivals.

First, that means avoiding transfers when possible. Transfers cause disruption. Ivan Gazidis, Arsenal's chief executive, says the club doesn't like buying players who will need time to adjust and who "might or might not be 5 or 10 percent better than the players we already have."

Second, it means knowing just when to sell. Wenger likes to sell players when they are at their most fashionable, but fractionally past their best. It's like selling a stock at the top of the market. He flogged Henry for $32 million at age twenty-nine, Vieira for $25 million at twenty-nine, Emmanuel Petit for $10.5 million at twenty-nine, and Marc Overmars for $38 million at twenty-seven, and none ever did as well again afterward. Beane notes, "Nothing strangulates a sports club more than having older players on long contracts, because once they stop performing, they become immovable."

Third, Wenger likes to buy players young and cheap. Thinking long-term, unlike most managers, he often signs players before they are ready for the first team. He therefore gets them at a discount—remember Robin van Persie or Cesc Fabregas—and has time to shape them. Van Persie said nearly six years ago, "Wenger is the only coach I've had who's kept his word. He told me he'd bring me slowly. The first month he didn't expect anything of me. Then he'd gradually give me more playing time. It began with two minutes. Now we're on half an hour." Today Van Persie is a star, as Wenger foresaw. Ferguson, too, has brought young players to stardom: Ronaldo and Rooney. The difference is that he bought them when everyone could already see they'd become stars. They were priced commensurately.

Last, Wenger is a realist. He knows that any player Arsenal can afford will lack something. Usually that something is experience: Wenger could afford to sign Van Persie at twenty-one, but couldn't have afforded him now. Sometimes that missing something is strength: Wenger knows it matters, and in his early years at Arsenal he had famously physical teams, but it's the quality he is most willing to forego in a player. When critics scoff that today's Arsenal players are physically weaker than Chelsea's, Wenger knows they are right, even if he'd never admit it. But he also knows he cannot afford players who are simultaneously experienced, very skilled, and strong.

His cut-rate Arsenal does better than you'd expect. It usually makes at least the quarterfinals of the Champions League. It is now challenging United and Chelsea for the Premier League. Weirdly, however, Wenger's critics often measure him against those much richer clubs, then complain when he loses. Beane sighs, "In those years of not winning, they've opened the Emirates. There's a debt service that comes with it. They have been able to service it and put themselves in a position to [potentially] win year after year. But sport has a habit of saying, 'What have you done for me lately?'"

Given how much wages determine soccer, Wenger almost cannot win. He tries to forget the fact. Some of his critics simply don't know it.

José Mourinho and Louis van Gaal
May 2010

José Mourinho "got angry, *angry!*" recalls Louis van Gaal. It was 1997, and the two men had just heard that Van Gaal would replace Bobby Robson as Barcelona's head coach. Mourinho, Robson's interpreter, must have feared his career would sink with his boss's.

Instead, Mourinho impressed Van Gaal, who kept him as an assistant. Thirteen years later, in Madrid tonight, Mourinho's Inter Milan faces Van Gaal's Bayern Munich in the Champions League final. Europe's foremost coaches look like opposites: the handsome Latin and the flat-faced Dutchman. They play like opposites: Van Gaal regards attacking soccer as a moral duty, while Mourinho believes only in winning. Nonetheless, they are spiritual twins. Both are outsiders, theoreticians, the sort of people whom soccer clubs rarely recruit as coaches.

Traditionally, good players later get jobs as coaches, even though the professions don't have much to do with each other. But neither Mourinho nor Van Gaal was a very good player. The Dutchman, a semipro at Sparta Rotterdam, was let down by his gangling body: One spectator remarked that he ran as if he had swallowed an umbrella. Mourinho peaked in Belenenses reserves.

Instead, both had a more relevant apprenticeship: decades of studying coaching. Asked why failed players often succeed as managers, Mourinho once replied, "More time to study." Van Gaal at age twelve would go to watch Rinus Michels train Ajax Amsterdam. At about that age, Mourinho was analyzing opponents for his father, manager of a little Portuguese club.

Even as a player, Van Gaal was effectively a coach. As playmaker, he would march around the center circle shouting instructions at his teammates. He would sometimes reorder Sparta's lineup in midmatch. Yet he later struggled to find coaching jobs. Few wanted a middling former player who looked peculiar and got up people's noses. Mourinho couldn't get coaching jobs because he hadn't played. Instead, he kept studying. At Barcelona, Van Gaal let him analyze prospective opponents. "I had to teach him how to look," the Dutchman says.

Both men spent decades earning the status that was handed free to former great players. When the two men finally became coaches, not at huge clubs, each took fewer than five years to win both the UEFA Cup and the Champions League. This wasn't coincidence. Each man had developed a theory of soccer. Mourinho has recorded his in his so-called bible, which no outsider is allowed to see. Van Gaal published his as a Dutch book, *Visie*.

Though Van Gaal's teams attack and Mourinho's don't, their "visions" are oddly similar. Like coaches in American football, both men know exactly where their players should be at any moment in the match. Van Gaal's former player Dennis Bergkamp told author David Winner, "I don't want to be disrespectful, but Van Gaal could have eleven machines on the field. Robots: you do this, you that." Mourinho likes robots, too. Both men distrust big-name players who might make independent decisions.

Both work harder than the plausible former stars in handmade suits who populate most coaching dugouts. Van Gaal, before a friendly against an amateur team, gave each Bayern player a sheet containing an analysis of his opposite number and match instructions. Mourinho claims to have watched the recent Inter-Chelsea game seven times. "This is not seven times putting the DVD in and letting the DVD run," he clarified. "I watched it seven times, and stop, and go back, and stop again."

Lately, the two men have been lauding each other. "He taught me the trade," says Mourinho. "Maybe one day I'll be his assistant," jokes Van Gaal, who doesn't normally do self-deprecation. Each senses how much the other needs praise. Mourinho's nonstop babbling about himself is often interpreted as a tactic designed to deflect pressure from his players. It's not: Just after his players' greatest triumph, the elimination of Barcelona, when there was no pressure to deflect, Mourinho upstaged them by charging around the pitch between the water sprinklers, celebrating for the television cameras. "*I* won this" was his message. Similarly, after Bayern became German champions, Van Gaal gave such a bombastic speech from the balcony of Munich's town hall that German satirists have been likening it to "balcony scenes" of past leaders. These men crave the respect so long denied them.

You might think their success will dissuade clubs from handing coaching posts to former stars. It won't. Soccer's traditions never die.

Fabio Capello
June 2010

In 1987, former player Fabio Capello took some psychological aptitude tests normally given to recent MBAs. Capello was working as an executive in the sporting wing of Silvio Berlusconi's media empire, and everyone could see he was bright. However, nobody expected him to score as highly as he did, writes his biographer Gabriele Marcotti. An impressed Berlusconi sent him for a year's high-level executive training. In 1991 Capello became coach of the empire's soccer team, AC Milan, and performed brilliantly.

He leads England into this month's World Cup as arguably the most successful manager of England ever. He is unlikely to win the tournament, but he has set a new template for the job. He has redefined what was once a chiefly ambassadorial role as a meritocratic one, best filled by a top-class coach from continental Europe, who descends on backward England as a sort of development consultant.

Capello was born in 1946 in the cold northern Italian town of Pieris, a dozen miles from the then Yugoslav border. His father, a schoolteacher and the local soccer coach, had recently returned from a German prisoner of war camp weighing just 105 pounds. Capello's upbringing was tough. Swimming, for instance, consisted of his father taking him to the nearby cliffs and throwing him from the rocks into the sea.

Capello became a top-notch player, who played thirty-two times for Italy and scored at Wembley for the country's first-ever victory in England in 1973. However, he was never single-minded about soccer. In the 1970s he became fascinated by the new *arte povera* movement, which made art out of rubbish and other discarded materials. He preferred the company of art dealers to players. He became a notable collector of modern art.

There was nothing artistic about his coaching. A pragmatist, he tailored his style to the players he had. All he cared about was winning. He was as tough with his players as his father had been with him, taking on even the biggest stars. "Aren't you ashamed of being so fat?" he roared when the Brazilian striker Ronaldo emerged from the shower. "He's a shouter," confirms his former player Clarence Seedorf.

Yet Capello holds no grudges, writes Marcotti. He judges people only on whether they can help him win in the future. In a rage at Real Madrid, he once said that David Beckham "will never play for me again." But Beckham did, helped Real win the league, and later served Capello's England team.

The craggy Italian won nine league titles in sixteen seasons as a club coach. Stefan Szymanski, a sports economist at Cass Business School in London, has calculated that only about 10 percent of managers consistently perform better with their teams than their clubs' wage bill would predict. Usually in soccer, the club with the biggest salaries finishes at the top of the league, and the club that pays least finishes at the bottom. Only a few outstanding managers, like José Mourinho and Alex Ferguson, have much of an effect on results. Capello heads the small elite.

Oddly, until 2000 England had never recruited from that pool. In a country that happily recruits chief executives and sometimes even monarchs from abroad, England's manager was one of the last jobs reserved by convention for an Englishman. Unfortunately, few Englishmen were elite managers. The country, long isolated from the European mainstream, had developed its own dysfunctional "kick and rush" style of soccer. This favored warrior virtues over thought. Accordingly, England produced few great soccer thinkers.

Worse, convention required that the England manager must have diplomatic gifts. That ruled out the best English manager of recent decades, the provocateur Brian Clough. Every Englishman who got the post ended up disappointing a demanding public. Before Capello, managing England was often called "the impossible job." Rather, it was a difficult job made impossible by a misguided recruitment policy.

Capello had long wanted his last coaching job to be with England. He had spotted the nation's unrealized potential. When he got the job with its salary of about £6 million (then about $12 million)—his appointment a symptom of the Europeanization of Britain since the 1990s—he scarcely even pretended to respect English traditions. Previous England managers had done the bidding of British tabloid newspapers. The best-known players were celebrities and so had to play at whatever cost. Capello, who does not care what the media say about him, broke this Hollywood-style star system. He banished the star Michael Owen from the squad, banished Steven Gerrard from central midfield, and used Beckham only as a humble substitute until the player disappeared from contention with a torn Achilles tendon. Capello banished the players' free-spending wives and girlfriends, or WAGs, from the team's camp: Rustenburg at this World Cup won't be the media circus that Baden-Baden was at the last one.

Above all, though, he has largely banished the old frenzied, blind English game—what soccer historian Jonathan Wilson calls England's "headless-chickenness"—even if it sometimes reappears like a genetic defect. Capello's England plays intelligent continental soccer. It values possession of the ball over speed. The results are telling: Capello's team has won 75 percent of its twenty-four matches. No previous England manager won more than 60 percent.

Crucially, too, Capello has given the tabloids nothing to work with off the field. He is a conservative, traditional Catholic—so much so, in fact, that in 2006 he praised the late Spanish dictator Francisco Franco in an interview with the Italian newspaper *La Repubblica*. What he liked about Spain, he said, was "the order Franco left behind."

In the UK he has wisely kept quiet about politics. He also lacks the free-range libido of another predecessor, Sven-Göran Eriksson, whose many relationships kept the tabloids busy. Capello lives a quiet, golfing life in London. He has made "the impossible job" seem almost a soothing leisure pursuit, like flower arranging.

His England will probably fly home in tears: It has generally lost against first-rank teams in friendly matches. However, Capello has redefined the job for a generation. His next few successors will surely be drawn from the elite of winning, monogamous continental European coaches.

Even after Capello's disappointment in South Africa, he continued to outshine all previous England managers. When he quit the job in disgust in February 2012, he had won 67 percent of his forty-two matches with England—7 percent more than any of his predecessors. But I was wrong that his successor would be drawn from the elite of winning continental coaches. Instead, England appointed Roy Hodgson.

Diego Maradona
June 2010

It was nearly midnight in freezing Johannesburg, but a bunch of us exhausted journalists were hanging on in a half-empty Soccer City for Diego Maradona. Argentina's manager gives press conferences that are more fun than most of the games here. His team had just beaten Mexico, its fourth straight win, and the celebrations seemed to be taking some time. Finally, the great man showed up, looking as ever like a tramp who had found a nice suit and two identical Swiss luxury watches, and proceeded to provoke journalists. "That's a stupid question," he told one. To another: "Listen, what are you actually aiming at?" When a journalist asked about Germany, Argentina's opponent in Saturday's quarterfinal, Maradona refused to answer but offered the man "carte blanche": "You may write whatever you want about what I think about Germany."

Yet when the suit from FIFA tried to end the press conference, Maradona objected, "Finally I get the chance to speak and he wants to send me away!" There was a message he wanted to convey, after two years in this job: "You see, as a coach, they said I had no idea, and suddenly I've won four games and they see me as someone else."

Here is Maradona triumphant. The critics said he knew nothing about coaching. They said someone else was running Argentina's tactics. It's now clear that Maradona truly is the boss. This is his team—for better or for worse. It's perfectly possible that on July 11 here in Soccer City he will be holding the World Cup aloft for the second time in twenty-four years, and shortly afterward running naked through Buenos Aires as per promise. Yet it's also perfectly possible that Argentina will fail, and if so it will in large part be Maradona's fault.

Maradona was appointed in 2008 not so much for his supposed tactical brilliance but to incarnate the nation. It was a little like when cheerleader Kevin Keegan was appointed manager of England: Maradona was not a mere technician, but someone who stood for Argentina, who not only embodied Argentine soccer but at the last World Cup had come to Germany as a fan, an Argentine shirt taut over his belly, jumping up and down on the terraces to the chants of "If you don't jump, you're an Englishman."

Julio Grondona, eternal boss of the Argentine Football Association, had tried to surround the novice coach with experts. Maradona didn't want experts. He let his old septuagenarian coach Carlos Bilardo (under whom he'd won the World Cup in 1986) have a small role, but like many former players-turned-coaches, he preferred the company of old buddies. His adjutants here in South Africa, dressed in the same gray suits, are his former teammates Alejandro Mancuso and Hector "El Negro" Enrique. Neither has much coaching experience, either. It's just that Maradona goes way back with them. The greatest moment of Enrique's career was shoving the ball into Maradona's feet before the little man dribbled through half the English side to score the so-called best goal ever at that '86 World Cup.

Even when it came to picking players, Maradona surrounded himself with buddies. Juan Sebastián Verón, with whom he had played at Boca Juniors in the early 1990s, is now thirty-five and fading, but he made the squad. So did young Javier "Huesito" Pastore, whom Maradona loves for his ability to mimic anyone he encounters, from waiter to bus driver. World-class players like Javier Zanetti and Esteban Cambiasso, whom Argentina desperately needs but who don't seem to be part of the family, aren't in South Africa. Maradona's logic seems to be that he selects on passion, feeling for the shirt. That translates into selecting only people who totally buy into his project. "I was talking to Carlos Bilardo and other people in the team," Maradona mused here the other night, "and we were talking about the good vibrations we feel." It's more fun with your mates.

Bilardo, although never quite rejected, has never quite penetrated this phalanx of buddies. He and Mancuso openly loathe each other. In December Bilardo said that Mancuso "encouraged the separation" between himself and Maradona and that he'd tell all on the radio. In the event he didn't. Maradona himself crushed the squabbles by noting who was boss. "No one is going to impose anything on me, not even suggest a player. They didn't do that to me when I was fifteen, and now I'm forty-eight."

This is quite true, and something almost everyone missed before the World Cup. Maradona simply isn't the sort of guy to defer. Nor is he cowed by the responsibility of coaching a team at a World Cup. He's always saying here how comfortable he is at World Cups: "I have seen many things, and perhaps others have not done what I have done." To him a World Cup is as familiar an environment as a favorite vacation destination is for normal people.

And of course he knows soccer. So although he listens to others, he, in the phrase of George W. Bush, is the decider. Last week Argentina beat Greece, with the substitute Martin Palermo scoring a late-second goal. Speaking about himself in the third person, Maradona revealed afterward, "Enrique, Mancuso, and Maradona discussed whether Palermo or Higuaín should come on. Enrique and Mancuso wanted 'Pipita' [Higuaín], so I said 'Yeah? Bring on Martin then.'"

But just because Maradona is the decider, it would be wrong to assume that he determines events. The role of the coach in soccer generally is overestimated. In our recent book *Soccernomics*, sports economist Stefan Szymanski and I showed that players' salaries determine almost by themselves where a club finishes in the league. The typical coach doesn't matter much. Because the coach appears after the game to explain why his team won or lost, we start to believe that he shaped the result. In fact, he is usually better understood as his team's spokesman.

At a World Cup, it would be ludicrous to think that the best players in the country, with many years of professional experience, need to be told by a coach just what to do. Argentina has a very mature culture of soccer tactics; this is not New Zealand, or England. Here in South Africa Maradona often consults with a forum of senior players: Verón, Javier Mascherano, and Gabriele Heinze. On the field, they can shape matters. Maradona also happens to possess the best player on earth, Leo Messi, who is in the habit of winning games single-handedly. "If you have such a sensational team, it's easy," said Maradona after his boys whipped South Korea 4–1. Perhaps he was trying to be modest, but it was true.

Certainly, a "Maradoniano" team is taking shape. Messi has finally become, in Argentine soccer parlance, the team's "owner," running things from central midfield, as Maradona wanted—after all the coach's previous plans for Messi failed. The team has scored four times from set pieces, which Maradona claims to orchestrate. They don't play the defensive Bilardista *antifutbol* associated with the old coach.

But the mark of Maradona is also visible in the team's failings. In the absence of Zanetti and Cambiasso, there is no decent right-back and only one ball-winning midfielder in Mascherano. That means Argentina often goes long periods without possession. "What I didn't like is that we left the ball so often to Mexico in the second half," Maradona complained in Soccer City. "It's our ball." But that's the team he created.

We may yet get to relish that naked run (or waddle). But if so it will have as much to do with Mascherano or Messi or the glorious Carlos Tévez as with the fat chap who does the press conferences and his kitchen cabinet.

*Maradona's struggle to find work after the World Cup is a sign of the times. He spent months looking for a job, advertising his availability to English clubs but getting no response, before finally signing for Al-Wasl in Dubai. The club fired him in July 2012, soon after its entire board had resigned following a trophyless season. He hasn't found a managerial job since.

Fifteen years ago, there was still a widespread belief in soccer that a great player would generally become a great coach. His sheer presence would motivate his players to exceed their limits. That's why Bryan Robson was given all the spending money he wanted at Middlesbrough and was touted as a future England manager practically before he had unlocked his office door. It's also why Keegan was named manager of England in 1999.

Now, though, soccer is a bit more professional (see the profile of Mike Forde in Part III), and no club with any sense will touch Maradona.

Malcolm Allison
October 2010

Thinking of Malcolm Allison, who has died at age eighty-three, two very different images spring to mind. At Crystal Palace in 1976, he invited the porn actress and vicar's daughter Fiona Richmond to join him in the team bath. Naturally, press photographers were on hand to record the moment.

That was "Big Mal," the extroverted hedonist known to tabloid newspapers and people in soccer as "a great character." But then there is the thinker Allison: sitting at a table in Cassetari's café in the late 1950s, debating tactics with teammates from West Ham United, moving salt and pepper shakers around to make points about formations. Several of those teammates, inspired by Allison, also became leading soccer managers. One, Bobby Moore, captained England to victory in a World Cup. Allison could have helped make English soccer a thinking game, but instead he morphed into "Big Mal."

Allison was born in Dartford, Kent, in 1927, son of an electrical engineer. He was a bright boy, a reader, but he deliberately failed his entrance exams for grammar school because the school didn't play soccer. After the war he served as a soldier in occupied Vienna, and there he first tasted continental soccer. He turned out for the local side, Admira Wacker. He sneaked into the Soviet zone to study the Red Army team and noticed how much they trained with the ball, whereas English teams of the day mostly ran laps.

Back at his club, Charlton Athletic, he told the manager that his training methods were useless. He was promptly sold to West Ham. He made his debut there in 1951 and soon became captain, but in reality was almost the club's de facto manager. In an era when players were expected to be deferential, Allison often ran practice and helped pick the team. He followed coaching courses and kept learning from the Continent. In 1953 the great Hungarians thrashed England 3–6 at Wembley. Allison loved the way their players changed positions during play, something almost unknown in England. He always favored passing soccer against the rugged English tradition of punting balls long. In short, he was a continental thinker about four decades before they began taking over English clubs. Allison had continental style, too: he favored Italian clothes and alone in his playing era wore his shorts very short.

In 1957 he was diagnosed with tuberculosis. Part of a lung was removed, and he now lacked the stamina for soccer. Seventeen-year-old Moore replaced him as West Ham's center-back, but in a sense this was a triumph for Allison. Moore said in his autobiography, "Malcolm had taught me everything I know. . . . When Malcolm was coaching schoolboys he took a liking to me when I don't think anyone else at West Ham saw anything special in me. . . . It's not too strong to say I loved him." Moore's famed passing game was founded on a piece of advice Allison had given him: Even before you get the ball, know where you are going to pass it.

Inevitably, Allison became a manager, with Bath City and then Plymouth. He got his big break in 1965 when Joe Mercer, Manchester City's manager, hired him as his assistant. Between 1968 and 1970 City won the league, the FA Cup, the League Cup, and the European Cupwinners' Cup. It was City's zenith, and Allison's too. He coached the team while the calmer Mercer ran the business and was the club's public face. Allison, who wrote the provocatively titled *Soccer for Thinkers*, was ahead of his time in the realms of fitness, diet, and motivation as well as tactics. Colin Shindler, City fan and author of *Manchester United Ruined My Life*, describes how Allison brought players to Salford University to have blood samples taken to measure their stamina. "In 1971 this was unique in British soccer and, predictably, was regarded by the players as a complete waste of time," writes Shindler.

Yet by then Allison had already begun the downhill slide that occupied most of the second half of his life. During the World Cup of 1970 he had worked as a television pundit. Handsome, articulate, and fond of smoking cigars on screen, he drew viewers. Women mobbed him in the streets. He became "Big Mal." "Allison did not win a single thing in English soccer after the birth of Big Mal," notes his biographer David Tossell. "It seems to be more than coincidence."

At City, Allison insisted on being promoted from coach to manager. Shindler says he proved "a brilliant coach and a rotten manager." Allison left the club for Crystal Palace in 1973, and from then on was known chiefly for what he did outside soccer. London offered gambling, nightclubs, champagne, and blondes. Among his claimed conquests was Christine Keeler, siren of the Profumo affair.

Big Mal was a showman, famous for his sheepskin coat and fedora hat, though he could also give team talks shirtless, and took off even more to bathe with Richmond. He created that seventies phenomenon: the manager as hedonistic performer. Newspapers egged him on. A former "runner" for the press in Fleet Street in his youth, Allison understood media, and he fed journalists quotes and stories, sometimes while drunk. He would promise "to take soccer to the moon" or to "frighten the cowards of Europe." He screamed at referees.

All these were distractions. He began to go from job to job: Plymouth and Manchester City again, Middlesbrough, Kuwait, Galatasaray in Turkey, and even Memphis, where he was fired before his first game. ("You're not really a manager until you've been sacked," Big Mal liked to say.) His brief American experience prompted him to advise Middlesbrough to dye their pitch orange. When he later sued Middlesbrough for wrongful dismissal, it emerged that in a three-month stay at a local hotel he had run up a bill of £3,500 for brandy, champagne, and cigars.

He did win the Portuguese league with Sporting, but mostly he floundered without adult supervision. Like many of his contemporaries in English soccer, he was eaten away by alcohol. Wives and girlfriends came and went. He ended up alone with his Alzheimer's in a one-room apartment in Middlesbrough. The Allison of Cassetari's café and *Soccer for Thinkers* had disappeared long before—his loss, and English soccer's.

Jorge Valdano
January 2011

Jorge Valdano is trying to explain what Real Madrid is about—a question he's better equipped to answer than perhaps anyone else—and the club's director of soccer reaches into the past, to talk about a fellow Argentine-turned-Madrilene. "You could say that Alfredo di Stefano incarnates Real," says Valdano. Di Stefano was the linchpin of the great Real that won the first five European Cups, from 1956 to 1960. Valdano explains, "After a defeat it was best not to look at Alfredo, because his eyes would be spitting fire. When things were going badly, he'd forget about beauty and just pursue the result. Everything that has happened at this club, in one way or another, has been influenced by the spirit of di Stefano. This is a club with a very bad relationship to defeat."

Valdano is speaking as Real Madrid's director of soccer, as a former player and coach of the club, but also as a gifted writer. Perhaps nobody inside the game can talk soccer better than he does. Ask him a question and he pauses a beat or two, before answering in complete sentences in his precise, Argentine-inflected Spanish.

We're sitting in Real's offices inside the Bernabéu stadium one evening, an hour before a game. On one wall is a black-and-white picture of di Stefano's team. It shows the players standing up in open-topped cars, dressed in summer suits, driving through Madrid amid cheering crowds. General Franco's policemen accompany them on motorbikes. The photo is Real triumphant—the club's natural state. But in Valdano's four spells at the club since he first came here in 1984, Real mostly hasn't been like that.

There is something dysfunctional about post-Franco Real, and Valdano's journey of these past twenty-five years helps illuminate what. The club has struggled to redefine its identity and regain the dominance it had in di Stefano's era. Its present failure is baffling. There's an almost iron law in soccer that money brings success, and Real is the world's richest club: It had income of more than $565 million in the 2008–2009 season. Yet on the field it reliably gets humiliated by the world's best team, its eternal rival, Barcelona. Real had better hurry up and win something soon—ideally the Champions League in London this May—for Valdano's sake and its own.

Valdano was born in 1955 in a small town in the Argentine pampas. "When I was small," he told me once, "I often heard: 'You're in a country where nobody is hungry, where it's unthinkable that there'll ever be war, and where you have the most beautiful women in the world.' Now we only have the most beautiful women in the world." He has called Argentina "the world's first undeveloping country."

But Valdano grew tall and strong on the then bounty of the pampas. He turned out to be good at everything, the man other men wanted to be. He devoured Jorge Luis Borges, briefly studied law, dressed as elegantly as he spoke, became a goalscoring striker, and in 1975 arrived in Spain to play for the little Basque club Deportivo Alavés. Franco died that same year, and so Valdano found himself a young left-wing intellectual in a free country just as young left-wing intellectuals in Argentina were being dropped from military helicopters into the River Plate. This shaped his thinking about soccer.

He admired the bony, chain-smoking closet communist Cesar Luis Menotti, the Argentine coach who brought the country its first World Cup in 1978. Menotti believed in "a soccer of the Left": a creative game in which working-class people expressed their natural genius. By contrast, "soccer of the Right" was the thuggish game played by certain Argentine teams, whose players read up on the personal problems of their opponents in order to unsettle them, just in case biting and spitting failed.

Valdano, a subtle and funny man, only partly bought this spiel, yet the soccer he describes in his books is a *Menottista* soccer. It's the soccer he always wanted his teams to play. That makes it so striking that last spring Real hired as its coach José Mourinho. The little Portuguese favors a defensive style that looks suspiciously like "soccer of the Right." (More about Valdano and Mourinho later.)

As a player Valdano won two league titles with Real. However, his great moment was winning the World Cup with Argentina in 1986. Valdano scored in the final, and just as thrillingly got the chance to observe his teammate Diego Maradona from up close.

Valdano with Maradona, as in most of his relationships in soccer, was a literate, educated person who had wandered into an alien world. Other players often mock him as a pseudointellectual, and call him *El Filósofo* (The Philosopher), a nickname that's intended as insult. On Spanish television's satirical puppet show, Valdano's puppet was always blathering on about Plato.

Valdano never hides his bookishness, but he doesn't think it's very relevant. He knows that reading books doesn't help you win soccer matches. I could describe Maradona's goal [the dribble against England in 1986] much better than he could," he once told me, "but I could never have scored it."

This evening in Madrid's offices we get talking about winning World Cups. Several of Real's players pocketed one with Spain last year. Had that reminded him of his own triumph? "It seems pornographic to me that twenty-five years have passed, because I remember it as clearly as if it were yesterday. But when the Spanish players were being given their medals, my daughter asked, 'Where's your medal?' My wife went off to search for it. Eventually, she found it. It's now in a place where I can't get to it," he said, and laughed. Still, he insists he hardly ever thinks about lifting the cup.

A year after that, hepatitis forced him to retire from playing. He became a writer, and a coach, and in 1994 he returned to coach Real. The club was then in its dark decades. It hadn't won its pet prize, the European Cup, since 1966. Worse, in 1992 Barcelona had won the trophy for the first time, and Catalans had taken to mocking Madrilenes for only winning the cup "in black and white."

In fact, Spanish soccer was experiencing the same shift in power as Spanish politics: from the center to the regions. Under Franco, Real's hegemony had been unchallenged. The general himself had made a point of catching the club's games on the radio, taking a transistor with him if he went out partridge shooting, writes Jimmy Burns in *When Beckham Went to Spain*.

None of this is to say that Real was a "fascist club," as its detractors sometimes charge. In fact, notes Burns, during the Spanish civil war the club was briefly run "as a Soviet-style workers' federation." Yet Real did benefit from Franco. It's not that he fixed referees or gave Real money. He didn't need to. A dictator typically concentrates his country's resources in the capital city. That's where he, his bureaucrats, generals, and secret policemen live. It's the last place where he wants an uprising. And so capitals and their soccer teams thrive under dictatorships. Every team from a dictatorship ever to win the European Cup (now called the Champions League) came from a capital city. By contrast, winning teams from democracies almost all come from provincial towns.

After Franco died, Spain's regions rose. Barcelona in particular grew richer, and its soccer team improved. Real's decline fed the daily hysteria that grips the club. In Spain there are newspapers and television stations that live off Real. "This is a club that moves amid great turbulence. It's a universal focus of news," says Valdano. He tries to remain ironic amid the hysteria.

When a journalist laid out two tape recorders in front of him prior to an interview recently, Valdano commented, "Ah! One to record my words, the other to record my thoughts."

But at Real, the hysteria often crowds out everything else. The club's inherited obligation is to rule Europe with the world's best players playing attacking soccer. It's an obligation no other club has. When Real stopped meeting this obligation, it got caught in an endless cycle of hubris and despair. The club's president would hire a coach, buy new players, say that this at last was the perfect team, as good as di Stefano's, and when they lost three matches running, he'd throw everyone out and start again. Valdano himself was sacked months after leading Real to the Spanish title in his only full season as the club's coach. At Real, the coach's function is to be a human sacrifice.

Real's wealth did eventually buy more titles: the Champions League in 1998 (immediately after which the club sacked the winning coach) and 2000. UEFA, the European soccer association, named Real the club of the twentieth century. And in the summer of 2000, the Madrilene construction magnate Florentino Pérez was elected the club's president with a mission to restore the glory days of di Stefano. Pérez made Valdano his technical director in charge of signing players. After a hiatus when Pérez was voted out of office in 2006, the two men returned to power in 2009. Today they are still chasing di Stefano's legacy, watched from the stands by an impatient octogenarian di Stefano.

Pérez's big idea was to buy *galacticos*, the world's greatest players. Di Stefano's team, too, had been full of *galacticos*. Santiago Segurola, a writer on soccer and buddy of Valdano's, has a nice theory about this. When Pérez was four years old, in 1951, his father began taking him to the Bernabéu stadium to watch Real. Pérez loved his dad. And so some of his happiest childhood memories were formed in that great concrete bowl, watching di Stefano's team. Pérez, explains Segurola, has a Freudian relationship with Real. In Pérez's mind, that great team of the 1950s is tangled up with his beloved father. By trying to reassemble the 1950s team—now with Cristiano Ronaldo as di Stefano and the Brazilian Kaká as Raymond Kopa—he is communing with his father. John Carlin in *White Angels*, his book about Real, describes the photograph he once saw hanging over Pérez's bed: Pérez posing on the Bernabéu grass among four of his *galacticos*. As the psychiatrist in

Fawlty Towers says of Basil Fawlty: "There's enough material there for an entire conference."

In name Valdano was Real's technical director, but working for the mercurial Pérez he often seemed more spokesman than policy maker. His job was to turn the club's actions into beautiful words. It might have been frustrating, but everyone in soccer, even Jorge Valdano, wants to stay on the boat, especially at Real, and so everyone does what it takes. In 2003 I sat in this same room listening to Valdano tell me that Real's team would consist entirely of *galacticos* and homegrown players. In his fine phrase, Real wouldn't sign "middle-class players."

In 2002 Real had won its ninth Champions League. But after that Pérez's *galacticos* stopped producing. There were too many chiefs and almost no Indians. From 2004 through 2006 Real won exactly zero prizes. Looking back this evening, Valdano admits, "We lacked players of—you could say—the middle class. This time, as well as signing Cristiano Ronaldo and Kaká, players with another profile have arrived to bring a greater stability. You always need players like Xabi Alonso. Guys who might not look spectacular, but who can read a match. Who can destroy a counterattack by taking one step left or right."

While Pérez was out of office, in 2007 and 2008, Real won the Spanish league twice. Pérez and Valdano returned for the 2009–2010 season, and again won nothing. In Pérez's two eras in charge Real has spent hundreds of millions of euros in transfer fees, almost certainly more than any other soccer club, and has gone through more than a coach a year. The club's debt was nearly $800 million in 2008, and surely more now. Meanwhile, pundits are debating whether the current Barcelona side is the best soccer team ever, better than di Stefano's Real.

When I ask Valdano about his second spell as technical director, he says, "That's what is more difficult: Barcelona. It's the strongest Barcelona in history."

Isn't Barcelona's beautiful game—invented by Valdano's own hero Johan Cruijff—exactly the soccer Valdano has always had in his head? "No," he smiles. "I'm from South America, not from Europe. I've always been a great admirer of Cruijff. But for me, Brazil of 1970 was the platonic dream of soccer."

Still, doesn't Barcelona benefit from a fixed style? That gives the club a stability that Real seems to lack. Valdano interrupts:

The leader of Barcelona is the style of play. Now, at the head of Barça is a person who has taken the respect for this culture to the point of exaggeration: Pep Guardiola [the current coach]. In Madrid it was always different. At Real there is an enormous passion for triumph. There's an admiration here for the player who gives everything. That's why a player like Angel di Maria has had such rapid success here. And there's also a desire for spectacle. But that's the order of things here. In Barcelona that order is reversed. First it's the play, then the result.

I once witnessed Real's "enormous passion for triumph" close-up in Valdano himself. It was a few minutes after Real had lost a group match in the Champions League away against Milan. The defeat didn't matter much. Real eventually progressed to the next round anyway. When I passed Valdano on the staircase leaving the San Siro stadium, I greeted him cheerily. He glared at me, "eyes spitting fire," as he had described di Stefano after a defeat, and strode off. The usual courteous funny *Filósofo* had vanished. Like Real, Valdano has a very bad relationship with defeat.

That's why last spring the club hired the coach who is, match for match, probably the winningest in soccer history. It was unfortunate that a couple of years earlier Valdano had described the defensive soccer played by Mourinho's then team Chelsea as "shit on a stick." Unveiling the Portuguese at a press conference, Valdano admitted that he had once been "aggressive" about Mourinho's style. However, he added, the two men had "resolved our differences in a personal meeting." Since then Valdano, Pérez, and Mourinho have formed an uneasy trinity.

Some companies get so obsessed with their internal processes that they lose sight of outcomes. In appointing Mourinho, Real showed that it has the opposite problem: it's so obsessed with outcomes that it barely seems to care about processes.

Why did Valdano appoint his ideological opposite? He says, "My idea of soccer is expressed in five books, and in the teams I coached at Tenerife, Real Madrid, and Valencia. All my teams had the same style. But in the position I am in now, I'm an interpreter of Real Madrid—not of my own ideas. And Real Madrid, at this moment, with our reorganization of the team, needed a very strong leadership, and nobody represented that better than Mourinho."

"In two years we have replaced almost the entire team. Now we have a side with an average age of twenty-four. Marcelo is twenty-two, Özil is twenty-two, Khedira is twenty-three. It's a team with a lot of future." The young men have played well under Mourinho, especially if you forget the 5–0 thrashing by Barcelona on November 30.

How has the Portuguese changed Real? Valdano says:

If this team has a quality, it is its devotion. We haven't yet lost a point because the players weren't trying hard enough. Surely, that must have something to do with the coach's personality. His way of working, with very clear ideas, is well suited to players today. When I was a player I liked to have more liberty than obligations. Today they seem to prefer having more obligations than liberty. They seem comfortable with a demanding coach who imposes a regime on them. We do have personalities here. We have Iker Casillas, captain of the world champions. We have players of great intelligence like Xabi Alonso. And Cristiano Ronaldo, with his tremendous character. But I think these players—and this club—needed a coach with these characteristics.

Is the Mourinho he sees the loud and shouty one that the rest of us watch from afar? Valdano replies:

No! In the way great players and coaches are perceived in the media, there is often a colossal misunderstanding. The Mourinho you see from a distance would not have the support of all his players—let alone of his ex-players. Almost nobody who has worked under his discipline speaks badly of Mourinho. I've seen the same thing with many players, like Raúl: great players who are nonetheless great unknowns. It's incredible in this society of the image, with the projection in the media that players have today, that this situation is so common.

Actually, admits Valdano, even he now struggles to penetrate to the players. "Twenty-five years ago, the contact between the club and the player was very direct. It was all much simpler. A player was the club's employee, with rights but above all obligations. Now there are many layers between club and player. Sometimes your interlocutor is still the player himself. But sometimes the interlocutor is the player's father, the player's agent, the player's communications director, the player's girlfriend. The complexity has increased."

One thing hasn't changed: Real's "enormous passion for triumph." The club is currently chasing Barcelona in the Spanish league, and seeking its tenth European title, *la décima*. Valdano promises: "When Barcelona awakens from its dream, *el Madrid* will be there, to occupy the place it's always had in the history of soccer."

Well, possibly.

In May 2011 Valdano lost the power struggle with Mourinho and was sacked by Pérez.

Billy Beane
April 2011

At first you think it's the junk room: a cellar where they dump old, broken things. But gradually it dawns on you: This really is the Oakland A's clubhouse. Billy Beane, the A's general manager, is sprawled on a battered sofa, his giant feet on the grubby beige carpet. It's February, the off-season, but here and there a yellow-and-green baseball shirt hangs in one of the players' open lockers. The Oakland Coliseum has barely changed since 1981 when my dad drove me up from Palo Alto, a rabid eleven-year-old A's fan, to see the A's beat the Red Sox 4–3 on a Tony Armas homer. It must now be the most dilapidated stadium in the Major Leagues.

In this very junk room not long ago, Beane and Brad Pitt sat eating takeout pizza from Zachary's in Berkeley. Pitt was hanging around with Beane, preparatory to playing him in the movie *Moneyball*, and as Beane explains, "He's not the kind of guy you can just walk down to the local restaurant." Pitt also sneaked a visit to Beane's house, in the hills near Oakland. "I didn't think it was a big deal," Beane says, "but my wife and the nanny seemed to think it was. They were up at five in the morning getting ready, which is the first time my wife's got up at five in the morning."

Beane spends a lot of time sitting in this junk room watching European soccer on the big television. While he watches soccer, the A's players watch him. They're bemused as to what their boss sees in the girls' sport. Beane remembers sitting on his battered sofa last year when Arjen Robben volleyed in the shot that knocked Manchester United out of the Champions League. Beane, nearly fifty now, jumped vertically into the air and whooped. An A's player looked up from his locker and laughed: what an absurd sight. You didn't often see Beane whooping when his own team won a ball game.

"Just watch that goal," Beane instructed the player, and because Beane is the boss and six foot four and still sports the Charles Atlas physique that once lured half the baseball and football scouts in the United States to his parents' house in San Diego (his exercise machine stands beside the battered sofa), the A's player watched the replay. And the second replay. Finally the A's player got it: That skinny bald little European with knock-knees was as great an athlete as the A's player himself. "Wow," said the A's player, though maybe he said it only to please the boss.

Like millions of other Americans this past decade, Beane has come to follow soccer with the almost unhealthy fervor of a convert. "I watch as many of the games as I can," he tells us this morning in the junk room. Often he's up watching at five thirty in the morning. Sometimes he has to battle his wife for the remote control: He'll be watching Fox Soccer Channel, and she wants to see the baseball highlights on *SportsCenter*. However, his study of soccer goes much further. On his morning commute through the northern Californian hills, or while the A's are playing in the evening, he often listens to obscure soccer podcasts—for up to five hours a day, according to the *Toronto Star*. "I'm a bit of a junkie," he admits.

And he's also a soccer revolutionary. Five thousand miles from Europe, almost unseen by the media, Beane influences the thinking of Chelsea and Manchester City. He regards Arsène Wenger as a soul mate, and you could even call him the brain behind John Henry's Liverpool. Beane and his followers are now changing soccer just as he previously changed baseball.

Sometime in late 2009, an e-mail arrived in my in-box from Billy Beane. "Sorry to intrude," it began. Chelsea's soccer operations director, Mike Forde, had given him my address. Beane had read my book *Soccernomics* and wanted to chat. Of course he'd read the book. He reads all soccer books. He was once raving to me about David Goldblatt's 978-page history of soccer, *The Ball is Round,* and when I said that if he liked I could put him in touch with Goldblatt, he exclaimed, with what sounded like genuine excitement, "That would be great!" In fact, he seemed to admire Goldblatt in much the same way that Goldblatt and I admire great athletes like Beane.

Beane and I began phoning and e-mailing each other to chat about soccer. I first met him in real life in October 2010, at a conference in London. He turned out to be an unusual mix: an amiable Californian, with a boyish quiff and big eyes behind his round glasses, and at the same time a bonehard American businessman. I found the contact enjoyable, but also slightly surreal. I had trouble seeing Beane as a real person. Like millions of other readers, I already knew him from Michael Lewis's book *Moneyball.* To me Beane was above all a great literary character, like Winston Smith or Holden Caulfield. Once we became e-mail buddies, I was often reminded of Woody Allen's story *The Kugelmass Episode,* in which sweaty old twentieth-century Professor Kugelmass finds himself having an affair with Madame Bovary from the nineteenth-century novel. Sometimes, when Beane rang me from the highway in the California morning, I knew what he was going to say before he said it. I'd already read it in *Moneyball.*

We know most of the life story from the book: son of a naval officer in San Diego grows up to be brilliant teenage athlete, a living Greek statue, courted by Major League baseball clubs and college football programs. In the junk room this morning, I ask him whether as a kid he ever played soccer.

"Not once," says Beane.

Did he never even kick a ball?

"We had a hybrid game at junior high which we called speedball, which would really disgust anybody from outside the United States. You could actually catch it in the air and throw it. I did have a Pele poster on my wall from the Cosmos. Most Americans in the '70s knew Pele. They weren't quite sure what he did, but they knew of him."

In the classic American high school divide, Beane was both jock and nerd. His parents, who had married young and never had a shot at college, wanted Billy to use his brain. "Our family wasn't particularly well off," says

Beane. "Really, the reason my dad introduced me to sports was the ability to acquire a college scholarship. It was just a way to pay for college."

That's why in 1980 the Beane family was excited when Stanford tried to recruit him as a quarterback. Beane likes to joke that if he'd accepted the scholarship, you'd never have heard of the guy who was then Stanford's quarterback, John Elway. The A's media officer, a feisty lady who used to work at Stanford, likes to retort that if Beane had gone to Stanford he'd have spent three years riding the bench behind Elway and nobody would ever have heard of Billy Beane. Anyway, Beane turned down Stanford. The New York Mets were offering him $125,000 to play baseball, and the military middle-class kid felt he ought to take the money. As Lewis records in *Moneyball*, a family friend advised the Beanes to sink the $125,000 in a real-estate project. The project tanked, and the $125,000 evaporated. Beane missed out on college.

"I don't look at it as a regret now," he says in the junk room. "I'd say *missed opportunity* is probably a better word. The people that you're going to school with, what you're exposed to in future world leaders, senators—I missed that opportunity, and I don't think you can really put a price tag on that. But it was a great life lesson." Beane (although a Republican) has tried never again to make a decision based on money alone.

As I've gotten to know him slightly, I've come to think of this missed opportunity as his great formative moment. Over the past thirty years, Beane has created his own Stanford. His scientific revolution in baseball, the clever people and books with which he surrounds himself, and his current deep study of soccer: It all seems to me an attempt to catch up on the education he missed at age eighteen.

Beane began playing Minor League Baseball, but from the beginning he had inklings of having chosen the wrong profession. He recalls:

When I was eighteen, the general manager of the New York Mets was a gentleman named Frank Cashen, a lawyer by trade. And he walked into the park, and there was just a certain air about him. And I remember saying to one of my teammates, 'I think we've got this wrong. We all want to get to the big league; that guy over there in the bow tie is the guy you want to be.' I wanted to be the guy picking the players. I wanted to be the guy running the club. And as I've gotten older, I wanted to be the guy running the business, because it's such an important part of sports now.

Beane never became the great player the scouts had seen in him. "As a baseball failure—" I begin my question.

Beane pulls a pained face: "Can we? . . . Do we have another? . . . Is there a synonym that we can use? How about, 'My relative success'?"

He did after all make the Major Leagues. In 1990 he was a twenty-seven-year-old outfielder with the Oakland A's. That was when he walked into the A's front office and said he wanted to quit playing and become an advance scout. As Lewis notes in *Moneyball*, nobody ever quits Major League Baseball at age twenty-seven to become a scout. But Beane wanted to be the guy with the bow tie.

Naturally, he treated his new career as a kind of further education—graduate school, if you like, at the University of Billy Beane. The great thing was that baseball at the time had recently acquired its very own revolutionary intellectual movement: sabermetrics. The sabermetricians, a grouping of mostly weird-looking nerds whose dean was the Kansas janitor Bill James, were very much outside professional baseball. When Beane became a scout, James was already a cult hero, yet hardly anyone inside the Major Leagues had ever heard of him. But as soon as Beane heard about the sabermetricians, he wanted to read their stuff. To this day he still keeps James's *Baseball Abstracts* in his office, as revered relics. "I'll never throw them away," he says. "I actually have some of the original ones that almost look like academic papers, typewritten."

The story of *Moneyball* is how Beane became general manager of the A's and reformed the club along sabermetric lines. "We just stole these ideas from smarter people than ourselves," he says now, and then corrects himself: "*Stole*, that's the wrong word." (Beane spends a lot of his mental energy trying to find the right words.) "We borrowed these ideas that had been written about even long before Bill James."

Beane hired smart young statisticians from the Ivy League, like the twenty-four-year-old Harvard grad Paul Podesta. Their job was to find undervalued players, and to further Billy Beane's education at the same time. Beane is so proud of their conjuring with numbers that he sometimes forwards their e-mails to his friends, as if to say: go figure. Sometimes, when Beane is very busy, and the nerds want to explain another algorithm, he'll just say, "Cut to the conclusion." But mostly he considers them an enrichment of the University of Billy Beane.

As *Moneyball* records, stats worked for the A's. Whereas other clubs did things because they'd always done them that way, the A's came up with new ways of running a baseball club. They dropped the idiotic ancient strategies of base stealing and sacrifice bunting. They stopped recruiting batters for their batting average and began recruiting them for their much more telling on-base percentage. Whereas other clubs tried to recruit living Greek statues like the eighteen-year-old Billy Beane, the A's were quite happy to sign fat players. "*Big-boned* is the term we prefer to use," chuckles Beane. Always, they were trying to find players who had been undervalued by other clubs. Inevitably, he looks for an analogy in soccer. What the A's were doing, he says, was "looking for the next Gareth Bale, paying £500 for Gareth Bale and seeing him perform at a certain level and then turning 'round and selling him."

Other people began to notice the A's. In 2002 John Henry, owner of the Boston Red Sox, tried to lure Beane to Boston. He offered him a minimum of $12.5 million over five years, more than a GM in baseball had ever been paid. Beane first said yes, but then he said no. He wasn't going to make a decision based on money again. Instead, Henry hired a twenty-eight-year-old Yale graduate named Theo Epstein as GM.

The A's never had the money the Red Sox did. Beane says, "We are in a big media area, but we share it with a bigger club. I guess, we were sort of Everton to some extent."

"Smaller," I say. "More like Wigan," and Beane agrees.

The Wigan of the Major Leagues punched above its weight for years. The A's won the American League West four times between 2000 and 2006. With a bit more luck they might have made it to a World Series. (Beane reckons that success in the baseball playoffs, like success in the knockout rounds of a soccer World Cup or Champions League, mostly comes down to luck, because it is decided over so few games.) The A's weren't lucky.

And there the story might have ended, with Beane a minor celebrity at a small club, but for the fact that he had met a clever guy who lived just down the road from the Oakland Coliseum, in Berkeley: Michael Lewis. (I owe a particular debt to Lewis because his first book, *Liar's Poker*, explains so clearly what a bond is that it got me through my job interview at the *Financial Times* in 1994. Seventeen years on, I'm still at the paper.)

The University of Billy Beane is always on the lookout for visiting professors. Lewis, the master of business books, was the perfect candidate for a man who has educated himself largely from business books. "I consider him both a friend and an incredibly stimulating person to be around," says Beane. Partly for that reason, and partly because Beane is a canny businessman who knows the value of publicity, he let Lewis hang around at the Coliseum for a year. In 2003 Lewis published *Moneyball*. Suddenly everyone in baseball knew what Beane and his fat A's had been doing.

More and more clubs began to copy them. Baseball, says Beane now, "has turned into more of a science—I think more of a science than even people will publicize." As German author Christoph Biermann writes in *Die Fussball-Matrix*, the best book so far on soccer and data, *Moneyball* is the only book that changed a sport. But *Moneyball*'s influence goes even further: It changed other sports, too. In 2004 the first NBA team hired a full-time statistician. Now they all have statisticians. And from there, the statistical revolution spread across the Atlantic to sports like rugby, cricket, and even soccer.

The conquest of baseball by *Moneyball* methods was formally sealed in 2004, when the Red Sox of John Henry and Theo Epstein won the club's first World Series since 1918. In 2007 they won another. In a way these were triumphs for Beane, but they weren't visible triumphs.

Once almost everyone in baseball went *Moneyball*, the A's lost their advantage and stopped punching above their weight. (Those who scoff that *Moneyball* was wrong because the A's haven't been winning lately don't seem to understand the basic principles of imitation and catch-up.) It's surely no coincidence that in recent years, as the A's have tailed off somewhat, Beane has developed an obsession with soccer.

It began when Beane's wife had a birthday. Like most men, Beane couldn't think of a present. He panicked. Luckily, he says, "I had a cheap flight to London. So I said, 'Hey, honey, we're going to London for your birthday.'"

"I didn't go over to London anticipating falling in love with soccer," he claims now. But inevitably, he did treat the trip as a sort of seminar in English culture. Every morning in London he'd study the British newspapers. He noticed that they barely ran a word about the NFL or baseball. Instead, they just went on about soccer all the time. On romantic strolls through town with his wife, Beane noticed that in front of almost every pub was a chalkboard with the times of that day's televised soccer matches. From the A's junk room he recalls, "I'm a big college football fan here, and it was very similar to how college football is in the South: SEC football where you have this passion and you have a large number of massive fans in this small area."

Back home in California, he started studying for his major in soccer. "I just literally—and it's been going on for a decade—have read every piece of literature I could find on it," he says. "The history of baseball's part of my DNA. Ironically, the history of the Football Association is almost identical in terms of length as Major League Baseball. So I had this whole new sport that I had to learn 150 years of history, and instead of starting at age five I started at a much older age. It's never stopped for me. It continues because I have so much to catch up with."

But Beane is a jock as well as a nerd, and the other thing that drew him to soccer was the athleticism of the players. It turned out they weren't little wimps at all. Watching them, Beane saw, "These are the exact same guys that are playing our sports. They just chose this sport. Had they grown up in the United States, they would be playing at the highest level at whatever sport they did." For instance, when other Americans ask him what this guy Lionel Messi is like, Beane will say, "Well, just imagine if you had Barry Sanders—who's one of the greatest running backs in the history of the NFL—his quickness and his ability to change direction, with the vision of Steve Nash on a basketball court. That's Lionel Messi."

Just around the time that Beane got interested in soccer, something fortuitous happened: People in soccer got interested in him. Mike Forde, a Briton then working as performance director for Bolton Wanderers, who happened to have gone to college in Beane's hometown, San Diego, and who loved American sports, read *Moneyball*. "To be able to make contact with these people is really something that would have never happened had the book never been published," says Beane. Forde visited the Coliseum, where Beane bombarded him with questions about soccer. Only right near the end did Forde manage to steer the conversation to what Beane did at the A's.

Frenchman Damien Comolli, who had worked for Wenger at Arsenal, and then briefly been technical director of Spurs, also dropped by. What the visitors really wanted to know was: How do you use stats to evaluate sportsmen? If *Moneyball* had worked in baseball, might it have some use in soccer?

Beane became friendly with Comolli, Forde, and a German expat in California named Jürgen Klinsmann. When Klinsmann later became manager of the German national team, he hired more sports scientists than anyone in soccer had ever seen (some of them Americans, which was another taboo) and guided Germany to a surprising third place at the World Cup of 2006. Afterward Klinsmann joined Bayern Munich and sent Beane a Bayern shirt with BILLY BEANE on the back. Beane was happy with the shirt, but admits he is too self-conscious to wear it into the local Starbucks.

Beane had become a soccer junkie. However, he still spent his days surrounded by baseball junkies paid to think and talk about baseball all the time. That couldn't last. The University of Billy Beane needed a small soccer faculty. One day, when the A's were looking for a new young statistician, Beane interviewed an MIT economics graduate named Farhan Zaidi.

At this point in the conversation, Beane summons Farhan and his laptop to the junk room. Farhan is a cheery, small, round brown guy with a sense of humor. He's the kind of person you'd expect to meet late one night after a gig in a bar in a college town, not in a professional sports club. At MIT he specialized in behavioral economics ("Like that's real useful," teases Beane). But when Farhan came for his job interview at the A's, Beane quizzed him on one topic: Oasis, the favorite band of both men. When it then transpired that Farhan was a soccer junkie, too, he was hired. "I tried to direct the conversation in each of those directions," Farhan admits now.

In between crunching baseball stats, the two of them have been talking soccer ever since. As Farhan says, "We spend so much time together that if all we ever talked about was the numbers on spreadsheets, we would have killed each other a long time ago."

Farhan had been to the World Cups of 1998 and 2002. When the World Cup 2006 in Germany came around, they both reasoned that they really ought to go, even if it happened to fall in the middle of the baseball season. Together with the A's owner Lew Wolff, they played hookie and flew over for eight days. "We were just like college kids with backpacks, shorts, going to every match we could," Beane recalls.

He was then still a bit naive about soccer. During England-Trinidad he went to the bathroom and missed one of England's two goals. But, he says, "You go through life and you think about the best trips you've ever taken, and we all have a list of two or three that we'll always remember, and that by far was the most enjoyable trip I've ever taken." Even better, while they were away in Germany, the A's won every game. Every day they'd phone home, and their colleagues would say, "Don't hurry back." In fact, someone said, if Beane and Farhan would just emigrate to Europe, the A's would probably win the World Series.

After that World Cup, whenever the A's players teased Beane about soccer, he'd tell them, "The rest of the world can't be wrong." The main thing that had struck him in Germany was the emotion of the fans. You didn't see that so much in American sports. In Beane's view, "Wherever I see emotion, I see opportunity." He drew two conclusions from his German visit: Where there's emotion, there's money to be made. And where there's emotion, people are probably making emotional decisions.

Rational *Moneyball* thinking might have a place in soccer, too.

A few people at a few English clubs had already begun to try. Wenger had been using computer programs to value players since his time at Monaco in the 1980s. Bolton's manager Sam Allardyce, whose somewhat Neolithic appearance hid a Beane-esque mind, was always interested in any newfangled ways of getting more bang for his buck. Allardyce hired university graduates like Mike Forde, who spent their days working out questions like: If a striker averages ten goals a season in the French league, how many goals would he typically score in the Premier League? Do inswinging corners produce more goals than outswingers? At what average age do attacking midfielders begin to fade?

In 2005 Beane's best friend in soccer, Comolli, became technical director of Spurs and did his best to turn them into a sort of London version of the Oakland A's. Comolli used the new match data that were becoming available (on numbers of tackles, kilometers run, shots on target, shots stopped, and so on) to value soccer players. Using these *Moneyball* methods he signed a Brazilian goalkeeper with big ears, barely any international caps, and no reputation outside the Dutch league: Heurelho Gomes. (Beane's followers in soccer have learned over the years how to value a keeper. The crucial stat is the percentage of shots *from inside the penalty area* that the guy stops. If you credit him with every shot he stops, you'll be rewarding him for picking up rollers from thirty yards—the sort of easy balls that keepers of the best teams see a lot of. This is one of the many examples of the gradual refinement of *Moneyball* thinking in soccer.)

In 2007 Comolli paid $14 million to bring an unknown seventeen-year-old left-back named Gareth Bale to White Hart Lane. It seemed an absurd sum. Bale came from little Southampton and had played only a couple of internationals for not very fashionable Wales. But on the phone to Oakland, Comolli would talk about him with great excitement.

A couple of summers ago, when Spurs visited California, Beane got to see Bale up close. He recognized the type at once: "An eighteen-, nineteen-year-old kid, broad shouldered, lean." Bale was fast, athletic, *and* strong—a most unusual combination. Beane says, "If he was in the States he would never have touched a soccer ball. He'd have had no chance. He'd be playing wide receiver for the New York Jets, he'd be playing centerfield for a Major League Baseball team, or he'd be a shooting guy for an NBA team." The great athletes, whatever their sports, are each other's brothers. By the time Bale was twenty—long after Spurs had kicked out Comolli—it had become clear that he was a sort of Superman.

Later, Comolli took his *Moneyball* methods to St. Etienne in France. St. Etienne almost never bought players, because it had no money. Rather, its main financial decisions were about whether to offer players new contracts. If you had a starting player who was thirty years old, and you gave him a new two-year contract, that might cost you $3 million. At thirty, the guy was still good. But how could you know if he'd still be good enough at thirty-two? Comolli would look at his statistical trends: In recent seasons, had the player been making 10 percent fewer sprints each year, was the pace of his sprints falling sharply year by year, was his number of passes in the opponents' half declining sharply? If the trends were all heading downward fast, you wouldn't offer him a new contract. That's *Moneyball*: You never pay for past performance, only for future performance.

Men like Forde and Comolli were learning from Beane how to apply data to sport. But, I ask Beane in his junk room, did he learn anything from European soccer clubs? After all, they too had built up over a century's worth of sporting know-how.

Beane has to think about that one. Eventually, he says, "They were so much further ahead of us in terms of nutrition." He thinks some more, and finally he has it: "They dress nicer. I like the fact that when they walk in they all have their blazers on. We could never get our guys to do that."

Otherwise, watching television every day on his battered sofa in the junk room, Beane sees a pretty emotional sport.

Normally Beane follows European soccer from a distance of 5,000 miles. A year ago he told me, in much the same tones of wistful awe in which he'd spoken of David Goldblatt, that he hoped one day to meet Arsène Wenger. Then one day it happened. In October 2010 Forde organized a conference about sports and data at Chelsea. Beane was flown in from California, to be on a panel with Wenger chaired by Comolli. I too got a small role at the conference: as interviewer of an obscure Qatari soccer official, Mohammad bin Hammam, who had then not yet brought the World Cup to his country or announced his candidacy to replace Sepp Blatter as president of FIFA.

The first night of the conference, about a hundred of us participants gathered for dinner at Marco, Marco Pierre White's restaurant at Stamford Bridge. At the cocktails I spotted Beane: I looked up toward the ceiling, and there he was. So he wasn't just a literary character. We began chatting about soccer and data. Comolli joined us, and the three of us sat down at a table. The first course was served. We kept talking about soccer and data. After a while I looked up and saw that the restaurant was empty. Everyone else had finished eating and left. Hours had passed without us noticing. Though I discovered that evening that Beane was a Republican, he turned out to be just as much fun in real life as in the pages of *Moneyball*.

The next day Beane debated Wenger—or so I'm told, because on Wenger's orders no journalists were admitted. But afterward the two men came to the room reserved for speakers, accompanied, oddly enough, by Tony Blair's soccer-mad former right-hand man, Alastair Campbell. They planted themselves on the sofa and sat talking (I timed them) for three hours. The two soul mates had found each other. (Campbell said nothing. As a former member of the Blair government, he was probably happy just not to be kicked out.)

On the last morning of the conference I had breakfast at Stamford Bridge with Beane and Comolli. Beane showed up with the morning papers tucked underneath his arm. The news had broken that John Henry, the Red Sox owner, was also in England. He'd flown over to buy Liverpool. Beane had sent him an e-mail suggesting they meet, but it wasn't going to work out, as Beane had to fly back to California that afternoon. However, Beane was enthused by the impending deal. Henry had perfected *Moneyball* at the Red Sox. Imagine, mused Beane, if he could do something similar in soccer. Beane said, "John understands numbers, and in sport it's about numbers. John is a very rational person."

"He tried to hire you," I said.

"Well, that's the irrational part of him," said Beane.

I live in Paris. A few weeks after that breakfast in London, I was in a café eating my morning croissant when I noticed a news story in the French sports daily *L'Equipe*: Comolli was leaving St. Etienne. The paper said he was unhappy at the club, but it also predicted that later that day he'd be joining Liverpool. So it proved. It was clear where John Henry had been getting his advice on soccer hires. Henry was indeed planning a *"Moneyball* of soccer," hampered only by his near-total ignorance of the sport. It must have been useful to be able to ask Mr. Moneyball himself to point him in the right direction.

A couple of months after Comolli moved to Anfield, he used data to sell Fernando Torres and buy Andy Carroll and Luis Suarez. "When you find yourself handling three of the biggest transfers in English football history in the last days of the market, precise figures allow you not to do that blind," he told a British newspaper.

A lot of calls now ping back and forth between Anfield and the Coliseum. In the A's' junk room, Beane says, "Damien, you can call him anytime. He's up all the time. I'll e-mail him and it will be two in the morning there, and he'll be up and he'll say, 'Hey, I'm up, watching the A's game,' because he watches a lot of A's games on the computer. The guy never sleeps." It seems that Beane has become an unpaid consultant to Liverpool's *Moneyball* project.

At the end of the interview in the junk room, I give Beane an old baseball card of himself to sign. "Billy Beane: Outfield," it says. It's from 1987, when he was back in the Majors with the Minnesota Twins. The season before, according to the card, he'd batted just .213. (Of course, the card doesn't record what we know now is his far more significant, "OPS," the combination of on-base percentage and slugging percentage.)

Beane takes the card from me and studies it. "I think this is at the old Cleveland Stadium," he says, even though about the only one thing you can see behind the young Beane in the picture is a batting cage. "You know, you take these when you're twenty-two, and you don't think that you're going to be immortalized for the rest of your life, and you sure wish you'd shaved that day." I realize then how much of his life he's spent being seen through a slightly distorted medium: through baseball cards, and through that Greek statue of a body, Michael Lewis, and now Brad Pitt.

Beane goes off with the A's stadium manager to find a sandwich. Then he comes back, and he and Farhan sprawl on the battered sofas of the junk room and talk soccer, baseball, data, and irrationality off the record for half the afternoon.

Comolli's tenure at Liverpool ended when he was fired in April 2012. He is widely regarded as a failure who tarnished the image of data analytics in soccer. However, that view is too harsh. Certainly, his purchases of Stewart Downing, Jordan Henderson, and in particular Andy Carroll didn't pay off. However, selling Fernando Torres for $79.5 million while signing Luis Suarez for $36 million now looks pretty smart. No man who brought Suarez and Gareth Bale to the Premier League can be all bad.

Alex Ferguson
December 2011

When Sir Richard Greenbury ran the British clothing chain Marks & Spencer, he used to take Alex Ferguson out for lunch and pump him for management tips. That was smart. Manchester United's manager celebrated his seventieth birthday on December 31 as the most trophy-laden individual in soccer's history. Ferguson wins prizes not merely because United can afford excellent players. Stefan Szymanski, economics professor at the University of Michigan, has compiled a "Soccernomics index" of overachieving managers in England, the men who have reached the highest league positions relative to their clubs' wage budgets since 1974. Ferguson ranks second in the index, after Liverpool's Bob Paisley. In other words, the Scot adds exceptional value to his teams. Better, he seems capable of doing so unto eternity.

This isn't because he has a brilliant understanding of soccer. "Ferguson is not a genius," writes his biographer Patrick Barclay. Brian Clough was a better judge of players; José Mourinho is a better tactician. As United's former goalkeeper Peter Schmeichel said, "There are thousands of better coaches. But management? The handling of men? There's nobody better." Following are some of Ferguson's management secrets.

Identify yourself with your company's brand. Ferguson made himself unsackable at United partly by converting himself from mere employee into embodiment of the club's values. Doing that took study. After arriving at Old Trafford in 1986, he interviewed long-serving staff about United's history and listened to fans. He gradually absorbed three tenets of United's brand: United teams must attack, the world is against United, and United is more a cause than a soccer club. When he said, "I am like the keeper of the temple," he meant that the cause has become almost unthinkable without him.

Hone your strongest character trait into a weapon. In another manager, this trait might be niceness or sensitivity. In Ferguson's case, it's his temper.

Bobby McCulley, who played for the first club Ferguson managed, little East Stirlingshire in Scotland, said later, "I've never been afraid of anyone before, but Ferguson was a frightening bastard from the start."

Ferguson's temper is genuine, but he has learned just how to use it. An early colleague recalls him as a young manager practicing screaming at a friend behind the stand and then asking, "Does that sound okay?" Ferguson's famed "hairdryer" treatment—when he berates someone from so close that his breath blows his victim's hair—is finely honed.

John McEnroe's autobiography helped teach Ferguson when to switch off his rage. The tennis player would use his temper early in a tournament, to intimidate opponents and referees, but he'd stop before the final, when he needed calm.

Cultivate every interest group inside your company. As a young manager at St. Mirren, Ferguson got fired (for the only time in his career) after fighting with his chairman. He hadn't fully grasped that the man's consent was central to his project. "Even if you hate your chairman, you have to find a way of getting on with it," he concluded. Ever since he has worked to keep his club's board, players, fans, and sponsors onside. One leader of United's fans says Ferguson would sometimes chat to him for hours on the phone, keen to know what supporters thought. Ferguson worries much less about outsiders—referees, journalists, and other clubs—whom he treats as parties to the permanent conspiracy against Manchester United.

Gather information everywhere. Alastair Campbell, Tony Blair's former aide and a friend of Ferguson's, recalls attending a lunch in Ferguson's honor at the League Managers Association. "You could feel his gravitational pull on other managers in the room," says Campbell. "There were dozens of managers there, past and present. He knows them all. He calls them all the time. He hoovers up information all the time." Years after players have left United, they still get calls from Ferguson. He makes time to do this by working more hours than other managers. He cultivates his contacts unto death: Barclay writes that perhaps nobody in soccer attends more funerals.

Seek total control, but recognize when you cannot have it. Ferguson once listed for Campbell the three main qualities required for leadership: "Control. Managing change. And observation."

As any dictator knows, fear plus information equals control. Ferguson knows everything about his players, even their bathroom habits. (If someone goes to the bathroom more than usual, he investigates.) Dissidents generally get exiled. However, after United's best player, Wayne Rooney, flirted with joining Manchester City last year, Ferguson forgave him. He knew Rooney was irreplaceable.

Don't let other people cause you stress. Days before the 1997 election, Campbell felt stressed. People already sensed that Blair would win, and so they stopped bothering the prime minister–in-waiting with practical problems and began bothering Campbell instead. On the phone Campbell confided to Ferguson, "I'm feeling the pressure." Ferguson replied, "You know what I do in those circumstances? You've got to literally imagine you are putting blinkers on. People want to get into your space. Only you decide who gets into your space." He advised Campbell to tell petitioners, "I think you can resolve this yourself."

Remember that crises blow over. Ferguson has been through so many: Eric Cantona's karate-kicking of a spectator, the boot he himself kicked at David Beckham in 2003, the dimly remembered "Pizzagate" spat with Arsenal, and more. Ferguson never adjusts his strategy to crises, because he knows that they pass.

Always be unsatisfied. "The sweetest moment for me," he often tells interviewers, "is the last minute of a victory. After that it drains away quickly. The memory's gone in half an hour. It's like a drug, really. I need to reenact it again and again to get that last-minute feeling, when you're shouting at the referee, 'Blow that bloody whistle.'" Ferguson knows that satisfaction is fatal. Every trophy he wins is just a notch toward a target he never wants to meet.

Raymond Domenech
December 2012

Review of Raymond Domenech, *Tout seul: Souvenirs* (Flammarion, in French)

As almost every French person knows, at halftime during France's hopeless defeat to Mexico in the World Cup of 2010, the forward Nicolas Anelka shouted at his coach, Raymond Domenech, "*Enculé!* [Usually translated as "bugger," or worse.] Do it yourself then, with your shit team! Me, I'm quitting." All those involved being French, what shocked Domenech most is that Anelka addressed him with the familiar *tu* instead of the formal *vous*. This encounter led to another quintessentially French moment: after Domenech and France's soccer federation expelled Anelka from the squad, the players went on strike mid–World Cup. The phrase "the bus of shame"—the bus that the players sat in one day, refusing to practice—has entered the French language. Domenech shared the blame for the national disgrace. Today he is a pariah in France.

His bizarre new memoir, *Tout seul*, is his attempt to explain how things got so bad. It's unlike any other soccer memoir, often unintentionally hilarious, and filled with character assassinations of almost every major French player of his era, from Anelka to Zinedine Zidane. Domenech says he could have written it only with two years' distance; one hardly dares imagine what he would have said in the heat of the moment. It's a story of modern France and modern soccer. But above all it works as a business book in reverse: a study in how not to manage people.

A working-class boy from Lyon, Domenech grew up to be a violent mustachioed soccer player. He played eight times for France in the 1970s and later became coach of France's youth teams. In 2004 he used his political skills to procure the top job. ("The network, Gérard Houllier used to tell us at the coaching courses, the network . . . ") During six years managing France he kept a diary, which is the basis for *Tout seul*.

From the start, Domenech was a solitary figure inside the French soccer establishment. First, he writes, others didn't consider him "legitimate" because he hadn't been a great player. Second, as an intellectual by soccer standards (he is a keen amateur actor), he was inclined to look down on his players. And last, as *Tout seul* reveals, he didn't possess people skills.

The team he inherited had long been run by the players. In 1998 and 2000, when France won the World Cup and then the European championship, Laurent "Le Président" Blanc, the team's captain, would ceremonially punch any player who disrupted the collective. (In 2010 Blanc succeeded Domenech as France's manager.)

Domenech set out to deprive his players of power. Nobody's advice was required. Doctors and physiotherapists who were too close to the players were ousted. No wonder that Zidane, his captain at the World Cup of 2006, told him, "I feel I'm not of any use as captain. The players ask me what's happening, and I can never answer them."

Still, after a poor start, a brilliant Zidane led the French to the World Cup final against Italy. But in Berlin, Zidane head-butted Italian Marco Materazzi—a moment now immortalized in a statue in front of the Centre Georges Pompidou in Paris—and was sent off. France lost, agonizingly, in the penalty shoot-out when David Trezeguet's kick hit the underside of the crossbar and bounced out. That's how close Domenech got to winning a World Cup.

Domenech—who constantly breaks soccer taboos by revealing intimate moments behind closed doors—describes the locker-room scene after the defeat. He made a speech praising Zidane, who was retiring from soccer immediately, and asked the players to applaud their captain. "There was only the grinding of teeth," he recalls, "and my applause was not spontaneously followed. . . . Certain players really hated their captain." They could not forgive Zidane for sabotaging victory, he says. Nor, it seems, could Domenech.

He notes that Zidane was a serial offender, sent off thirteen times previously. And he has an interesting theory about Zidane's self-destructive head butt: it looked, he writes, as if Zidane was "taking revenge on his own glory, as if he felt his success was as miraculous as it was unbearable." Perhaps there is something in this.

That head butt ended a glorious French era. I live in Paris, and over the next four years I spent many freezing evenings in the Stade de France watching Domenech's France play soul-destroyingly ugly soccer. For the most part, Domenech blames the players. After 2006 Zidane et al. exited, to be replaced by the first generation of soccer players to have become millionaires on signing their first contracts. Soccer had changed in the 1990s, with fortunes flowing in from television and the "Bosman ruling" that gave players greater freedom of contract. When Domenech broke into Olympique Lyon's first team as a teenager around 1970, he earned nine hundred francs a month, or about what his dad made in the factory. When Karim Benzema was a teenager at Lyon thirty-five years later, he earned more than three hundred thousand dollars a month, writes Domenech.

These young men had different habits. They would sleep all afternoon and then sit up into the early morning having endless conversations. They "erected friendship into a supreme value, yet would break it because of an insult or a reported comment." They disrespected authority.

From the start, Domenech seems to have regarded many of his players with contempt. "It is always difficult to know what these immature boys have in their heads," he writes at one point. By the end, rereading his diary for the last World Cup, he feels "rising inside me a fund of hatred that I cannot contain." His sketches of his players—highly respected figures internationally, many of them longtime stalwarts of English clubs—are startlingly candid. There's almost an entire psychobiography here of Anelka alone. A few samples will have to suffice:

On Samir Nasri: "In a group he always pushes where it hurts, and reveals the sore spot instead of soothing it. And as a playmaker, he is just illusory. . . . As the quality of his game isn't excellent, the balance is worse than meager."

On William Gallas: "He will never be a leader. . . . Nobody could bear his attitude." When Domenech once refused to give the players a Sunday off, Gallas threatened to play badly in a qualifying match.

On Florent Malouda: "Glory has made him pretentious."

On Hatem Ben Arfa, Domenech cites the verdict of a senior player: "Punches, without hesitation."

On Anelka, seen playing for Chelsea: "It's a bizarre impression: he serves no point yet has an exceptional aura. You are reminded of Cantona."

Benzema's lack of responsiveness in conversation reminds Domenech of a "young Anelka."

Franck Ribéry, France's best player, is repeatedly depicted as a narcissist with learning disabilities who refuses to play anywhere but left wing.

Even Thierry Henry is shown playing the disc jockey and not bothering to warm up when substituted before that fatal France-Mexico match.

Then there are all the conflicts between players. Domenech doesn't take Nasri to the World Cup in 2010 because the midfielder and Ribéry loathe each other, "angry over a story of money and family." Gallas also dislikes Nasri. Malouda, Gourcuff, Henry, and Patrick Vieira all clash with Ribéry. Players won't pass to Yoann Gourcuff. The list goes on.

No doubt this French generation is a bit of a menagerie. It's often said that the hardest job in international soccer is managing England, but at least English players are mostly obedient. The media and public demand it of them, because the historical role model for an English soccer player is the soldier. They order these matters differently in France.

Nonetheless, Domenech's complaints aren't good enough. If you are a soccer manager, you can't just whine about young people today. You have to work with them. Great managers, such as Alex Ferguson or Guus Hiddink, can work with almost anyone (in Ferguson's case, even with Cantona). And the players whom Domenech savages have all succeeded at their clubs. Admittedly, club managers have more control than national managers over the weapons of pay and career. But national managers can offer glory: a World Cup trumps any Champions League, and players know it. High pay hasn't spoiled all soccer players: of the thirty-two teams at the 2010 World Cup, only one went on strike.

In short, the problem is mostly Domenech. Partly, it's because he stuck with one unhelpful bit of the old corporate culture of the French team: an old-fashioned rhetoric about the values of soccer and of France. In "the bus of shame," Domenech spoke to the striking players "of the dignity of their country, the judgment of their families, the honor of soccer." They weren't persuaded. Probably nobody under thirty-five who actually works in soccer believes this sort of thing. *Tout seul* never mentions the issue of ethnicity, but these players overwhelmingly grew up in black and brown ghettos far from the French mainstream. What, they might have reflected, had France ever done for them?

In the end he cannot reach them, mostly because he's bad with people. About the only hint of empathy he shows to any player is when he writes that Ribéry, "for various reasons, was in a psychologically difficult phase." However, he immediately adds, "In my eyes it was unimaginable to give in to his caprice." Domenech worships the collective, but not the people in it. The title *Tout seul*, presumably intended to evoke pity, contains another truth: he had no friends.

From autumn 2006 onward, Domenech appears increasingly tired, angry, and apparently depressed. The media tear him apart. Unlike, say, England's last manager, Fabio Capello, he seems a sensitive man, and sensitivity is a handicap in this job. He now realizes he should have resigned earlier. "Happy are those who can stop at the summit," he reflects in 2009. He continued partly because he saw himself as a battler, partly because he couldn't face a shameful exit, and partly, surely, because he wanted the pay. In any case, staying was a selfish decision.

The team was already splintering at Euro 2008 (even worse than the World Cup, he darkly hints), and Domenech's own reputation suffered when after France's elimination, with the nation already angry, he ignored an interviewer's questions about the shambles and instead proposed to his girlfriend live on television. (His girlfriend was furious too.) Two years later in South Africa, his team disintegrated live on international television.

Writing about that last World Cup, he finally drops his cocksureness and admits mistakes. For instance, he had decided not to take Henry to South Africa but ended up picking him—for "emotional reasons," he claims, but in truth probably because his nerves were shot and he couldn't face the public uproar that Henry's ejection would have provoked. He blundered again in South Africa by reading out his players' declaration of their strike to the TV cameras—thereby associating himself publicly with a reviled act of which he disapproved. (His first thought, on seeing the declaration, was to wonder who had written the long words for them.)

Domenech returned from South Africa so despised in France that his three-year-old son asked him, "Papa, are you going to go to prison?" Two years later, things have scarcely improved. "At the head of my next team," he fantasizes at one point, "I'll probably change my manner of functioning." But if that team comes, it might be in a desert or on a Pacific island. Domenech currently works for France's coaches' trade union and as a pundit for a small cable TV channel. He dedicates *Tout seul* to "members of my family, who had the heavy burden of carrying this name for six years." He wrote the book, he explains at the end, for fear "that all that will be left of me is the memory of a bus. I wanted to leave another trace."

But all that will be left of him probably is the memory of a bus.

So remarkable was Domenech's memoir (particularly by contrast with the more obedient English soccer culture) that the UK's New Statesman made this the lead review of its books section that week—an unheard-of honor for a soccer book published in French. As of January 2014, Domenech (now sixty-two years old) still hasn't found a new job in soccer.

Arsène Wenger
January 2013

"Spend some f****** money!" Arsenal fans chanted as their team lost again at Chelsea last Sunday. The cry echoed around the world on Twitter. Its target, Arsenal's manager, Arsène Wenger, had heard the argument before.

Wenger, now sixty-three, arrived at Arsenal in 1996 and led the club for eight glorious seasons. He's since led it for eight and a half inglorious ones. Arsenal has won no trophies since 2005 and now stands a miserable sixth in the Premier League. The Frenchman is becoming a figure of derision. Many fans complain that although Arsenal has $246 million in cash—an unheard-of sum for a soccer club—Wenger refuses to buy the expensive players who could compete with Chelsea, Manchester United, or Barcelona. He stands accused of practicing soccer's version of austerity—at a club that looks to be a model of financial good health.

Wenger and Arsenal retort that the soccer economy is a bubble: clubs are spending beyond their means and risking collapse. The argument is at bottom an argument about the soccer business. Has Wenger, almost the only actual economist in soccer, called the soccer economy right? Will Arsenal's prudence finally pay off one day?

Wenger was born in Alsace in 1949, four years after France retook the region from Germany. As a toddler he spoke not French but the Alsatian German dialect. His parents ran a café in tiny Duttlenheim. Wenger today is upright, tense, and often angry in public, but when I hosted him at a long sponsors' evening years ago, I found that in private he became a jolly mime and raconteur. Those café skills obviously ran deep.

Wenger has a mathematician's brain. He graduated with a degree in economics from Strasbourg University, and it taught him about valuations and the importance of data. When he weighs potential signings, he judges like an economist pricing assets as much as like a coach seeking quick wins.

A mediocre soccer player, he soon emerged as a born soccer manager. Raymond Domenech recalls that in 1992, when Wenger was coaching Monaco and Domenech Lyon, Wenger persuaded him to sign a player from

Monaco named James Debbah. Domenech duly bought—only to discover fast that Debbah was less wonderful than advertised. When Domenech complained, Wenger shrugged: he was simply protecting his club's interests.

Later he coached in Japan, where Japanese perfectionism left a mark on him. Then Arsenal's vice chairman David Dein decided that this obscure professorial Frenchman was just what Arsenal needed.

English soccer in the 1990s was so insular (indeed xenophobic) that many managers didn't even watch World Cups. In this world Wenger was bound to triumph. It just so happened that the best young soccer players then were French. Wenger had the pick of them. Stars like Patrick Viera, Thierry Henry, Robert Pires, and others turned the club long nicknamed "Boring, Boring Arsenal" into the best and most exciting in England.

Wenger found stars elsewhere, too, because he spends half his life watching satellite footage from obscure leagues anywhere. He has always had a wonderful eye for a player. Arsenal's scouts were everywhere, and he bought cheap. Dein negotiated the transfer fees and salaries, and if he wanted to pay a few pounds more than the more stringent Wenger thought fair, he'd pay it.

In 2004 Wenger's "Invincibles" became English champions without losing a match. It was their third championship in seven seasons, even though rivals Manchester United were much richer. Then the Invincibles lost at United in October 2004, and nothing has been quite the same since.

By then, soccer was already changing. A Russian oligarch named Roman Abramovich had bought Chelsea and begun spending fortunes on players. But the change didn't merely involve money: everyone in England had copied Wenger. Clubs stopped feeding players baked beans and began watching matches worldwide. The pioneer was falling victim to catch-up.

Abramovich's Chelsea began winning titles. When Wenger loses, he rages and punishes himself. He hated the idea that some random sugar daddy could buy himself a championship, as if it were a vacation villa. He complained that Chelsea were using "economic doping, because their resources were artificial." Wenger appears to share the widespread French suspicion of rootless international capital.

In those years he either made or went along with two fundamental decisions: One, Arsenal would build a big new stadium so as to boost revenues.

Two, Arsenal would remain financially conservative. It wouldn't spend riskily. These are the hallmark policies of the latter Wenger years.

The Emirates Stadium opened in 2006. Mostly, it has worked out: the sixty thousand seats sell out almost every match, for the largest regular crowd in London's soccer history. Arsenal's ticket prices are the highest in English and probably global soccer, with this year's cheapest season tickets costing nearly $1,600. Consequently, Arsenal now earns $5.28 million per home match, or about double its rival Spurs. The club's total revenues last season were $389 million, sixth in European soccer.

Yet moving stadiums was scary. Most of the approximately $700 million required was borrowed. Suddenly, the most conservative English club was drowning in debt. Things got scarier when the financial crisis hit in 2008, while Arsenal was selling converted apartments at its old Highbury stadium. Every season Wenger had to sell players, partly to pay off the Emirates mortgage.

With hindsight, Wenger was always going to choose a cautious spending policy. It's in his nature. The wilder side to Wenger's nature was Dein, but Dein left Arsenal amid board ructions in 2007, and since then Wenger has been freer to be himself. That has often entailed his refusing to sign a player who cost a touch more than Wenger's own valuation.

Second, choosing austerity was inevitable because it's in Arsenal's culture. The club has been cautiously run for decades. That tradition must have attracted the current majority owner, the American Stan Kroenke, who treats sports clubs as serious businesses. Ivan Gazidis, Arsenal's quiet-spoken chief executive, one of the least flashy men in soccer, son of a South African antiapartheid and anti-HIV activist and doctor, told me, "We don't spend more than we have. In soccer that is seen as conservative. That tells you a little bit about the environment we're in." Arsenal's "policy of sustainability," Gazidis adds, "should be familiar to more people given the economic state of the world, but soccer has continued to be a little bit of a bubble."

In fact, the environment of overspending rivals probably only encouraged Wenger's caution. Many pundits have long predicted a great reckoning, of soccer clubs ceasing to exist when they couldn't pay their debts—especially after the financial crisis hit and even some big banks went under. Michel Platini, president of the European soccer association UEFA, said in 2009, "If this situation goes on, it will not be long before even some major clubs face going out of business." Stefan Szymanski, economics professor at the University of Michigan, suggests Arsenal was waiting for the moment when prices collapsed and it could snap up great players cheap.

But that moment never came. It turned out that soccer clubs weren't like normal businesses. In normal business, if you rack up unpayable debts, you close down. However, soccer clubs rack up unpayable debts and live. No English club has folded for good since tiny Wigan Borough during the Great Depression in 1931.

True, smaller British clubs are forever going insolvent (though the only Premier League club ever to do so was Portsmouth in 2010), but then they do deals with their creditors, usually repay a small fraction of debt, and march merrily on. No creditor or bank manager wants to kill off a beloved ancient institution. And anyway, at bottom a club is just a name. If the club's holding company folds, a new limited company is simply created using the old club name, and the club continues on. Asked if he expected clubs to start disappearing, Gazidis says, "I don't see an immediate prospect of that, especially in England."

Arsenal's cautious spending therefore seems exaggerated. If the club thought that big soccer clubs were as vulnerable as other profligate businesses, it was wrong. Clearly, it shouldn't have copied Leeds United, which amassed a particularly spectacular debt mountain that eventually required the sale of Leeds's almost entire team and ended in a fall to the third tier of English soccer. However, Arsenal chose the other extreme. The "Swiss Rambler," a British financial professional based in Switzerland who runs a respected blog on soccer finance, calculates that since 2007, the club has made total profits of £195 million (about $322 million), of which about $294 million came from selling players. He estimates, "Arsenal could safely spend £50–60 million (about $80–96 million) from cash resources." That itself might not dislodge the two Manchester clubs. (Gazidis says, "Although the stadium took us forward, it didn't take us forward far enough.") However, such spending could get Arsenal closer. Red and White Holdings, which represents Alisher Usmanov and Farhad Moshiri, who own nearly 30 percent of shares between them, also wants Arsenal to spend more.

Arsenal's wage costs have risen sharply in recent years and last year reached $237 million, or 61 percent of turnover. Gazidis thinks that spending a bigger slice of turnover on wages would be to enter "dangerous territory."

But the Premier League's average wages-to-turnover ratio is 70 percent. And Manchester City, Chelsea, and Manchester United pay comfortably higher wages than Arsenal.

Separately from economics, Wenger made another fundamental misjudgment. He dreamed of building a team produced in Arsenal's youth academy rather than bought as adult stars. Yet in sixteen years, the academy has produced perhaps a handful of Arsenal-class players.

Here's another truth of soccer: it's almost impossible to predict whether a great untried teenager will make a great adult player. The body and mind change too much in that phase of life. Cesc Fabregas was a great fifteen-year-old who became a great adult, but he was the exception, and anyway in his prime he left Arsenal for bigger Barcelona. Wenger's youth policy was built on a false premise. Only once a teenager has achieved success in actual professional soccer—as did Cristiano Ronaldo, Wayne Rooney, or Gareth Bale—can you know he is the real thing, and by then richer clubs than Arsenal will be chasing him.

Some think a prince is now riding in to prove Wenger's conservative policy right after all: "financial fair play," or FFP, as UEFA's new policy is called. It essentially requires that European clubs stop spending more money than they have. The "FFP rules" are full of loopholes, and even when they take full effect in 2018 may not require clubs to break even, but FFP does already seem to be limiting clubs' spending slightly. The Premier League is considering similar rules for England.

But it's unlikely that FFP will transform soccer. More probably, says Szymanski, clubs and UEFA will both give a bit. UEFA's main concern will be to stop penniless clubs from risking insolvency. Clubs with sugar daddies, like Chelsea and Manchester City, who face less risk, may be cut more slack. In any case, some of these clubs are already finding ways around FFP. City has signed a ten-year deal believed to be worth $560 million with Etihad Airways for stadium naming rights and shirt sponsorship—a flabbergasting sum. Critics note that Etihad, like City's owners, comes from Abu Dhabi. They hint that the deal allows City to inject outside money while evading the FFP restrictions. However, UEFA might struggle to prove in court that the $560 million was excessive or that Etihad and City's owners were linked. Presumably, then, deals like this will be left to stand. In the end, FFP may change soccer less than Arsenal would hope. Gazidis says, "Are there loopholes in the way FFP works? Quite possibly. FFP is not part of our strategy."

To sum up: neither a collapse of the soccer economy nor a sudden blossoming of Arsenal's youth academy nor FFP is likely to come along and save Wenger. On the upside, Gazidis does expect Arsenal to get richer, as longstanding commercial deals expire and get replaced by bigger ones. Arsenal's revenues look set to hit $480 million next year. Meanwhile, interest costs on the club's debt have dropped to a manageable $21.6 million, with net debt at $158 million. The burden of the stadium is lifting. "We're coming through a period of risk to a period of less risk," acknowledges Gazidis. Last week Arsenal climbed down from a previous tough stance to offer forward Theo Walcott a new contract that pays him a reported $144,000 a week plus bonuses—a sign that austerity is being eased.

However, other clubs are finding new revenues, too, as countless Asians and Americans start switching onto the Premier League. Contrary to the doomsayers, English soccer's economic rise may have only just begun. That probably means Arsenal's new revenues won't be enough to lift it back into prizewinning zones—certainly not in time for Wenger.

The prize he wanted most was the European Champions League. In 2007, at the Champions League final in Athens, I sat one row ahead of Wenger and his fellow coaches Marcello Lippi and Gérard Houllier, so close that I was swathed in the fumes of Lippi's illicit cigars. All match Wenger looked grim, angry, as if he had to contain himself to stay seated. After Milan beat Liverpool, he sat silently for a while, then began bashing his hands together in applause. "You see?" he said angrily. "You only need an ordinary team to win the Champions League." He must still have hoped it would be him with a great Arsenal one day. Now it probably never will.

*I missed a trick in writing this article. A week after it was published in the Financial Times, the newspaper printed a letter from a Mr. D. Cornock Thomas in London. He pointed out that since 2002, Arsenal's share price had risen by nearly 1,200 percent, compared with a rise of just 60 percent in British shares in general. In other words, Wenger's austerity hadn't been winning any trophies, but it was doing a great job for Arsenal's shareholders. As Cornock Thomas wrote, "No wonder the board of Arsenal plc, which includes Stan Kroenke, the principal owner (who owns slightly less than 70 percent of the shares), is happy with his performance."

I'm not suggesting that Wenger pursued austerity as a sly way to boost Arsenal's share price. Rather, he pursued the policy because he thought it was right and because it suited his prejudices. But as I suggested very briefly in the article, Kroenke was delighted for him to keep pursuing it. Kroenke's family owns various American sports franchises, including the St. Louis Rams of the NFL. Like most American owners in the English Premier League, he regards sports as a business. Wenger is the perfect profit-maximizing manager for him, if not for Arsenal fans who would prefer to win prizes.

Josep Guardiola
April 2013

We all see that Barcelona is brilliant. The only problem is understanding just how it does it. That's where my friend Albert Capellas comes in. Whenever he and I run into each other, we talk about Barça. Not many people know the subject better. Capellas is now assistant manager at Vitesse Arnhem in the Netherlands, but before that he was coordinator of Barcelona's great youth academy, the Masia. He helped bring a boy named Sergio Busquets from a rough local neighborhood to Barça. He trained Iniesta and Victor Valdés on their youth teams. In all, Capellas worked nine years for his hometown club.

During our last conversation, over espressos in an Arnhem hotel last year, I had several "aha" moments. I have watched the Barcelona of Pep Guardiola umpteen times, but only now am I finally beginning to see. Barcelona is great not merely because it has great players. The team also has great tactics—different not just from any other team today, but also different from Barcelona teams pre-Guardiola. Barça is now so drilled on the field that in some ways, it is more like an American gridiron football team than a soccer one. Its luscious game isn't nearly as spontaneous as it looks.

Before getting into the detail of Barcelona's style, it's crucial to understand just how much of it comes from Guardiola. When a Barcelona vice president mused to me five years ago that she'd like to see the then thirty-seven-year-old Pep be made head coach, I never imagined it would happen. Guardiola was practically a novice then. The only side he had ever coached was Barça's second team. However, people in the club who had worked with him—men such as the club's then president, Joan Laporta, and the then director of soccer, Txiki Beguiristain—had already clocked him as special. Not only did Guardiola know Barcelona's house style inside out. He also knew how it could be improved.

Guardiola once compared Barcelona's style to a cathedral. Johan Cruijff, he said, as Barça's supreme player in the 1970s and later as coach, had built the cathedral. The task of those who came afterward was to renovate and update it. Guardiola is always looking for updates. If a random person on the street says something interesting about the game, Guardiola listens. He thinks about soccer all the time. He learned from another Dutch Barcelona manager, Louis van Gaal, but also from his years playing for Brescia and Roma in Italy, the country that pretty much invented defending. Yet because Guardiola had little desire to explain his ideas to the media, you end up watching Barça without a codebook.

Cruijff was the single most formative influence on Guardiola. When the Dutchman returned to the Nou Camp as head coach in 1988, he did something that few Barça coaches had ever done before: he went to the fields where the youth teams played. There he saw a skinny kid in central midfield hitting perfect passes. "Take that boy off at halftime," he told the boy's coach. "Why?" asked the coach. "Because I'm putting him on the first team," said Cruijff. Guardiola went on to spend a decade on the first team.

Cruijff was perhaps the most original thinker in soccer's history, but most of his thinking was about attack. He liked to say that he didn't mind conceding three goals, as long as Barça scored five. Well, Guardiola also wanted to score five, but he minded conceding even one. If Barcelona is a cathedral, Guardiola added buttresses. Even in his last, somewhat disappointing, season, his team conceded only twenty-nine goals in thirty-eight league games. René Meulensteen, Alex Ferguson's assistant manager at Manchester United, told the Dutch magazine *Voetbal International*, "Pep Guardiola's Barcelona made the biggest change at the top of soccer, and I'm especially talking about how they played without the ball. They applied very fast and coordinated pressure to win back the ball as quickly as possible." Following are some of Guardiola's innovations, or the secrets of FC Barcelona.

Pressure on the ball. Before Barcelona played Manchester United in the Champions League final at Wembley in 2011, Ferguson said that the way Barça pressured their opponents to win the ball back was "breathtaking."

That, he added, was Guardiola's innovation. Ferguson admitted that United hadn't known how to cope with it in the Champions League final in Rome in 2009. He thought it would be different at Wembley. It wasn't.

Barcelona starts pressing (hunting for the ball) the instant it loses possession. That is the perfect time to press because the opposing player who has just won the ball is vulnerable. He has had to take his eyes off the game to make his tackle or interception, and he has expended energy. That means he is unsighted and probably tired. He usually needs two or three seconds to regain his vision of the field. So Barcelona tries to dispossess him before he can give the ball to a better-placed teammate.

Furthermore, if the guy won the ball back in his own defense and Barcelona can instantly win it back again, then the way to the goal is often clear. This is where Messi's genius for tackling comes in. The little man has such quick reflexes that he sometimes wins a tackle a split second after losing one.

The Barcelona player who lost the ball leads the hunt to regain it. But he never hunts alone. His teammates near the ball join him. If only one or two Barça players are pressing, it's too easy for the opponent to pass around them.

Meulensteen says, "You see that few teams have the individual skills to play themselves out from under pressure. Guardiola saw that very well. But Barcelona's is also the playing style with the highest degree of difficulty. You need players with the tactical qualities to shift very quickly from possession to defense and who are physically capable of doing that constantly. It's a very short moment of hunting the prey."

The "five-second rule." If Barça hasn't won the ball back within five seconds of losing it, the players then retreat and build a compact ten-man wall. The distance between the front man in the wall (typically Messi) and their last defender (Javier Mascherano, say) is only eighty to a hundred feet. It's hard for any opponent to pass their way through such a small space. The Rome final of 2009 was a perfect demonstration of Barcelona's wall: whenever United won the ball and kept it, they faced eleven precisely positioned opponents, who stood there and said, in effect, "Try and get through this."

It's easy for Barcelona to be compact, both when pressing and when drawing up their wall, because their players spend most of the game very near each other. Xavi and Iniesta in particular seldom stray far from the ball. A packed midfield, without out-and-out strikers, enhances the compactness. Cruijff has said, "Do you know how Barcelona win the ball back so quickly? It's because they don't have to run back more than 10 meters [30 feet] as they never pass the ball more than 10 meters."

More rules of pressing. Once Barcelona has built its compact wall, it waits for the right moment to start pressing again. The players don't choose the moment on instinct. Rather, there are very precise prompts that tell them when to press. One is if an opponent miscontrols a ball. If the ball bounces off his foot, he will need to look down to locate it, and at that moment he loses his overview of the pitch. That's when the nearest Barcelona players start hounding him.

There's another set prompt for Barça to press: when the opposing player on the ball turns back toward his own goal. When he does that, he narrows his options: he can no longer pass forward, unless Barcelona gives him time to turn around again. Barcelona doesn't give him time. Their players instantly hound the man, forcing him to pass back, and so they gain territory.

The "3–1 rule." If an opposing player gets the ball anywhere near Barcelona's penalty area, then Barça goes Italian. It applies what it calls the "3–1 rule": one of Barcelona's four defenders will advance to tackle the man with the ball, and the other three defenders will assemble in a ring about seven or ten feet behind the tackler. That provides a double layer of protection. Guardiola picked up this rule in Italy. It's such a simple yet effective idea that you wonder why all top teams don't use it.

No surprises. When Barcelona wins the ball, it does something unusual. Most leading teams treat the moment the ball changes hands—"turnover," as it's called in basketball—as decisive. At that moment, the opponents are usually out of position, and so if you can counterattack quickly, you have an excellent chance of scoring. Teams such as Manchester United and Arsenal often try to score in the first three seconds after winning possession. So their player who wins the ball often tries to hit an instant splitting pass. Holland—Barcelona's historic role models—does this too.

But when a Barcelona player wins the ball, he doesn't try for a splitting pass. The club's attitude is: he has won the ball, that's a wonderful achievement, and he doesn't need to do anything else special. All he is supposed to do is slot the ball simply into the feet of the nearest teammate. Barcelona's logic is that in winning the ball, the guy has typically forfeited his vision of the field. So he is the worst-placed player to hit a telling ball.

This means that Barcelona doesn't rely on the element of surprise. The team takes a few moments to get into formation and then pretty much tells its opponents, "Okay, here we come." The opposition knows exactly what Barça is going to do. The difficulty is stopping it.

The only exception to this rule is if the Barça player wins the ball near the opposition's penalty area. Then he goes straight for the goal.

Possession is nine-tenths of the game. Keeping the ball has been Barcelona's key tactic since Cruijff's day. Most teams don't worry about possession. They know you can have oodles of possession and lose. But Barcelona aims to have 65 or 70 percent of possession in a game. In the 2011–2012 league season, it averaged more than 72 percent.

The logic of possession is twofold. First, while you have the ball, the other team can't score. A team like Barcelona, short on good tacklers, needs to defend by keeping possession. As Guardiola once remarked, they are a "horrible" team without the ball. Second, if Barça has the ball, the other team has to chase it, and that is exhausting. When the opponents win it back, they are often so tired that they surrender it again immediately. Possession gets Barcelona into a virtuous cycle.

Barça is so fanatical about possession that a defender such as Gerard Pique will weave the most intricate passes inside his own penalty area rather than boot the ball away. On almost all other teams, the keeper at least is free to boot. On the England side, for instance, it's typically Joe Hart who gives the ball away with a blind punt. This is a weakness of England's game, but the English attitude seems to be that there is nothing to be done about it: keepers can't pass. Barcelona thinks differently.

José Mourinho, Barcelona's nemesis, has tried to exploit the club's devotion to passing. In the Bernabeu in December 2011, Real Madrid's forwards chased down Valdés from the game's first kickoff, knowing he wouldn't boot clear. The keeper miscued a pass, and Karim Benzema scored after twenty-three seconds. Yet Valdés kept passing, and Barcelona won 1–3. The trademark of Barcelona-raised goalkeepers—one shared only by Ajax-raised goalkeepers, such as Edwin van der Sar—is that they can all play soccer like outfield players.

That characteristic will be key in Barça's hunt for Valdés's successor. The club may well choose to sacrifice core keeping skills in favor of ballplaying ability.

The "one-second rule." No other soccer team plays the Barcelona way. That's a strength, but it's also a weakness. It makes it very hard for Barça to integrate outsiders into the team, because the outsiders struggle to learn the system. Barcelona long had a policy of buying only "top-ten" players—men who arguably rank among the ten best players on earth—yet many of them have failed in the Nou Camp. Thierry Henry and Zlatan Ibrahimovic did, whereas even David Villa, who knew Barcelona's game from playing it with Spain, has often found himself on the bench.

Joan Oliver, Barcelona's previous chief executive, explained the risk of transfers by what he called the "one-second rule." The success of a move on the pitch is decided in less than a second. If a player needs a few extra fractions of a second to work out where his teammate is going, because he doesn't know the other guy's game well, the move will usually break down. A new player can therefore lose a match in less than a second.

That's particularly true at Barcelona, whose system has such a complex orchestration. Soon after Cesc Fabregas returned home from Arsenal, he said, "Barça has a very specific system, and everyone has to adjust to it. Everything has been studied down to the last millimeter. In my first matches I really had to adjust. I was so used to Arsenal, where I could roam around the whole pitch without worrying about anything. Here it's really very different. Everyone has his own position, and you can never lose it from sight. I had to go back to my youth days at Barça to master the basic principles again."

Barcelona needed Fabregas precisely because he had once mastered those basic principles. An even better example of this staffing principle is Pedro: not a great player, but because he was raised in the Masia, he can play Barcelona's game better than stars from outside. The boys in the Masia spend much of their childhood playing passing games, especially Cruijff's favorite, six against three. Soccer, Cruijff once said, is choreography.

Nobody else thinks like that. That's why most of the Barcelona side is homegrown. It's more a necessity than a choice. Still, most of the time it works pretty well.

No doubt, Guardiola will want to transplant most of this system—plus new ideas he has thought up in Manhattan—to Bayern Munich. But in a team of Germans who grew up without these principles, such a complex knowledge transfer could easily fail.

I later read in Dennis Bergkamp's excellent "nonautobiography," Stillness and Speed, that when you play for "dominating" teams like Barcelona, Arsenal, and Milan, "as soon as you lose the ball, you win it back again—in their half—as soon as possible. Or if you can't win it in three or five seconds, then you come back in position and make the compact thing, again with the correct distances between the players. Attacking, the distance is maybe twenty-five yards on average. Defensively, it should be closer, about ten or fifteen. That's so important." Bergkamp's words show the existence of a European family of dominating teams, each of them borrowing from the other's codebooks. If Guardiola stays in Munich for a while, Bayern too may join that family.

Barcelona won't quite abandon the Guardiola style, but since his departure the club has been less religious about it. In September 2013 Barça beat Rayo Vallecano 4–0, but had less possession than its opponents for the first time in 316 games. Gerard Pique explained around that time that Barcelona's opponents now "know what we are going to do" and that the team therefore needed to vary its approach. "We're trying to find the balance between playing more directly and playing as always," he said. All styles of soccer have to keep evolving, even tiki-taka, and Barcelona is quite right to keep updating Guardiola's cathedral.

Alex Ferguson
May 2013

Soon after Sir Alex Ferguson became manager of Manchester United in 1986, his team lost to Wimbledon, and he lost his temper. He began throwing things around the locker room. A jockstrap landed on a player's head and sat there like a pigeon, because the player didn't dare move. The Scot was giving his team the famous "hairdryer" treatment: screaming at them from so close that his breath blew their hair. Meanwhile, the player he most wanted to berate was hiding in terror in a freezing bath.

It's a scene from another era. Now that Sir Alex is hanging up his hairdryer at age seventy-one, the last manager who truly ruled his club is leaving the game. The era of "the Boss" is ending not just at United but across soccer.

Sir Alex was born in Glasgow in 1941 into the sort of close-knit industrial community that no longer exists in Britain. His father worked in the shipyards. Both his parents were union representatives. Sir Alex became one too, at age nineteen, as a toolmaker's apprentice.

A journeyman striker in the 1960s, he watched the manager rise to dominance in the British game. Previously, power in most clubs had resided with the directors. These local businessmen picked the team and treated the manager as a sort of secretary. But in the 1960s, says Stefan Szymanski, sports economist at the University of Michigan, technocrats were ousting amateurs. Managers such as Matt Busby, Bill Shankly, Jock Stein, and Don Revie became stars. They ruled their clubs like dictators, for long spells, typically choosing their own moment of departure. This was Sir Alex's model when he entered management with tiny East Stirlingshire in 1974.

Of course, managers then weren't quite omnipotent. Sir Alex's second club, St. Mirren, fired him after he quarreled with the chairman. But he later triumphed with Aberdeen, and when he joined United he expected to get time and space "to build a football club, rather than just a football team."

Soccer players in 1986 were still humble figures. They called the manager "Boss." They weren't free to leave their clubs even after their contracts expired. They weren't rich: United's total wage bill in 1986 was somewhere over $4 million, says Szymanski. Most players were British or Irish and therefore culturally familiar to Sir Alex. He always expected to control their lives like a strict but loving father. His former goalkeeper Edwin van der Sar praises his warmth, saying, "You could discuss anything with him. Once he came to stand beside my goal in training to tell me how proud he was of his grandson, who had performed at a Christmas concert with my son. In between I'd have to make a save, and then he'd continue talking."

Whereas other big clubs came to seem like airport transit lounges, United—with their ritual quiz nights on European trips—still resembled a northern English working-class family that happened to be made up of multimillionaires.

But the floods of TV money—more and more as fans in new countries began watching—were changing soccer's balance of power. The new sums were too big to be entrusted to the manager. Instead, trained financial professionals such as United chief executive David Gill handled the money. Meanwhile, the European Court of Justice's Bosman ruling of 1995 had given players much greater freedom to move between clubs. Their wages soared. Today, says Szymanski, at least twelve United players earn $5 million or more.

Soccer players gained power. In all of European soccer, Sir Alex was one of the few managers who still dared wield the hairdryer. (The *Sun* newspaper greeted his retirement with a front-page picture of a red hairdryer, knowing that readers would instantly associate it with him.) His unique longevity, success, and personality made him untouchable. Players knew they couldn't beat him in a power struggle. In Sir Alex's United, Sir Alex alone was indispensable.

Still, even he noticed the new player power. Cristiano Ronaldo, whom he had talked of as a son, joined Real Madrid in 2009. A year later, when Wayne Rooney threatened to leave, Sir Alex ended up granting Rooney's demands for more pay.

Meanwhile, the soccer manager's power was being challenged from another quarter. The new breed of owner is an international plutocrat who demands control over spending. In 2005 the Glazer family from Florida used borrowed money to buy United. The Glazers have since drained more than $850 million from the club to service their debts. Had they let Sir Alex spend that sum, he would surely have bettered his thirty-eight trophies with United. But it wasn't his decision. Even he was no longer the Boss.

Now the breed is extinct. "No manager will ever again have such power, no manager will ever get six years to win his first championship, and no manager will ever get away with the hairdryer, at least at the highest level," says Szymanski. Look at that other prominent manager, José Mourinho at Real Madrid, currently losing a power struggle with goalkeeper Iker Casillas. Madrid's fans recently booed Mourinho, who will surely leave Madrid. He had overestimated a manager's power.

Just as tenures of corporate chief executives are shrinking, soccer managers are becoming short-term fixers. In 1992 the average manager's tenure in England was three and a half years. Now it's little more than a year. By summer, of the ninety-two managers of English league clubs, only Arsenal's Arsène Wenger will have held his job more than seven years.

Sir Alex's successor, David Moyes, will be just one power broker among many at Old Trafford. Good luck to him with handling Rooney, whom he once sued for libel. If anyone's now the "Boss" at United, it's Rooney.

Ferguson's latest autobiography (see below) grimly confirms the end of the Boss in soccer. "In modern football," he writes, "celebrity status overrides the manager's power. In my day you wouldn't whisper a word about your manager. You would fear certain death. In my later years, I would hear constantly about players using their power against managers, and the player receiving the support of the public and even the club." Perhaps he feels better off out of it.

Alex Ferguson
October 2013

Review of *Alex Ferguson: My Autobiography* (Hodder & Stoughton)

"The only person I ever coached who was totally unaffected by his mistakes was David Beckham," writes Sir Alex Ferguson in this mixed bag of afterthoughts to his career. "He could have the worst game possible and still not believe that he had underperformed in any way. . . . In a way, it was a great quality."

Vignettes like that make this autobiography worth reading. Ferguson understands people—a skill honed while running pubs in Glasgow—and he observed a lot of people in his twenty-seven years managing Manchester United Football Club before retiring in May. Phil Neville was a player to whom you could say, "Phil, I want you to run up that hill, then come back and cut down that tree," and he would reply, "Right, boss, where's the chainsaw?" Paul Scholes hit such an accurate long ball that "he could choose a hair on the head of any team-mate answering the call of nature at our training ground." Australian goalkeeper Mark Bosnich was, "in my opinion, a terrible professional." Roy Keane's mood swings "would determine the whole mood of the dressing room." And Ferguson disliked Owen Hargreaves.

Unfortunately, though, this book (written with Paul Hayward) offers only scraps of something that many readers will crave: a great manager's secrets of management. This is a memoir, not a business book.

There are fragments of a Fergusonian management manifesto. He unfolds his belief that if you give people total loyalty and trust, they will give it back to you. (That explains the endless tributes to supporting characters, which make the book's early parts read like a long retirement speech.) Behind closed doors, you can scream at people. In public, you must always "protect them from outside judgements," however accurate. That, he writes, is "the one constant principle of my time as a manager."

His need for control seems to have been pretty constant, too. Ferguson writes of Beckham, "You cannot have a player taking over the dressing room. Many tried. . . . [T]hat was the death knell for him." Beckham, he believes, had begun working harder at being a fashion icon than a soccer player. Consequently, after leaving United, "he never attained the level where you would say: 'That is an absolute top player.'"

Keane, too, was banished for taking on the manager. Ferguson—who places himself on the left of the UK's Labour Party—once advised Labour prime minister Tony Blair to fire disobedient superstars in his cabinet, because control was paramount. Only later did Ferguson realize that Blair had had his finance minister (and future successor), Gordon Brown, in mind.

Other supposed Fergusonian methods turn out to be less important than presumed: the media deconstructed his every word, imagining that he was playing "mind games" to upset opposing managers. Usually, he says, he wasn't.

He says little about soccer tactics, confirming suspicion that his brilliance lay exclusively in man management. He does ponder whether United should have played more defensively against Barcelona in the lost Champions League finals of 2009 and 2011. Defense, he writes, wouldn't have been United's way. It would have "put myself through torture, put the fans through hell." Instead, "I wanted a more positive outlook . . . and we were beaten partly because of that change in emphasis." It's a fascinating dilemma. Often, though, the insights disappoint. Here is Ferguson on assessing players: "The demarcation line was always: what can they do and what can they not do?"

We learn more about the private man. He explains that his wife's sister's death—which left his wife feeling alone—helped push him to retire. As for pursuits, "[Horse] racing taught me to switch off, along with reading books and buying wine. That side of my life developed really from 1997, when I hit that wall and realized I needed to do something else to divert my thoughts from football." Among other things, he began to obsess about John F. Kennedy's assassination, collecting conspiracy theories and memorabilia—including a copy of the Warren Commission's report signed by Gerald Ford. But he also became a serious reader of American history, encouraged by Gordon Brown. (Ferguson's network within the British establishment may be unparalleled.) His library seems to consist largely of biographies of leaders, with a large section on despots.

Ferguson himself didn't tolerate dissidents or free media, yet this is a surprisingly good-tempered book. It has kind words for former enemies such as Liverpool and the Irish racing owner John Magnier, though he does patronize Arsenal's Arsène Wenger.

It adds up to an entertaining read, but less than Ferguson deserves. He attempts jokes, but humor isn't his forte. It's a shame, too, that the book seems to have been written too fast, presumably to get it out before Christmas and earn a payday that Ferguson doesn't need.

Perhaps managerial greatness always arises from an unrepeatable combination of person, place, moment, and luck and therefore cannot be taught by a business book. Other managers can't simply decide to be like Ferguson. Despite that lecture about control, Blair lacked the power to discard Brown as Ferguson had Beckham. If it were possible to copy Ferguson's management secrets, everyone would have done so long ago.

Carlo Ancelotti
January 2014

"I have a lot of power," grins Carlo Ancelotti, manager of Real Madrid. "Here I can decide: training at six in the morning! Training eleven in the night! But my style is not to impose. I would like to convince the players of what they are doing. This takes more time."

We are sitting in the coaches' office at Madrid's spiffy new training ground, just north of the city. The Italian, his chubby frame bulging out of a bright-blue Madrid tracksuit, is puffing on a cigarette, confident that the club president isn't about to walk in and catch him smoking, as happened at a previous club he could mention. Madrid's president, Florentino Pérez, mostly leaves his head coach alone. Ancelotti landed at the world's richest club last summer, after a whistle-stop European tour during which he managed AC Milan, Chelsea, and Paris Saint-Germain within three years. Though much lower profile than peers like Jose Mourinho and Arsène Wenger, Ancelotti has won soccer's biggest prizes. Now his task is to win Madrid the Champions League, its record tenth—the mythical "*la décima.*" Nobody better than this international crisis manager to explain how to handle superstar players (currently Cristiano Ronaldo and Gareth Bale), difficult club presidents (previously Silvio Berlusconi and Roman Abramovich), and the global media. Here are the management secrets of a nice guy.

To gather them, I have got a lift from the airport with Ancelotti's assistant manager, Paul Clement. The English former gym teacher met the Italian at Chelsea and is tipped for a solo managerial career soon. Clement drives through the soft December sunshine to the training ground, where even on this quiet afternoon a couple of dozen journalists, TV cameras, and autograph hunters are waiting by the gate for something to happen.

Yet inside the training ground, life feels tranquil. Everything possible has been done to keep the hysteria outside the gate. Clement parks opposite a gleaming white Batmobilesque sports car belonging to Bale, the Welshman whom Real bought from Tottenham Hotspur this summer for a reported world record fee of $132 million.

The main building is almost empty. In the quiet coaches' room, Ancelotti's son Davide, a polite, slender young man who works on his father's staff, is reading the pink Italian daily *La Gazzetta dello Sport*. The surrounding hillsides have gone a wintry brown, but just outside the window of the coaches' room, a dozen groundkeepers are tending the impossibly green practice field. Ancelotti keeps his staff happy: The previous evening, he took fifty colleagues to the Basque restaurant Mesón Txistu and picked up the bill himself.

Today Ancelotti distributes excellent espressos, sits down, and lights up. Occasionally his mobile phone vibrates, but he ignores it. Talking slowly in his serviceable English, sometimes doodling with a green pen, he exudes an unhurried calm.

"Carletto," the farmer's son from Emilia-Romagna, has spent his adult life in pressurized environments. A canny midfielder in Italian soccer, he learned leadership from his coaches—notably the Swede Nils Liedholm, who managed him at AS Roma in the 1980s. "When we played in the north, we wouldn't go by plane, because he was afraid of flying," reminisces Ancelotti. "We took a train from Rome to Milan. The train left Rome at midnight. But Liedholm went to bed early! So he would get on the train at 9:30 pm and go to sleep at ten as usual. The players would get on at midnight and not sleep. The worst preparation!" On match day the team would arrive at the stadium hours early and hang around the changing room. To keep the players calm, Liedholm would get Roma's doctors to tell jokes. Later, as coach, Ancelotti usually performed the pre-match jokes himself—even before Champions League finals. Ancelotti understands something about top-level soccer: Most players don't need to be motivated for a match. They need to be calmed down.

Liedholm, who treated players as adults, was his model for the coach as human being. Other coaches taught him how not to do it. Ancelotti recalls, "I had managers who said, 'You have to do this because I tell you to.' I didn't understand this. I cannot be—*come se dice?*—authoritarian."

In 1987, when Ancelotti was twenty-eight, already with ruined knees, Milan's coach Arrigo Sacchi brought him north. Sacchi saw him as an on-field "conductor of the orchestra," a midfielder without pace or exceptional skill but with a soccer brain. "Usually the most intelligent player is a midfielder," Ancelotti reflects, and lists the cleverest he has managed: "I could say [Andrea] Pirlo, I could say Xabi Alonso, Thiago Motta, Didier Deschamps. All midfielders."

Ancelotti the midfielder didn't adapt instantly at Milan. The club's owner, Berlusconi, used to complain: "We have an orchestra director who can't read sheet music!" In Jonathan Wilson's book *Inverting the Pyramid*, Sacchi remembers promising Berlusconi to teach Ancelotti "to sing in tune in our orchestra. Every day, I would make [Ancelotti] come an hour before training with some kids from the youth team, and we would go through everything. Eventually he sang in perfect tune." Sacchi's Milan won two European Cups playing perfectly orchestrated attacking soccer. When Ancelotti retired from playing in 1992, he was a believer in Sacchi's 4-4-2 formation. He says: "In my experience, it was the only way to play soccer."

He became Sacchi's assistant manager with Italy's national team, then joined Reggiana in his home region. The club was tiny, yet initially he found the stress of management almost unbearable. "I said at the end of the first year, 'I do this three or four years, and after this, holiday.'" Chuckling, he quotes Liedholm: "This is the best job in the world, with the exception of the matches." But gradually Ancelotti learned to live with the pressure, to the point where he now claims: "My ass is earthquake-proof." Knowing that he can be sacked any day no longer stresses him. Nowadays he enjoys even matches.

After Reggiana he coached Parma. There, he had the chance to sign the "divine ponytail," Roberto Baggio. But Baggio wanted the role of playmaker, or "number ten"—a position that didn't exist in Sacchi's system. Ancelotti recalls, "I said no, you have to play striker. Baggio went to another club. That year Baggio scored twenty-five goals—for Bologna! I lost twenty-five goals! Big mistake." The incident changed Ancelotti's thinking: No system, he decided, was more important than the players. He became adaptable by conviction.

He moved up to Juventus and then to Milan. When you manage Berlusconi's club, you have to manage Berlusconi. Ancelotti—who in his autobiography jocularly calls Berlusconi "He" with a capital "H"—did this masterfully. He grasped the key facts: Berlusconi owned Milan, and the coach's job was to please Berlusconi. Ancelotti says: "The tradition at Milan is to play a good style of soccer—differently from Juventus, where the most important thing is to win. When Berlusconi bought Milan, it was this." Accordingly, Ancelotti constructed a very attacking line-up. "This was the only reason to play Pirlo, Seedorf, Rui Costa, Kaká, Shevchenko at the same time." Here was another discovery: No system is more important than the club president.

Some leading managers tolerate no intrusion from their chairmen, but Ancelotti let Berlusconi tell the pre-match jokes in the changing room. Before Milan played Juventus in the Champions League final of 2003, Ancelotti even let Italy's then-prime minister sit in on his team talk. "I handed out sheets of paper with the formation and the plays," wrote Ancelotti in his autobiography. "He wanted copies for himself. (Later I saw them published in a book by Bruno Vespa; the chairman passed them off as his own . . .)." Ancelotti recounts all this with a smile, but indulging Berlusconi was part of his job. Better yet, Milan beat Juve on penalties. Ancelotti became one of just six men to win the Champions League as both manager and player.

In 2005 in Istanbul he lost the trophy to Liverpool in an unforgettable final. Milan led 3–0 at halftime, then conceded three goals and lost on penalties. Yet later that night, a relaxed Ancelotti could be seen sitting in the hotel bar, chatting cheerily with acquaintances about the sights of Istanbul. He'd done his work. Now he was off duty. Looking back, he explains: "Because the team had done the maximum to win this game. So I couldn't be angry. I think this was destiny." Anyway, he adds: "Soccer is the most important of the less important things in the world."

He insists he has no regrets about Istanbul: "What can you do when in six minutes they score three times? It's impossible to change something, because there is no time. I was a manager for eight hundred games in my career. If I had to choose two games that my team played really, really well, it would be this game. Another was the semifinal in 2007 against Manchester United."

In 2007, after Milan reached the final again, Milan's squad gathered around a big screen at their training ground to cheer on Liverpool in the other semifinal against Chelsea. "We were shouting and howling against Chelsea," says his autobiography. "Liverpool team hats and toy trumpets were pulled out at one point." The cheering worked. Liverpool beat Chelsea, and in the final in Athens Milan took revenge for Istanbul, winning 2-1. Afterwards Ancelotti and the players told jokes all night, trying to fix the victory in their minds forever.

At multinational Milan, he learned to coach players from everywhere. Once he had to brief his squad on a practical joke being prepared at the expense of newcomer Mathieu Flamini. "First you tell the Italians, in Italian," he recalls, "then you tell the Brazilians, in pseudo-Italian, and then you tell Beckham, with grunts and gestures." (Like most of Ancelotti's jokes, this one is told fondly: Beckham is a friend.)

The cross-cultural skills would come in handy. Ancelotti had dreamed of staying at Milan forever, but Berlusconi reduced funding, the team declined, and in 2009 Ancelotti joined the exodus of highly skilled Italians fleeing a bad economy. Chelsea's owner, Roman Abramovich, had hired his combination of people skills and tactical nous.

Ancelotti remembers: "The first time I met Roman Abramovich, he said, 'When I see Chelsea I don't recognize it is Chelsea—the identity, the style of play.'" Ancelotti's job was to give the team an identity.

In London, he continues, "the only problem was the language. Difficult to speak, difficult to show emotion. But the team was organized." Chelsea won the Premier League in 2010, and then went into the FA Cup final against Portsmouth aiming for the league-cup "Double"—something the club had never achieved.

Before the final, Ancelotti did something unusual: after naming the starting eleven, he asked them to decide the match strategy themselves. He recalls: "Everyone said one thing. For example, [goalkeeper Petr] Cech said, 'You have to control the space behind, to avoid the counterattack.' That season we played sixty games, and sixty times I made the strategy. So I think the players understood very well what they had to do."

Still, why did he take the risk before such a big match? "I was sure the players followed the strategy, because they made the strategy. Sometimes I make the strategy, but you don't know if the players really understand the strategy. Sometimes I joke with the players: 'Did you understand the strategy?' 'Yes, yes!' 'Repeat, please!'" Chelsea beat Portsmouth 1-0 to complete the Double.

Ancelotti has often contrasted his own flexibility on tactics, his lack of ego, and his chilled manner with a man who could be the anti-Ancelotti: Jose Mourinho. When Ancelotti's Chelsea played Mourinho's Inter Milan in 2010, Ancelotti reports in his autobiography: "We met in a corridor at the San Siro [stadium] and we made a pact: 'No more bickering, no more controversy.' Six words, a handshake, and in ten seconds we had an understanding." After Chelsea won the league, Mourinho texted him: "Champagne." When Inter won the Italian league, Ancelotti texted him: "Champagne, but not too much." Nonetheless, Ancelotti's autobiography ironically invokes Mourinho as "the Great Communicator, He who Knows, the Lord of the Press Conference, the Immense Provocateur, the Special Coach," etc. This, by contrast, is his self-description: "Here comes the fat boy with a bowlful of Emilian tortellini."

No manager lasts long at Chelsea. In 2011, Paris Saint-Germain's new Qatari owners lured Ancelotti to France. There he encountered a new set of national peculiarities. He says, "The problem of the English player: Sometimes it's difficult for them to understand that they *don't* have to work 100 percent in training. There are some training sessions where it's important not to work 100 percent. The French don't understand why they have to work 100 percent every day."

Paris wasn't professional enough. "PSG was a good experience because it was the first time in my experience to build something new. It's different to arrive at Chelsea or Real Madrid, where you have already a good organization of the club, a good team. At PSG you have to build everything from a low, low level," and he rubs his hand over the table to indicate ground zero. Some club executives in the past have accused him of being lax with players, but in Paris he had to intervene.

The team's changing room was divided into ethnic factions. "We had the South Americans, the French, the Italians. The relationship is not easy. The South Americans like to play with each other. The Italians the same. The players were not used to having a winning mentality. Training was at 11 am, usually. The players were used to coming at 10:30, train—and 12:30, one o'clock to leave the training ground. To change this was not easy, to tell them: 'You have to stay after training, to eat properly, to drink properly, to rest.' You cannot miss one day. It was important to have [Zlatan] Ibrahimovic, the best player with good professionalism. He was a model for others to follow in training sessions, because he concentrated every time. We took six months to have results." In 2013 PSG became French champions.

Almost immediately, Ancelotti was off to Madrid. In the small world of top-class soccer, President Pérez had been greeting him for years with the words: "Carlo, some day you will be my coach." In 2006, Ancelotti had even signed a contract with Madrid, but Milan hadn't let him go. In summer 2013, the time came. Madrid wanted an antidote to Mourinho. The Portuguese had coached Real for three years, imposing his characteristic defensive soccer in big matches and trying to crush uppity players.

Abiding by the truce, Ancelotti will no longer criticize Mourinho, but he does say of his own task at Madrid: "The goal is to play soccer a little bit differently, because the culture of this club is to play"—he blows out his cheeks, searches for the right word—"spectacular soccer. The supporters here are exigent. They don't like to see counterattack. They like to see a team that has control of the game, with possession. We are trying to follow the history, the tradition of the club."

What makes Ancelotti attractive to big clubs (especially those that treat coaches as disposable) is that in a profession dominated by big egos, he is happy to adapt to his surroundings. In each new country Ancelotti looks for little differences: "In England in general, teams have less tactical skills defensively. In France the teams are hard, physically, because there are a lot of African players. And in Spain, teams have the *pleasure* to play soccer. You have to adapt your methodology to these differences."

Adapting when moving countries sounds obvious, but many players and managers cannot do it. "It's not easy," says Ancelotti, "above all for players that leave England. I think of Ian Rush, Michael Owen." The Welsh striker Rush returned from a bad year in Italy in 1988 complaining, "It was like another country." Owen left Real Madrid after a year, homesick for English food and weather.

So how is Gareth Bale adapting to Madrid?: "Bale didn't have a lot of problems, because he is a humble man, not very demanding. He doesn't want too much."

Can Bale speak any Spanish?: "He is starting to speak. My job is to help him be comfortable on the pitch, comfortable with teammates. We have a lot of players that speak English."

One of them is Cristiano Ronaldo. He is Madrid's best player but hardly an easy-going guy. Ronaldo wants Madrid to play the way he wants. How does Ancelotti manage such a big talent? "Managing talent for me is difficult to understand. For me, it's managing people. Managing Ronaldo is the same for me as managing Carvajal or Morata [two of Madrid's more junior players]."

In fact, says Ancelotti, superstars tend to be easier to manage than "normal players" because "usually they more are professional than the others. Ronaldo is really professional," and Ancelotti blows out his cheeks in admiration. He's happy not to have to do any policing. "I don't like to control the private life of the player, because I'm not the father, I'm not the brother."

Ancelotti finds players far more professional nowadays than when he played in the 1980s. The average player today "controls more his private life, his style of life." And the average player today eats less tortellini. Under Liedholm at Roma, Ancelotti marvels, "We arrived at the hotel before a match and everyone could choose from the menu! There was no diet."

"When I played, the feedback was: The best training was, the day afterward you wake up with pain in your legs. If you were not able to go upstairs, it means that was fantastic training!," he guffaws. Nowadays players wear GPS's in training and physical trainers calibrate the right workload for each player day by day.

Players today don't engage in power struggles with managers, says Ancelotti. Has he ever had a player he couldn't work with?: "No." Or a player who couldn't work with him?: "No." He puffs away on his cigarette. Madrid's players are obedient, and smart enough to adapt even if he changes formation mid-match: "When you manage top players, they understand quickly." Xabi Alonso, in particular, is practically a coach on the field.

Madrid has wonderful players and the highest revenues of any club in any sport ($792 million last year). So why hasn't it won the Champions League since 2002? Ancelotti dodges the question with his trademark chuckle: "I don't know. This is a question even the club is asking itself. In ten years they didn't reach the final. This is a little bit strange. But they played three semifinals in a row. This is not bad."

To make Madrid's wait even more irksome, Real's next Champions League would be its record tenth. Ancelotti is tasked with delivering "*la décima*," starting with the round-of-sixteen encounter with Schalke of Germany in February 2014. Oh, and Real also has to win the Spanish league, in which the club currently stands third. How does Ancelotti cope with the daily pressure? "Because I have experience of this world. It doesn't matter what happens around me. I'm not so depressed when the result is not good, I am not so happy when results are good. I don't feel there is a lot of pressure on my shoulders, because I love this job. The pressure on a manager is normal." Then he walks me to reception and arranges my taxi.

One of his predecessors in Madrid's hot seat, the Dutchman Guus Hiddink—a man whom Ancelotti resembles in girth and tranquility—once explained how any manager in Spain should deal with the fear of being fired. "*Finiquito*" is what Spaniards call the termination. In Hiddink's telling: "Being sacked isn't considered a disgrace here. It goes like this: You're called in to see the club president. 'Mister,' he says, 'mister, it's better if you don't continue.' He hugs you, and says, 'Go see the treasurer tomorrow.' The next day you go see the treasurer, you get your check, you go to the corner of the street, and you're given a suitcase full of money. Boom, done in one go. In Spain you're killed romantically." No doubt Ancelotti will eventually experience *finiquito*—perhaps after winning *la décima*, more likely before. He won't treat it as a disgrace. It will be just another anecdote to serve up to old friends over tortellini one evening in the Emilia-Romagna. Then he'll get another top job, because few other leading managers are internationally adaptable nice guys who can rub along with everyone from Ronaldo to Berlusconi.

PART III:
Some Other Soccer Men

Anthony Minghella
April 1998

When Anthony Minghella was filming *The English Patient* in the North African desert, the *Portsmouth Football Mail* was delivered to him every week. Usually, the news was bad. "Part of following a club is accepting that it can have bad spells lasting years," says Minghella. Or in his case a lifetime.

The English Patient won nine Oscars, but Portsmouth, his team, is now odds on to be relegated to Division Two, the third tier of English soccer. The game against Ipswich is crucial. And so Minghella, his father, and his young son troop into Fratton Park, as the family has done for decades.

These three swarthy gentlemen stand out among the pasty locals. Minghella grew up on the nearby Isle of Wight, where his father made ice cream, but the family origins are Italian, and several Minghellas were interned in the UK during the war as enemy aliens. The director's father, a chirpy old man born in Scotland, was spared that.

With their mixed descent, the Minghellas could have been characters in *The English Patient*, which features a Hungarian count, a Sikh sapper, a French Canadian nurse, and an English rose. At Fratton Park all that seems far away. Whereas the film is beautiful—set in Tuscany and the Sahara, featuring Ralph Fiennes and Kristin Scott Thomas—the Portsmouth fans tend toward obesity, and the day is unfeasibly cold. Yet Minghella is entirely at home here: he is a genuine Portsmouth nut, not a celebrity masquerading. He gives me a ham-and-mustard sandwich and fills me in on the merits of the team's fullbacks. In his contentment he resembles the Scott Thomas character lying in a warm bath with her lover, Almasy:

"When were you most happy?" Almasy asks.

"Now," she replies.

"When were you most sad?"

"Now."

"What do you love?"

"Portsmouth Football Club," Minghella might have answered, but Scott Thomas says, "Water. Your handwriting."

Sadly, at Fratton Park it is clear from kickoff that Ipswich is much the slicker side. Within minutes a Portsmouth defender is forced to commit a vicious foul.

"Good for you!" shouts Minghella.

I ask him about Alan Ball, Portsmouth's new manager, famous for producing teams that manage simultaneously to play ugly soccer and lose. "I don't want to talk about my attitude to Alan Ball," Minghella says, perhaps worried that I will take Ball to a showing of his next film. "Do I get frustrated? Heartbreaks! You want so much for them to play good football, more than anything else." He wishes Portsmouth could find a continental European manager.

I ask him to tell me about his next film, but just then David Johnson scores for Ipswich. Minghella crumbles. As Almasy phrases it, "My organs are packing up. I'm a bit of toast."

After the goal, the Portsmouth crowd starts chanting "Play Up Pompey" and Minghella joins in. "Portsmouth have performed mediocrely for decades," he says, "but it's supported as if it were a great club." Eighteen thousand passionate spectators: Minghella, who wrote plays before he moved into film, says there is a lesson here for theater. "If you look at a football game, it speaks actively to its constituency. But if you are writing a play, you don't know who exactly it is for."

But the quaint 1950s chant fails to stimulate the appalling Portsmouth team. This is no game for a neutral; Minghella apologizes to me.

"I'm enjoying watching Ipswich," I reply.

"That was a terrible thing to say."

He recalls Terry Venables, the former England manager, taking over for a doomed spell as Portsmouth's chairman. "We had such hope," says Minghella. "There's always some messiah around the corner, some rock billionaire."

His wistfulness seems strange. After all, Minghella has just directed a film that has grossed more than $300 million. Has the club never asked him to help out? "I'd love to be a director," he says—he means a soccer club director, not a film director—"but I'm sure it would make absolutely no difference. I don't have that kind of financial wherewithal."

Halftime comes with the score still only 1–0—Ipswich is being merciful—but the future looks grim. A man in front of us opens Bernard Crick's biography of George Orwell.

We eat more ham-and-mustard sandwiches, and Minghella tells me about his next project. Called *The Talented Mr. Ripley*, a film about Americans arriving in Europe in the 1950s, it will star Matt Damon and Gwyneth Paltrow and goes into preproduction in Italy in a few days. Much of the planning seems to involve trying to get tickets to the World Cup in France this summer.

Soccer also dominated the making of *The English Patient*. While Minghella edited the film in Berkeley, California, he would drive to San Francisco at six in the morning to watch a satellite feed of Euro 96. Every time England played he would go berserk, watched by an aghast Michael Ondaatje, author of the antitribal novel on which the film is based.

Will Minghella ever put soccer into a film? He says:

I love the fact that football is entirely apart from my working life. But football has been a useful paradigm for thinking about the work I am doing.

Football has high drama, but in the most rigid of forms. In football there is unity of time, place, and action, as Aristotle recommended for drama. Very few outcomes are possible—it's rare for more than four or five goals to be scored in a game—yet moment by moment it is very exciting. That is a real lesson to writers. I wish every film had as exciting a shape as most football matches.

Minghella, his son, and I turn to the subject of our playing careers and discover that we are all right-halves. *The English Patient* damaged Minghella's chances of soccer fame—he broke his ankle on the set—but one day he plans to get fit and start again. He assures me that Daniel Day Lewis, the actor, is also a keen player. As for Matt Damon, "I gather his great sadness in life is that he wasn't tall enough to play basketball."

Nowadays, Minghella just watches his son, even if he slightly regrets the fact that the boy supports Manchester United. His son offers, "I support United, but I like it more when Portsmouth win, because they don't win so often." Minghella is pleased.

In the second half Portsmouth improves, led by its center-forward, John Aloisi, an Italian Australian. Later, Ball sends on Paul Hall, a Jamaican forward. "Incomprehensible that Hall didn't start," Minghella complains.

Has he met many of the players? "I've said hello to Andy Awford a couple of times. And I once presented some awards with Paul Walsh."

Suddenly, just as Portsmouth seems certain to equalize, Ball takes off Aloisi. "Extraordinary decision," mumbles Minghella. Indeed, Portsmouth immediately collapses.

The Ipswich winger, Bobby Petta, a Dutchman of Indonesian Christian descent, starts tearing Portsmouth's defense apart, and only boredom and laziness keep Ipswich from scoring a few more.

The match ends, Portsmouth has lost, and Division Two looms. The three Minghellas smile wanly. Minghella's father distributes kisses and disappears.

"Grandpa always looks like he doesn't care," says Minghella's son.

"Oh, he cares a lot," says Minghella. "He's just better at hiding it than we are."

Minghella tells me that Portsmouth might yet survive, as long as rival strugglers Manchester City lose to Middlesbrough and . . . But he looks distraught, like Almasy being taken prisoner as his lover lies dying in a desert cave.

"The afternoon got colder," says Minghella. Or as the count phrased it, "You can't kill me. I died years ago."

Poor Minghella died in March 2008, aged fifty-four, after a botched operation. Portsmouth hadn't won a prize in his lifetime. Two months after his death, it won the FA Cup. I thought of him that day.

Jacques Herzog
May 2005

Jacques Herzog, the Swiss architect, sits in a leather armchair looking out over the Munich soccer stadium he has just built. Thin and shaven-headed, Herzog exudes nervous energy as he scours the gray stands.

In 2001 Herzog and Jacques de Meuron, his business partner and friend since kindergarten in Basle, won the Pritzker Prize, architecture's equivalent of the Nobel. They got it mainly for their Tate Modern Gallery in London, but Munich's Allianz Arena will displace the Tate as their best-known building next year when it hosts the opening match of soccer's World Cup. Hundreds of millions of people will see it. The Allianz Arena—named by the insurance group—opens with friendly matches next week. Herzog won't be there: He is booked for the opening of an exhibition of his firm's work at the Tate.

Today he is seeing his finished stadium for the first time. He has just marched through it in yellow helmet, raincoat, and sneakers. What does he think? He sighs, "Like always, unfortunately, you discover those little things that you would have liked to have done otherwise, and that jump at your eye. But it works very well, I think." What should he have done differently? "Let's say, I wish I had added a bit more color. But the people, and the illumination, that's also an integral part of the whole thing." When the stadium's full, he says, you'll hardly notice the gray stands.

Few famous architects had sullied their hands with stadiums before Herzog and de Meuron did so in Basle (for the club they support, FC Basel) and Munich. They are still building Beijing's Olympic Stadium for the 2008 Games. All this signals a new era: Stadiums are becoming keynote urban buildings, as cathedrals were in the Middle Ages and opera houses more recently. When Norman Foster's new Wembley opens in 2006, it will be his first stadium in more than forty years in architecture.

Months ago, in the converted villa in which he works in Basle, Herzog mused about stadiums, "This is a new issue, like museums were at some point. It was for a long time the domain of more technically oriented people. It was totally neglected. It was done with very little money. A lot of stadiums were built with pride by the community, but if you look very closely, lots of things were not thought through."

Over the past century, after many mistakes (and while Americans have approximated the ultimate baseball ground), Europeans have learned what makes the ideal soccer stadium. The Allianz Arena is Herzog's attempt to build it. Some things he has gotten right. Some he hasn't, because cities have changed. In sum, his attempt illuminates the nearly 3,000-year history of stadiums.

The first one, Olympia, opened in Greece in 776 BC and lasted 1,145 years. The Colosseum in Rome survived about half as long, until the sixth century AD. After that people got along fine without stadiums for nearly 1,500 years, notes Simon Inglis, the great chronicler of the breed. (Few topics are so dominated by one writer, evidence of how much stadiums have been neglected.)

After the Victorians invented modern team sports, stadiums reappeared, still looking rather like the Colosseum. These early British grounds were built on the cheap: barns to house the devoted. Most of the legendary ones—Old Trafford, Anfield, Highbury, Ibrox, Twickenham, Craven Cottage—were partly or wholly the work of an obscure Glaswegian architect called Archibald Leitch. When Leitch died in 1939 he seems to have had just one obituary, a brief notice by the Institute of Mechanical Engineers, which didn't mention stadiums. In a sign of what Americans call the "ballpark renaissance," Inglis has just published a biography, *Engineering Archie: Archibald Leitch—Football Ground Designer*.

Leitch didn't bother making his stadiums look good. His clients didn't care about looks. To quote Inglis's maxim on soccer stadiums, "Form follows whatever the club chairman's builder pal from the Rotary Club could come up with at a cut-price." Herzog, who has possibly never heard of Leitch, says, "The stadiums I love—Anfield or Old Trafford—are ugly stadiums on the outside."

Yet Leitch created what would become Herzog's inspiration: the traditional English stadium. The type was usually surrounded by terraced streets. To save space, its stands towered steeply from the edge of the field. There was no athletics track, because athletics didn't pay. The stadium's roof was cheap and simple. The great baseball grounds of the early twentieth century, such as Boston's Fenway Park and Chicago's Wrigley Field, looked similar.

Comparisons between religion and soccer are overused, but European stadiums undeniably took over certain functions from the emptying cathedrals. It was increasingly in stadiums that twentieth-century citizens gathered in community, sang, cried, and felt part of something larger than themselves. An English stadium, says Herzog, was "the living room of a religious community." The stadium also became the home of civic pride: the biggest and best-known building in many cities.

Traditional stadiums started disappearing in the United States first. By the 1950s, most American families owned cars. They moved to the suburbs, and the stadiums followed them because there wasn't enough parking in their old neighborhoods. As fans grew richer, they also demanded more food, toilets, and comfort. Stadiums had to be big, with parking garages, and next to a highway.

In 1988, just when everyone was sure the "urban ballparks" were dying out, a minor-league baseball team opened one in the decaying city of Buffalo. Pilot Field stood not in the suburbs but downtown. It even made reference to the old urban buildings around it, with its white brick and big arched windows. The seats were very near the foul lines. Fans liked this "retro ballpark," and they came in droves. Pilot Field, incidentally, was built by an architecture firm called HOK. Though little known outside sports, HOK is responsible for most extant baseball stadiums, Sydney's Olympic Stadium, Cardiff's Millennium Stadium, Arsenal's future stadium, and Wimbledon's new center court.

Pilot Field (now called Dunn Tire Park) inspired minor-league baseball teams everywhere to build retro ballparks. In 1992 the major-league Baltimore Orioles opened Camden Yards, and that settled the matter. Camden Yards, built by HOK, is downtown, in redbrick, and has an asymmetrical field with real grass just like the old ballparks. At the front is a statue of local boy Babe Ruth. Fans love it, and retro ballparks have since conquered the major leagues.

In Europe, the ballpark renaissance has taken a different turn. Few European city centers have the deserted stadium-size spaces found in the downtowns of the United States. In Munich and across the Continent, the new stadiums are outside town. Here too, however, architects have learned from the past. The new stadiums don't have athletics tracks, which ruined the atmosphere by keeping fans far from the action. Soccer and athletics simply don't mix.

What soccer fans crave in a stadium is communal emotion. Leitch's stadiums offer it. He built perfect places for soccer, chiefly because he put fans near the pitch. His grounds inspired the Allianz Arena. "It's somehow an attempt to go back to the roots of soccer," says Herzog, "to take some of these archaic ingredients. The Shakespearean theater, probably it was even a model for the soccer stadium in England—this closeness between the actors and

crowd. If you can achieve this proximity, the people become the architecture."
The Swiss quips that the Allianz is "too good for Germany." "I would rather
have made the stadiums for Manchester United or Liverpool," he says.

Sitting in the Allianz's top tier, he points almost straight down toward
the pitch. The stands here climb as steeply as the law allows, keeping all
66,000 fans close to the action. There's no track: There would be little point,
as soccer now attracts more spectators than any athletics event. The roof is
simple and dark and shuts out all but a small patch of sky, leaving fans with
nothing to look at except the field. This is the traditional emotional soccer
stadium—"the witch's cauldron," as the Germans call the type—taken to
its extreme.

It's a perfect place to watch soccer. However, it is traditional only while
you are watching. The arena's catacombs are stuffed with restaurants and
business lounges unthinkable in Leitch's day. These novelties irritate some
fans, including apparently Herzog himself. Striding through the business
club, he gestures at the ceiling: "It's gold, or goldish, referring to the Master-
card or whatever." He accepts this corporate lacquer as inevitable. "Older
versions of soccer stadiums were working-class cathedrals. Here there is no
more working class: It's a totally different public. It's a kind of contemporary
opera house. You could ask me, do I like the name Allianz Arena? No, I don't.
But this is a fact. We cannot be moral in this respect."

The arena's worst breach of tradition, however, is on the outside. The
stadium is in the middle of nowhere, near an industrial terrain. Herzog has
hit upon a clever device to connect it to the world: During games, the stadium lights up on the outside. It will glow red when Bayern Munich play,
blue for 1860 Munich, and white for Germany. But whereas in the Basle of
Herzog's childhood, cheers for a goal would resound through the surrounding neighborhood, now even the drivers passing the arena on the highway
won't hear them.

The other thing lacking from the Allianz Arena are the details that, as
Herzog has observed, make a stadium feel like home to the fans: a clock, a
statue, the sign in Liverpool's tunnel saying "This Is Anfield." The Allianz
Arena lacks local touches, Herzog admits, partly because the stadium was
built for three different home teams, and partly because the teams scarcely
bothered talking to him. He explains, "Even though architecture is so visible

now, soccer is still much more in the living room of the whole world, so soccer teams don't need architecture to highlight their identity."

As we sit in a business lounge, a familiar figure materializes on the turf below: Michael Ballack, Germany's greatest current player. The script has him leading Germany to victory in the World Cup next year. Today he is filming an advertisement. Herzog starts, "Ballack is here! It's amazing how young they look."

Ballack, by contrast, would probably never have recognized the old gent upstairs. Stadiums may be the new cathedrals, but their architects are not yet the new soccer players.

Not all Herzog's stadiums get built. When I visited the firm's offices in Basel in 2008, I was introduced to three bright young people who were designing a "stunning waterfront stadium" for Portsmouth FC. Peter Storrie, the club's then chief executive, said at the time: "We have only one word to describe this stadium: perfection."

Unfortunately, the perfect stadium has not yet been built. Early in 2010, when a debt-laden Portsmouth appeared in bankruptcy court, the spendthrift club became the new symbol not just of spendthrift English soccer but of spendthrift Britain itself.

Franz Beckenbauer
January 2006

On a roof terrace in Lisbon, Franz Beckenbauer makes the X-thousandth speech of his life. "I loved Lisbon before I had ever been here," the most celebrated living German reveals in that soothing Bavarian singsong, "because aged about twenty I read all of Erich Maria Remarque's work, some of it several times, and I loved *The Night in Lisbon.*"

Even seasoned Franz watchers are surprised. Few people have read any of Remarque's novels other than *All Quiet on the Western Front*, let alone several times, and anyway, Beckenbauer was supposed to produce a bland hymn to Portugal. The Kaiser has charmed yet another audience.

Every year is Beckenbauer's year, but 2006 is more so than usual. The man who won one World Cup as a player, another as a manager, and a third as a campaigner when he snagged this year's event for Germany is now organizing the tournament. His niche in the postwar German psyche just keeps expanding.

Beckenbauer is the phoenix from Nazi Germany's ashes. Conceived in the country's darkest winter, he was born in a bombed-out Munich in September 1945, Germany's "Hour Zero." His father worked in the post office. The Beckenbauers didn't eat meat often. Franz worked as an insurance agent and signed a semiprofessional contract with Bayern Munich, then a smallish local club.

He became a libero, a defender with a free role, and a unique German player. The country's soccer, still shaped by a Nazi ethic, mostly produced *Kämpfer*, or battlers, like the German team that won the World Cup in the mud of Berne in 1954. But Beckenbauer ran with a straight back, his head up, and with such elegance that he was seldom tackled: It would have seemed like lèse-majesté.

Off the field he exemplified the ambitious young money-oriented Federal Republic. Never a hippie or a lefty, Beckenbauer was an instinctive bourgeois. He was barely of age when he married the first in a parade of elegant blondes, bought himself a semidetached house with a mortgage, and took elocution lessons. He always allied himself with the establishment: with the right-wing Christian Social Union in Bavaria, every big German company or television channel, and the country's biggest tabloid, *Bild Zeitung*.

But he also, always, had charm: good looks, wit, and a lightness of touch. When I asked one of his fellow world champions of 1974 whether Beckenbauer was a tough nut, the man replied, "No! He is so nice. If you speak to him, the next time he sees you, he will remember everything about you, drape his arm around you, ask how you are."

When soccer became commercialized, Beckenbauer was present at the birth, plugging soup on television in the midsixties. It was the start of four decades as the poster boy of German industry. Having represented almost every German multinational, he is now practically their collective face. The former teammate mimes Beckenbauer ducking as companies throw money at him: "Here's €1 million! Here's another €1 million!"

Beckenbauer's first apotheosis came in 1974, the last time the Federal Republic hosted a World Cup. The team started off badly. After it lost a grudge game against East Germany, its manager, Helmut Schön, panicked. He sent out his captain, Beckenbauer, to represent him at a press conference. Beckenbauer told the press that from now on Germany would play more "realistic" soccer. Several players were dropped—probably at the captain's instigation—and a little later, Beckenbauer was lifting the World Cup in his hometown. His smile as he does it is one of the great happy images of the Federal Republic.

During that World Cup Beckenbauer had also banned a German tradition: swearing an oath of loyalty to the fatherland in the locker room before each match. He thought it didn't motivate multimillionaire players. It wasn't that he feared overblown German patriotism: Beckenbauer appears to have spent very little time contemplating the Nazi past. Rather, he just wasn't interested in it. His own date of birth absolved him from German sin. He saw little point in looking back. Campaigning in 1998 to bring the 2006 World Cup to Germany, he said, "All over the world they're still showing those old films harking back to things that happened forty, fifty years ago. That gives a wrong impression of this country. . . . A World Cup gives you a chance to present yourself to the world for a solid five weeks."

The rest of his playing career after 1974 passed in glory with only one blip: In 1977 it was revealed that he hadn't paid all his taxes. Shamed, and with another marriage collapsing, he fled to New York to play for the Cosmos. There he learned decent English, an essential attribute in his later global rise.

He retired as a player in 1982. Two years later he was appointed Germany's manager, charged with saving the country's decaying soccer. In 1986 he took his team to the World Cup final in Mexico. The side played ugly, battling soccer, and during its matches the eye was drawn easily to the elegant figure of Beckenbauer, standing upright beside his dugout, with such poise that one overlooked his startling checkered trousers. He always, then and thereafter, took care to disassociate himself from the shortcomings of post-*Kaiserzeit* German soccer. Days before that final, chatting to friends, he said the names of several of his players aloud and guffawed. "What was so funny?" he was asked. "Just think of it," said Beckenbauer. "In a day or two these guys could be world champions!" They weren't: They lost to Argentina. "Luckily, because if we'd won it would have been a defeat for soccer," Beckenbauer wrote later.

In 1990 his German team did win the World Cup, though again without playing beautifully. Beckenbauer as manager always produced "realistic soccer" rather than the beautiful game he himself had played. That night in Rome, while his players went wild, Beckenbauer strolled alone across the pitch, gold medal around his neck, looking around him like a man walking his dog. He later explained that he had been saying good-bye to soccer.

It was more an auf Wiedersehen: See you later. He soon returned in his third incarnation as soccer politician. Alone among soccer's former greats, he was born to the role: Beckenbauer isn't a squabbler like Johan Cruijff or a dullard like Bobby Charlton or a drunk like George Best or a recovering drug addict like Diego Maradona or a weak character like Michel Platini or a talking puppet like Pele. Despite being German, Beckenbauer is liked worldwide.

At home he no longer has to ally himself with the establishment. It tries to ally itself with him. Every German politician tries to attach himself to the Kaiser. When Beckenbauer would drop in on his former fan Gerhard Schröder in the chancellory, and Schröder would crack open a bottle of red, it was clear which man needed the meeting most. When Schröder pushed through a major tax reform, German comedian Harald Schmidt joked, "And the greatest surprise is: without the help of Franz Beckenbauer!"

Nothing seems to damage him in Germany: not his constant contradictory statements to the nearest microphone nor the inevitable split with his latest blonde. The former teammate told me, "The thing about Franz, his greatest gift is in his . . . ," and the teammate gestured at his crotch. "But he makes all his women happy! They all go away with money." Beckenbauer, with his facility to laugh about himself, always happily admits his mistakes, and the German public always forgives him. In a country sick of upheaval, he represents a reassuring continuity. The Federal Republic is no longer very successful at soccer or anything else, but Beckenbauer still represents the Germany that wins with a smile.

The smile falters only when he is criticized. Then he throws a tantrum. Last week he did so when a German consumer group said some of the World Cup stadia were unsafe. Beckenbauer duly appeared in *Bild* newspaper—his representative on earth—and announced from Cape Town that the group should stick to "face cream, olive oil and hoovers."

Usually any attacks on Beckenbauer came from the critical intellectual Left—a lot of people in Germany. Beckenbauer reads books but disdains intellectuals, and they tend to disdain him as too rich, greedy, right-wing, unapologetic, celebratory, and Bavarian.

Now the incarnation of Europe's critical Left is taking him on. Danny Cohn-Bendit, "Danny the Red" of the 1968 student revolutions, has founded an *Allianz gegen Franz*, or "Alliance against Franz." It aims to stop Beckenbauer from becoming president of the European soccer association UEFA. The argument is that Beckenbauer, who is already president of Bayern Munich, would devote his reign to making the world safe for the big clubs.

He probably would, and he probably will. If Beckenbauer stands next year, he will surely win. He always does. As the only soccer official who is popular with the European public, he would have a power almost unprecedented in the game. If he carries on like this, his ancient nickname of Kaiser will require an upgrade.

Mike Forde
November 2009

It's taken too long, but at last European soccer clubs are starting to learn from American sports. Mike Forde, Chelsea's soccer operations director, visits the United States often. "The first time I went to the Red Sox," he says of the Boston baseball team, "I sat there for eight hours, in a room with no windows, only flip charts. I walked out of there saying, 'Wow, that's one of the most insightful conversations on sport I've ever had, with guys that don't know who Beckham or Ronaldo are. It wasn't, 'What are you doing here? You don't know anything about our sport.' That was totally irrelevant. It was, 'How do you make decisions on players? What information do you use? How do we approach the same problems?'"

Forde, holding forth excitedly from his comfy chair at Chelsea's health club, is tapping the statistical revolution that has swept American sports. The revolution's manifesto was Michael Lewis's baseball book *Moneyball* (2003). Earlier this year, Lewis proclaimed, "The virus that infected professional baseball in the 1990s, the use of statistics to find new and better ways to value players and strategies, has found its way into every major sport." In soccer, Forde is spreading the virus.

Forde worked at Bolton Wanderers before Chelsea, and he looks like a soccer man: trim, graying, regional accent, nice suit. That helps him deal with hidebound soccer men who are wary of fancy numbers spouted by dowdy statisticians. "Letting even a top-level statistician loose with a more traditional soccer manager is not really the right combination," says Forde.

He studied psychology in San Diego, and that early American experience proved key. He often visits Billy Beane, hero of *Moneyball*, general manager of the Oakland A's baseball team, and a soccer fan who grills him on English soccer's latest goings-on. Recently, though, Forde has been studying basketball, a sport more like soccer. "Basketball's ahead of us," Forde admits. However, he says England's biggest soccer clubs now have people in roles like his. "We as a nation are probably more open to the American experience than maybe the French are, the Italians are. Maybe we'll be quicker to adapt the *Moneyball* ideas because of that."

Adapting those ideas began a decade ago, when clubs started to buy data on the number of passes, tackles, and miles run for each player per game. Forde remembers the early hunt for meaning in the numbers. "Can we find a correlation between total distance covered and winning? And the answer was invariably no." People from the England rugby team told Forde that possession won matches. Yet that didn't work in soccer. "If you had 55 percent possession, the chances of winning were *less* than if you had 35 percent possession."

But the data can help clubs evaluate individual players. After all, says Forde, "Most of the elite clubs are probably spending 70 percent of their revenues on 2.5 percent of their workforce. Really all we've got is talent."

Clubs are always buying the wrong players. Forde sees his task as "risk management": reducing the game's uncertainties. For instance, he studies data covering a player's whole career to avoid the old trap of signing someone just when he's in top form. A player, explains Forde, spends minimal time in the ideal state of flow. "The player thinks that's his normal standard. It's not. My job is to see what form he regresses to."

The search is still on for the best data to evaluate players. If a forward is tearing up the French or Dutch league, you need to predict his strike rate in the tougher Premier League. Forde says, "We've created our own algorithm: The guy scores fifteen goals in France. Is that ten in England?" Finding criteria to assess defenders is harder. "Is it tackles? Well, look at Paolo Maldini: He made one tackle every two games."

The holy grail would be discovering the key to victory. "I don't think we're there yet," Forde admits. But he says, "If you look at ten years in the Premier League, there is a stronger correlation between clean sheets and where you finish than goals scored and where you finish." Billy Beane would be proud.

Ignacio Palacios-Huerta
June 2010

If Uruguay's Diego Forlan ends up taking a penalty against Ghana on Friday night, we have a pretty shrewd idea of where he will put it: in the opposite corner to his previous penalty. Forlan has a pattern of hitting one spot kick to the right of the keeper, the next left, the next right, and so on. He is trying to shoot in a random sequence, but failing. And one man has spotted it.

The man is Ignacio Palacios-Huerta, economics professor at the London School of Economics, who is watching the World Cup from his native Basque country in between bouts of child care. Palacios-Huerta played professional soccer in Spain's third division, and then began looking at penalties as a real-life case study of game theory. He has studied more than 9,000 penalties since 1995, and now probably knows more about penalty takers than all the teams in the tournament. Their ignorance amazes him: "I have nothing at stake. They have lots: the whole nation."

You rarely anymore hear coaches or players grumble that shoot-outs are "a lottery," but their planning for them mostly remains antediluvian. Germans, for instance, revere the crib sheet that their keeper Jens Lehmann had tucked into his sock during their victorious shoot-out against Argentina in the last World Cup. Yet the sheet, scribbled on a piece of hotel notepaper, is ludicrously simplistic. It lists seven Argentine penalty takers and their supposed preferred corner: "Messi left," for instance.

Palacios-Huerta notes that almost no regular penalty taker has a career-long bias toward one side. Lionel Messi, he says, randomizes his penalties almost perfectly. "He can also change his mind at the very last instant," notes Palacios-Huerta. Sometimes Messi waits for the keeper to shift his weight very slightly to one side, and then shoots to the other corner.

Four years on, some teams may have crib sheets more sophisticated than Lehmann's. One team in the quarterfinals has an hour's film of penalties taken by its opponents, plus a penalty database. That's why it was silly of England's coach, Fabio Capello, to announce his designated penalty takers before playing Germany. He gave the opposition time to study their habits.

But Palacios-Huerta thinks that even today's most sophisticated teams probably just count who shoots how often to which corner. "I would be supersurprised if they do any kind of statistical test," he says. He himself runs two. The first is: Does a particular kicker follow a truly random strategy? If the kicker does, then the direction he chooses for his next kick—right of the keeper, through the middle, or left—cannot be predicted from his previous kicks. A random kicker is like a man tossing an honest coin: Whether he throws heads or tails this time cannot be predicted from his previous throws.

But people in real life struggle to follow random strategies. Often they fall into patterns, and Palacios-Huerta gets excited when he detects someone's patterns. Argentina's Gonzalo Higuaín, for instance, kicks too often to the right. And the keeper whom Higuaín may face in a shoot-out on Saturday, Germany's Manuel Neuer, also fails to randomize: Too often, Neuer dives to the opposite corner from his previous dive, going first right, then left, then right, and so forth.

Next Palacios-Huerta tests the kicker's success rate with each strategy. The kicker should have an equally high scoring rate whether he shoots right, middle, or left. But both Argentina's Sergio Agüero and Germany's Miroslav

Klose, for instance, score more often when shooting right of the keeper. That would logically encourage them to aim right on Saturday.

Only rarely does Palacios-Huerta find a kicker with a very skewed strategy, but England's Frank Lampard is such a man. For years, Lampard randomized his kicks beautifully. But this season, notes Palacios-Huerta, "he has kicked thirteen out of fifteen times to the right of the goalkeeper—and the two lefts were in the same game when he had to retake the same penalty three times."

No wonder Lampard has recently developed a habit of missing penalties. Keepers are figuring him out. Portsmouth's David James, for instance, chose the correct corner for Lampard's penalty for Chelsea in the FA Cup final—perhaps with help from Palacios-Huerta, who had sent Portsmouth a briefing note before the game. In the event, Lampard's shot went wide. Admittedly, Kevin-Prince Boateng missed his penalty for Portsmouth in the match, but then he had ignored Palacios-Huerta's advice to kick left of keeper Petr Cech.

The patterns of individuals are only a secondary matter, though. The most important moment in any shoot-out occurs before it even starts. The referee tosses a coin, and the captain who calls correctly gets to decide whether his team takes the first kick. Always kick first, says Palacios-Huerta. The team that takes the first penalty wins 60 percent of shoot-outs. That's because the team going second shoots under great pressure: It keeps having to score just to stay in the game. In Tuesday's shoot-out, for instance, Japan was the likely loser the moment Paraguay's captain, Justo Villar, won the toss and chose to start. Paraguay duly won.

Few seem to know this initial advantage exists, notes Palacios-Huerta. Television commentators rarely even mention the toss. Bookmakers don't shift their odds immediately after the toss is done—a mistake from which gamblers could benefit. And at Euro 2008, Italy's captain, Gianluigi Buffon, may have decided the outcome of the tournament when he won the toss for a shoot-out against Spain and let the Spaniards shoot first. They won, of course—not necessarily gladdening the heart of the Basque Palacios-Huerta—and then won the tournament.

Ignorance about penalties could decide this World Cup, too. Palacios-Huerta sighs, "I don't think serious analysis of the data has arrived yet in soccer, but it's coming. I think the world will be a different place in a decade or so."

Declaration of interest: I recently helped set up a soccer consultancy called Soccernomics, which aims to advise clubs and associations. Ignacio became our penalty expert. He did his first (unpaid) work during the World Cup. First we supplied England with his analysis of Germany's penalty takers, but that game, surprisingly, didn't go to a penalty shoot-out.

When Holland reached the final, I e-mailed a Dutch official I knew slightly. I explained what we could provide. Was the official interested?

He was. Ignacio pulled all-nighters and finished the report on the Saturday morning before the final. We sent it to the Dutch. At lunchtime on Sunday—matchday—someone inside Holland's camp e-mailed us: "It's a report we can use perfectly."

In Soccer City, with the final scoreless in overtime, I reread the report on my laptop between Dutch yellow cards. It turned out that Spain was finishing the match with only one experienced penalty taker still on the field: Fernando Torres. Spain's two most regular kickers, David Villa and Xabi Alonso, had been substituted. The Spaniards must have viewed the impending shoot-out with anxiety.

I checked our report's findings on Torres. He had a slight tendency to kick to the keeper's left, but critically, 76 percent of his shots were "low." Sometimes Torres shot "midheight," but never high. Clearly, Holland's keeper Maarten Stekelenburg, should go to ground fast against him.

The only remaining Spanish player to have taken even five penalties as a pro was Cesc Fabregas. The report's finding: "He has a strong tendency to kick left [of the keeper]. Looking at his videos, it seems hard for him to kick to the right."

No other Spaniard still on the pitch had any significant penalty-taking experience. However, that fact itself was telling. According to Ignacio, infrequent penalty kickers hit 70 percent of their kicks to their "natural" side: right of the keeper for right-footed kickers, left for left-footed ones. That's the easiest way.

As for Spain's keeper Iker Casillas, over the fifty-nine penalties that we observed him, he did better diving to one corner than the other. Kickers scored considerably more when kicking to their "nonnatural" side against Casillas. Right-footers should therefore aim to his left and left-footers to his right.

Sitting in the stands, I started to get excited. Perhaps I was about to help the team I support win a World Cup. Alternatively, perhaps I was about to help it lose one. And then, five minutes before the shoot-out was to begin, Iniesta scored.

Johan Cruijff
December 2011

"This isn't Ajax anymore," wrote Johan Cruijff in his column in the Netherlands' best-selling newspaper, *De Telegraaf*, on September 20, 2010. The father of Dutch soccer, who first wandered into the Amsterdam club sixty years ago as a toddler from down the road, said he was willing to come back and take charge. "We need to put a big broom through it," he wrote.

He was given his broom, and it was big indeed. For the past year, Ajax has lived through a bloody Cruijff-led coup. There have been episodes of racism and sexism and a court case by Cruijff against his fellow directors at Ajax. All these conflicts will be familiar to any follower of Holland's soccer these past forty years. Cruijff invented the Dutch game in his own image: he is arguably the most creative thinker on the sport, but he is also very quarrelsome. The phrase "the neurotic genius of Dutch soccer," as David Winner subtitled his book *Brilliant Orange*, derives from this sixty-four-year-old Barcelona mansion dweller.

There is an instructive comparison between Cruijff and his fellow baby boomer Franz Beckenbauer. Both ran their respective countries' soccer, but Cruijff never learned Beckenbauer's gift for getting along. In part, this is because Beckenbauer is from Catholic Bavaria, whereas Cruijff is from the Netherlands. The great historic influence on Dutchness was Calvinism. Calvin taught that you must be true to yourself, follow your own heart. As Cruijff put it, "You must die with your own ideas." Beckenbauer—never on a quest for authenticity—knew how to work with other people. Cruijff couldn't. Beckenbauer is a politician, Cruijff a revolutionary, and politicians are the ones who tend to end up with power. Beckenbauer became a World Cup–winning manager of Germany and then organizer of a World Cup, while Cruijff never managed Holland because the job negotiations ended in quarrels after a misunderstanding over a fax.

Cruijff thought quarrels were essential. The *"conflictmodel,"* he called it. The notion was that conflicts were a motor of creativity, because they got everyone thinking and gave them something to prove. Certainly, Dutch soccer seems to thrive on intellectual ferment. When a country of 16 million people reaches three of the last ten World Cup finals, something is working.

But you can have too much ferment. With Cruijff, almost everything ended in quarrels. In 1981 he returned to Ajax with a broken thirty-four-year-old body and won the club two more titles, but then departed for Ajax's archrival, Feyenoord, after quarrels. He returned to Ajax again as a coach in 1985, but left after quarrels in 1988. He went off to coach his other love, Barcelona, where he left after quarrels in 1996. He hasn't had a full-time job since.

The early retirement was partly by choice (one made by many Dutch baby boomers) but partly by necessity. The man was impossible to work with. He commuted between his mansion in Barcelona and his pad in Amsterdam, tried to procure coaching jobs for old friends (inevitably, people he had quarreled with during his career), and had fun.

Eventually, he grew restless. One evening in February 2008, he staged his Fourth Coming at Ajax. He showed up unexpectedly at a meeting of Ajax's members' council, began to speak, and was installed by acclamation as the club's new dictator. But seventeen days later he drove out of the stadium and flew home to Barcelona. He explained that he had wanted to revolutionize Ajax's youth academy and fire loads of people, but the club's coach-elect, Marco van Basten (Cruijff's own soccer son, with whom he had quarreled in the past), had said no. "And then I've got no more business at Ajax. I've taken my hands off it," concluded Cruijff.

In 2010 he put his hands back on. He'd hit on a classic sixties idea: the talent should run the business. Instead of those old directors in suits with whom he'd always quarreled, he dreamed of "a club run by athletes." In fact, there is nothing very new about this. Most soccer clubs are in practice run by athletes: the coach and technical director are almost always former players. At some clubs, like Beckenbauer's Bayern Munich or Daniel Passarella's River Plate or Michael Jordan's Charlotte Bobcats in basketball, the former athletes even run the board. It's not clear why this should be a great advantage, yet the notion was the core of Cruijff's coup.

The coup began brilliantly, as if he'd studied up on revolutionary manuals. He'd long since seized control of the Dutch airwaves: both the *Telegraaf* newspaper and the mighty soccer magazine–cum-TV program *Voetbal International* are his mouthpieces. His initial arrival from Barcelona was a coup de théâtre that recalled the Ayatollah Khomeini's flight from Paris to Teheran in 1979 or Lenin's journey from Zurich to Russia in his sealed train.

Cruijff's mistake was then to return to retirement. He flew home to Barcelona and let his surrogates—former players like Dennis Bergkamp and Wim Jonk—run the revolution. It was as if Khomeini had returned to Paris to sit on a *terrasse* drinking wine and watching the girls go by. A management consultant and professor named Steven ten Have was appointed Ajax's new chairman, presumably because Cruijff thought he'd be good at filling in forms. The new board included only two former Ajax players, Cruijff and Edgar Davids. Cruijff's fellow directors could rarely reach him anyway, because he was usually in Barcelona and doesn't have an e-mail address. But he still wanted his own way. He demanded that the board appoint the former Ajax winger Tscheu La Ling (with whom Cruijff had quarreled as a player) as technical director. The board, concerned about Ling's murky business past, refused.

The smoldering row blew up at a board meeting in the summer of 2011, when Cruijff told Davids, "You're only here because you're black," and explained to another director, Marjan Olfers, that she was on the board strictly because she was a woman. After the remarks leaked, Cruijff shrugged them off in a *Voetbal International* broadcast: "'The baldie, that squinter, that redhead,' what does it matter? That's spoken language in soccer."

Meanwhile, his fellow board members had gone behind his back and appointed his archenemy, Louis van Gaal, as Ajax's general director. Van Gaal is actually Cruijff's lost twin: an exact contemporary, from the same neighborhood in Amsterdam-East, also fatherless since childhood, also a seventies Ajax player (albeit in the reserves) who became a great obstinate coach with Cruijffian ideas about soccer. Yet the two hate each other. The antipathy seems to have started when a traditional Dutch St. Nicholas Day's celebration at Cruijff's house in Barcelona went badly wrong. Regardless, Van Gaal's appointment enraged Cruijff. The other board members explained that they hadn't been able to e-mail Cruijff the news, and anyway, he'd only have leaked it to his loyal media.

In December he and the other former players took the board to court. The Cruijff team won: the judge delayed Van Gaal's appointment until Ajax's shareholders had approved it. The shareholders—mostly a bunch of lifelong Ajax members—won't approve it. At a meeting at Ajax, they also told the

Ten Have board to leave. Whenever Cruijff spoke at the meeting, there was hysterical applause. The man still retains some magic.

Yet this is probably the final act of the long psychodrama. Given Cruijff's history, it's not hard to predict that this will end in quarrels. After that, one struggles to envision a successful Sixth Coming. Dutch soccer is slowly escaping the grip of its maker. Cruijff himself is impossible. Only his ideas will live on.

At the time of writing, the Cruijff junta remains united and in control of Ajax. Its stated aim of making the club a contender for European trophies again shows no signs of coming true, though.

Andrea Agnelli
April 2013

Andrea Agnelli, president of Juventus Football Club, points to a photograph on his office shelf. It shows a small boy in shorts, with a mop of brown hair, standing beside some sunny rural field where Juventus are playing. The boy is Agnelli himself; the man sitting on a bench in the photo is his late father, Umberto, who ran Juve fifty years ago.

The current Mr. Agnelli, now thirty-seven, inhabits a surprisingly modest office in the club's mansion smack in the middle of Turin. As Juve's president since 2010, he has presided over the club's return to its habitual place at the top of Italian soccer. Juventus will soon pocket yet another Italian championship—possibly as early as Sunday, if it beats local rivals Torino and second-place Napoli doesn't win. However, this proud club isn't where it wants to be: at the top of Europe. In part, that's because Juventus has fallen victim to the problems of Italy itself. "Is Italian football interesting to watch today?" Agnelli asks. "Half the stadiums are empty; there is violence. I mean, it's not the best product." Italian soccer—corrupt, beset by violent thugs, economic decline, parochialism, and lack of government—offers almost too perfect a metaphor for Italy itself. Like Ferrari (also in the Agnelli stable), or Gucci, or a brilliant corner café, Juventus is aiming for something very difficult: to be a pocket of excellence in a decaying country.

The Agnellis are often called "Italy's royal family." Giovanni Agnelli, Andrea's great-grandfather, thought there might be a future in horseless carriages and in 1899 cofounded a company called Fabbrica Italiana di Automobili Torino, or Fiat. In 1923 Giovanni encouraged his son Edoardo to become president of Turin's soccer club, Juventus. "The ninety years' ownership makes us the longest-lasting ownership in any sports franchise globally," says Andrea Agnelli. "Juventus and Fiat are the two eldest ownerships we have." The family's other assets, bought by the Agnellis' investment company, "came and left. Juventus and Fiat are the common denominators of the history of the family." Agnelli also sits on the board of Fiat, the world's seventh-biggest automaker, where his cousin John Elkann is chairman. (Andrea's half brother Giovanni Alberto was groomed to run Fiat, but died of cancer in 1997 at age thirty-three.)

You wouldn't instantly spot Agnelli as a quasi-royal. He speaks like the trained international business manager he is, as if keen to prove he isn't some airheaded heir. Yet his modest office, understated yet immaculate charcoal gray suit, and near-perfect English (polished at boarding school in Oxford) are characteristically Agnelli. "Reserved, stylish, elegant, 'British'" is the family "myth," says John Foot, historian of Italy and author of *Calcio: A History of Italian Soccer*. Foot writes that generations of Agnellis have watched Juve, bought players, fired managers, and talked soccer to a usually fawning Italian press. Andrea's handsome white-haired uncle Gianni Agnelli, nicknamed *l'Avvocato*, "the Lawyer," ran Fiat yet was known to many Italians chiefly as the figurehead of Juventus. The club's 1980s playmaker Michel Platini, who won three Golden Ball awards as European Player of the Year, gave one of them to *l'Avvocato*, saying, "This is something you cannot buy, not even with your money." "Is it real gold?" Gianni asked, and Platini replied, "If it was, I wouldn't give it to you."

Juventus is nicknamed *la Vecchia Signora*, "the Old Lady," but Agnelli notes another description: "Juventus is known as 'the girlfriend of Italy.' It's probably the woman everyone wants to be with." Whereas most Italian clubs bear their city's name and are tied up with feelings of local belonging, Juventus bestrides the nation. Gianni Agnelli once said, "Not having the name of a city has brought us great popularity. It makes us national." Few institutions in divided Italy can make that claim. Juventus estimates it has 11 million

Italian supporters, many in the poor South that sent generations of peasants to Turin to work in Fiat's factories.

Andrea Agnelli credits the "stability of leadership" by the family for helping Juve become Italy's strongest club. In truth, Fiat's millions probably did more to push a team from a midsize provincial town to greatness.

How was Agnelli raised to think of Juventus? "Winning," he replies. From his office shelves he plucks a child's drawing. Under the heading "Juventus You Are a Queen," it shows a penalty flying into a goal. Nine-year-old Andrea drew it in 1985, after Platini's penalty defeated Liverpool in the European Cup final at the Heysel stadium—a match now chiefly remembered for the thirty-nine Juve fans crushed to death in a crowd riot before kickoff. Agnelli apologizes: as a child, he didn't understand the context; what he registered that night was victory.

His own favorite Juventus team, he says, was the European champions of 1996. He quotes a phrase from Juve's then captain, Gianluca Vialli: "In the tunnel going onto the pitch, I remember looking at our opponents who were thinking, 'Why are we playing against this team, because we have already lost?'" But Agnelli adds, "The current team has great potential. I feel it's mine, whilst with the others I was, let me say, a privileged observer. This is my creature." And his creature has started to win.

Yet Juventus's many enemies see another, darker, side to the club's story. They charge that Italy's leading soccer club, backed by Italy's leading family, has used its web of connections to ensure victory. In a country given to conspiracy theories, this charge sticks. The question of whether referees support Juventus has prompted scuffles between members in Italy's parliament. But sometimes (especially in Italy) conspiracy theories are true. Juve's enemies felt vindicated when it emerged in 2006 that the club's then general manager, Luciano Moggi, spent much of his working week on his cell phone, arranging which referees should be appointed for Juventus's matches and which for rival teams. The scandal known as *Calciopoli* (each new Italian match-fixing scandal gets its own name) was the nadir of Juventus's history. One image sums up the despair: that summer of 2006, club executive Gianluca Pessotto sat in an upstairs window clasping a rosary and let himself fall backward onto the asphalt below. Thankfully, he survived.

Italian justice rarely offers closure, and still nobody quite agrees who did what in *Calciopoli*. Agnelli says of Juventus's role, "It was not match fixing." He notes that the club was only ever found guilty of "unsporting behavior," not "sporting fraud."

I retort, "But Moggi was phoning referees' bosses!"

Agnelli replies, "Moggi, and a lot of other people, as later came out."

He sticks to the Juventus line: the club was made the scapegoat for a systemic disorder in Italian soccer. It was stripped of its championships of 2005 and 2006 and sent down to Serie B, Italian soccer's second tier. A year later, Juve won promotion. "Our brand is enhanced now by our tremendous comeback story," Agnelli says. "That gave us the opportunity to restate, in a louder way, how strong we are and how focused on leading the Italian system."

But *Calciopoli* tarnished Italian soccer, worsened suspicions between clubs, and was followed by the *Calcioscomesse* scandal, in which more than twenty clubs (but not Juventus) were accused of match fixing. Juve's current coach, Antonio Conte, was banned from the dugout for four months last year for having failed to report match fixing he witnessed while coach of little Siena.

This is the context in which Agnelli leads Juve. The beautiful Italian game of old is disappearing. I wrote in my first book, *Soccer Against the Enemy*, twenty years ago, "When the soccer fan dies, he goes to Italy, where he finds the best players in the world, matches shown in full on public TV, and numerous daily sports newspapers. Nice weather, too." For me as for many fans then, Italian soccer was hopelessly mixed up with memories of frothy cappuccinos, copies of the pink *Gazzetta dello Sport* studied at café tables, and sun-kissed stadiums as safe as family restaurants at a time when hooligans ravaged English soccer.

But Italian soccer isn't beautiful anymore. As with many things in Italy, Silvio Berlusconi must take some blame. When he was prime minister, Italy became a country where Berlusconi voters and Berlusconi haters watched Berlusconi's team, Milan, thump teams subsidized by Berlusconi's government on Berlusconi's pay channels, in a league run by Berlusconi's right-hand man, Adriano Galliani, and then watched the highlights on Berlusconi's free channel. The only thing Berlusconi didn't do was carry out his government's laws for making stadiums safer.

By 2010 Juventus no longer even headed what remained. "It was having issues recovering from the 2006 events," says Agnelli. "So we decided we needed a family member in charge." Being keen on sports management, he was the obvious choice. The family owned more than 60 percent of the club (the minority shareholders included the Gaddafi family).

In 2011 Juventus finally opened its new stadium. Creating it had taken seventeen years. Most Italian clubs play in run-down municipally owned grounds that they cannot afford to leave, even if they could navigate the local bureaucracy. Only Juventus owns its home.

Last Sunday night I saw Juve play Berlusconi's Milan there. It's a very twenty-first-century stadium: there are even two crèches ("baby parks," in Italian) for spectators' kids. The forty-one thousand spectators sit close to the pitch, English style. Two hours before kickoff I stood by the corner flag and saw how a player here could look straight into individual fans' faces just yards away, separated from him only by Plexiglas, watching them scrutinize him. In Juve's locker room I found the hairdryers (essentials of life for Italian soccer players) plugged in and ready to go. There were hot and cold baths, four treatment tables, and a dinner table set with a fruit basket where the players would eat right after the game. This was modernity—a rare commodity in Italian soccer.

In some Italian stadiums you worry about firecrackers falling on your head, but the stands at Juventus felt safe. As Agnelli says, this is the sort of clean environment that encourages people to behave. Before kickoff, Juve's Ultra fans unfurled three vast banners: on them, two little cartoon players from Milan and Inter, Juve's main rivals, gazed upward at the tower of Juve glittering with thirty league titles and one to come. The stadium applauded the excellent drawings. This was Italian fan culture at its best.

But some Juve fans racially abused Milan's black midfielder, Kevin-Prince Boateng. And the game itself plunged one firmly back into today's impoverished Italy. A decade ago, Juve versus Milan was possibly the best game in global soccer; no longer. Andrea Pirlo, Juve's last great outfield player, turns thirty-four next month, and their great keeper, Gianluigi Buffon, is thirty-five. Juve's passing was awkward and slow. Watching poor Mirko Vucinic labor up front for Juve, you longed for the days when Platini and

Zbigniew Boniek graced that space. No wonder almost all the journalists in the press stand were Italians: Juve-Milan has become a provincial affair.

Watching the game, you understood why Juve recently got thumped in the Champions League by Bayern Munich and why Coach Conte had said afterward, "In the coming years I don't see a possibility for an Italian team to be successful in the Champions League." At least Juve remains supreme in Italy. It beat Milan 1–0 on a penalty after Milan's substitute keeper bizarrely and unnecessarily floored Juve's Kwadwo Asamoah. When I fell asleep in my hotel room after midnight, a platinum-blonde woman and three aging male pundits on state TV were still debating the penalty's validity. Either way, by Sunday "the Old Lady" could have her twenty-ninth title (or thirty-first, depending on whom you believe).

This is the Italian morass in which Juventus is trying to thrive. But what to do? England's Premier League, Agnelli says, makes about $2.6 billion a year from television rights, about half of that domestic and half foreign. Italian clubs make about $1.3 billion, of which almost 90 percent is generated inside Italy. Agnelli even envies English advertising boards: "You are reading messages in Chinese across all Premier League stadiums. We access multinational companies, but we access their local budgets. We want to be talking to their headquarters."

In soccer, money determines success. Agnelli sighs: "Rather than a final destination for top players, we are now a transit league." Juve's revenues last year were $280 million, less than half Real Madrid's and Barcelona's. For now, the club needs infusions of Agnelli money: its net debt has hit $200 million after several years of losses, though the new stadium has recently helped Juventus move into modest profit.

Agnelli still benchmarks Juve against Europe's best, and he looks abroad for role models. "If one was to look at a perfect situation for a top team," he says, "it's a mixture of what you find in England, in Germany, and in Spain." From England, he would take the stadium and its vendors on game day; from Spain, the freedom of big clubs to sell their TV rights individually rather than having to share them with small teams; and he envies how "corporate Germany" sponsors German clubs. That's the fantasy for Italy. "Now is this possible?" he asks. "No."

Take something as apparently simple as selling replica shirts, he says. British and German fans flock to buy their teams' new shirts. "In Italy we buy counterfeit shirts. Fake is a problem of this country." People in a constantly shrinking economy don't want to pay full price. Or there's the struggle for Italian clubs to build new stadiums: "Italy has been talking for ten years about passing a law that incentivizes building these stadiums," Agnelli laments.

I point out that most of the problems he complains about are problems of Italy—of the country whose economy grew slower than that of any country except Haiti and Zimbabwe in the decade to 2010. Agnelli's father, Umberto, once said, "The team has followed the evolution of the nation." Today, is the nation dragging down the team? "Correct," Agnelli replies.

He's cautious about talking politics, but thinking about broader solutions for Italy, he looks to the UK. He says:

> Maybe we should go back to analyzing British history more, from [1970s prime minister Jim] Callaghan to Lady Thatcher and how the eighties saw England rewriting its future in a very aggressive and disciplined way. Now, does Italy have the same discipline that England showed? I wish. I hope. But if I was to comment on the last sixty days [in which Italy has had neither new government nor a president], of national institutions evaluating how to move forward, we haven't shown the same capacity as England.
>
> Italian football, as much as Italy, needs structural reforms. Italy a few years ago was at a crossroads: do we want to tackle this and stay competitive? We chose to do nothing. In football, you need a concerted effort: violence, stadiums, trademark protections. Now there isn't even a government, so we haven't got a minister of sports.

If big soccer clubs really were the globalized behemoths without local souls that their critics see, life would be easy for Juventus. Then the club could forget Italy and play the international market. But even giant soccer clubs are irredeemably local. Most of their spectators, sponsors, rivals, and a great chunk of their paying TV viewers live inside their own borders. Juventus won't sink with Italy. But with the country in its current state, not even the Agnelli family club can thrive.

INDEX

Vincent Lignier

Simon Kuper is the award-winning author of *Soccer Against the Enemy*; *Ajax*; *The Dutch*; *The War: Football in Europe During the Second World War* and, with Stefan Szymanski, the national bestseller *Soccernomics: Why England Loses, Why Spain, Germany, and Brazil Win, and Why the US, Japan, Australia—and Even Iraq—Are Destined to Become the Kings of the World's Most Popular Sport*. Kuper writes a weekly column in the *Financial Times*, and has previously written soccer columns for the *Times* and the *Observer*. In December 2007, he won the annual Manuel Vazquez Montalban prize for sports-writing, awarded by the Colegio de Periodistas de Catalunya and FC Barcelona's foundation. In 2011, he was named Britain's Cultural Commentator of the Year by Editorial Intelligence. He lives with his family in Paris, France.

The Nation Institute
Nation.

NATION
BOOKS

Founded in 2000, **Nation Books** has become a leading voice in American independent publishing. The inspiration for the imprint came from the *Nation* magazine, the oldest independent and continuously published weekly magazine of politics and culture in the United States.

The imprint's mission is to produce auth(
ground and shed light on current social a
established authors who are leaders in their
to cultivate a new generation of emerging a
of our books we aim to positively affect cul

Nation Books is a project of The Nation Insti
established to extend the reach of democra
independent press. The Nation Institute is
programs: our award-winning Investigative F
breaking investigative journalism; the widely   .....
TomDispatch; our internship program in conjunction with the *Nation* magazine; and Journalism Fellowships that fund up to 20 high-profile reporters every year.

For more information on Nation Books, the *Nation* magazine, and The Nation Institute, please visit:

www.nationbooks.org
www.nationinstitute.org
www.thenation.com
www.facebook.com/nationbooks.ny
Twitter: @nationbooks